Robert A. Lovett
and the Development
of American Air Power

D0863748

Robert A. Lovett and the Development of American Air Power

David M. Jordan

McFarland & Company, Inc., Publishers

Jefferson, North Carolina

LIBRARY OF CONGRESS CATALOGUING-IN-PUBLICATION DATA

Names: Jordan, David M., 1935– author.
Title: Robert A. Lovett and the Development of American Air Power / David M. Jordan.
Description: Jefferson, North Carolina : McFarland & Company, Inc.,
Publishers, 2019 | Includes bibliographical references and index.
Identifiers: LCCN 2018050517 | ISBN 9781476675497 (softcover : acid free paper) ∞
Subjects: LCSH: Lovett, Robert A. (Robert Abercrombie), 1895–1986. | United States.
Department of Defense—Officials and employees—Biography. | Cabinet
officers—United States—Biography. | United States. Army Air Forces—
History. | Air power—United States—History—20th century. | World War,
1939–1945—Aerial operations, American.
Classification: LCC UA23.6 .J67 2019 | DDC 355.6092 [B]—dc23
LC record available at https://lccn.loc.gov/2018050517

BRITISH LIBRARY CATALOGUING DATA ARE AVAILABLE

ISBN (print) 978-1-4766-7549-7
ISBN (ebook) 978-1-4766-3477-7

Front cover: Robert A. Lovett, 1943 (Library of Congress);
B-24 Liberator bombers over the Mediterranean Sea
in World War II (U.S. Army Air Forces)

Printed in the United States of America

*McFarland & Company, Inc., Publishers
Box 611, Jefferson, North Carolina 28640
www.mcfarlandpub.com*

To my old law partners and close friends,
Charles Potash, Andy Cantor and Bill Landsburg,
and to my late stepson Steve

Table of Contents

Acknowledgments

In putting together this biography, I had a great deal of assistance. The first mention must go to my college classmate and friend Joe Illick, a former history professor at San Francisco State University. Joe not only suggested Lovett to me as a possible subject but also was good enough to read and critique my chapters as I went along with the story. At the Yale Library's Manuscripts and Archives Division, I had much assistance from Judith Ann Schiff and the rest of the staff while I went through the Lovett papers. Brian Kiss of Yale's Sterling Memorial Library was a big help, as was June Can of Yale's Beinecke Rare Book and Manuscript Library. David Clark, Pauline Testerman, and others helped out at the Harry S. Truman Library and Museum in Independence, Missouri, as did Stephen Plotkin and Maeve Kennedy at the John F. Kennedy Library. Christina Barber, archives and special collections specialist at the Amherst College Library, helped me. Rosa Grier at Temple University's Paley Library and Tammy Kiter at the New-York Historical Society were also helpful, as was Deborah Cordonnier at Princeton's Firestone Library. Cathy Skitko, Louis Jeffries, and Mary Selan helped me go back into Lovett's prep school days at The Hill School. Breanne La Camera, Carrie Hintz, and Tara C. Craig gave me assistance at the Columbia University Center for Oral History. My classmate Bob Aldrich assisted with Henry Stimson, and my high school and law school classmate Skip Corson, my Princeton classmate Lyell Henry, my law partner Bill Landsburg, and Sue Stuard, Jane Unkefer and my daughter Diana gave additional help. The whole staff at the Radnor Memorial Library, particularly Maryanne Buck, contributed all along the way. And so many others at various libraries and institutions whose names I didn't get helped out in many different ways. My wife Jean was always with me, even when it involved riding along on trips to New Haven or Independence, Missouri.

Preface

As the United States emerged as the dominant power on the global stage in the years following World War II it was led by statesmen of the Roosevelt and Truman administrations: Averell Harriman, Dean Acheson, George Kennan, John McCloy, Charles Bohlen, and Robert Lovett, the apt subjects of a joint biography, *The Wise Men: Six Friends and the World They Made*, published in 1986 when America's world image was becoming tarnished. These friends had been born around the turn of the century, were educated in Ivy League institutions, and had succeeded in their professions. They were relatively well known in their own times, but perhaps least so the very modest Robert Lovett.[1] But before that time, as it was written, "Bob Lovett was one of the half-dozen most influential civilians in the conduct of World War II and made immeasurable contributions to the development of American air power."[2]

Lovett was awarded a Presidential Medal of Freedom by John F. Kennedy that bore the inscription "Servant of the Republic." Those words perhaps as well as any convey an idea of who Lovett was and what he did. The writer David Halberstam described Lovett as a man with "a sense of country rather than party."[3] Robert Lovett's services to his country were substantial and covered many years. From his accomplishments as a naval aviator in the First World War to his building up of the army air force that helped to win World War II, from his service in the State Department in bringing the Marshall Plan and NATO into being and his work in the Defense Department during the Korean War to his efforts as a member of several of Eisenhower's boards of consultants, his counsel to Kennedy during the Cuban Missile crisis, and even his advice as requested by Lyndon Johnson, Lovett was right in the middle of so many historical events of the twentieth century. (He and his wife, Adele, were even, in the years before the Second World War, occasional participants in the doings around the Algonquin Round Table, in Manhattan.) One historian and prominent Eighth Air Force officer said that Lovett "has come down through the years by unanimous acclaim as one of the most brilliant and effective of all the World War II policy makers." Newsman Arthur Krock of the *New York Times* wrote that Lovett was an "able administrator in war and peace who, in my reportorial judgment, had no superior in able, wise, and devoted public service during two Administrations."[4]

And of course before, after, and in between his tours of duty in Washington Robert Lovett was an active partner in Brown Brothers Harriman and Company at 59 Wall Street, so his doings as an international banker need to be mentioned as well. He got no headlines for any of that, but he had a far better knowledge of Europe when he went to work for the government than most had, and his encounter with a couple of German aviators while he was overseas on bank business turned out to be rather important in his War Department work. But now, in the second decade of the twenty-first century, who knows Robert A. Lovett? Why does his name so often produce a blank stare? Lovett, for all of his accom-plishments, was always willing—eager at times—to let someone else get the headlines, the press coverage, the acclaim. He was not interested in pub-licity and he actively avoided it most of the time; he just wanted to get his job done and done right. Long after Lovett had left the service of the government, he received letters from publishers, men who were aware of what he had done, telling him that they would be happy to publish his memoirs, his reflections on the active life he had led. Robert Lovett's response was always about the same, that George Marshall declined to write any memoirs and Lovett agreed with that. So there is nothing in the way of a Robert Lovett autobiography.

Even his personal papers, donated to the Yale University Library by his grandchildren, are not complete. Lovett maintained that his papers from his serv-ice in the government—the years in the War, State, and Defense departments—belonged not to him but to the govern-ment, so he left them all in Washington, where they have to be searched out in various locales, as any writer doing gov-ernment research knows all too well.

Lavinia Lovett and her young son Robert in Texas (Robert Abercrombie Lovett Papers [MS1617]. Man-uscripts and Archives, Yale University Library).

Years after the end of World War II, a friend wrote to Lovett and quoted a letter he had just received from Haywood "Possum" Hansell, one of the leading air force generals in the war. "Bob Lovett," Hansell wrote, "is a very great man. His stature is not generally appreciated. It is high time that his fine contributions to the air war and to the ultimate development of the Air Force should be understood."[5] For his accomplishments, it was felt, he deserved a biography of his own. In pursuing this aim it was necessary for me to keep in mind a thought that Lovett himself expressed, after he was out of government service: "How in the world an author can ever marshal his facts in an orderly fashion, and find his way through a maze of dreary documents, will continue to baffle me."[6]

1

Texas, New York, Pottstown
and New Haven

Huntsville, Texas, in 1895 was a small town of about 2,000 people, the seat of Walker County, 70 miles north of Houston in the East Texas Piney Woods. Its main claim to fame was that the beloved Sam Houston had lived there many years before, and in fact 316 acres in the center of town were occupied by the Sam Houston Normal School, which, when it was opened in 1879, became the first teacher training school in the southwestern United States.

On September 14, 1895, Huntsville saw the birth there of Robert Abercrombie Lovett, the son of Robert Scott Lovett and Lavinia Chilton Abercrombie Lovett. Robert Scott Lovett, the son of a plantation owner in east Texas, was a highly regarded railroad attorney, usually called "Judge" by his friends because of a very brief term in the court system. Lavinia's grandfather, on the other hand, had been a member of the Texas Supreme Court, and her father served in the Texas senate. Among her forebears she had numerous Confederate officers, and Lavinia, a native of Alabama and a graduate of Randolph Macon College, believed in keeping the antebellum spirit alive.

Robert Scott Lovett had married Lavinia in 1890 when he was thirty years old and practicing law in Dallas. His reading for the bar had resulted in a law license, which he used to attain a high standing and widespread recognition of his good qualities. Bernard Baruch, who served on the nation's War Industries Board, which Lovett chaired during the First World War, said that Lovett "had an extremely dignified carriage and a leatherlike countenance which made me think there must have been some Indian in him" (however, he was, as was his son, all Scottish).[1] Lovett had been doing railroad work since 1884 for the Houston East and West Texas Railroad, and in 1892 he joined a Houston firm. After several years he moved his family to Houston, which then had a population of about 40,000. He became general counsel for all Southern Pacific Railroad lines in Texas.

Both the Lovetts and the Abercrombies had come over from Scotland, where, as son Robert later wrote, "our forebears … undoubtedly were minor border cattle thieves, bagpipe players and porridge merchants." He recalled "from conversations with my father and mother … our branch of the family came over from Scotland in the early 1700s and settled in Virginia Colony." The Lovetts later "moved southwesterly into what is now North Carolina," then into the western part of Georgia, Hancock County, "from which the younger sons moved west into Texas somewhere around the 1830s or 1840s."[2]

One memorable day in 1903, young Robert's father had a business visitor in Houston, a gentleman named Edward Henry Harriman, who wanted to talk railroad business with

Judge Lovett. While the two gentlemen were consulting—in a meeting the outcome of which was Judge Lovett's becoming legal counsel for all of the vast Harriman railroad interests—eight-year-old Robert encountered Harriman's son Roland, who was about the same age. Let Roland tell what happened in his father's private railroad car and why he thought Robert Lovett was "a most obnoxious brat":

> My father, essentially an out-of-doors man, did all he could to keep physically fit. He even installed a horizontal bar on which to exercise in his business car. I frequently accompanied my father on his business trips … and being the youngest and the puniest—I was instructed to make daily use of that bar. My "chin-up" record I remember was about one every other day. At about this juncture, about 1903, on a trip down Texas-way, Judge Robert S. Lovett plus a kid my own age joined the party at some frontier cow-town—probably Houston. While the men were talking business, Bob—for that's who the kid turned out to be—and I were turned loose on the car to amuse ourselves. Of course, Bob spotted that bar and started chinning himself twenty or thirty times and cavorting about in a manner to put the "daring young man on the flying trapeze" to shame, ended up in a whirlwind of giant swings. Watching him with awe and envy, I was not aware we had other witnesses to the performance till my father's voice came over my shoulder: "Roland, why can't you do that?"[3]

Of course, after that questionable start, Roland Harriman and Bob Lovett became the closest of friends over many years, while their fathers became the closest of business associates and Judge Lovett moved to New York City, summoned there by E.H. Harriman in order to keep close tabs on the Harriman interests. He did not choose willingly to leave Texas, but business necessities required that he be in New York. At Harriman's death in 1909 Judge Lovett succeeded him as president and chief executive officer of the Union Pacific and Southern Pacific railroads. Young Robert was about ten when the move to New York City was reluctantly made by the family. After several years in the city the Lovetts moved to Locust Valley, on the north shore of Long Island, where the Judge built an elegant home, called Woodfold.

It was quite a change for young Bob Lovett, moving from a small town in the wide-open state of Texas to the biggest city in the country. In New York City he attended the Hamilton Military Institute, a grade-school military academy, for five years, riding his bicycle from the family home on Central Park West to school and back every day. When Robert came home from school each day his father, who had taken note of his son's extraordinary memory, would quiz him on what he had seen on the way to school and on the way home, insisting on an accurate report of details. If the Judge considered young Robert's observations accurate he would reward him with twenty-five cents, if inaccurate he would dock him a quarter. Robert's photographic memory would serve him well over the years.[4] Later in his life, Robert Lovett wrote about his memory, "the somewhat unusual gift which I had in my younger days but which appears to be fading now that I am almost 71." He went on to explain: "When considerably younger, I had what was generally called a photographic memory. While it was largely visual and frequently seemed to operate involuntarily, I think some early preparatory training by my father may have had something to do with it."[5]

Young Robert had a French governess named Marie Lucie Gay, and he claimed he "resented the idea that I had to talk French." Nevertheless, years later he decided that his "mediocre knowledge of the language has stood me in good stead for so many years"— both in business and in government service—because of "Mlle. Gay's stern character" in teaching him the language.[6] He spent a considerable part of his summer holidays either at the Harrimans' fishing camp at Klamath Lake in Oregon or at their ranch, called "the Railroad Ranch," near Big Springs, Idaho. "Roland was about my age, one month difference in age," he recalled. He was closer with Roland than with Roland's older brother Averell. "Averell was three or four years older," Lovett recalled. "I never saw as much of Averell as I saw of Roland ... who became my closest and oldest friend."[7]

In 1909 Robert was sent to a boarding school, The Hill School, in Pottstown, Pennsylvania, some 32 miles northwest of Philadelphia. He worked hard at his studies and in his ninth-grade year led the whole school with the highest grade-point average. In his junior year he was cited for "excellence" in both English and ancient history.[8] In October 1913 the school newspaper reported that young Bob had written a new school song, "which has already appealed to everyone who has heard it."[9] His senior yearbook at The Hill said of Lovett that he was "born for success he seemed," and he led his class in grades his senior year and served as business manager of his yearbook and as manager of the Dramatic Club—he had come a long way from Texas. Young Bob was also a cheerleader, was in the "Q.E.D." debating team, sang (basso) in the chapel choir, and tumbled on the gym team. In his senior year, it should also be noted, Lovett was voted second by his classmates as "Biggest Sponge," second as "Biggest Bluffer," and first as "Most Popular with Masters" (hmmm). He cofounded the Shakespeare Club at the school and acted parts in *The Merchant of Venice*, *Twelfth Night*, and *A Midsummer Night's Dream*. He graduated in 1914 and was one of 46 Hill School boys who headed off to Yale University.[10]

During that summer of 1914, Lovett became enamored of a neighbor on Long Island Sound, a young beauty named Adele Quartley Brown, whose father, James, was the senior partner in the Wall Street banking firm of Brown Brothers. Adele was about five feet eight inches tall, with light blond hair and blue eyes. (Lovett himself was five feet ten inches, with brown hair and hazel eyes.) James Brown liked to give tennis parties for his three daughters, and Bob Lovett and the Harriman brothers went to lots of them. "When he kept coming over," Adele later said, "I thought he wanted to see one of my sisters, but when he *kept* coming over, I found out he had wanted to see me all the time." She and Bob Lovett became quite involved with one another.[11]

He and Roland Harriman, called "Bunny" by his friends, both entered Yale University, Harriman in 1913, Lovett a year later. Lovett reminisced about their youth together: "We shared a little pup tent on these camping trips and we were so dead tired we generally went to sleep right away, but when we stayed awake we'd talk about what we'd do after college. And we agreed that some day we'd get together and work together." They did not plan college with each other—Bunny Harriman went to Groton while Lovett was at The Hill School—but they both wound up in New Haven at Yale.[12]

Before starting at Yale, though, Lovett traveled to Europe that summer with his family, and at one point he hired a motorcycle and headed off to Switzerland. Some five miles out of the town of St. Moritz, Lovett took a bad spill on freshly spread tar. He managed to make it into St. Moritz, where he was taken under the wing of an American doctor named Harold H. Fries. Dr. Fries took care of Lovett's bruises, cleaned the tar off his suit, and introduced him to his daughter Gladys. Bob Lovett was not romantically interested in Gladys—Adele Brown was waiting for him back home—but that autumn he introduced Gladys Fries to his good friend Bunny Harriman. Six months later Gladys and Bunny were engaged. They were married in 1917, the start of a long and happy life together. Bunny always gave his friend Bob credit for that union.[13]

Soon after his motorcycle spill Bob Lovett arrived at Yale. He was a serious student on the New Haven campus, and he found that his preparatory work at The Hill had put him well ahead of many of his classmates. He majored in humanities and economics and was eventually voted by his classmates as among the "most brilliant," "most scholarly" and "hardest working" in the class of 1918, as well as the "most thorough gentleman." When his freshman Latin instructor became seriously ill during the Christmas break, Lovett took over and taught the class for the balance of the year. Not surprisingly, he was elected to Phi Beta Kappa in his junior year.[14]

Lovett was also a member of the Elizabethan Club, after a paper he wrote as a sophomore in which he suggested that a line in *Hamlet*—"The play, I remember, pleased not the million; 'twas caviar to the general"—referred to Shakespeare's own *Troilus and Cressida*, which most authorities up to then had assumed was written after *Hamlet*. This was quite a literary discovery, but it tended to confirm what one of his classmates said about him: "It's just that when he starts to find out something about anything, boy, he finds out everything!"[15]

Still, he was not a gregarious collegian. He had a standoffish, reserved personality and was far from the most popular member of his class, though he was respected by all for his brains, his accomplishments, and his sense of humor. Rail-thin, shy, and rarely smiling, nonathletic on a campus where brawn was celebrated, and blessed with a photographic memory, he was regarded by some of his classmates as a patrician snob. "Observant, serious, brooding at times, and always impeccably tailored in clothing and manner," Bob Lovett "revealed little of himself even to those who thought they knew him well."[16] Even so, he found much to do outside of the classrooms, though he loathed athletics. He sang as second tenor in the glee club and managed the drama society, the Dramat. In the summer of 1915, Lovett and Bunny Harriman spent a month in neutral Switzerland while the war raged through Europe. They traveled up and down the mountain roads and passes by auto and motorcycle, being careful to avoid freshly spread tar, and sampled Swiss wines and cuisine.

The social event of the year at Yale was Junior Promenade Week, and Bob Lovett was named as floor manager for the prom itself in his junior year, which took place on February 6, 1917. The floor manager of the prom was considered the social leader of the class, and Lovett relished the role, sharing the spotlight for the week with the lovely Adele Brown. He hired two dance orchestras for the prom, one from New York City and the other locally in New Haven, and he it was who stepped out on the floor at 9:30 p.m. in his white tie and tails and signaled for the music to start.[17]

At Yale, of course, Lovett was aware of the legendary senior societies, which had much to do with social and extracurricular life there. Membership in one of the societies constituted just about the apogee of campus achievement and distinction. The oldest and most prestigious of these societies was Skull and Bones. It was customary on "Tap Day," a Thursday afternoon in mid–May, that 15 members of the junior class would be tapped and taken into Skull and Bones, while others would be tapped for the—thought to be— lesser societies, Wolf's Head and Scroll and Key.[18]

What went on in the Skull and Bones Tomb, the windowless, forbidding-looking structure on High Street in New Haven, was never discussed publicly, though it was learned that members would gather several nights a week in a darkened room to explore the self-revealed beings of their fellow Bonesmen. The secret symbol of the society was the number 322.

According to Bones lore, the great Greek orator Demosthenes died in 322 BC, when, as the story went, Eulogia, the goddess of eloquence, ascended into heaven, not to return to earth until 1832, when she happened to take up residence with Skull and Bones, which was founded that year. Since then, Bonesmen have traditionally signed their letters to one another with "322."[19]

Bob Lovett would be tapped for Skull and Bones, thereby becoming a Bonesman for the rest of his life, but the actual facts of his entry into the society and his membership therein were quite different from those of the routine Bonesman. That, however, is a part of the story to be told further along.

2

The Yale Unit

While Bob Lovett and Roland Harriman spent the summer of 1915 frolicking about Switzerland, Lovett's friend and classmate Frederick Trubee Davison spent the same summer serving as a volunteer for an ambulance crew in Paris, transporting the broken and maimed bodies of the soldiers fighting against the Germans. While in France, Davison spoke with members of the flying unit called the Lafayette Escadrille and was quite impressed with the pioneer work in military aviation that this group was performing. When he returned to campus in the fall, Davison spoke to his friend Bob Lovett about the possibilities in aviation, its future, and what young men should do with it. Davison said, "In 1915, I at least saw enough of the fellows over there to know that if we ever got into the war, where I personally wanted to be was in the air service.... When I went back to college in the fall, I picked out Bob Lovett and poured it into his ear. We made a sort of compact that if war came we should go into aviation."[1]

While the combatants in Europe were using much more advanced aircraft, airplanes in the United States were in many cases not much improved over the one the Wright brothers had flown in 1903. There had been much legal interplay over the years since then between the Wright brothers and Curtiss and other air pioneers over patent and other monetary claims by the Wrights, as a result of which the development of American aircraft had been held back. Flying in America, despite the efforts of Curtiss and others, had lagged well behind that of Germany and Great Britain. A high-level review by the U.S. Navy had stated that, at that time, "the airplane was a toy."[2]

On June 23, Bob and Trubee got together at the lavish Davison home at Peacock Point on Long Island, not far from the Lovett house, Woodfold. They sat down and worked out a list of friends from Yale to invite for a session of summer flying and, if all developed as they thought it might, to become the nucleus of a unit to fly in the war that was coming. From this list they were able to round up a crew of nine. Several of them lived nearby, but others were some distance away. Eventually, they all gathered to live the summer in a large upstairs room in the Davison house. Trubee assured them that his family would finance the summer of flying (Trubee's father Henry just happened to be the senior partner at J.P. Morgan & Co.).

About thirteen miles below Peacock Point in Port Washington, the Trans-Oceanic Company, run by Lewis Rodman Wanamaker, son of the department store mogul, maintained a ramshackle flying boat station and school. It was to this operation that Davison and Lovett took their friends. At the station there was one flying instructor, a gruff pilot named David McCulloch. There was one impediment to flying lessons for the young Yalies: they must have permission to fly from their parents. At a time when flying in an airplane was widely considered to be almost suicidal, this looked to be a major problem. Aerial enthusiasts John Hayes Hammond and Henry Woodhouse of the Aero Club met with the boys and Trubee's mother at Peacock Point, and the men explained and extolled flying to her. McCulloch too worked on Mrs. Davison, telling her that a well-instructed flyer was a safe flyer and that he would keep her boys safe. "A dead aviator is of no use to anyone," he assured her.[3]

Mrs. Davison was converted. She said that as long as her husband agreed she was "willing to aid as much as possible in preparing my son to serve his country as an aviator."[4] Henry, her husband, came home from a fishing trip and, though expressing initial doubts about Trubee's project, gave his consent after a conversation with Hammond and Woodhouse. Eventually, McCulloch took Mrs. Davison up for a flight, and after that she had little trouble in getting the other boys' parents to consent to the flying experiment.

Along the way Trubee Davison made a couple of trips to Washington to meet with Josephus Daniels, secretary of the navy, to see how the navy might work with a group of young aviators. Daniels, a newspaper publisher from North Carolina with little exposure to the ideas of aircraft, applauded young Davison's interest in aviation, but he was most dismissive of any idea of naval sponsorship of an air reserve group. Any funding for the summer's training was totally out of the question. Back from Washington and unhappy with the navy's disinclination to offer any backing, Davison, Lovett, and their cohorts began their actual training with McCulloch. They were trained in stripping down airplane engines and maintaining bracing and cables, learning all the things that could go wrong in an airplane's interior as well as what to do should any of them happen.

When training started, in mid–July, the Trans-Oceanic had one plane on hand, a two-seat, dual-control, 90-horsepower F-boat—called the *Mary Ann*—built by Glenn Curtiss. Each morning the boys piled into Bob Lovett's automobile for a wild ride to Port Washington. McCulloch gave each of the boys a flight in the *Mary Ann* and then went on to teach them how to do it for themselves. They learned what to do if an engine stalled, which often happened with those early flying machines, and how to adjust the fuel mixture. McCulloch applauded the courage they showed, but he emphasized that courage without skill could lead to disastrous results. They got to know the *Mary Ann*, the only plane at their disposal, inside and out—how to remove a motor, pull it apart, and reinstall it in the plane. Each evening, the boys would return to the Davison home, "hot, tired, and dirty, and more enthusiastic than ever," recounted Mrs. Davison.[5] In August, Henry Davison purchased another F-boat plane for the group and there was more flying available. Late in the summer Trubee Davison became the first of the Yalies to solo, and he was followed soon after by Bob Lovett and later by Artemus "Di" Gates.

Subsequently, of course, Bob Lovett, Trubee Davison, and their colleagues had to report back to New Haven to begin their junior year at Yale, where the student newspaper praised them for doing "the work of the pioneer."[6] Throughout the fall, every Sunday many of the young airmen visited the navy's submarine base at New London, Connecticut, where they participated in flying exercises. They were now enrolled in what was called the Yale Aero Club. Trubee learned that Lieutenant John H. Towers, one of the principal leaders of the small U.S. Navy Air Corps, was in New York, so he made a point of visiting Towers and telling him what the Yale Unit was doing and how their offer had been rejected by Daniels. Towers was impressed. Soon thereafter Davison made another trip to the nation's capital, this time to visit Towers in his Navy Department office. When Davison told him that all of his group were prepared to leave college to form a navy flying unit, Towers responded, "If this is the case, you ought to go." He said the Aero Club members should enlist promptly in the naval reserve and then depart for Palm Beach for their training. Towers even made final arrangements with the reluctant Josephus Daniels. Davison, before leaving on his train home, wired Bob Lovett back at Yale: "We're off!"

Back on campus, Lovett raced from room to room, spreading the word that the members of the Yale Unit had only five days to enlist, close their rooms and make arrangements with the college to leave, pack up their warm weather gear, and say their good-byes. By that time, Henry Davison had recruited a close friend, Colonel Lewis S. Thompson, to take the Yale Unit in hand, to oversee their activities and to make sure that their training was adequately funded. By the end of the morning after Trubee Davison's visit with Towers in Washington, Thompson had raised $200,000 to cover the unit's expenses. The members of the Aero Club then traveled to New London to enlist in the naval reserve as the navy's first air reserve squadron. Trubee Davison was given the rank of lieutenant junior grade, while Bob Lovett and those who had soloed received the rank of ensign. The others were made petty officers or engineers. On March 28, with their gear packed, the new reservists were off to Palm Beach and the United States Navy. As the "Millionaires' Unit," as it was called in some newspapers, went to war, it was recognized that its members were the first group of boys called out of college for military training. Many more would be called, but they were the first.

As Bob Lovett and his fellow reservists rode their train south, they had quite a lot on their minds. They were not really sure where they stood in the military world. They had followed Trubee Davison without knowing just what lay ahead of them, and of course Davison did not know either. They were not sure how long they would be training, and they did not know if the navy was going to expend any funds in their support. And, though enlisted in the U.S. Navy, they knew little of the navy's ways—its organization, procedures, rules, and way of life. On the way south, Davison was designated the unit's "first officer," Bob Lovett the "second officer," and Curt Read the "business manager." Still, rank and military discipline were ideas that were foreign to the men of the Yale Unit.

At 4:30 the morning of March 29, the train arrived at its final stop at West Palm Beach, and the sleepy-eyed young men left the sleepers for the humid South Florida night. As they moved slowly toward the Trans-Oceanic Air Station, they were startled to be greeted by Dave McCulloch, drunk after an all-night carouse with friends. With McCulloch leading the way, they checked out the Trans-Oceanic facilities—a shed enclosing a small machine shop, five plank runways going off into Lake Worth, and the wreckage of old boats along the shoreline. There were no hangars; what frail aircraft were there were perched on stands out in the weather. Following the jolt of that inspection, they hired cars to transport them and their bags three miles to Palm Beach, where they checked into the lush Breakers Hotel on the ocean, although Colonel Thompson soon decided the expensive Breakers was not the place for these high-spirited young men. He soon took over the entire 50-room Salt Air Hotel, closer to the Trans-Oceanic location in West Palm Beach, for $75 a day, and moved his young Yalies there, each with a private room and a shared bath.[7]

From New Haven word came that Yale's Emergency War Council had passed, on March 28, the following resolution, which gave to all a feeling of satisfaction: "Any student applying for leave of absence because of orders from the United States Government which affect him personally, will be allowed to leave the University immediately; and if he is an undergraduate in good and regular standing at the time of leaving, who has advanced into Junior year, due credit towards a degree will be given him for satisfactory work in the Army or Navy."[8] Soon the unit got down to business. Davison divided the group into seven crews, each with a flying machine and a leader from among those who had already soloed. The head mechanic and McCulloch got them right into mechanical learning and flight instruction, and the seven groups were soon competing with one another.

Each day the trainees were flying from 6:00 a.m. to 11:00 a.m., with lectures from 2:00 to 3:00 in the afternoon, then back to flying and hangar work until 6 o'clock. With the instruction they were given, they turned out to be as good at mechanics as they were at flying. The formal connection to the navy was represented by Lieutenant Edward O. McDonnell, who arrived at West Palm Beach to serve as the unit's commanding officer. McDonnell, an Annapolis graduate, wore the Medal of Honor for his exploits at Vera Cruz in the Mexican action of a year earlier. He instilled some navy discipline and order into the ranks, and his young men added some freewheeling spirit to the young officer, who very much enjoyed his new association.

The trainees bought and installed seaplane radio sets and made some progress in picking up stray radio bits while they were in the air. "On one occasion Bob Lovett intercepted a tender missive which threw him off his balance.... It was sent from Havana and said, 'Love and caresses. Galli Thea.'" Lovett was of course able to put this sweet message behind him; he had plenty of love and caresses waiting for him at home, from Adele Brown.[9]

While the training was going on, a very Yale-like event took place in West Palm Beach. Early in the spring, one society at Yale suggested that Tap Day take place immediately, since some juniors would be leaving the campus soon for military duty. Skull and Bones demurred because its members had not finished its election process; Tap Day was put off to April 19. When that day came around, the three societies were represented in West Palm Beach to perform a special Tap Day proceeding. The juniors gathered at noon in the lobby of the Salt Air Hotel, and the representatives of the societies appeared. They proceeded to tap their chosen. Robert Lovett was one of those tapped by Skull and Bones. Trubee Davison, John Vorys, Di Gates, and Alphie Ames were also designated Bonesmen. Six were tapped for Scroll and Key, and the two tapped by Wolf's Head declined their invitations. The society representatives sent the appropriate word back to New Haven. Lovett's formal initiation into Skull and Bones did not take place until some time later, when he was at Dunkirk, France.[10]

With Tap Day out of the way, and with the training and instruction imparted by McDonnell and McCulloch, the members of the unit were soon considered worthy of moving ahead. On June 1, 1917, they took a train north for stationing at Huntington, Long Island, where Colonel Thompson had located and secured for them an estate of 75 acres and 1,400 feet of shorefront on Huntington Bay, with a fine mansion for the boys to live in. Thompson had then hired workmen to construct hangers, runways, a radio shed, a machine shop, and docks. He had Kate Davison, from nearby Peacock Point, to keep an eye on the progress of the work. As the train neared Philadelphia, rumors were heard that foreign agents were plotting to blow it up, so it was routed off the main line onto a siding. The scheduled stop in Philadelphia, as well as one scheduled for Pennsylvania Station in

New York (where family members waited to greet some of the young flyers), was cancelled and the locked-up train continued on to Huntington, where Colonel Thompson had things in pretty fine order for the training to continue.

By this time, however, Thompson needed more money. He duly sent telegrams to the unit's backers, who came through with additional infusions of cash to cover the construction costs at Huntington and the cost of a 60-man staff. To these would be added the expenses of keeping the flimsy aircraft flying as well as the purchase of motor parts, radios, and spares. Thompson also ordered khaki naval aviator uniforms, which the flyers found when they arrived. The navy supplied two new seaplanes for the trainees' use, and Harry Payne Whitney furnished another machine. The boys continued to work in five-man teams, but there were now enough aircraft that everyone could spend some time aloft each day. The training moved ahead, and by the end of June each of the boys had soloed. They then began preparations for the navy's pilot's license tests, which were scheduled for the end of July. The test involved a written exam as well as a flight test in which the pilot being tested ascended to a height of 6,000 feet, spiraled down, cut off his engine, leveled off at 3,000 feet, and then brought his plane to a landing within 200 feet of a marker placed on the water.

While the tests loomed ahead, the young fliers went through other routines, practicing firing machine guns from the air, shooting at kites that were moving, and working on landing approaches that would bring them right to the spot they wanted. Using compasses and charts, they started taking longer flights, working their way back to base. They also enjoyed flying over the beaches, estates, and towns in their neighborhood, showing off a bit, all under the supervision of Lieutenant McDonnell. The press reported on the young fliers' progress from time to time, and a photo of the unit mustered on the Huntington dock appeared in the *Saturday Evening Post*, illustrating an article entitled "The Aviator's Sixth Sense." Later on, the *Washington Post* ran a series of photographs of the members of the unit in various poses, duly identifying the young men with their accomplishments at Yale along with their fathers' names.[11]

The flying trainees were also happy to impress the "Wireless Girls," also known as the Girls Radio Unit, a group of seven pretty young women who had been recruited by Kate Davison in April 1917. The group, which included Alice Davison (Trubee's sister), Adele Brown (Bob Lovett's girlfriend), and Priscilla Murdoch (the girlfriend of Kenneth MacLeish, by then part of the Yale Unit), took radio lessons in New York City and relocated, not surprisingly, to Huntington in June. The young ladies were glad to share experiences with the flyer-trainees, who, if a flying boat was free, were happy to take them up for a ride over Long Island Sound and the nearby countryside.[12]

Saturday, July 28, 1917, a bright and clear day in Huntington, was scheduled for the young men to undertake the navy's qualifying flight tests, which were to be taken first by Trubee Davison, Di Gates, and Bob Lovett. All 28 members of the unit had passed the navy's written exam, and now all were ready for the flying part of the test. Trubee Davison was not feeling very well. The long days of hard work and stress as the leading officer of the unit had taken a toll; he had fainted on the dock the day before. Now, however, he said he felt fine. Soon all three pilots were in the air, in single-engine Curtiss F-boats, climbing to the required 6,000-foot ceiling to begin the spiral downward. Davison felt minor turbulence, overreacted to it in what was apparently a panic attack, and crashed nose first into the water. His plane was shattered, and he was trapped inside it. Only the quick thinking of Eddie McDonnell saved him; McDonnell dove off his boat in full uniform, swam to Trubee, and then, unable to lift him out of the sinking airplane, dove underwater to untangle the wires and broken planks around his legs. McDonnell rose to the surface, pulling Davison to safety, as the plane sank to the bottom of the sound.

Gates and Lovett landed nearby, their tests successfully completed, although few noticed that fact. Lovett and Dave "Crock" Ingalls quickly commandeered Curt Read's roadster and raced into the city to locate the Davisons' family doctor. They brought him to the New York Yacht Club landing on the East River, and Trubee Davison was then transported to the hospital. His back was broken, his body was severely damaged, and his naval flying days were over.[13]

The rest of the Yale Unit, with their leader suddenly taken from them, persevered as he would have wanted them to. Di Gates was qualified as Naval Aviator Number 65, Bob Lovett as Number 66. The other members of the unit passed their flying examinations, 27 in all, and were made available to the navy. The navy certainly needed them. At the time of Woodrow Wilson's declaration of war, the United States Navy had 22 operable seaplanes, 38 qualified pilots, and 163 enlisted men on aviation duty. The planes were mostly obsolete and the men barely trained. Across the sea, Germany was in 1917 producing more than 1,000 airplanes a month, but there was a paucity of technical and technological know-how in America. Still, Congress in July 1917 allotted $640 million toward the creation of an air force, and the U.S. made lavish promises of aircraft, pilots, and mechanics to its allies in Britain and France, promises there was no possibility of keeping.

In addition, there were very limited naval air training facilities prepared to create a force of naval aviation. Several of the members of the Yale Unit, recently licensed and eager to take on the enemy, found themselves sent to the newly created training stations in the United States, assigned to the development of more pilots for the navy. This development created much gloom among the members of the unit, who thought they should be fighting the enemy. To counter this mood somewhat, Lieutenant McDonnell requested that his two most senior officers, Bob Lovett and Di Gates, be sent to France. Such a move, he said, "would show that exceptional ability and industry will be rewarded."[14]

3

Off to Europe

As Lieutenant Eddie McDonnell had requested, the two young ensigns, Robert Lovett and Artemus "Di" Gates, sailed from New York on August 15, 1917, on an armed merchantman, the *St. Paul*, headed for England. It was not long before the reality of warfare loomed before them, in the form of four-hour watches in the dangerous stretches of the Atlantic looking for periscopes and, in the Irish Sea, of a zigzag course to avoid the ever-threatening German U-boats. Poor Bob Lovett was seasick for most of the crossing, and, as he wrote to Trubee Davison from onboard, "the last four days have been unmentionable." "It was awful!" he said. He concluded, "Ye gods, this is a cruel game!"[1]

The *St. Paul* landed safely at Liverpool, and the two young officers took a train south to London, where they soon enjoyed what there was of London society at that point in the war. They took in theatres and visited classy teashops; they purchased gloves and canes; and they accepted the compliments of those who were not yet accustomed to the sight of American military men. At night the two wandered through a dark and silent city while its defenders looked for Zeppelins and Gotha bombers coming across the English Channel with evil intentions. On August 30, 1917, Lovett and Gates crossed the channel and reported to naval aviation headquarters in Paris. Lovett soon sat down after a week to compose a letter to Trubee Davison, in which he first discussed the condition of France and the hope produced by America's entry:

> You must have remembered it as you saw it two years ago—you would be heartbroken now! She is staggering with the weight of the war's toll.... I can only account for her superb fighting by attributing that quality to something in each individual *poilu*—each man has a dash, a vision that carries him beyond himself. Her people were fed up with war and its suffering—they would never have been able to face the future if we had not brought hope just in time.... We hear stories of the men in the trenches shooting their officers from sheer desperation—anything rather than another winter in the hell of the front. Now however, with America's *promises* they are keeping at it splendidly.

He noted that Frenchmen "seem to think that the task of pushing Germany back is too great—they believe, understand, that we will win, but they don't think we will swamp Germany by a long sight." He had discovered "that the Germans are far superior in the air. I had expected it in seaplanes, but it is astonishing what those Huns are doing," and he described what the Gothas could do. The German fighters, too, had the Allied planes like the Spad beaten.

Lovett reported in his letter that "there are a number of Yale boys here in the Sig. Corps and in the Foreign Legion ... [and] it was great fun seeing them." He finished up by noting that he was "to be executive officer & officer-pilot in charge" at one base while Gates went to another: "We are both scared of the authority vested in our green selves." Then, he surmised, they were to "go to the fighting bases in time for the 'big fight.'" A few days later, Lovett wrote to Trubee's mother, telling her "the flying is great fun and we are with congenial officers so altogether we have nothing but thanks to give; if it never gets worse than this we will indeed be lucky."[2]

From Paris, Lovett and Gates were sent south to Saint Raphael, on the French Riviera, for further flight training to fly at full speed at low altitudes for long distances—but before too long Lovett was ordered back. He was sent to the brand-new American naval air station at Moutchic, opened on August 31 four miles from the ocean and thirty miles from Bordeaux, where he was given responsibilities much beyond what he felt himself qualified for. Those in charge, though, quickly recognized in Robert Lovett a man they could rely upon to carry out any duties assigned to him and to recognize essential details and remain focused on his objectives. Lovett wrote to Trubee Davison on September 24, when he was alone and in full charge of the station: "We are being treated much more considerately than we deserve.... The authority given me is alarming in that it is so loosely granted and we are so green."[3]

At Moutchic Lovett helped in chopping down trees, erecting hangars, and assembling the crated French FBA flying boats that were sent there. His commanding officer at Moutchic, Lt. Commander G.C. Dichman, wrote that Bob was "chief pilot, construction officer for seaplanes and organized the school and method of keeping the school supplied with machines," that "his handling of men was exceptionally good," and that he could not speak too highly of Lovett's "enthusiasm and energy with which he takes over his work." Lovett even made the first test of one of these seaplanes on September 27, a flight that marked the first flight ever by a naval flier at an American base overseas. Looking ahead hopefully, he said, "I am to see the real stuff ... in one month—as soon as our men are ready, and then patrolling will change to bombing, fighting and fire directing."[4] All, in Lovett's opinion at that point, was going well. He wrote to Kate Davison on November 29: "All of your unit are in the pink and doing splendidly; it is glorious fun over here and we are quite happy in hopes for the future. The worst is over I believe." That, of course was not to be true.[5]

In early December 1917 Lovett was sent off to Felixstowe, England, to a Royal Navy air base on the North Sea, where he found John Vorys and Al Sturtevant, two of his Yale buddies. Here, serving with the British, they flew escorts for convoys and patrols searching for German U-boats: "intensive patrol work ... by jingo it was fun." Soon Lovett "received a roving commission attaching me to the RNAS for 'duty with special attention to administration and organization data, with view to commanding a station.'" The British and American forces shared a common goal, and they worked very well together. Lovett was taken around to other British air bases, schooled in how the different units of military aviation fit together, and given bombing and gunnery courses. He managed to get to London for Christmas, where he and several other Yalies were able to celebrate the holiday, doing, as Crock Ingalls wrote in his diary, " a lot of what you do in London."[6]

It was with this training that Bob Lovett started to work out in his head a plan to revamp the navy's operations in Europe, "a wonderful stunt upon the success of which hangs our future profession," as he told Adele in a letter home, though he kept it a secret from his compatriots for the time being. This secrecy irritated some of those others. Gates wrote to Trubee Davison: "The same old Bob, very secretive and chasing all over the country with the wildest stories that never seem to match up."[7] In January 1918 Lovett was summoned back to Paris to serve as assistant to Captain Hutch I. Cone, the chief of U.S. naval aviation in Europe. Captain Cone had already assessed Lovett in a review dated December 16, 1917, writing "this young reserve officer is excellent in every particular, has splendid all around officer-like qualities and I cannot say too much in praise of him as an officer in the U.S. Navy."[8]

In Paris Lovett shared an apartment in the Latin Quarter with his unit's former CO, Eddie McDonnell. In February, when Cone took off for an inspection tour, 22-year-old Bob Lovett was left in full charge of all American naval aerial operations in Europe—and he handled everything that came along. He spent a good part of the winter going back and forth between Paris and Allied bombing stations, checking out aircraft and operations. As Yale flier Kenneth MacLeish wrote to his fiancée on February 22 about Lovett, "That boy has a better head and more ability than any two men in this branch of the service, and I'm glad they're beginning to appreciate the fact."[9] At one point, when Lovett was commanding one of the bases, it was visited by the assistant secretary of the navy, Franklin Roosevelt. The future president noted in his diary that he had met "the son of Judge Lovett ... [and] he seems like an awfully nice boy."[10]

Lovett was soon transferred to Couderkerque, near Dunkirk in northern France on the English Channel. Dunkirk was an Allied base, but it was well within the range of German bombers, who pounded it regularly from land, sea, and air. The Germans even moved "Big Bertha," their 15-inch howitzer, up to where it could pour its shells onto the station.[11] It was at Dunkirk that Bob Lovett, along with Di Gates, received his initiation into Skull and Bones, which brought back to him memories of his days in New Haven. "You'll never appreciate what the old place has meant to me over here," he wrote to Trubee Davison.[12]

It was here, also, that the theory of aerial warfare that had been forming in Lovett's head was brought to fruition—a theory he had been expressing in memos to his superiors. A seaplane's search for German U-boats at sea was a frustrating and usually unsuccessful mission, with the vastness of the ocean and the submarine's ability to drop beneath the surface out of sight. Lovett's experience in prewar railroad inspections with his father, the chief of the Union Pacific, had shown him that maintenance of a large number of railroad locomotives required a lot of down time for things like refueling and repairs. Would not a fleet of submarines require something of the same? And, he had learned, not to his surprise, that at any one time 85 percent of the German submarines were docked at their coastal bases for some sort of maintenance work. Why not concentrate on bombing the submarine pens on the shores rather than trying to find individual boats at sea? With the havoc that the U-boats were wreaking on shipping to Britain and France, the change in attack philosophy might have seemed obvious. However, because of the lack of resources to carry out missions against the pens at Bruges and elsewhere, these raids could hardly be made. To find out how they might be made and what would result, Lovett signed on as a rear gunner in a British flotilla of four Handley-Page bombers to attack what were considered the most risky bombing objectives in the whole European theatre.[13]

Armed with a full payload of more than a ton, the Handley-Page (which had a wingspan of 100 feet) had a range of about 200 miles, although its cruising speed rarely exceeded 65 miles per hour, which made it a target to enemy pursuit planes during the daylight. The planes could fly no higher than 7,000 to 8,000 feet, followed by a glide of

5,000 to 6,000 feet when on target, at which time they were very vulnerable to the air defense system of the Germans. On the night of March 23 Lovett climbed aboard the *Evening Star*, one of the four bombers, before it took off with 1,750 pounds of bombs for a flight over the North Sea, to the pens at the canals at the Zeebrugge Mole and Ostend, leading to Bruges. As Lovett later wrote, "the defenses far exceed anything one could imagine." Despite the fearsome antiaircraft fire, the mission was a success, with the bombs being dropped on target. Back on the ground, Lovett shook with exhilaration from the adventure, which he called "the greatest experience of my life."[14]

Lovett and his mates continued the nightly bombing runs for six weeks, with Bob describing in a letter to Adele Brown "sailing over a German base and dropping eggs on it while shrapnel bounces the machine about, and the searchlight stabs at you." Nevertheless, he noted that the antiaircraft response was becoming weaker each time. And, as he completed the raids on the submarine pens, he exulted, "I have at last been through it. I feel a different man."[15] He reported to headquarters what his own experience had shown him: "Due to the continuous expenditure of anti-aircraft ammunition, the continuous use of their guns, and the effect on the morale of the gun crews, their defenses became weaker each succeeding night." Further concentrated offensive missions could operate more safely at lower elevations and do more and more damage to the docks and installations below.[16]

Lovett's theory that sustained bombing lessened the enemy's strength was proving true, and he hoped that his recommendations for the U.S. Navy's first strategic bombing force would be accepted. He had played a key role in pushing for such a force: interviewing military officials and personnel with insights into the problem, drafting reports, participating himself in the bombing raids (while wearing, for warmth, a suit of long underwear made by his mother from white Angora wool), and compiling and refining policy proposals.

In April, Alice Davison (Trubee's sister and Di Gates's girlfriend) and Adele Brown started thinking about coming to France to be with their young men. They were soon discouraged by learning that they would have little chance to see them. As Ken MacLeish wrote to his young lady, "There's no such thing as leave. We used to be able to get forty-eight hours once in a while, but now that the big push is on, we don't get forty-eight minutes." The girls would continue to wait for their men on the other side of the Atlantic.[17]

In the meantime, Bob Lovett continued with the *Evening Star* on other raids, against railroads and ammunition dumps. On one raid in mid–April against a railway junction well behind the German lines, Lovett was startled to see that a 250-pound bomb was stuck in the rack after the initial bombing run. He alerted the pilot to the problem and then climbed down to the rack over the open bomb-bay door to try to loosen the bomb. The wind over the open hatch threatened to pull him out, while concussions from the antiaircraft fire knocked him about. The pilot decided on another run at the target and to try to shove the bomb free when they were over it. When he received the signal to let it go, Lovett pushed the bomb free, then took up his gun and started firing down the searchlight beams. As the plane headed back to base, he started singing wildly, "Have you seen the ducks go by for their morning walk? Quack, quack, quack, quack, quack, quack," as his fellow fliers laughed with him. Back on the ground, he said, "I could have cried I felt so lucky to have been through it and come out safely."[18]

Captain Cone accepted Lovett's recommendations for a strategic bombing group to take out the submarine menace, and on April 17 Cone sent a long cable to Admiral William S. Sims, commander of all U.S. naval operations in Europe, setting forth what should be done. This was the creation of the Northern Bombing Group, to consist of two wings, with nearly 300 airplanes requiring some 3,100 enlisted men to maintain them. The planes would be based at existing facilities around Dunkirk. Cone and Lovett certainly knew that their proposal was a major step forward in aviation warfare, and they were expecting that if the Northern Bombing Group should come into existence its operations would probably not get underway until 1919. But Cone, in his message to Sims, said, "Strongly recommend … program be undertaken immediately."[19]

Several days later, after the April 30 approval of the program by the secretary of the navy, Sims responded and told Cone to begin at once to organize the Northern Bombing Group for immediate activity, designated specifically to concentrate bombing raids on the Bruges-Zeebrugge-Ostend submarine complex. Cone named Captain David Hanrahan, who had no aviation experience whatsoever, as commander of the group. Hanrahan gave nearly unlimited authority to Lovett and Eddie McDonnell to carry out the unit's organization. The program at once encountered interservice opposition from the army, which felt that the navy should be kept away from attacking land bases. Lovett could not believe the opposition voiced by the Army Air Service. "What difference does the means make as long as the objectives are ours?" he said, noting that it was still submarine bases they were after. The secretaries of the navy and war managed to work out the objections, agreeing that operations against submarines in their bases were naval work.[20]

Hanrahan named Bob Lovett commander of the night bomber wing as well as commander of its first squadron. Lovett wrote to Adele: "Did I tell you that I am a wing commander now? … I'm insufferably stuck up now, have been presented to the king."[21] Lovett established headquarters for the night wing at a chateau in the town of St. Inglevert near Calais, south of Dunkirk. He set up three RAF fields nearby to serve as sites for the group's aerodromes. While waiting for planes he went to work to see how many of his Yale Unit mates he could bring back together in his wing. Before long he had gathered quite a few of them, and he was happy to tell Adele Brown in a June 15 letter he had "gotten all the old crowd together."[22]

Robert Lovett took care of most of the logistics of putting together the new bombing group, and when the group's operations against the Germans finally got under way late in the summer he had almost 1,500 men under his direct command. A buddy from Yale, Ken MacLeish, marveled at Lovett's abilities: "Without him, we would never get anywhere. They don't give men ability like that more than once in a million times." Lovett offered MacLeish command of a squadron, which MacLeish refused; he simply wanted to fly.[23]

In his night wing Lovett had under him 135 officers, including 88 pilots, as well as 1,336 enlisted men. Each night his leadership skills were tested as he got his men to their planes, the planes to the runways, and the bombers aloft on their way to the German submarine pens. After that, back in his room, he felt, as he told Trubee Davison, "absolutely alone with one's self in a strange place and knowing no one and nothing except war." At 22 years of age, warfare and the responsibilities placed upon him made a deep impression on his mind and spirit.[24]

On October 1, 1918, Lovett was given the rank of lieutenant commander in the United States Naval Reserve Force. He had just turned 23, but the promotion was commensurate with the responsibilities he carried and the work he carried on. As October moved along it was becoming more and more obvious that the German military forces, both on land and at sea, were collapsing and that defeat was soon to follow. Bob Lovett wrote a happy letter to Adele Brown rejoicing: "We've got the beggars on the run now and we'll break their ruddy necks before the month's gone."[25]

As the end of the war approached—to be marked by the armistice on November 11, 1918—Lovett was saddened to hear that two of his Yale buddies had been shot down, Di Gates on October 4 and Ken MacLeish on October 13. Hopes were high that both men may have become prisoners of the Germans and would be released at war's end. Gates was indeed captured and released on November 26. Of MacLeish there was no news until late December, when a Belgian landowner returned to his farm and discovered a wrecked Sopwith Camel and the body of an American flier. The papers found on his body identified him as Kenneth MacLeish.

The war's end of course saw the departure of most of the American military from Europe back across the ocean. Robert Lovett took with him not only the lieutenant commander's insignia he had won but also the Navy Cross awarded for all the excellent service he had performed for the United States Navy. As he departed, there went after him these words written by his commanding officer, Captain Hanrahan: "A most efficient, thorough, capable officer. High devotion to duty. Excellent organizer. Excellent command of men. An excellent squadron commander." That was Robert A. Lovett.[26]

4

Back from the War

Bob Lovett returned home from Europe in January 1919. He knew what the first thing he wanted to do was, and it was not a return to Yale. The university had notified its students who went to war that they would be given credit for the time spent in the service, so Lovett collected his degree without going back to undergraduate life. In this way he tripled the oddities of his Skull and Bones career: he was tapped for the society in Florida, not New Haven, he was initiated in Europe, not New Haven, and he did not put in his senior year as a Bonesman at Yale. Nevertheless, he remained a loyal Bonesman through the years.

No, what Bob Lovett did when he got back to Long Island was to sit down with Adele Brown and work out what their life together would be. They had become very close before he went overseas, and they had kept in fairly regular communication even with the Atlantic Ocean between them. Now they planned their marriage. In the couple of months before the wedding, young Bob lived with his parents and had the benefit of hearing his father describe the pros and cons of wartime industrial mobilization as he had experienced it during the war. Much of this discussion stuck in young Bob's head, to be brought forth many years later.

The wedding took place on Saturday, April 19, 1919, in Adele's parents' city home in Manhattan at 789 Park Avenue. At four in the afternoon 20-year-old Adele was escorted by her father to the makeshift altar, where the Reverend Charles Hinton, from the Episcopal church in Lattingtown, Long Island, near the homes of both the Browns and the Lovetts, was waiting. Bob Lovett had just joined Hinton's church, perhaps for the convenience of the marriage ceremony. Brought up as a Baptist, Lovett attended a Baptist church in New York City before going off to The Hill School and Yale, both places where the chapel services were Protestant but nondenominational. He attended the Episcopal church in Lattingtown over the years, but he was wary of identifying himself too closely with any specific church or denomination. However, he was quite satisfied to have Reverend Hinton perform the formalities on this day.[1]

For the ceremony, Adele wore a frock of white tulle over satin garlanded with rosebuds, and with a short satin train. Attended by her sister Angelica as matron of honor, she carried gardenias and wore "a rope of pearls" given to her by Bob, who had his father, Judge Lovett, as best man, with a crew of ushers from Skull and Bones and the Yale Unit: Charles Taft, Di Gates, Allen Ames, H.H. Landon, Jr., and Trubee Davison's brother Harry.[2] After Reverend Hinton pronounced Bob and Adele man and wife and an appropriate celebration that featured the Meyer Davis orchestra, the two of them headed off to the Far West for a honeymoon of several months. Robert had with him four volumes of Immanuel Kant's philosophy, provided by his father for light reading on the trip, but Adele was much more the center of his attention than Kant. Indeed, their first child, a daughter named Evelyn, was born on March 6, 1920.

The couple returned in September to Boston, where Robert was to take up the study of law at Harvard Law School. He had been urged to follow this course by his successful lawyer father. The law, however, turned out to have little appeal for Bob Lovett. Many years later he answered a law school questionnaire, saying that he had not planned to become a lawyer but came to the school "for intellectual stimulation and training." Asked for his emotional feeling about the law school as a student, he answered "mixed feelings"; he also said, "I got bored with law." After one year at the law school, he left it and entered Harvard's Graduate School of Business Administration, where he spent the 1920–1921 school year.[3]

One story from his law school year reflected on Lovett's photographic memory. At the final examination of a course in torts he took under Dean Roscoe Pound, there was a question about a particular case, and in his answer Robert quoted the case verbatim, complete with case numbers for his references. Robert's paper was returned to him with "Please see me, R.P." written across it. He dutifully went to the dean's office, and Pound said, "Mr. Lovett, you realize I must give you either an A or a zero." Lovett asked, "Would it help, Dean Pound, if I quoted the case to you now?" He then proceeded to do so, word for word, and Pound gave him the A he had earned.[4]

While he was in the Boston area, Bob Lovett got together with a former friend from Yale, Philip Barry, who was getting started on his career as a playwright. Barry's first play, *A Punch for Judy*, was being performed in Boston. Lovett and Barry stayed close over the years, to the point that Barry's widow many years later told a biographer, David Mays, that Bob Lovett was "perhaps her husband's closest friend."[5]

By this time, Lovett had realized that he had a bad stomach ulcer, one that would give him trouble for the rest of his long life; he lived as much as he could on soft foods, even baby foods, and he abstained from alcohol to protect his innards. When necessary, such as at formal banquets, he could put on a show of fine dining, but he was still pushing aside the heavy cuisine that he knew would cause pain. As he once said, "The doctors said I could 'eat anything at all,' just so long as it *shook* when they brought it in."[6]

A Harvard MBA degree from "one of those condensed courses following the war," Bob Lovett decided, was enough formal education. He had once thought of becoming a professor of economics, but his realization that the world of economics hardly resembled the real world turned him away from that. He started his business career at the bottom, as a runner and then a clerk for the National Bank of Commerce in New York City. "I started in as a night force, worked up to the proving force which came on midnight to 7:00 in the morning, and finally worked my way up into the loan department," Lovett recalled years later.[7] Then, as might have been foreseen, Lovett took his clerking skills to Brown Brothers, where he had previously worked as a summer messenger. Of course, it also happened to be where his father-in-law was the senior partner. "Mr. Brown persuaded me ultimately," Lovett said, "that if I was going to go into banking I ought to come to Brown Brothers…. And he had no son, and he wanted someone to follow him here." Lovett was happy to join Brown Brothers, with whom he not only served an enjoyable apprenticeship, with Brown Shipley & Co. in London, but also became a highly respected international banker.[8]

In the early autumn of 1925 Lovett joined his father-in-law for what he called "a two weeks' dash over the Continent … an intensely interesting experience, and it wound up in a blaze of glory in Brussels where we tried to secure the N.Y. end of the exchange work in connection with the stabilization of the Belgian franc." On the trip Lovett and James Brown "really got to know each other" and "it was a happy time for me." He described his father-in-law as "a delightful companion … great fun." Brown pumped him about his future ambitions, "whether private banking was more or less congenial and interesting than joint stock commercial banking." Late in the trip, James Brown revealed that the partners of Brown Brothers had authorized him to invite Bob Lovett to become a partner. Lovett, dumbstruck at the offer, "accepted joyously and with positively indecent haste." It was quite a journey.[9] In 1926, Robert A. Lovett formally became a partner in the Wall Street firm. He would retain his Brown Brothers connections virtually to the end of his life, although with scrambled leave-takings on those occasions when he went to work for the government. Shortly after attaining his partnership, Bob was happy to become a father once more, when his son, Robert Scott Lovett II, usually called "Robin," was born in March of 1927.

Bob Lovett described his father-in-law as "a smallish man … very ramrod straight, extremely well turned out, very debonair." Educated in Switzerland before returning to Columbia University, Jim Brown spoke French "and was almost the epitome of a highly educated, cultured man." His specialty was the Latin banks, in Belgium, France, Switzerland, and Italy. Asked to describe his father-in-law's manner, Lovett recalled that "he was rather austere … [and not] a gregarious person." As to his own relations with Jim Brown, Lovett said, "He was utterly delightful and behaved as a father-in-law should, keeping his hands off the marriage."[10]

Brown took Lovett on several other trips to Europe to introduce the young partner to banking friends abroad and to international banking—"The Banque de France, the Banque Nationale de Belgique, the Banque Nationale Suisse," Lovett remembered. "All the central banks were his specialty. That's how he knew the government business so well over there…. We just went around to all of our contacts over there." Lovett described the "very large travelers credit business when I first came over here." The Brown Brothers Letter of Credit was the most highly regarded traveler's aid at that time, and Brown Shipley, the copartnership in London where Lovett had worked briefly, was at 123 Pall Mall, "the best known address in London then."[11]

Lovett took up the same specialty his father-in-law had, overseas banking. He remembered going to Europe at least twice a year—seven days over, seven days back—and at least three weeks "to do the tour of the Latin Union countries," Belgium, France, Switzerland, and Italy, and then Germany and the Teutonic countries, places like Hamburg, Dresden, Essen, and Berlin, "another week." Bob Lovett was reputed to be, in the international banking business, "tactful, diplomatic, and suave." He "was generally gone about three months at least of the year on those trips." When he did these trips, he had to leave Adele at home— "too expensive and moved too fast…. I used to do 21 towns in 20 days. And there was no flying then … [so it was] automobiles and trains."[12]

Of course, he was not overseas all the time. On his daily commutes from Long Island to Wall Street, Lovett listened to the radio and indulged in one of his fancies—swing music. "Really got to love the stuff," he reminisced years later, "men like Benny Goodman, Dorsey, Shaw…. Irving Fazzola, a really excellent clarinet player, Teddy Wilson, Dave Tough, Pee-Wee Russell … got to know them all."[13]

In 1922, Lovett met in the banking business a young man named James Forrestal, with whom he soon became fast friends. Forrestal, who had shocked his classmates at Princeton by dropping out of the college several weeks before graduation, had gone on to become a successful bond salesman at William A. Read (later Dillon Read) on Wall Street. He had served in the navy during the war (even earning his wings as navy pilot #154), but he never went overseas and returned to Wall Street and big-time finance afterwards. Forrestal and his partner Ferdinand Eberstadt "earned fortunes in their daring corporate rescues and reorganizations."[14]

Lovett introduced Forrestal and his gorgeous ex–chorus-girl wife, Jo, to people like Philip Barry and got him into the Racquet and Tennis club in town and the prestigious

Bob Lovett and his wife, Adele, in 1951 (Associated Press).

Piping Rock Club in Locust Valley. As a Forrestal biography has it, "There is no doubt that the Lovetts became the Forrestals' principal sponsors and mentors in New York society." At one point in the '20s, the Forrestals and Lovetts shared a rented summer house. Bob Lovett was one of Jim Forrestal's closest friends for the rest of Forrestal's often troubled life.[15] As Lovett wrote late in his life, Forrestal was "an old and close friend of mine…. [W]e saw a great deal of each other outside of business and had a large number of friends in common." He recalled, "Jim liked to be seen, at the opera, at the right parties, and especially in the company of good-looking girls."[16] The Forrestals, mainly through the Lovetts, became very active in the social life of the North Shore of Long Island, along with Alice and Di Gates, Evie and Stuart Symington, and others. Forrestal and Lovett often played a round of golf together. Adele Lovett became a close friend of Jo Forrestal, a former *Vogue* writer, and Adele was able to laugh away Jo's sometimes eccentric doings. "She was an attractively natural woman who said and did exactly as she pleased," Adele said.[17]

Other close friendships developed in Bob Lovett's career. At one point a lawyer named Henry C. Alexander was assigned by his law firm, representing Brown Brothers, to work closely with the partnership as its general counsel. Alexander became a very close friend of Lovett, who "knew him to be of complete integrity with the courage to state the facts that a trained lawyer is able to dig out." Lovett said Alexander's "personality and his courteous treatment of his associates and those with whom he made contact, was an invaluable asset." Some years later Alexander brought his fine qualities to the air force's World War II bombing survey, much to Lovett's delight.[18]

Over the course of the years, the members of the Yale Unit gathered for an annual dinner, where they could reminisce about the war years, talk of their present endeavors, and speculate about the future of flying. At their gathering in 1926 they decided to create a trophy for speed flying, and they chose to name it after their old benefactor Lewis S. Thompson. In April 1928 the L.S. Thompson Speed Trophy became official, "to be awarded from time to time for breaking the world's maximum speed record." After the donation to the National Aeronautic Association of the USA, the Yale Unit gentlemen had little further to do with the Thompson Trophy.[19]

While steadily employed at his growing banking practice, Bob Lovett also became involved to some extent in the railroad business, primarily through the influence of his father and his good friends, the Harriman boys. In 1893, the Union Pacific Railroad had, as had a number of railroads in that depression year, fallen into bankruptcy. In 1897 E.H. Harriman, from his vantage point on the Illinois Central, took over the Union Pacific and with his particular talents rebuilt it into one of the nation's premier roads. As Bob Lovett described it many years later, Harriman extended the Union Pacific to the point where its network and its relations with other roads covered one-third of the country's railroad mileage. "Where others consolidated small railroad principalities into kingdoms," Lovett said, "Harriman federated their kingdoms into an empire and became the greatest railroad builder of them all."[20]

We have seen earlier how E.H. Harriman took Judge Lovett, Bob's father, into close association, both personally and in the railroad business, moving him from Texas to New York in the process. When Harriman died in 1909, Judge Lovett succeeded him as the primary power in the Union Pacific. From then until his death in 1932, the judge presided over the line's executive committee in New York, watching over the operational headquarters in Omaha, Nebraska, and dealing with the war, government intrusions, competition from other railroads, the growing trucking business, and the crash of 1929. Judge Lovett handled matters so well that the Union Pacific continued to thrive when other lines struggled.

While the judge kept a steady grip upon the Union Pacific, its affiliated lines, and its non-railroad ventures, his son kept an eye on things as well. Young Robert obviously had none of the responsibilities his father had, but he was a stockholder, had been elected a director in 1926, and became a member of the line's executive committee. He was very interested in the railroad business, foreseeing that a day might very well come when he would have some of the same obligations his father had. From time to time he joined his father on trips to the West to see firsthand how the railroad was operating and what might be done to improve those operations.

Judge Robert Lovett passed away in 1932. "While things will never be the same without the Judge," his son wrote, "I have the highest possible recollections of him and the greatest pride in him."[21] Averell and Roland Harriman, two of Bob Lovett's closest friends—heirs (through their mother) to their father's stockholding in the railroad—stepped in to take over the leadership of the Union Pacific executive committee in New York, and they welcomed Bob Lovett's ideas and contributions, such as drawings of diesel locomotives he brought back from Germany.[22]

Lovett had always been a close friend of Roland Harriman (called "Bunny"), and over the years had become friends as well with Roland's older brother Averell. Lovett had seen that when Averell got into anything he would do whatever it took to be successful. He recalled from college days that Averell took over Yale's freshman crew and did everything he could to make it a winner, even taking a six-week leave from sophomore class to learn how the Oxford crews operated in England. Later he made himself into a star polo player. "He went into any game lock, stock, and barrel," Lovett recalled. "He would get whatever he needed—the best horses, coaches, equipment, his own bowling alley or croquet lawn— and work like the devil to win."[23]

Bob Lovett's time to run the railroad had not yet come, but in 1940 he suggested that it might be time for the railroad to get into the field of airfreight. Always interested in flying (he had joined the National Aeronautic Association of USA in August 1928, and Bunny Harriman said, "He was sneaking over to some flying field and flying a rented plane just to get his hand in again"), Lovett submitted a paper headed, "Memorandum Concerning Air Express and Air Freight Operations in the United States." He pointed out that "the Union Pacific has pioneered in the development of many aspects of transportation, and the present time may be a most appropriate one for it to blaze the trail again." His paper defined the airfreight issue with clarity and foresight, but the timing was a bit too early. Nevertheless, what Lovett picked up while the Harrimans were in charge would be of great help to him at a future time.[24]

While dabbling in railroad administration, Robert Lovett was deeply involved with his work at Brown Brothers. Before he even became a partner (1925) he did a study of various banks and how they operated. He found that Harriman Brothers, a private banking business down the street on Wall Street, had little business and too much capital, while Brown Brothers "had too much business and little capital. So a merger was perfectly obvious." In 1930 he was one of those in his firm who pushed for a merger with the firms of W.A. Harriman and Co. and Harriman Brothers and Company. Clearly the longtime friendship of Lovett with Averell and Roland Harriman was a factor in the merger. As Roland Harriman wrote later, "The first thing I want to emphasize about my own part in this merger is that there was an intimate friendship between the younger partners of Brown Brothers and Averell and myself, and also, of course, with Knight Woolley, the managing partner of our firm Harriman Brothers, and Prescott Bush, vice-president of W.A. Harriman & Co.... [P]ractically all of us had been at Yale together."[25]

The Harriman companies were operated in a more aggressive style than the more conservative Brown Brothers, but as it turned out the new firm, called Brown Brothers Harriman & Company, was a great success, combining the modes and practices of the two groups. It helped, of course, that Prescott Bush, Knight Woolley, and Roland Harriman of the Harriman companies and Ellery James and Bob Lovett of Brown Brothers were all members of Skull and Bones.[26] When asked years later what he most enjoyed doing at Brown Brothers Harriman, Lovett said, "I think it was the working out the financing of some of the stuff abroad." He mentioned financing the PLM railroads (Paris-Lyon-Mediterranée) and the Chemin de Fer du Nord (French Northern Railway) as well as "an awful lot of the shipment between England and this country, and a little bit from India and South America.... There was a variety of things. In other words, the thing that appealed to me in the banking end was the variety."[27]

His partners saw in Lovett one who loved solving problems, many of which he would take home in his briefcase at night. Bunny Harriman noted, "He was a fool for anything unsolvable." One problem he noted while in Europe on business was the coming troubles with Germany; he managed to get almost all of the Brown Brothers investments out of Germany in the 1930s.[28]

From his post on Wall Street, Lovett observed the changes in American life, from the Great Depression to the coming of the New Deal under Franklin Roosevelt, which he did not applaud. He did not consider himself in any way a politician, but as a thinking member of society he had his conservative ideas on how things were or were not working out. In 1934, in a letter to his brother-in-law, Lovett lamented "a great majority of people have not recognized and done something about the insidious, sinister changes which are being made in our form of government ... [and] we probably won't wake up until it is too late."[29] In a sour letter to his Yale Unit buddy John Vorys, who had been elected to Congress as a Republican from Ohio, Lovett wrote, "As a Mugwump by birth and inclination, I cannot see anything in the record of the New Dealers to distinguish them from the pinkish, social reform government of Blum in France, or the stubborn fumbling Baldwin-Chamberlain school of political thought in England. Both belong to the 'everything's-just-going-to-be-dandy' school of politics.... I have an awful feeling that we have progressed merely from the era of wanting to have two chickens in every pot to the next step which is to have two pots on every chicken."[30]

When Averell Harriman and two partners put together a magazine called *Today*, with its first issue coming out in October 1933, it featured articles and editorials by Raymond Moley, one of FDR's "brain trust" who had worked his way out of the administration with his temper and tactlessness. Lovett looked at what his friend Averell was putting forth and decried it as Moley's "personal journal." "Moley's pet hates," Lovett wrote, "may increase circulation but I think pornographic stories will accomplish the result more quickly and do the cause of liberalism less harm in the long run. The magazine is becoming increasingly cheap and increasingly colored by Moley's own views." Harriman managed to tone down Moley somewhat and the magazine thrived, eventually in 1937 merging into the weekly *Newsweek*.[31]

In the spring of 1937 Bob Lovett had an article published in the *Saturday Evening Post*. Entitled "Gilt-Edged Insecurity," it was a warning to stock purchasers that, despite the name, securities were not always that secure. He had originally written the piece as a memorandum for his firm after a study he had done at Harvard, but Marty Summers of the *Post* and the writer John O'Hara, Lovett's friend, felt it deserved a broader circulation. Lovett wrote: "Consider the absurdity of applying the word 'security' to a bond or a stock. It is hard to find a sillier misnomer.... Now, most of us have been taught that 'security' means freedom from danger or risk. Its use, therefore, to describe paper evidence of debt or ownership, both fairly bristling with risks, is clearly misleading and no doubt tends to support the myth of unchanging value, absolute safety, and so on."[32] Many years later, Bunny Harriman, in his autobiography, wrote of Lovett's "wonderful article" in which "Bob proved that what is a blue chip today might be a loss leader tomorrow."[33]

Through his time at Yale, Lovett had become good friends with writers like Philip Barry and Archibald MacLeish (Kenneth's older brother), and, as he liked to associate with their kind, Barry provided the introductions for him. Working in New York, Lovett, along with Adele, found time on occasion to join with the group of writers who had established what was called the Algonquin Round Table in that well-known hotel on 44th Street. They became friends with Robert Benchley, Dorothy Parker, Harold Ross, Robert Sherwood, Lillian Hellman, Franklin P. Adams, Donald Ogden Stewart, along with their tablemates at the Algonquin, and other literati, such as William Faulkner, Joel Sayre, and John O'Hara, who joined the group on occasion. At times actresses Tallulah Bankhead and Greta Garbo entertained the crowd.

Dorothy Parker called the Lovetts' home, Woodfold, formerly his father's, a "lovely, soap-bubble-tinted house." She introduced Faulkner to the Lovetts and appeared to be a close friend of Adele Lovett, who was said by Parker's biographer to be "a witty and elegant blond clotheshorse who cultivated the Round Table writers and made a big effort to befriend Dorothy." Ms. Parker "gave the impression of reciprocating Adele Lovett's esteem for several years, even dedicating a book to her, although Adele and her Brahmin manners grated on her nerves." After some time, though, as Adele said, she "dropped us like hot potatoes." So much for Dorothy Parker, about whom Nora Ephron said, "The idea of Dorothy Parker was far superior to the living version, who was good with a one-liner but not much fun to be around."[34]

With or without Ms. Parker, the Lovetts were happy to host dinner parties to enter-

(Left to right) Bob Lovett, Trubee Davison, Artemus "Di" Gates of the Yale Unit, 1916 (Robert Abercrombie Lovett Papers [MS1617]. Manuscripts and Archives, Yale University Library).

tain their literary friends at their large and handsome duplex apartment at 625 East 83rd Street overlooking the East River and later at their home in Locust Valley, on Long Island. Bob and Adele became good friends with William Faulkner, who came to New York often in those times, sometimes with his wife, Estelle, but usually alone. The couples first met in 1929, but they saw each other quite a bit through the 1930s. "I knew Bill Faulkner fairly well and, of course, had great admiration for his talent and pleasure in his company," Lovett said, "… a man of special qualities and learning and of kind and courtly manners."[35] Frequently Lovett or Adele would hear from Ross or someone else in the group that Faulkner had been seen in the city. Lovett would then call him at the Algonquin and invite him and a few others to their home. On other occasions, before the end of Prohibition, Lovett would join Faulkner and others at New York speakeasies, even though Lovett, with his ulcers, did not drink.[36]

A piece Faulkner wrote, "Turn About," which appeared in the *Saturday Evening Post* in March 1932, was based on a story Bob Lovett told him from his time in the war, seeing the boys of the Coastal Motor Boats lying drunk in the gutters of Dunkirk before and after their dangerous raids against German submarine bases.[37] Robert Benchley liked to tell a tale of an evening spent at the Lovetts' home in Locust Valley, when his banker-host was called away from the dinner table to take a phone call. Benchley and Donald Ogden Stewart heard Lovett on the phone, saying, "Yes…. Yes. Why, yes! Let Austria have eight million dollars." For the rest of the evening, Benchley said, he was known as "Give Austria Eight Million Dollars Lovett." The next day Stewart sent Lovett a telegram reading, "YOU HAVE MADE ME THE HAPPIEST LITTLE COUNTRY IN THE WORLD. [signed] AUSTRIA."[38]

In 1928 Lovett was appointed to the board of trustees at The Hill School. He added this service to a number of other nonbanking activities. At that time he was a director of several railroads besides the Union Pacific. He was also a director of the American Acceptance Council and a trustee of the New York Trust Company as well as a number of insurance companies, a trustee of the Boys' Club of New York, on the board of managers of Presbyterian Hospital, and a trustee of the Brooks School in Massachusetts. Over the years these extracurricular commitments would increase, to include such outfits as the Union Sulphur Company, the Provident Fire Insurance Company, the United States Guaranty Company, and the Commercial Pacific Cable Company, as well as the Metropolitan Museum of Art, the Babies Hospital, the Neurological Institute, and the Carnegie Foundation for the Advancement of Teaching. Bob Lovett was highly regarded for his work with these nonbanking organizations. An officer in the Carnegie Foundation said, "Lovett is the kind of man who will take a trusteeship and fulfill its obligations on the hunch that somewhere in this cosmos he may be able to do some good for someone else."[39]

Lovett still possessed a great interest in flying. In the late 1930s, the people at Brown Brothers often noticed him disappearing from the office for an afternoon. "We knew something was in the air and, come to find out, it was Bob," recalled Bunny Harriman, thinking back to Lovett's flying lessons he took at the Hempstead Aero Club. After that Lovett made a practice of flying a rented plane—a "puddle-jumper" or "grasshopper," he called it—to keep his hand in.[40]

So the years of the '30s passed by, with Bob working hard for Brown Brothers Harriman and even taking piano lessons in December 1938, he and Adele becoming well known in New York society, and Bob getting to Europe on a regular basis and looking hard at what was happening there. He wrote a paper about it in June 1939 in which he said, "[T]he situation is in such an unholy mess that it is virtually impossible to appraise the real facts. One can, however, be fairly confident in stating that so far no way has been found of liquidating the present situation short of war."[41]

Then one evening, as he was finishing up dinner in a hotel restaurant in Milan, Italy, he fell into a conversation with two gentlemen.

5

To Washington

Robert Lovett continued his banking travels in Europe, even as he saw Adolf Hitler's war breaking around him. He was doing business in Italy before heading to Switzerland, "at the request of the Swiss National Bank, on matters connected with gold." One spring afternoon in 1940 he was finishing up dinner in a hotel in Milan, eating soft foods as usual, when he spotted two gentlemen in German Luftwaffe uniforms at the bar, one of whom he knew slightly.

Lovett walked over to converse with them—two well-known fliers named Erhard Milch and Ernst Udet (whom he had met previously in America) who spoke English—and they were quite happy to go on at some length about their knowledge of the Luftwaffe, their country's aircraft industry, and all the things German flying could, and soon would, accomplish. The two were not simple airmen but had considerable stature in German aircraft, as well as in Hermann Goering's air force, and they knew very well what they were talking about. Milch was state secretary of the Reich Aviation Ministry and later air inspector general, while Udet, who had been the second highest-scoring German flying ace in World War I with 62 kills, was involved in the early development of the Luftwaffe and had since 1939 been director-general of equipment. Udet, who had spent a good bit of time in the United States in the '30s in stunt piloting and air films, had also developed friendships with leading American airmen like Eddie Rickenbacker, Charles Lindbergh, and Jimmy Doolittle. At the bar in Milan, Lovett listened carefully to their boasting and made mental notes of much of what the two told him. "They gave me some very valuable information," he later recalled.[1]

Lovett's trip to Europe was curtailed at that point by the German invasion of France, so he took a ship home. He had been mightily impressed by the talk of his Luftwaffe companions, and he was sorely concerned about whether the United States could compete aviation-wise with Hitler's Third Reich. As interested as he had always been in aviation and aeronautics, Lovett felt that he should examine the present aircraft capacity of the U.S. He had no illusions that the war now encompassing Europe would not soon pull in the United States, and he was much concerned about America's readiness for such a war. When he got back to New York he took care of the banking matters before him and soon embarked on a personal inspection tour of the American aviation industry. Over the years he had kept in touch with those most involved in the manufacture of aircraft in this country, and he set out to visit with them.

Initially Lovett visited factories in the East such as Grumman and Republic, and from there he headed in October 1940 to the West, combining a railroad inspection trip with visits to plants such as Lockheed, Northrup, Vultee, Douglas, and North American. He was in most cases well acquainted with the heads of these facilities, and he sat down and talked with them about their businesses. "I was appalled to find that we were way behind the progress abroad, both in Britain and in Germany," Lovett said later. "In fact that if it had not been for certain of our orders received from France and Britain, we could fairly be said to be asleep."[2] Lovett and the aircraft executives completely agreed that the American aircraft industry was not prepared for the demands that a mid-20th-century war would impose on it, and they urged Lovett to get the word back to Washington.

When he returned East, Bob got together with his close friend Jim Forrestal, who had recently left Wall Street to become undersecretary of the navy, to tell him what he had learned and show him the notes he had taken. Forrestal had long been impressed by Lovett; some months earlier, when Forrestal was being pressed to take a job as an administrative assistant to Franklin Roosevelt, he had written to his friend Tom Corcoran, who was pushing him to take the job: "I think there are better men available. Bob Lovett is one who comes to my mind."[3]

Forrestal was captivated by Lovett's message about the aircraft industry's deficiencies and by a follow-up letter Lovett sent him on July 1, and he suggested that it should be conveyed to former judge Robert Patterson, who was then serving as an assistant to the secretary of war, Henry L. Stimson. Forrestal set up a luncheon meeting for Lovett to talk with Patterson. Patterson was all too aware of America's weakness in these military areas, and Lovett's portrayal of the aircraft situation troubled but did not surprise him. At the end of the lunch Patterson, deeply impressed with Lovett's understanding of his subject, asked him to put his thoughts on the aircraft business in writing.

On November 22 Lovett sent off to Patterson a five-page report, "outlining," as he put it, "several of the views I expressed to you in connection with a report on a recent visit I made ... as part of a continuing effort I have made to keep up with the industry." The report was headed "NOTES ON CERTAIN PROBLEMS IN CONNECTION WITH AIRPLANE PRODUCTION" and was broken down into four parts, "General Comments," "Planes," "Training Program," and "Kicks Heard in the Industry." Lovett said, "It is my impression that the government will not get the plane production now being talked about from present or planned aircraft plants." He added, later, "This is a quantitative war. The airplane industry has, so far, been qualitative." The program, he said, "must be enlarged in order to get adequate facilities and to make mass methods possible without too much sacrifice of quality." Too many types of aircraft were being built, some not right for warfare, with inadequate armament and firepower; mass production of the specific types of planes agreed upon for military usage was necessary. He suggested an increase in the training of non-college men for pilots so that the possibilities for military airmen would be much enlarged. And, he concluded, "plants are too concentrated geographically, causing them to bid against each other for labor, thus injecting an element of instability in the wage situation." These comments, Lovett said, duplicated "fairly accurately the remarks made to Jim Forrestal and are those which he asked me to pass on to you, on the chance that there might be something of interest in them."[4]

Indeed there were items of interest there. On November 25 Patterson wrote Lovett, asking if it would be possible for him to come to Washington to meet with and go to work for Secretary Stimson. "Your comments on the airplane situation," he added, "were greatly appreciated." The next day Lovett responded, saying, "I shall be very glad to come down to Washington any day that suits Secretary Stimson."[5] On November 28 Patterson brought Lovett in to talk with Stimson, "with a view," as Stimson wrote, "to having his assistance in the Department." Stimson "was very favorably impressed" with Lovett, who had, he found, "a very good first-hand view of the problems of the industry. We talked the whole matter over with him and it cleared my mind as to some of the steps forward."[6] On December 18 Stimson, who had obviously received quite a recommendation from Judge Patterson, received Franklin Roosevelt's approval for the appointment of Lovett and John J. McCloy as special assistants to the secretary of war, and the following day the appointments were officially made (at a salary of $8,000 each).[7]

On the 19th, knowing that he would be appointed to the government job, Lovett had submitted letters of resignation to his business connections—he was a director of the Union Pacific Railroad and four of its subsidiary lines, as well as four other companies—sold his stock holdings so he would have no conflicts of interest, and severed his partnership ties to Brown Brothers Harriman. He resigned from the boards of eight philanthropic organizations, ranging from the Metropolitan Museum of Art to the Boys' Club of New York. In his letter to the chairman of Union Pacific's executive committee, he said, "I know you can appreciate how much I dislike the necessity for doing this, but, in the present national emergency, I would never feel right if I didn't take a crack at the job which seems to have got off to such a bad start."[8]

Lovett sat down with Henry Stimson on the afternoon of December 20, to tell his new boss what he knew and thought about the nation's air program. As Stimson had foreseen, it was not a pretty picture. America's aircraft production capacity was low and what planes were being produced were being diverted to commercial airlines and Lend-Lease programs, to the detriment of the army air force; training facilities were sadly inadequate and there were few experienced flying officers; and there was in the armed forces little understanding of what an air war would encompass. Stimson, at the conclusion of their meeting, asked Lovett to sum up his knowledge of the air program and its difficulties in writing, which Lovett did ten days later.[9] Stimson noted in his diary for that day that Lovett had come in to see him "and talk over his work. He is to have special charge of matters pertaining to air work—airplanes—and the more I see of him the better I like him."[10]

Stimson assigned the Wall Street banker to assist with the aircraft program as planned. And assist he did. Patterson wrote Lovett after the war had ended: "I still believe that the best day's work I ever did was when I persuaded you to come to the War Department … back in 1940."[11] Judge Patterson was moved up to the newly created post of undersecretary of war and, as it was reported, "two other civilians of proven ability have been appointed to key posts in the War Department … John J. McCloy … and Robert A. Lovett…. Mr. Lovett, who had a distinguished record as a Navy aviator in the World War, will be concerned with aviation problems." And problems there would be.[12] A third assistant was soon appointed, Harvey H. Bundy, who had worked with Stimson in the Hoover administration. Lovett, McCloy, and Bundy soon found that they worked very well together, much to the benefit of the American military effort.

Actually, Lovett had been thinking about a government job for a while, especially after his meeting with the German flyers and his tour of the airplane factories. Even before that, he had fended off an approach by commerce secretary Jesse Jones about taking a job in that department. In mid–September, Lovett had written to his friend Arch MacLeish (who was then Librarian of Congress): "After a lot of soul-searching, I find myself more and more convinced that, if there is anything which I can usefully contribute to the Government in the present emergency, it will probably lie in one of the fighting forces and in connection with the Army or Navy air program." He felt that the growth of the air forces was "the most effective method of attaining the strength in arms which we need so badly.… If I ever get asked to do that kind of a job, I will be down there on the next plane." Obviously, Henry Stimson did not have to twist Bob Lovett's arm very much.[13] Lovett had hardly arrived in Washington before he was the subject of a scurrilous attack on the floor of the U.S. Senate. On December 23, isolationist senator Rush D. Holt (D-WV) rose to insert in the record a false statement about Lovett and his overseas connections. At Lovett's request, Senator Morris Sheppard of Texas corrected the Senate record.[14]

In the meantime, Lovett went to work for Henry Stimson (who just happened to be a fellow member of Skull and Bones, as was Harvey Bundy) on matters connected with the air force, and Stimson in no time came to regard Lovett as indispensable. As a matter of fact, Lovett recalled, Stimson "dealt with McCloy and me as though we were his sons, having no children of his own so that it was a very close relationship," though at times Stimson called them the "Imps of Satan."[15] By late February 1941, Joseph Alsop and Robert Kintner were writing in their column that "in the short time he has been in charge of the air problems at the War Department, Lovett has shown enough good sense, decision and imagination to equip several Government officials."[16] Stimson's biographer noted that one of Bob Lovett's valuable assets was "the sense of what was really possible and the sense of what was really ridiculous. He was, in fact, one of the funniest of men, full of brief sophisticated witticisms, rueful humors and a perception of incongruity that expanded in the bureaucratic circumstances where such perceptions ordinarily wither away. He was, in other words, both sure in action and wise in counsel."[17]

Robert Lovett got down to business in the War Department. He soon discovered that his working conditions would be far different from what he was accustomed to at Brown Brothers. The apartment he and Adele rented at 2021 Connecticut Avenue in Washington, formerly that of General Pershing, was a considerable step down from his digs in Manhattan and his fine house on Long Island, and the old Munitions Building on Constitution Avenue where the War Department was centered was far less elegant and refined than the quarters at 59 Wall Street, where Brown Brothers' partners worked. Lovett quickly established a seven-day workweek for himself in the War Department, generally from 8:30 in the morning to around seven o'clock at night. On Sundays he sometimes managed to leave the office at about one-thirty in the afternoon, after which he often went to the movies.

Bob Lovett soon came to recognize that Henry Stimson, even while treating him as a son, had a low boiling point but that his explosions soon played out. One morning he walked into Stimson's office while the secretary was reading some report that was making him very unhappy. When Lovett interrupted, Stimson began yelling at him for his insolence and invasion of privacy. Lovett simply backed out of the office, closing the door behind him. Seeing McCloy in the hallway, he said, "Good morning, Jack. The Secretary wants to see you right away," smiling as McCloy walked into another outburst. Of course, Lovett and McCloy, on the frequent occasions when they were invited to Stimson's home in northwest Washington, Woodley, delighted in telling these tales to Mrs. Stimson, while the secretary joined in the laughter.[18]

Lovett missed his old secretary, Hazel Pierson, especially when he encountered the clerical help provided him at the War Department. One memorandum to Secretary Stimson had to be completely retyped when "B-17" appeared as seventeen letter "B's" each time the plane was mentioned. Sorting the mail within the War Department offices took something like three days. Lovett immediately started to do what he could to straighten out the administrative chaos with which he felt surrounded. He knew he had to do that even as he began working on the aviation problems he had been hired to deal with.

6

Lovett Goes to Work

Robert Lovett's principal motivation for taking a job in the War Department was his conviction that the United States was sure to enter the war already convulsing Europe, that airpower would be a major factor in such a war, and that America was poorly fitted to compete with Germany in that area of aviation. With this as his driving force, once he became accustomed to the working conditions in the War Department, Lovett was ready to go to work. He quickly recognized that his first major project was to make sure that his superior, Secretary Stimson, knew and approved of the steps that Lovett was convinced had to be taken. Once Henry Stimson was on board, what Lovett aimed at "was a steady, businesslike, and unbeatable increase of American air power."[1]

As mentioned previously, Bob Lovett sat down with Stimson in several head-to-head meetings, the first on the afternoon of December 20, 1940, his first day on the job, to give the secretary a straightforward summary of his views and opinions on the strengths (few) and weaknesses (many) of the aviation program as it stood. Lovett emphasized that the problems needed "immediate vigorous treatment." Stimson emphasized that Lovett was to take charge of matters pertaining to air work. He asked Lovett to set down his views on the air program in written form. Several days later, Stimson met with Robert Patterson, Jack McCloy, and Lovett "to straighten out the work that is now in view and get the new men like Lovett and McCloy on their respective jobs." It did not take much to do that. A week later Stimson wrote in his diary about the bomber situation in which "Lovett, by the way, is turning out a very helpful man in this matter." Over the next months the secretary found that Lovett was very helpful in handling numerous and different kinds of problems, most dealing with aviation but not all.[2]

By December 30 Lovett had prepared the written summary of the air program Stimson had asked for, advising the secretary that "air power is not merely a question of our existing number of planes and squadrons" but "is increasingly a question of industrial capacity to produce today, tomorrow, and next year." He stressed to Stimson the issue of lead time for building an airplane. "Production for 1941 … is now largely over the dam. The time deadline is approaching if we expect to get the benefit in 1942 from any increase in our production program over the present totals." With the U.S. having only about a third of Germany's air production capacity at the time, Lovett told Stimson that additional plant facilities must be provided for air frame, engine, and aircraft guns if there was to be any chance of producing 5,000 planes a month by the end of 1942. He called for some aircraft plants to be put on a 24-hour-a-day, seven-day-a-week schedule. He felt that research into new equipment should be separated from regular production, with experimentation in new technology limited to a few plants, but research was certainly essential. "We must go ahead with all possible speed on advance research and experimentation," Lovett reiterated, "and not rest content with making present types of air frames and engines." Another emphasis in Lovett's December 30 letter to Stimson was on the urgent need for heavy-bomber production. "If there is one lesson that this war has taught," he said, "it is that defensive weapons will not win the war." Accordingly, the bomber program should be materially increased "as rapidly as possible."[3] "Lovett's job," as one article summed it up, "has been the gigantic one of coming in at the last possible moment and helping to make American air power equal, and superior, to an enemy war machine that had been in preparation for ten years and longer." It was a job Lovett carried out superbly, as the Germans and Japanese ultimately discovered."[4]

Lovett found early in his tenure that there was a singular lack of specific information, much of it statistical, pertaining to the Air Corps; he could not even find out exactly how many airplanes there were in the country. As one of his future aides has written, "Lovett was almost at wit's end. He had been a prominent investment banker in New York and understood how crucial the flow of information is to good management. But the air corps he had inherited was tiny, gung ho, and so informal that he had almost no data with which to plan and control operations."[5] Lovett learned of a report a clerk in the Interior Department, Charles B. Thornton, had written on financing low-cost housing that had attracted attention. He persuaded young Thornton to join the Air Corps, got him a commission as a second lieutenant, and put him to work.

When Thornton asked to see the Air Corps plan for the defense of the country, he was shown, after much stalling, a plan for the aerial defense of New York City. "Tex" Thornton, as he was known, soon became one of Bob Lovett's most senior and closest deputies, working on statistical planning, with the aid of Harvard Business School, to make sure that there was accurate knowledge of whom and what the air force had at which place at any time they might be needed. Thornton, after he had set up a widespread reporting system, was able to give Lovett a blanket air-power statement each morning, telling him how many planes, pilots, bombs, ground crews, and even spare parts were available that day. "Thornton," as one of his subordinates wrote, "had no interest in building an empire of clerks. His vision was much more sophisticated. He thought the system and the data, if used intelligently, could help win the war." Bob Lovett felt the same, and he was very happy to have "Tex" Thornton on his team.[6]

Harvard Business School turned out to be just the right place to train officers in statistics. One of those who became a teacher in the program there, a young Californian specializing in analytical control, was Robert S. McNamara. He was such a standout at the business school, a relentless worker day and night, that Thornton soon drew him away from Harvard and into the air force. Working at first on some problems with the B-17, McNamara was soon put to work by Lovett and Thornton on the mass of facts, statistics, operational analyses, and program systemization that developed into the B-29 bomber so essential to the latter stages of the war. In 1943 McNamara and another young Harvard professor, Myles Mace, began working directly with the Eighth Air Force in England and accepted commissions in the army. During the next three years McNamara served in England, Kansas, India, China, Washington, the Pacific, and Ohio, producing information on which the air force could rely. When he left the army as a lieutenant colonel in 1946, McNamara was awarded the Legion of Merit by General Arnold for his services. Robert Lovett had paid particular attention to what McNamara produced.[7]

One problem Lovett had to handle early on was that of British pilots brought to the U.S. to learn how to operate the B-17 Flying Fortresses that would be sent over to England under Lend-Lease. Stimson was disgusted when the army's judge advocate general ruled that as foreigners they could not be trained on American fields. Lovett took the matter in hand, arranged for TWA to fly one of their four-engine planes to Canada, to have some B-17s flown north of the border, and to have the training of the British pilots take place there. "They put this thing through in record time," Stimson noted, "and by the next morning— New Year's Day—Lovett had arranged for the whole affair."[8] Interestingly enough, Lovett spent New Year's Day working at his desk, keeping two stenographers busy. He did not even go out for lunch but had a snack of crackers and milk at his desk. As columnist Drew Pearson noted, Lovett's job was "to wield an ax on the mountain of red tape that has the Air Corps tied in a knot," which was taking some determination to carry out. (Lovett had described the army's general staff as being so heavy with dead wood it was a fire hazard.)[9]

Before long Lovett had embarked on plans to increase the estimated output of airplanes for the spring of 1942 from 3,000 a month to 5,000 in order to satisfy American needs as well as those of the British. One of the principal reasons for the lag in American airplane production was a great shortage of engines. "The task is enormous and difficult," Joseph Alsop and Robert Kintner wrote, and it "would seem hopeless, if it were not for the presence in the War Department" of Lovett, "brought in to head the air production effort." Lovett, they said, "seems to have found his way already through the administrative labyrinth to the heart of the problem." With Lovett tackling the air problem "squarely and boldly, the future is not so dark as it was."[10]

It was not long before Stimson, who quickly recognized Lovett's qualities and abilities, recommended to President Roosevelt that the position of assistant secretary of war for air should be filled. Trubee Davison had held the job from 1926 to 1932 in the Coolidge and Hoover administrations, but it had been vacant since then. Soon thereafter, on April 10, 1941, Roosevelt nominated two assistant secretaries of war, sending the names to the Senate, where they were quickly confirmed. One was McCloy, to the position from which Patterson had just moved up to become undersecretary in charge of the army, and the other was Lovett, as assistant secretary of war for air. "Both men," it was reported, "have been serving as special assistants to Secretary Stimson, and both promotions were on his recommendation." Lovett's title changed, but the work he would do was the same that he had been doing since coming to Washington in December. His energies would be directed to two principal ends: promotion of substantial aircraft production and streamlining the organization of the army air force.[11]

When asked about his politics, Lovett said he thought he was registered as a Republican in New York but added that didn't "mean anything" since he votes as a "Mugwump." It was clear, in any event, that political leanings would have little to do with his new job.[12] While awaiting swearing-in to his new post, Lovett attended the dedication ceremony in Caldwell, New Jersey, of Curtiss-Wright's new propeller plant. At a press conference there he predicted that "three or four months from now you will see American equipment in the air which has no equal." While his timing may have been a bit optimistic, it was clear what Robert Lovett was set to do for the Air Corps. "Air power," he said, "is measured by productive capacity, not by the number of planes." He added that "the aluminum shortage is affecting production to a certain extent, and by the time we lick the aluminum shortage we will probably be up to our ears in a steel shortage." Nevertheless, Lovett said, "in the tough days ahead we're going to ask the aircraft industry to do what seems like the impossible—and it is going to do it somehow." He acknowledged that the production of propellers had been a bottleneck in the aircraft program, but that problem would be relieved by awarding propeller contracts only to "know-how" companies like Curtiss-Wright, whose unfinished plant was already turning out 600 propellers a month, only a few less than the entire aircraft industry was producing annually when the war in Europe had started.[13]

Lovett and McCloy were formally sworn in to their new positions in a ceremony at the War Department on April 22. "Quite a little company gathered for it," Stimson noted, including Adele Lovett. That evening Bob and Adele were dinner guests of the Stimsons at their Woodley home, along with Harvey Bundy and Justice Felix Frankfurter and their wives.[14]

After dinner, over brandy and cigars in Stimson's study (with Lovett and his ulcers passing up both), the gentlemen discussed at length Lovett's new position and the many challenges he would face in building up the Air Corps. Frankfurter confessed that he found the procurement process rather confusing, and Lovett explained to him as best he could the dealings with the several boards, commissions, and councils the president had established, as well as the authority the air force possessed in these matters and where it was lacking. The Office of Production Management (OPM, consisting of William Knudsen, labor leader Sidney Hillman, navy secretary Frank Knox, and Stimson) had control over the provision of raw materials, the allocation of machine tools, and the procurement of manufacturing facilities, as well as the handling of the flow of materials and tools to the manufacturers. In addition, there was an army-navy Munitions Board, which was directed to cover the allocation and stockpiling of raw materials between the two services, and a Joint Air Advisory Committee, which set priorities for utilization of the production capacity for aircraft manufacture. With a couple of other members named by Stimson, it was renamed the Joint Aircraft Committee, which Patterson said had the "power to schedule the delivery of, and allocate the capacity for, aircraft and aircraft components in the official program for all customers, Army, Navy, British, and other foreign and commercial." With all of these agencies and boards, some with overlapping authority, Robert Lovett dealt to make sure that the production required for the air force to fight the upcoming war would be carried out properly. He had to make sure that appropriate strategic goals were established and that the aircraft industry, such as it was and such as it became, met the necessary production goals. One day in May Lovett told a reporter, "I know that we don't know just who we're going to fight, or just where, but what the hell difference does that make? We're going to fight someone and we're not going to do it in our own front yard. We're going to get them, and nothing goes and gets like the Flying Fortress" (the nickname for the B-17 bomber).[15]

A problem that would vex the War Department for some time was that of out-of-date airplanes. Lovett discussed this in testimony before a Senate military appropriations subcommittee in June: "A lot of the airplanes which are in production today are of necessity obsolete, in that they represent designs drawn three or four years ago and which have been in production for a year and a half."[16] Later in the year, in September, a movement developed to reduce the size of the 90,000-man American army. Even Walter Lippman encouraged such a move in a September 20 column headed "The Case for a Smaller Army." General

George Marshall, the chief of staff of the army, was summoned to the White House for a conference to discuss such a reduction in order to make more material available "for other purposes." Lovett and McCloy wrote for him a long memorandum presenting the dangers of reducing the army. With the Russians nearly losing Moscow, the British failing in the Middle East, and the Japanese threatening, the free world would be horrified if the United States set out to reduce its army. "Abandonment of maximum effort in any form," Lovett and McCloy wrote, "would be considered a step toward appeasement, for a negotiated peace is at the root of the Lippman article—not a complete victory." At the White House meeting, Roosevelt glanced at the Lovett and McCloy memorandum and assured Marshall that he had no idea of interfering with the plans to build up the U.S. Army.[17]

In the department the question came up one day as to what form of a directive Lovett should have, to indicate his authority. General Henry H. "Hap" Arnold, commander of the Air Corps (and deputy chief of staff), told him, "You ought to have some directive to give you authority." So Lovett asked Stimson if he ought to have a directive. Stimson scoffed and asked, "What do you need a directive for? Has anybody challenged your authority?" "No," Lovett replied. Stimson followed up. "You just tell them that whatever authority the Secretary of War has, you have. That is my directive to you."[18]

Though he had numerous difficulties with the various agencies dealing with the War Department, particularly in his early months there, Bob Lovett felt after the war that the department as it was set up for World War II had been overall "enormously effective, because there were very few of us" actually running matters—the secretary, the undersecretary, the assistant secretary, and the assistant secretary for air. "At the end, we had something over twelve million people to look out for, with I don't know how many million civilian employees at arsenals, shipyards, etc. There was never any question about civilian authority, or who ran what. It was run as a cohesive group. You could get decisions, and you didn't have to horse around with twenty or thirty committees to get an answer to things. You made a decision yourself—having been given a clear authority, and having been given a clear line as to overall policy. It just worked like a charm."[19] Interestingly, much of the War Department's work was done by Stimson, Patterson, McCloy, Lovett, and Bundy, all of whom were Republicans working for a Democratic administration, and most of those heading the department were Wall Street bankers or lawyers. The important thing was, of course, that they got the job done, with very little political interplay.

As Lovett settled into his position, he took note of the situation in the Air Corps, above and beyond the question of aircraft manufacture. The corps' 1939 provision of 24 air groups had gone up in 1940 to 41 then to 54 and in the spring of 1941 to 84, but the airplanes to fill the groups were lacking, and, as Lovett testified to the Senate committee in June, many were obsolete when they came off the production line. As of July 31, 1941, the total combat planes available were only 1,221, and 458 of these were "undergoing modernization, service tests, or repair." Requirements for pilot training had soared from 1,200 a year to 30,000, and pilot trainees were required to have had at least two years of college education, a standard Lovett had deplored in his November 22 letter to Patterson. Obviously, the necessity for many more military airplanes fostered a corresponding need for many more trained pilots, and this was one of the principal issues Robert Lovett would face.[20] He was able, with Patterson's cooperation, to keep procurement for the Air Corps relatively streamlined: "Requirements were established by the Air Force, the producer was selected, the specifications were drawn, everything else was handled, in a procurement sense, through Wright Field, except that the contracts were signed by Judge Patterson as Under Secretary of War."[21]

Lovett was able to achieve, through his suggestions to Henry Stimson that were then passed on to the White House, a very helpful and necessary direction from President Roosevelt. On May 4, FDR wrote to Stimson: "The effective defense of this country and the vital defense of other democratic nations requires that there be a substantial increase in heavy bomber production." He went on to say, "We must see to it that the process is hastened and that the democratic superiority in the air be made absolute." This was just the push Lovett needed for dealing with the various boards and authorities as well as with the navy; it was what he felt was essential to the burgeoning air force and to the monthly production of 500 big bombers. "Now that we've got the go-ahead," Lovett told inquiring reporters, "we're going to show them the goddamdest group of bombers they ever saw."[22] Those who were watching for the needed increase in heavy bombers were happy to applaud Bob Lovett. "It is all to the good," wrote one authority, "that such a program has at last been approved, and a great deal of credit must be given to Robert A. Lovett … who since the middle of December has been rigorously handling many of the problems arising from the rapidly expanding Air Corps program."[23]

Lovett kept at it. "The job is up to us," he wrote Hap Arnold. "This matter is of such urgency … that it should be given the right of way and made the first concern of everyone in the Air Corps." And Bob Lovett would make sure that it would be the first concern of one and all.[24] Several days later Lovett wrote to the Army-Navy Munitions Board and the Joint Aircraft Committee for priorities for the raw materials and production facilities needed for an increased heavy bomber program. On May 16 the Joint Aircraft Committee furnished "Aircraft Report 8-E," setting the schedules and priorities for the bomber program the president had indicated. This report gave A-1-B priority, the highest priority actually awarded (A-1-A was held in reserve), to the heavy bomber program. There soon arose a dispute whether the A-1-B applied to subcontractors as well as to prime contractors. The navy, which relied far less on subcontractors than did the army's manufacturers, attempted to restrict the priority to principals. Lovett recognized that this represented a fearful delay to the big bomber program. He wrote to Patterson: "Most of these delays are the result at the outset to give subcontractors a priority rating equal to that of the principal contractor." He said he was concentrating on getting adequate priorities for subcontractors as well as obtaining "machine tools for those production lines which must come into being in order to enable us to meet the schedule."[25]

Matters came to a head in late June when Admiral John H. Towers, chief of the Navy Bureau of Aeronautics, tried to withdraw the navy's approval of "Aircraft Report 8-E." Navy undersecretary Forrestal called a meeting on June 27 with Towers, Lovett, Knudsen, Admiral Harold Stark, and several other naval officers. Towers complained that the big bomber program was interfering with the manufacture of naval aircraft. Lovett broke in, saying that Towers was correct and that was the purpose of the priorities given the Air Corps. Stark questioned whether Roosevelt had actually intended to give the heavy bomber program such an edge, and Lovett, well prepared, then read the letter FDR had written to Stimson, unambiguously giving preference to the heavy bomber program.[26] Shortly thereafter, Lovett and his old friend Forrestal got together and worked things out. It was not interservice competition that was the real problem but an overall inefficient system that worked against both the army and the navy. It was agreed between the former Wall Street bankers that the OPM (Office of Production Management) would be pressured by both the army and the navy for much faster action on 21 items that most affected production. The joint effort produced some satisfactory results from the OPM, and Lovett told Judge Patterson that they were much encouraged by the OPM's "recognition of the problem."[27]

Lend-Lease also presented issues for Lovett and the Air Corps. The War Department had been holding back on airplanes that were supposed to go to Russia, and Roosevelt took it upon himself to see that the scheduled planes were sent. The Russian army, of course, was bearing the brunt of the war against the Germans at that time, and aid was essential. Nevertheless, Lovett was concerned that the aid to Russia was competing with his aircraft program. Although he was forced to concede the shipment of planes to Russia, he was bitterly opposed to shipping machine tools. "It seems to me unsound to permit such vital items as tools to be sent out of this country without determining what the effect, if any, will be on our own production program," he told Stimson. Nevertheless, despite Lovett's protests, essential machine tools went to the Soviets by the end of the year.[28]

One of the primary issues facing Stimson, Lovett, and the War Department was the role the Air Corps would be playing in the coming activities. Both the army and the navy considered airplanes and their pilots to be auxiliary to their own operations, for reconnaissance, transportation, and other non-fighting purposes, but, as the warfare in Europe was demonstrating quite clearly, aircraft functions were now, as Stimson set it down, "independent action quite divorced from both the land and the sea … [and] requires greater freedom and unity of action for air." Some pressure was building for making the Air Corps completely independent from the army (and the War Department), but Stimson and Lovett were agreed that a fairly large measure of autonomy, rather than independence, was the best course for the Air Corps in 1941.[29]

Over the next few months there were various discussions within the War Department, discussions involving Stimson, Lovett, General Marshall, Hap Arnold, and others concerning the steps to be taken toward autonomy for the Air Corps. Lovett described "the so-called autonomy program, which I was in charge of developing, and which General [Joseph] McNarney and General [Hoyt] Vandenberg, [Lauris] Norstad, [Lawrence] Kuter and one or two others drafted," with Arnold, "as a preliminary design of the type of autonomy which would make it possible for the Air Force to operate efficiently, both in procurement and in the field."[30]

Progress was made, but no final agreement was reached. Even so, there were problems within the air force that needed attention, stemming from the division of authority existing between the so-called chief of the Air Corps, General Delos C. Emmons, in charge of training, procurement, research and administration, and General George Brett, the commanding general at General Headquarters Air Force, presumably the striking force for purposes of combat. And the commanding general over them was Henry Arnold, supposedly above both parts. Lovett sized it up: "Who commanded what, and how would it work?" The organizational chart, he said, "resembled nothing in the world as much as a bowl of spaghetti."[31]

Lovett wrote the papers pointing out the weaknesses of the program as it stood: it "might be all right to fight a war against the Seminole Indians, up on Lake Okeechobee, but it was a hell of a way to have to go into a war against the ablest enemy we ever faced."

Secretary of War Henry Stimson hands commissions to his new assistant secretaries John McCloy and Robert Lovett (right), April 22, 1941 (ACME).

With his push and the cooperation of the generals in the separate divisions, the lines were quickly set in proper order with the issuance of Army Regulation 95–5 on June 20, 1941, creating the Army Air Force, giving it a fighting arm (Air Force Combat Command) and a service arm (the Air Corps). "As soon as we got the thing cleared up," Lovett recalled, "we set up a proper straight-line organization," with the general commanding the air forces (Arnold) commanding everything.[32]

Observing the inner workings of the War Department on the question of air force autonomy, columnists Alsop and Kintner recognized that "the compromise is understood to be largely the work of three men," Stimson, Marshall, and "the extremely able new Assistant Secretary for Air Robert A. Lovett." If the compromise were to go through, they wrote, the Air Corps would gain "control of the two most important functions—deciding what sort of planes and how many planes to buy, and recruiting and training its flying officers."[33] Stopping off in Salt Lake City late in May 1941, Lovett said the American air force would soon be "the finest in existence, with striking power second to none." He quickly added, "What we need is time—as much as we can get." The Pacific Coast aircraft industry was doing a fine job, he said. "Two years from the date we started building up our air force, we will have the best in the world, but only if the American people decide they want it," he went on. "The public must realize they can't get both planes and every conceivable luxury at the same time."[34]

The autonomy issue was still unresolved when, on June 12, FDR's aide Harry Hopkins called Stimson from the White House to say he had heard that a piece of legislation creating an independent Air Corps was in danger of passing in Congress. Hopkins said that President Roosevelt was against this bill, and he hoped Stimson would talk Speaker Sam Rayburn out of it. First, though, Stimson called in Marshall and told him about it. Marshall and Lovett got their people together and finally tied together the final strings of the Air Corps reorganization they had been working on, giving it autonomy and unity. The relationship of the army air forces to the army was now, as Lovett had pictured it, similar to that of the Marine Corps to the navy. *Time* magazine later commented on the Air Corps' achievement of autonomy: "How he did it, Bob Lovett will not say. It was probably done by peaceful argument in the many conferences with War Department top men.... However he did it, he did it. Lovett's hand did not show, but the results did."[35] Autonomy, Lovett recalled, "was, I think, an extremely important step—not just because I was so intimately associated with it, but the development of the Strategic Air Command naturally was the outgrowth of that type of autonomy." An army officer on the ground, he suggested, would have little interest "in bombing someplace a thousand miles away."[36] Robert Lovett was quite aware of the importance of the steps taken. He wrote the introduction to a special air forces issue of the magazine *Flying and Popular Aviation* in September 1941:

> The establishment of the United States Army Air Forces will in time be regarded, I believe, as one of the real milestones in the march of American Aviation toward the goal of air power. Its establishment is the result of impartial and careful study of the lessons of European use of aircraft under combat situations. It represents, furthermore, an effort to develop air power in such a way as to permit it to function smoothly under our existing Governmental procedure and to cooperate easily and effectively with the War and Navy Departments at all times. The Army Air Forces now have a degree of autonomy which has long been considered necessary. For the first time since its organization the destiny of the Air Forces lies largely in its own hands. America can have just as good an air force as it wants. We think the people want the best. That is what we are going to try to give them.[37]

With that achieved—making the Army Air Force an autonomous organization within the War Department—Stimson felt he had "something with which to meet this threat of an independent Air Corps created by legislation." After "a long talk with Lovett in the afternoon," Stimson called Rayburn, who told him there was no chance of the "independent Air Corps" bill being passed, and he himself was against it.[38] Columnist Drew Pearson commented that "the really important feature of the new Air Corps set-up" was that Robert Lovett would "have charge of deciding on new models and types of Army aircraft." "Because he shuns the limelight and works without hoopla," Pearson wrote, "only insiders know that Lovett has been militantly battling the red-tape brigade since he entered the War Department last December: and that the reorganization plan 'was largely Lovett's work.'"[39]

One factor that helped the reorganization was that Arnold and the other Air Corps generals were willing to accept at the top of the line a civilian boss, Lovett, because they knew that he himself was a pilot, that he had fought in the World War, and that he had flown planes at an earlier date than almost all of them, except Arnold and a few others. So in the Air Corps there was no real division between the civilian and the military. Lovett, Arnold wrote later, was "of towering importance to our Air Force." In addition, a very close relationship developed between Bob Lovett and Hap Arnold. Their offices were next to one another, and the two of them were very often in consultation on issues that arose, moving easily through their connecting doors many times a day. Lovett recalled the situation: "As I say (and I think you'll find references to this in Hap's books) the relationship was a very, very close, congenial one, with great respect on both sides, and a very happy one."[40]

Indeed, Arnold in his memoir, *Global Mission*, described Lovett as "a man who possessed the qualities in which I was weakest, a partner and teammate of tremendous sympathy, and of calm and hidden force." When Arnold was ready to explode, "fully intending to tear the War and Navy Departments to pieces, Bob Lovett would know exactly how to handle me. He would say, with a quiet smile: 'Hap, you're wonderful. How I wish I had your pep and vitality! Now ... let's get down and be practical.' And I would come back to earth with a bang." An Arnold biographer put it this way: "Lovett's tact and political savvy balanced Arnold's fervor and aggressiveness. They made a perfect team at the high-command and political level."[41] With Lovett to run interference, Arnold found his relations with Stimson going well. "Bob Lovett did a grand job in every way," Arnold said. "He was a trouble shooter de luxe." Asked what qualities made Lovett so valuable, Arnold mentioned "his business background and his aviation background, plus plenty of good sound horse sense." One other quality that often came in very handy was Lovett's fine sense of humor and quick wit; there were sometimes situations where that wit became very valuable.[42]

The workings between Lovett and Arnold were evident to the other leaders in the Air Corps, and this had a good effect. As General Emmet "Rosy" O'Donnell wrote to Lovett after the war, "I have always had the deepest admiration for you, ever since the days when you and Hap Arnold established the kind of relationship that should exist between the secretary and Chief in the running of the Air Force."[43] Lovett recognized that solidarity of view between himself and the military leaders of the Air Corps was essential. "Once the competence of the individual had been tested, you were accepted by this top band of brothers. In being so accepted, there was none of this division between the civilian and the military. It simply did not exist."[44]

On a personal basis, in 1941 Bob Lovett was reexamined medically, and no evidence could be seen of the duodenal ulcer for which he had been kept on a rigid diet for nine years. As a result, Lovett was permitted to smoke and drink in moderation. He was in a couple of years smoking about a pack or so of cigarettes a day and drinking an occasional old-fashioned. But his health problems were not gone.

7

The Big Problem

Robert Lovett found that he fitted in very well in the War Department. He got along fine with his highest boss, Henry Stimson, with his slightly-less-high bosses Bob Patterson and George Marshall, and with those who were basically his equals, Hap Arnold, John McCloy, and Harvey Bundy. As one of the leading air force histories put it, "This team of Stimson and Lovett, Marshall and Arnold was to hold together through the war … [because of] the ability of its several members to work harmoniously together."[1]

Lovett and Stimson had convinced Franklin Roosevelt that the production of heavy bombers was of prime importance, to the discomfiture of the navy. So as 1941 moved along Bob Lovett turned as much of his attention as he could to the major problem facing him—and the nation: how to get those heavy bombers produced, armed, and manned. He quickly recognized the major aspects of the bomber problem: getting major manufacturers to making the planes, working up production of the armament and equipment for those planes, ensuring the presence of sufficient manpower to produce the airplanes, having the big companies subcontract work where appropriate, and, finally, providing adequate trained personnel to man the bombers when they were ready to go.

Late in 1940 Walter Reuther, the young vice president of the Detroit chapter of the United Auto Workers, had presented to Donald Nelson, chairman of the War Production Board, a plan to convert Detroit's auto plants, which sat idle for substantial periods of the year, to the mass production of airplanes. The Reuther Plan, as proposed, would by various steps "transform the entire unused capacity of the auto industry into one huge plane production unit." Lovett, recognizing the problems facing the Air Corps in getting planes produced, was taken with Reuther's plan to pool machine tools in a central facility; better to have one plant fully equipped to produce something, he told Patterson, than to have a multitude of plants that couldn't produce anything because of equipment shortage. Lovett arranged to help Reuther in several functions looking toward the implementation of his plan. Unfortunately, because of the sweeping nature of Reuther's various proposals, the powers behind the auto manufacturers and big business were able by March 1941 to shoot down the Reuther Plan. Bob Lovett, the War Department, and the Air Corps would have to work on the necessary aircraft buildup using the tools and procedures available, slow though it might be.[2]

Patterson, as undersecretary, maintained the ultimate authority for procurement, but he was happy to share that responsibility for air matters with Lovett, whom he recognized as a highly competent administrator. Lovett knew it was his job to make sure that the aircraft industry, as it developed, met the Air Corps' production goals and that these goals were attuned to proper strategic considerations. He and Hap Arnold visited many of the country's aircraft factories in the summer of 1941. Lovett's activities during his first year in office were necessarily constrained by the fact that he was preparing for a conflict in which the nation was not yet involved. Things changed considerably after Pearl Harbor. At first the OPM and later the War Production Board neglected to furnish the proper priorities to the air force manufacturers, subcontractors, and suppliers, and this failure required active participation in the process by Robert Lovett. A further area in which Lovett became much involved was helping to strengthen the management of a number of aircraft manufacturers that were not run well, a failure that affected their production capabilities.

Machine tools were, in those early days of the increased production targets, a considerable problem. Without tools being in the right places, production broke down. Lovett suggested to Patterson that he ask the OPM to assign priorities by project, assuring that they could "have one plant completely equipped" rather than having "several plants all lacking a certain proportion of tools so that none of them are in operation." He asked Patterson not to seek priority ratings for manufacturers of engines, propellers, and landing gear "until they have received the machine tools necessary to balance the capacity of the existing air frame sections of the industry."[3] Lovett of course could not resolve all the problems of tools for subcontractors, but he was able to intervene in quite a few specific situations and his interventions gained time for the flawed priority system to improve generally. And if something looked wrong, he was quick to act; as one aircraft official said, "There's nothing soft about Lovett. If he ever gets the idea that some aircraft plant is chiseling, he gets mean as a snake."[4]

In the summer and fall of 1941 the attitude in the aircraft manufacturing industry was one of business as usual: "Hey, the war's over there in Europe, not here." Lovett had encouraged manufacturers to add extra shifts in order to make more efficient use of the available facilities, but this had yielded few results. He wrote to Major General Oliver Echols, Chief of the Materiel Division of the Air Corps, in mid–July that it was "evident that many plants are not at present operating on a full weekly basis." Such a situation, he said, "cannot be accepted as normal, and until accelerated production is attained, every effort must be used to make up the deficiencies by overtime activity."[5]

Henry Arnold recognized that Lovett "carried more than his share of the air expansion load." When Lovett found the shortage of machine tools and "unequal distribution among the various industries engaged in war production," he "took that case up and worked it out with the OPM." Lovett, Arnold recalled, "had to deal with one such problem after another." When the various aircraft manufacturers cited the lack of important parts for production slowdowns, Lovett "took that problem up and worked it through the various agencies until a just solution was found." One of the first things he did was reduce the nine men who had to be involved in air production decisions to two.[6]

In October 1941 Lovett had an opportunity to bring before the public the state of the air force and what it could—and should—be, presenting the subject in an address to the University Club in New York City. After describing the air force program, he concluded, "If this country makes up its mind to it, and puts the first things first," which meant no strikes in the aircraft factories, "we will give you an Air Force that can look any aggressor in the eye and tell him to go to hell—which in my opinion is where he belongs."[7]

Many of the aircraft manufacturers suffered slowdowns due to machine tool shortages. In mid–August, Lovett sent an open letter to all of the major machine tool producers, urging them to adopt a seven-day workweek with a 24-hour schedule. He also urged William Knudsen to beef up the machine-tool division of OPM, bringing in new staffers with no obligations to, or fears of, the machine tool companies. A couple of months later Lovett went after the machine tool industry himself. He wrote to Clayton Burt, who headed the Defense Committee of the National Machine Tool Builders Association, complaining of the machine toolmakers' requirement for signed orders before commencing production. Lovett said that the pressing shortage of machine tools, along with the knowledge that new aircraft plants were being built, should certainly assure the toolmakers that they would have no problem at all in disposing of their products. The industry's insistence on signed orders before undertaking any work, he told Burt, was "unpatriotic," since it slowed down production. In addition, he wrote, "it would seem not unreasonable to assume that industry, in a time of national emergency, would take every possible step to turn out the essential elements in national defense at the greatest possible rate." Other industries, he pointed out, had done their best to get around government red tape and he said "the machine tool industry can not relieve itself from responsibility for its maximum output of every one of the critical tool items." Lovett's efforts relieved some of the machine tool problems but many persisted into 1942.[8]

Congress, in its usual way, was a bit tardy in providing appropriations to the War Department, which slowed down production, but Lovett found a unique way to alleviate that issue. He got in touch with Jesse Jones, head of the Reconstruction Finance Corporation, explained to Jones that money was limited although the eventual appropriations from Congress were almost assured, and asked if Jones could help the Air Corps in its production problem. When Jones asked how much the Air Corps needed, Lovett quickly answered with a figure of two hundred million. Jones promptly produced a letter giving the War Department a loan of $200,000,000, and Lovett was immediately able to get reluctant manufacturers to work on production.

Aircraft production increased in 1941 with help from Bob Lovett, but it was still not up to the quantity he regarded as essential for the oncoming hostilities. However, what there was proved to be very good. On September 11 Stimson produced Lovett at his weekly press conference to talk about the American planes coming into production, which would be used at the upcoming Louisiana maneuvers. Lovett was careful to state that our planes were "the finest in the world … in quality," while stating "with great candor" that there were still great problems with quantity. "Production is now beginning to roll," Lovett said, "and our share of it from here on should enable us to equip combat units at the rate of about one squadron every other day." He added that this rate would be increasing in the coming months.[9] A couple of weeks later Lovett attended the Louisiana maneuvers and said they presented "a very fine picture. Our boys," he went on, "are doing a fine job under difficult and adverse conditions." Though a squadron of combat planes was being delivered every other day, this were still hardly enough. He summed up the Louisiana maneuvers as a showing by "the best group of Air Forces qualitatively that there is in the world—better than any in Europe," even though "quantitatively we are terribly behind, as everyone knows."[10]

On the afternoon of December 7 Bob and Adele were on their way home from the movies in Georgetown—Greta Garbo in *Ninotchka*—when they learned of the Japanese attack on Pearl Harbor. Bob told Adele, "I can't believe the Japs would be such damned fools as to do a thing like that!" He went home, got his shaving things and some fresh linen, and hurried over to his office, where he stayed for the next 72 hours, handling all sorts of emergency tasks and putting the Air Corps on a suddenly necessary wartime basis, after meeting with General Carl Spaatz (temporarily in charge of the Air Corps, with Hap Arnold on the West Coast) and intelligence chief Maj. Lauris Norstad.[11]

The next morning Stimson and Lovett met with British air marshal Sir Arthur Harris to arrange for the British to send back at once for the defense of Hawaii 250 planes already supplied to the RAF by the U.S. The impression Harris got of the two was that "they were dazed, and Stimson himself hardly able to speak," though this of course could have simply resulted from lack of sleep.[12] Lovett knew what had to be done. He fired off a cable to Edsel Ford, who was running his father's auto company. "We are going to raise our sights all along the line," Lovett said, emphasizing "the vital part which we are counting on the Ford Motor Company to play" in making airplanes. The Ford plant built at Willow Run, Lovett went on, "is the keystone in the arch of the big government plants, and for that reason we are most anxious for it to get into operation at the earliest possible date." The mile-long factory Ford had built at Willow Run outside of Detroit was essential in constructing B-24 bombers using Ford's well-developed assembly-line techniques.[13]

The United States declared war on Japan after the Pearl Harbor attack and on Germany and Italy a few days later. Several days after Pearl Harbor, George Marshall brought to the War Department a recently promoted brigadier general, Dwight D. Eisenhower, to head up the War Plans Division. Bob Lovett and Dwight Eisenhower became good friends in the War Department; the letters between the two over the years in the Lovett Papers at Yale are all signed "Ike" and "Bob," no matter the time or position held.

New Year's Day 1942 was not a holiday, at least not in the War Department. Lovett, Stimson, and McCloy were there working, and they "went over different matters that are important, each one [Lovett and McCloy] bringing up what he thought had been neglected for a while, in order to have a sort of round-up of the matters before the Department."[14] On January 6 Franklin Roosevelt gave to the nation his State of the Union address, in which he set forth American objectives. "Our own objectives are clear," he said, "the objective of smashing the militarism imposed by war lords upon their enslaved peoples, the objective of liberating the subjugated nations—the objective of establishing and securing freedom of speech, freedom of religion, freedom from want, and freedom from fear everywhere in the world" (these quickly became known as the Four Freedoms). The president went on to speak of the necessary increases in military production, including "our production rate of airplanes" to produce 60,000 planes in 1942, including "45,000 combat planes—bombers, dive bombers, pursuit planes," and in 1943 to increase that to 125,000 airplanes, including 100,000 combat planes. Needless to say, FDR's speech to Congress produced a "great public impact … at the time."[15]

Lovett was not happy with the aircraft goals set forth in the president's speech. He knew that the numbers Roosevelt presented were unattainable and that efforts to meet those goals were likely to result in easy-to-build light airplanes and fewer numbers of heavy bombers, the air forces' real need. Lovett produced for Stimson an analysis of the president's plan and the harmful results it would likely produce, an analysis Stimson relied on at a January 12 meeting with Knox and Knudsen to go over Roosevelt's "objectives." As they discussed "whether the President has set us an impossible proposition," they agreed "that much depended on the classes of planes," exactly what Lovett feared. Stimson stressed to his colleagues "the fact that we should frankly tell the President of our difficulties with his program rather than to go ahead blindly" with unrealistic and possibly harmful goals. The group found Lovett's analysis persuasive but declined to refer the matter back to the president.[16] Lovett was able to convince Donald Nelson of the OPM that the aircraft projections were unrealistic, and Nelson told the president in May that his 1942 goal could not be attained. However, Roosevelt stuck with his numbers.

As time passed by and projections were overtaken by production numbers, Lovett was able to get Stimson, Knox, Forrestal, Patterson, and Di Gates, along with General Marshall and Admiral Ernest King, to present to the president a recommendation to reduce his numbers. With the position taken by such a group, Roosevelt agreed to reduce his airplane production number for 1943 from 125,000 to 107,000, although Lovett felt that even this reduction was not realistic. He believed that the aircraft companies could actually produce between 92,000 and 96,000 planes. In March 1943 he wrote Harry Hopkins, blaming the expected shortfall on a lack of sufficient aluminum and the replacement of obsolete models with "new, superior designs." As he said to Hopkins, "By facing the facts frankly at this time, I believe … that we will get more planes rather than less by removing doubt and confusion in the services, the industry and the public."[17] Nevertheless, the unrealistic production numbers remained as the nation's goals, and Robert Lovett pushed ahead to try to come as close to meeting those goals as was possible, while keeping firmly in mind what kind of airplanes were absolutely necessary to be produced.

There were other problems. The Army and Navy Munitions Board had set forth priorities that placed furnishing naval vessels ahead of aircraft, intending to redress the damages to the fleet resulting from the Pearl Harbor attack. To Lovett, this made little sense; airplanes were more important for the war effort in early 1942 than were ships. And new aircraft carriers without planes to fly from them would be useless. As he wrote to Patterson, "Aircraft is one of the few combat weapons now actually being used against the enemy." Stimson and Patterson agreed with Lovett's argument and managed, with the help of Harry Hopkins, to have the Army and Navy Munitions Board give aircraft production a higher priority.[18]

Another serious matter was a shortage of aluminum, a problem Lovett had foreseen a year earlier. In 1940 Lovett's friend Averell Harriman (then working for the OPM) and Bob Patterson called on Harold Ickes, the secretary of the interior, to see whether a bloc of power from the Bonneville Dam on the Columbia River could be allocated to the Aluminum Company of America (Alcoa) in order to expand aluminum production rapidly. Ickes refused, on the basis that such a move would strengthen Alcoa's monopoly position. He wanted the power contract to go to Reynolds Metal Company, an award that Harriman and Patterson felt would hurt the defense effort. But Ickes refused to change his position, a stance Lovett told Harriman "cost the country many hundreds of vitally needed aircraft by delaying our aluminum expansion."[19]

Lovett went back and forth with A.H. Bunker, head of the aluminum and magnesium branch of the OPM (and an executive of Alcoa), over aluminum production and aircraft needs. Bunker kept insisting that there would be sufficient aluminum to build the projected number of planes, but Lovett quickly perceived that Bunker was thinking in terms of fighters rather than the bombers Lovett knew had to be produced. Lovett's computation of the actual need for aluminum produced a figure of 2.5 to 3 billion tons, twice what Bunker had estimated would be available. Lovett told him that the need was to "overproduce rather than underproduce" since it would be "impossible to guess what the future requirements are under war conditions."[20] Shortages of materials like aluminum continued to dog aircraft production. In March 1942 Bob Lovett advised Harry Hopkins that Ford could double its daily production of 2,000-horsepower motors if it could be provided with sufficient aluminum. It was a shortage that was gradually alleviated.[21]

One unexpected issue that arose after the inception of the war was the question of Charles Lindbergh and what could or should be done with him. The hero of the nation in May 1927 for his unprecedented solo flight from New York to Paris, the object of the nation's pity in 1932 upon the kidnapping and murder of his son, Lindbergh had become a divisive public figure with his isolationist views in the America First campaign, his bitter challenges to the policies of Franklin Roosevelt, and his favorable views of, and acceptance of a medal from, Nazi Germany in 1938. Nevertheless, with America now at war, Charles Lindbergh claimed he wanted to do his part, so he set up a January meeting with Stimson to see what he could do. Stimson, Lovett, and Arnold had a couple of meetings with Lindbergh, the outcome of which was their advising him that there was no place for him in the War Department or the air force and that he should rejoin Pan American or TWA, where he had worked previously, to carry on technical work there.[22] With Lovett's approval Lindbergh went to work for Ford in Detroit and performed some useful functions for Ford's aircraft business during the war.[23]

Another matter came up, this one related to a situation in Texas. A young congressman from the 10th District in Texas, Lyndon Baines Johnson, had gone off to war shortly after Pearl Harbor, and his wife, Lady Bird Johnson, ran his office during his absence (until FDR ordered congressmen who had gone into the military to return to Washington). Lady Bird was aware that the people in Austin, in her husband's district, were anxious to get a major military installation there, and she went to talk with Robert Lovett about it, showing him the advantages of the 10th District. She also asked Lovett, in the event a base could be installed, if she could learn of it ahead of time so that she could issue a press release and her husband receive due credit. As it turned out, on September 19, 1942, the Del Valle Army Air Base, seven miles east of Austin, was activated on 3,000 acres leased from the city. Congressman Johnson's name figured prominently in the announcement.[24]

Although there were all sorts of problems following the sudden onset of war (not all of them as potentially touchy as Charles Lindbergh), Lovett was gratified to find that almost all of the little impediments to getting things done properly had disappeared. Washington's red tape gave way to wartime necessities. However, not all production delays could be blamed on government red tape or shortages of machine tools or other material deficiencies. Lovett recognized that there were problems with some of the aircraft manufacturers and their leaders themselves. With the expansion of the industry brought on by the heavy demand suddenly imposed upon it, there developed problems with management that caused slowdowns in coming out with the finished product. Bob Lovett well understood the essential role management at the top played in the production picture. When William L. Batt, vice chairman of the War Production Board (under Donald Nelson), asked in December 1942 for recommendations for the Joint Labor-Industry Conference, Lovett was critical of Robert Gross of Lockheed and Glenn Martin of the Glenn L. Martin Co., but he praised

Lawrence Bell of Bell Aircraft, Guy Vaughn of Curtiss-Wright, and J. Carlton Ward of Fairchild Engine and Aircraft, whom he saw as "really a star."[25]

Lovett had already been involved in the criticism of what was being done by companies in the aircraft business. Dismayed at the slow pace of activities at the Republic Aviation Corporation, Lovett arranged for Ralph Damon to move from American Airlines to Republic to work things out. Another slow producer drew a Lovett letter in the summer of 1941 when he wrote Vincent Bendix of the Bendix Corporation that "we are very much disturbed" at the company's poor production of machine gun and turret assemblies. Finished aircraft, he told Bendix, sat idle because of the Bendix "failure to meet even approximately" the terms of its government contracts.[26] Lovett was most concerned with the failings of the Glenn L. Martin Company, which he regarded as "the most serious problem the Army faces." He felt that Martin himself, a prima donna type, was the major drawback to the company's production. Using bankers holding loans to the company as well as minority shareholders on the Martin board, Lovett was able to get Martin eased upstairs and replaced as president. After that, the company's production difficulties lessened considerably.

Curtiss-Wright was another aircraft company with troubles. The Truman Committee, acting as the Senate's watchdog on wartime government contractors, had ascertained that the Curtiss-Wright plant at Lockland, Ohio, was putting out engines for the air force that were defective. Lovett then asked William Knudsen to make up a board to investigate, and Knudsen's board determined that lax inspection was enabling the shipment of many defective engines. The Truman Committee's report agreed with Knudsen's conclusions, but by this time Lovett had already taken away the "A" rating of Curtiss-Wright, the removal of which required much closer inspection practices.

When the company began a series of advertisements in newspapers around the country denying that it was doing anything wrong, Senator Harley Kilgore, a member of the Truman Committee, made a number of surprise inspections at various Curtiss-Wright plants around the country and reported to Lovett on what he had uncovered. Lovett assured Kilgore that the problems he had found had been discovered earlier by the air force. "We insisted on a change in management," Lovett said. "They've agreed to that. We've insisted that they get some outside help." And Lovett had worked on that; new management was on its way, he told Kilgore. "We've had to do it with, oh, three out of five companies all the way through. The government always has to step in in some form or other." Engine production at Curtiss-Wright improved thereafter.[27]

On the whole, though, Lovett was favorably impressed with the work of the aircraft industry. One of the problems, he quickly noticed, was with the government's procurement and contract policies and the doubts they engendered in the manufacturing companies. He realized that he was in a position to intervene in problems between the manufacturers and government contracting agencies, of whom there were several. Whatever a particular company had in the way of a contractual or production problem, Lovett insured that his office could serve as a sort of court of appeals to get matters straightened out. Robert Gross of Lockheed even wrote to Lovett of the industry's "desire that you should be our father confessor on all important matters of policy."[28]

As matters moved along, the army air force gradually began to assume the role spelled out for it by the president in his call for a substantial heavy bomber striking force. *Time* magazine, in its February 9, 1942, issue, which featured a somber-looking Robert Lovett on its cover, said that the "sponsor of this striking power, in being and to be, is a man the U.S. scarcely knows: lean, articulate Robert Abercrombie Lovett." After reference to airpower zealots of the past, such as the late Billy Mitchell, the article went on to say that "Lovett's service is that he picked up all the pieces—the hopes and dreams of airmen, the tactical lessons of fact and theory, the wealth of U.S. design and production, its great reserve of manpower—and got something done about putting these ingredients effectively together." Since well before Pearl Harbor, Lovett worked on the striking power. "The theme song of his year in Washington," *Time* wrote, "has been bombers, bombers, bombers. Happily for the world, he put the song over."[29]

And, just to keep everything on the up-and-up, Robert Lovett, on April 27, 1942, registered with his Local Draft Board No. 1772 in Washington. At his age and because of his occupation there was obviously little chance of his being drafted, but he wanted to take no chances. He took advantage of his public position to give the nation his view of what was happening—in speeches on May 14 to the Marine Tool Manufacturers in Cleveland and on September 24 in New York City to the Russian War Relief luncheon. Bob Lovett wanted his countrymen to be as fully aware of matters as he could help them to be.

8

Manpower Issues

While he was tending to the various production problems in the aircraft industry Robert Lovett had to be involved as well in questions regarding manpower and, as it turned out, womanpower, both on the civilian side—making sure that those plants had enough people working in them to turn out the necessary airplanes—and on the military side, providing sufficient numbers of pilots and technical personnel to keep the planes flying and efficient.

Lovett recognized early on that there would likely be a conflict between military and civilian manpower requirements, and as a result he became very much involved in some of these issues. Obviously these involved labor to some degree, and Lovett had never been interested very much in labor situations. For those members of Roosevelt's administration who were veteran New Dealers, the growth of labor and its rights had always been a matter of priority, so there was necessarily tension between them and those officials of the War Department like Stimson, McCloy, and Lovett whose backgrounds were as Republicans in Wall Street. Bob Lovett was not a politician, but he was a Republican who had never had much sympathy with FDR's New Deal and many of its programs.

While Lovett shared most of Henry Stimson's economic and political views, his over-riding dedication to the development of a mighty bomber force caused him to forego some ideological positions in favor of other considerations calculated to achieve aircraft successes. He was not happy with the president's failure to put together a national manpower strategy with which to fight a world war, and as a result he got mixed up in numerous issues dealing with manpower. He approached those issues with the thought he conveyed in a letter to Patterson: "The Air Corps' program is more dependent on labor than anything. Good, willing, and uninterrupted workmanship are essential to the successful completion of it." He said there needed to be "a sense of unity of purpose between the men who build the planes and the men who fly them."[1]

Lovett was fortunate that Hap Arnold kept himself much involved with questions about air force personnel—assignments, promotions, and the like—leaving Lovett to concern himself most closely with problems of civilian manpower and how the aircraft business operations were manned. Nevertheless, there were also issues regarding military personnel in which Lovett became involved. The prewar air force—through 1939—trained roughly 200 cadets for flying in a year. The Air Corps in mid–1939 was made up of 26,000 people. In 1940 the number of trainees climbed to 1,200 and soon reached the number of 85,000 pilots per annum. By June 1944, Air Force personnel had reached 2,300,000, a considerable increase and one which strained to the utmost recruiting and training facilities.

The Air Corps had historically maintained very stringent requirements for those who sought to join, and these barriers held down numbers as well as minorities and recent immigrants. The requirements were caused by assumptions that flying airplanes in the proper manner demanded considerable intelligence to be developed further by formal training. Air Force recruiting guidelines, dating back to 1928, made clear the preference for "graduates of recognized colleges and universities." Application for flight training for pilots, navigators, or bombardiers called for nominations by three highly regarded citizens, a personal interview, rigorous physical exams, and passage of psychological and aptitude tests. Even those applying for ground technical positions had to go over similar hurdles. Many positions required college degrees in engineering, geology, chemistry or similar subjects.

When he first came to his job in the War Department, Robert Lovett felt that it was important to maintain the high quality of personnel that the existing standards promised. In February 1941 he told General George Brett, then acting commander of the Air Corps, of his "growing conviction that we will need, in fact must have, the highest grade men obtainable." Drawing on his recollections from the last war, Lovett said, "I am convinced that a program designed to interest young college men about to graduate ... will give the Air Corps a backbone of competent, trained men which can not be got any other way."[2]

It did not take long for Lovett to recognize that continued use of the longtime admission standards for the Air Corps would cause a shortage of air and ground crews, and this in fact was what happened in 1941. The Air Corps in 1940 and 1941 had set about intensely recruiting on college campuses across the country, with trained pilots visiting the campuses to set forth the idea that flying was the force of the future; nevertheless, this campaign failed to enlist the kind of response that the Air Corps needed. Not only did the numbers fall short, but there also developed considerable public criticism of how the Air Corps was doing its recruiting business. Lovett started to question the college requirement and the qualifying tests.

In April 1941 Lovett asked Hap Arnold for two copies of the current air force entrance exam; he took the test himself, and he had a friend, college professor Jay Stratton of MIT, take it as well. Both failed the test. Lovett then wrote to a number of college presidents to learn whether scores on the air force exam correlated with actual intelligence and aptitude. His friend Stratton told him that the highest score on the exam among undergrads at MIT was achieved by a young girl from Brooklyn from a family of musicians.[3] Lovett recognized that changes to the entrance requirements were needed, and it would be better that these be modest changes suggested by the air force rather than radical changes imposed by Congress. Accordingly, he wrote to Hap Arnold about complainers, he said, who question "the fairness of giving a stiff examination to a man who may have had 500 hours of licensed flying and be adequate in mathematics and deficient in a modern language or history." He believed the situation could be cleared with "elasticity of construction" of the "prevailing rules."[4] While Arnold delayed any action, Lovett sent him a paper he had prepared entitled "Intelligence vs. Education." He suggested dropping the longtime requirement of two years of college education; appropriate aptitude tests could provide a better measurement of native intelligence than could the successful completion of two years of college.[5]

General Carl A. Spaatz, high up in Air Force ranks, agreed with Lovett that the long-standing entrance requirements were "archaic ... too much emphasis on formal education which means nothing ... and no emphasis on native intelligence which may mean everything." Undersecretary of War Robert Patterson also felt strongly that the requirements should be modified. Still, Hap Arnold was reluctant to permit any lowering of pilot standards. Going around Arnold on this issue, Lovett urged Spaatz, chief of the air staff, to get into place new procedures for qualifying airmen, and Spaatz set up a committee to make recommendations, which recommendations he was quick to accept.[6]

The day after the Japanese bombed Pearl Harbor, with the United States formally into the war that had been anticipated for so long, Spaatz, with Lovett's approval, took action. He set up additional aviation cadet examining boards, gave to those boards the authority to accept cadets, replaced the two-year college requirement with a new test, and removed the existing ban on married men. The result of these changes was a fivefold increase in air force inductions, just what was needed to meet increasing air force requirements.

There was another issue regarding air force personnel that ultimately involved Bob Lovett, although it was not one he was looking for. This of course was the question of taking black men into the Air Corps. There was a long-standing tradition of discrimination in the Air Corps, stemming from widely held opinions that blacks were neither intelligent nor courageous enough to measure up to aviation standards. Lovett had not established any of the discriminatory practices in the Air Corps, either in admitting blacks or in treating them once they were in, but he felt no compelling pressure to change those practices. The whole question of blacks in the Army had brought about the appointment in 1940 of William H. Hastie, a notable figure in the black community and a former federal judge, as a civilian aide to Secretary Stimson in the area of African-American relations. Hastie, as was his obligation for the War Department position he held, looked carefully into various army activities as they affected the black race. It was not long before he realized that the most restrictive actions—and inactions—in the army were those of the Air Corps. The Air Corps had established a small training program for blacks at Tuskegee, Alabama, even though the program prepared its members to fly only single-engine airplanes. There was pressure from the black community to expand the program, which by its small size severely limited the opportunities for black men in the air forces. Lovett and Hap Arnold resisted the demands coming from the African-American community. It was the consensus of military leaders that black men lacked the technical ability to fly airplanes. Hastie lodged other objections to air force practices, presenting them to Arnold and Lovett. Basically, he charged that air force practices resulted in inferior training, continued widespread patterns of segregation, and, with all technical training for blacks confined to Tuskegee, unnecessarily costly because of duplication.

Later in 1942 Hastie learned from the press that the air force was planning to turn Jefferson Barracks at St. Louis into a segregated Negro training center. On November 26, he asked Lovett if there was any truth to the rumors about plans for Jefferson Barracks. Lovett on December 17 responded: "Present Air Forces plans do not provide for the conversion of Jefferson Barracks into an all-Negro post." This response was technically correct, although it avoided mentioning the coming plan to set up for blacks an officer candidate school and a cooks-and-baker school at Jefferson.[7] When in early January 1943 it was disclosed that Jefferson Barracks was indeed opening a new officer candidate school for blacks on January 15, Hastie promptly fired off a memorandum to Stimson, advising that he had now "no alternative but to resign in protest and to give public expression to my views." He said in his memo that "the failure of the Air Forces [by which he meant Lovett], after written request, to advise this office candidly and fully of a plan so soon to be publicly announced cannot be considered an excusable inadvertence."[8]

Following Hastie's resignation and the publicizing of his charges, the Jefferson Barracks proposal was quietly dropped, and certain other Air Force policies related to their black trainees and airmen were revised. When Hastie's former aide, Truman K. Gibson, was named his successor, Lovett was determined to establish a better relationship with Gibson than he had with his predecessor. The Tuskegee Airmen went on to perform very creditably for the air force in World War II as fighter pilots because of their single-engine training. Robert Lovett was certainly pleased to observe their performance. But few in the higher reaches of the air force or the War Department could take much credit for what these black pilots accomplished.

The great increase in the number of white men joining the Air Force brought about problems of its own, principally in the area of limited training facilities. With the influx of recruits the existing training centers were soon overflowing, and the air force leaders feared that they would lose desirable recruits to the navy. To cope with this problem, Hap Arnold came up with a plan, supported by Lovett, to subcontract with civilian flying schools. To protect the civilian operators of these schools from the draft Arnold arranged to secure Selective Service exemptions for them. As a result, within a month of Pearl Harbor 45 civilian flying schools were training at least 30,000 air force recruits. Bob Lovett pushed the matter further, with a plan to reduce elementary training from 66 weeks to 15 weeks, a plan that would get the trainees into air force hands much sooner.

In the spring of 1942 Lovett got together with his old Yale Unit pal Di Gates, who held the same position with the navy Lovett held with the army, to come up with a program to "develop a well-rounded, voluntary preflight training course" in public high schools, involving "physical culture and appropriate military training." This soon became the Victory Corps program, introducing pretraining courses into the high schools.[9] In another area, Lovett got involved with training mechanics because he felt there would soon be a considerable lack of specialists to meet the growing needs of the air fleet. Concerned both with inadequate numbers and unfocused training, he soon arranged for the best trainees to be transferred for specialized schooling to the factories making airplane engines. On a trip to the West Coast aircraft factories in August 1942 Lovett was gratified to find this program working very well. The manufacturers were volunteering to take on more trainees. "I believe it to be of the utmost importance," he told Arnold in a report, "that we take advantage of every possible means of supplying the combat units with specially trained mechanics."[10]

The training programs that Lovett and Arnold put into place produced excellent results. In October 1943 Lovett was able, in a speech to the National Safety Congress in Chicago, to tell of more than 3.5 billion miles flown by army air force pilots in a year with an accident rate less than the aerial average for the ten peacetime years before the U.S. entered the war. Thousands of lives, he said, were saved by the present air force system of training on the ground and in the air. "Every day there are 98,000 Air Forces men flying in this country as part of their training as members of combat crews," he said. "Every 20 seconds during the day a gunnery training plane takes off or lands at just one of our schools." With a huge expansion of flying time of pilots in this country, an accident-rate increase had been expected, but, to the contrary, there had been less than one accident for every 1,000 hours flown.[11]

While the numbers in the air force were growing at a gratifying rate, there were problems in the aircraft industry. The draft was taking too large a bite out of the aircraft factory workforce. Aircraft executives had unsuccessfully requested blanket exemptions from the draft for their employees. Lovett had initially resisted such pressures, but he soon recognized the problem and what it could produce. On January 28, 1942, he got together executives from the aircraft companies Boeing, Douglas, Curtiss-Wright, and Glenn Martin, along with a representative from Alcoa, the aluminum manufacturer, with Lewis Hershey, the director of Selective Service. The outcome of this gathering was a system for reciprocal communication between the aircraft industry and the Selective Service, with the industry being alerted to future draft requirements and Hershey's group being kept advised of critical skill needs and tight labor markets. This arrangement provided some relief to the aircraft industry, but it did not totally overcome the problem of autonomous local draft boards with quotas to fill.

As these various problems in the aircraft industry came to the surface, Robert Lovett soon realized that there was another, very nontraditional approach that could and soon would have to be taken. He came to believe that it was essential for aircraft manufacturers to make "a much greater employment of women and of men below and above combat ages, those with dependents and physical difficulties disqualifying them for military service." Lovett was one of the first to advocate a much-expanded role for women in the aircraft industry. He called for the elimination of restrictions upon the jobs women could hold; they would no longer be held to "feminine" jobs like sewing fabric for wings and would now be able to be used as welders. He also urged California's governor Culbert L. Olson to suspend the state's law restricting a woman's workweek to 48 hours.[12] As a result of the pressures by Robert Lovett and others, the percentage of women in the work force was enlarged from 1 percent in December 1941 to 39 percent in December 1943. "Rosie the Riveter, meet Bob Lovett!"

In the summer of 1942, the new War Manpower Commission (WMC), headed by Paul McNutt, took over the leading position in handling the civilian manpower problem. McNutt, a Democratic politician—former governor of Indiana and presidential aspirant—put together a program that was supposed to help manpower issues and provide benefits to labor. He directed the United States Employment Service (USES) to make up a list of essential occupations and to set forth minimal skill qualifications for these positions. The USES was also to supply to local draft boards a list of critical occupations for which there were shortages. McNutt also asked the War Production Board to keep him posted on manpower shortages in relevant industries, and he urged the setup of local labor-management committees to take on complaints against factories that failed to follow the government's manpower policies.

Robert Lovett found McNutt's procedure satisfactory, particularly since it utilized several ideas that Lovett and the aircraft manufacturers had tried out earlier. In October 1942 McNutt and Selective Service chief Lewis Hershey declared that the Selective Service would henceforth warn plant managers of the vulnerability to the draft of their employees. At the same time, the aircraft companies would prepare "Manning Tables," ranking their personnel by relative importance so the draft boards could go after men in reverse order. The table would reflect manpower needs of a plant at a particular time as well as anticipated hiring for meeting production schedules. The local War Manpower Commission (WMC) agents were to approve each company's proposal and then send it on to the local draft board. Lovett was not sold on the local emphasis, but he favored the Manning Tables approach. "While it will meet early congestion," he wrote, "it is hoped that it will solve most of these fundamental problems."[13]

With specific disagreements rising between local WMC representatives and local draft boards, Lovett sat down with General Hershey and worked most of them out. Although there were numerous complaints, he counseled patience while the Manning Tables approach was taking hold and would remove from him the onus of mediating particular disagreements. He wrote to Edsel Ford: "The appeals of the Secretaries and notices to the draft boards are really designed as temporary measures to serve until the Manning Table Program can become effective."[14] Nevertheless, Lovett was disappointed in McNutt, as his WMC was unable to bring down the turnover rate for skilled labor, which necessarily impacted aircraft production. He particularly disapproved of McNutt's reliance on local councils in the disputes that arose. The turnover of key personnel in major factories continued to rise, and the slowdown in production in the summer of 1943, particularly in the West Coast plants, especially worried Lovett. North American let Lovett know in July that because of manpower shortages it would need to make a choice between failing to produce sizable numbers either of B-25s or of P-51s. "Both of these types are of vital importance to us," Lovett wrote to Robert Patterson, so the North American "case gives very definite proof of the direct effect of the manpower situation on our combat plane needs."[15]

On August 18, 1943, much to Robert Lovett's dismay, McNutt's WMC issued a decree that kept local council control over deferment decisions, failed to include subcontractors in the affected program, and provided no blanket exemptions for critical aircraft workers. Lovett protested and appealed to Bernard Baruch, who supported his position in an appeal to James F. Byrnes, FDR's mobilization chief. Lovett got the industry's Aircraft War Production Council to oppose McNutt's August 18 memorandum. In a telegram to Byrnes and McNutt, the council said, "We believe that the plan is unsound, complex and unworkable to a degree which will retard rather than increase production." The wire went on: "If literally executed, the plan could transfer complete control of production to the War Manpower Commission and its committees [and] ... take complex problems of management and production from experienced hands and place them in inexperienced hands."[16]

McNutt resisted the efforts of the War Department and Baruch to overturn his program. He did, however, join with Hershey in late August 1943 to grant a two-month moratorium from the draft to all aircraft workers in the West Coast plants. In October 1943 Patterson and Lovett tried to get a six-month extension of the moratorium but were unsuccessful in the light of McNutt's opposition, but they were able to get another two months. Finally, on October 27, Byrnes settled things with a ruling that aircraft industries could name certain critical workers as "irreplaceable" and the Selective Service would have to grant them deferments. On November 23, Frank F. Russell, general manager of the Aircraft War Production Council, was happy to write to Lovett telling him of the ending within the last month of the "seriously disturbing downward trend of total employment" in the eight western aircraft companies, with both Boeing and Lockheed showing an increase of several thousand employees. Russell cited several factors for this progress, among them the 60-day draft moratoria and the six months' deferment of irreplaceable personnel as well as "the work of the community itself." Lovett was very pleased to see how his efforts were working out.[17]

Finally, after the problems of coming up with adequate manpower and womanpower were brought under control, there were the traditional issues of labor relations, issues in relation to which Robert Lovett took a rather traditional Wall-Street-Republican point of view. He believed that the handling of manpower problems and labor unrest by President Roosevelt and his administration could have been better, in line with the War Department's call for a more centralized, stricter approach. But, as the war progressed, production and manpower problems eased, and the air force became an ever greater factor in America's waging of the war.

9

Running the Air Force

While dealing with the problems of aircraft production and personnel, both in the air force and the airplane factories, Robert Lovett had as well the requirements of his day-to-day activities as assistant secretary of war for air to perform. He was not only the key civilian in making the air force as good as it could be, but he was also a central figure of Henry Stimson's staff in the War Department. Lovett was charged with maintaining the planes and bases in the United States but he also had to be a supporter of the air force overseas, especially the planes based in Great Britain. As a former flyer himself, he liked to utilize a particular epigram: "You don't have to be a damfool to be an airman, but it helps."[1]

Various issues came up from time to time. Sometimes it was dealing with a power assertion by the navy. On December 2, 1941, for example, British Air Marshal Arthur Harris needed Lovett to intervene when a spokesman for Admiral Harold R. Stark, chief of naval operations, attacked the heavy bomber program as an interference with naval needs and called for its reduction. The British were absolutely sold on the heavy bomber program as their greatest necessity and needed to be reassured that it would not be changed. Lovett was able to give this reassurance.[2] Another time the problem was criticism of the efficiency of the air force by a famous aviator, Alexander P. de Seversky. De Seversky, a World War I pilot and noted aircraft designer and manufacturer, was a follower of General Billy Mitchell and his theories of air power. In 1942 he published a book entitled *Victory Through Air Power*, which called for winning the war through the use of airplanes. The book attacked the navy for treating airpower as simply "an extension of old-fashioned sea power" and the army for treating "aviation essentially as 'flying artillery' or 'more effective reconnaissance,' as just an improvement of familiar textbook military precepts."[3] Walter Lippmann read de Seversky's book and pointed out that, with all the faults the author mentioned, "the growth of American air power is the outstanding achievement of the Government and of American industry." And when de Seversky called for "men who understand the air" to "rule the air," he overlooked "the Assistant Secretary of War for Air, Mr. Robert Lovett, [who] is conspicuously equal to his task. And the debt we owe him is greater than the country yet realizes."[4]

De Seversky's book was followed by another, *The Air Offensive Against Germany*, by reporter Allan A. Michie, which claimed the air force was misleading the American people as to the combat effectiveness and capabilities of its planes, which he said were inferior to those of the British and the Germans.[5] Lovett agreed with de Seversky on the ultimate use of air power but felt the author had misstated what the Army's airpower philosophy had developed into, and he felt that Michie's book misled the public on what the air force was already achieving and would do in the near future. He handled these public relations problems through a meeting with Stimson, McCloy, and his friend (and fellow Bonesman)

Archibald MacLeish, who was at that point representing the Office of War Information (OWI). Lovett suggested educating the public "as to the functions of the different kinds of airplanes ... showing that each of these planes was built deliberately for a particular and vital function and that it was impossible to use any one plane for all functions." Obviously, too, the capability of long-distance strategic bombing should be emphasized. McLeish was impressed with Lovett's views "and undertook to steer the OWI that way."[6]

There was growing recognition of Bob Lovett's achievements with the air force. In mid–January 1942, with many things going wrong militarily, one reporter stated that "many of the mistakes have been remedied since the quietly competent Assistant Secretary of War for Air, Robert Lovett, got settled firmly in the saddle and started herding his crusades successfully through the tricky passages of the White House." It was further noted that "thanks almost entirely to Lovett, U.S. heavy bomber production is really 'rolling,' and alterations in design have corrected deficiencies in defensive fire-power ... and Lovett has won his long fight to remove the stupid, snobbish 2-years-college requirement for air cadets."[7]

Several weeks later, as described earlier, Robert Lovett found himself on the cover of *Time*, with a stern look on his face and a heavy bomber flying behind him. In the article that followed, Lovett was compared to the late General Billy Mitchell, devoted as Mitchell was to the "thesis that air power is the decisive power." The rest of the article provided welcome publicity to the vast improvement to the air force Lovett was bringing about and contrasted him with Mitchell as "pushing the right button instead of wrecking the keyboard."[8]

In April 1942 thirteen bombers, ten of them North American B-25s, the other three B-17s, under the command of Brig. General Ralph Royce, flew 1,500 miles from Australia to an airfield on Mindanao in the Philippines. From there, on April 12 and 13, they carried out a series of raids against Japanese facilities on Luzon. Following the raids, Lovett sent telegrams of congratulations to North American and other aircraft factory workers in Los Angeles, Paterson, New Jersey, and Pittsburgh. "Docks were wrecked, ships were sunk, airfields and grounded craft destroyed," Lovett wired. "Your workmanship helped get them there and bring them back. We recognize that fact and know you join with us in pride in their accomplishment."[9]

A few days after the attack on the Philippines, Lieutenant Colonel Jimmy Doolittle led sixteen B-25 Mitchell bombers as they took off from the deck of the carrier USS *Hornet* 650 miles at sea from Japan for a flight in which they bombed Tokyo, Yokohama, and several other Japanese cities. None were shot down, although they encountered difficulties with their landings, mostly in China. This well-publicized exploit gave the American people some good news to follow all the bad news of the past several months, and it also gave them a glimpse of what air power could do. In May, Bob Lovett spoke to the United Nations Air Training Conference in Ottawa. He said, "While each of us unquestionably has his own particular problems, there are many of them that are common to all of us, and we welcome the opportunity to work out our program of team play on the training fields so that we may all do our jobs with precision and confidence as we fight wing to wing."[10] Early in June 1942, from the 3rd to the 6th, was the battle of Midway, north and west of Hawaii, another celebration of American air power with a decisive victory over the Japanese navy. This victory, however, was achieved through naval aviation, and the AAF could do nothing but look upon it with admiration.

On June 9 there was a diversion from army life as Bob traveled to New Haven at Yale's invitation to attend the college graduation. In what was called an unusual procedure, he and Artemus "Di" Gates—the "heavenly twins of Yale," as their citation read—received the honorary degrees of master of arts jointly, having distinguished themselves in the First World War as members of the Yale flying unit, came back to peacetime careers in banking, and now had "returned to direct the destinies of the nation's air forces in the most responsible positions which the government affords." As Lovett and Gates rose to receive their honors, they were applauded by a member of the Yale Corporation, F. Trubee Davison.[11]

After the U.S. entered the war, Henry Stimson called regular meetings of what he termed his "War Council," consisting of Patterson, Lovett, McCloy, and Bundy, as well as Marshall, Arnold, and whatever other generals or civilian aides he thought appropriate. At these meetings, usually weekly, there were discussions of general War Department business, as well as of matters of particular importance on any given day. Lovett was a regular attendee when he was in Washington. Later in the war Stimson met regularly with his "Civilian Staff," as he called it—Patterson, McCloy, Lovett, Bundy, George Harrison, and others.[12]

Stimson also made sure to invite his civilian assistants to dinner frequently at Woodley, the handsome estate in northwestern Washington he shared with his wife, Mabel, sometimes one aide at a time, sometimes two or more, and often with their wives. There was even, on Christmas Eve 1942, with Adele and Bob, the Pattersons, the Bundys, and a few others present, a concert at Woodley performed after dinner by some 55 musicians from the local army forces. "Everybody enjoyed it," Stimson wrote. "The singing was really beautiful."[13]

Lovett's position in the government made necessary a good bit of traveling, mostly around the country, sometimes to Europe. On occasion he accompanied Stimson on trips the secretary found necessary, but most of his traveling was on his own, often to the West Coast, where the major aircraft manufacturers were located, and frequently to army airfields, especially to Wright Field just east of Dayton, Ohio, a key to the continuing development of the air force. From 40 buildings at Wright in 1941 to more than 300 by 1944, there was also the Air Corps' first modern paved runway. Wright Field became a hub of research and construction, and as such it was always very much in Bob Lovett's mind.

In the middle of September Lovett got back to Washington from a trip to St. Louis, to be confronted by Stimson about bottlenecks in the Air Corps maintenance force. The obvious source of replacement for maintenance shortages in the military was draft-age men in the aircraft factories. Lovett assured the secretary "that they had this bottleneck in mind in the Air Corps and ... that there had already been a good start made in the bringing in of women" as replacements for those drafted. As noted earlier, the employment of women in the aircraft factories increased substantially and served to ease the problems quite well.[14]

On October 20, 1942, Stimson called in Lovett and McCloy to discuss his worry over the air coverage for the impending Operation TORCH invasion of French North Africa. Stimson, Marshall, Lovett, and others in the War Department leadership had been unhappy with the postponement of any cross-Channel assault upon the Germans because of the determination to invade North Africa, but with the matter settled they wanted to make sure that faulty air coverage would not compromise the attack. With assurances that the navy carriers assigned to the invasion were not to be taken away and the information that some fifteen four-engine bombers were being equipped to add to the air force already in line, there was a general consensus that adequate air coverage was assured. As it developed, the invasion of Morocco on November 8 was very successful, despite some early resistance by Vichy French forces.[15]

A bit later, on the morning of November 10, Lovett gave a widely reported talk at the annual meeting of the Academy of Political Science at the Hotel Astor in New York City. His point was to tone down the claims of certain aero-fanatics on the probability of air transport replacing shipping by vessel in the near future. His talk, later reprinted in the magazine *Air Transportation*, credited transport planes with great multipurpose accomplishments as "vital members of the combat team of our Army ... as vital to an air force as motorized equipment is to an Army Division." However, he went on, this fact had "fostered wild claims for air carriers and have, unfortunately, led to much loose talk, false hopes and misrepresentation of the transport plane's proper sphere and its possibilities." Air carriers, he said, provide "a supplementary *express* service, not a substitute *freight* service." Lovett pointed out the great difference between what a transport plane could carry and what a cargo ship could carry and concluded that the airplane was, and would continue to be, subsidiary to the cargo ship in the transport of major and weighty cargo.[16]

Lovett got a bit of press when a letter he wrote to congressman Overton Brooks (D–La.) was read in the House on January 28. In his letter Lovett revealed that the army's air accident rate was lower for 1942 than in the 10-year peacetime period from 1930 to 1940. Rumors were abounding that "50 per cent of personnel in army planes en route to our fronts are killed in transit." Lovett said this rumor was "vicious, reckless and completely untrue" and that 99.7 percent of army personnel transported by air in the past year were carried safely. This accomplishment, he went on, "is a superb one and an extraordinary tribute to the pilots, the machines and the operating and supervising personnel," particularly when these flights were being made to 10 active overseas air fronts.[17]

Through 1942 and 1943 and even extending into 1944, Lovett, along with Stimson and Marshall, was caught up in a struggle with the navy over the disposition and command of the campaign against the German U-boat. Through 1942 and 1943 the Nazi submarines wreaked terrible havoc on shipping along the Atlantic coast. Between the start of the war in late 1941 and March 1943, the U-boats destroyed seven million tons of Allied shipping, mostly in American areas. Oil tankers were a prime target, and the famed New Jersey seashore became coated with oil from the stricken tankers. Nighttime blackouts of the shore resort towns did not do the job as expected in protecting the ships from their underwater predators. Admiral Ernest King, who succeeded Stark as the navy's chief, believed firmly that any warfare having to do with the ocean had to be controlled by the navy. As Lovett recalled, "You could never deal with a subject such as submarines without getting into an argument with King or his representatives from the Navy."[18] King decreed that naval convoys were to be the weapon for fighting the submarine, and there should be no debate about that. Airplanes could fly along to protect the convoys, but that was about their limit. "We didn't believe that," said Bob Lovett, "and a very large element in the Navy itself didn't believe that, particularly the aviation part of it."[19]

On March 28, 1942, Henry Stimson intruded into King's world by sending Lovett and Hap Arnold to discuss with the admiral his proposal to use army airplanes against the submarines up and down the Atlantic coast. As might have been expected, they got nowhere. King believed that any and all antisubmarine warfare should be carried out and controlled by the navy. He (and navy secretary Knox) believed as well that aircraft were not effective submarine fighters. Of course they were ignoring the newly adopted radar with which sub-seeking army planes were soon equipped. Radar was a far-reaching weapon to be used along lines worked out by Stimson's radar consultant, Dr. Edward L. Bowles, along with Lovett.[20]

On July 7, 1942, Lovett produced for Stimson a letter to Secretary Knox proposing a rearrangement of antisubmarine command in the Atlantic, with supreme command still with the navy but with an army antisub air force without the necessity of roundabout communications between both army and navy headquarters. Stimson signed it and sent it on, but it got nowhere.[21] A week later Stimson reported happily of Lovett's telling him of a "'field day' which our airplanes had had over the Atlantic with submarines yesterday, having dropped bombs on some seven submarines." Lovett's account, Stimson noted, showed two things: first, "a very encouraging number of contacts with the submarines," and second, the navy's recent claim that the subs had been chased away from the Atlantic coastline was wrong, "as all of these contacts had taken place close to our Atlantic coast."[22]

Stimson and Lovett suggested to the navy early in 1943 the creation of "killer groups"—made up of escorts, small carriers, and army planes—equipped with the best new electronic and sonic devices to seek out U-boat "wolf packs." King and the navy turned this down despite the continuing heavy losses of merchant shipping. Finally, Stimson and his War Department team worked up a plan for separate army air units hunting submarines with land-based planes. After Lovett and the others worked out the details for a written report, Stimson took this to a meeting with the president on March 26. Roosevelt agreed on an experimental task force and agreed to Stimson's suggestion that it be on the entrance to the Bay of Biscay. Roosevelt then said, "I don't want to go over Knox's head. Cannot you and Lovett get Knox and Gates together and talk this over with them?" Stimson knew what the outcome of that was likely to be.[23] What this involved, of course, was the proposition to the navy that produced Admiral King's not-unexpected opposition. Over the next several months there was a steady back-and-forth between the army and the navy over the questions of what would be used and who would be in charge of it, with Ernest King's adamant opposition to most army proposals setting the tone.

Lovett got into the antisubmarine business again when he was in Algiers in June 1943. British Air Marshal Arthur W. Tedder complained to Lovett that navy command was blocking the proper and efficient use of army B-24s fighting U-boats in the Moroccan sea frontier. When Lovett got back to Washington, he took the matter up with General McNarney, who confirmed that "the disposition of this aircraft was entirely at the command of General Eisenhower," the navy having "no vested interest in the equipment." A couple of memoranda that followed placed the army antisub planes firmly in army control.[24] Nevertheless, in June, Stimson realized there would be only "further trouble between the Army and the Navy over these vital problems of jurisdiction," and the army withdrew from the antisubmarine war (but not in Morocco). "We have at least put a new spirit into them in regard to fighting of the submarines," Stimson concluded.[25]

In July, however, Bob Lovett had one last fling at antisubmarine problems. Major William Jackson returned from Europe with suggestions for fighting the U-boat in the Bay of Biscay, an area of prime importance to the British. George Marshall told Lovett to discuss the matter in detail with Admiral King, "giving him the benefit of information prepared by the British, relating to the importance of the Bay of Biscay." Lovett phoned King at 4:30

p.m. on the 27th, told him the situation, and offered to stop by and make available all the information the War Department had gathered on this matter. "Admiral King," Lovett reported, "showed signs of extreme irritation, to the degree that he made sounds like Donald Duck. He said that he wished the British would mind their own business … that he had not yet reached any decision with respect to the final disposition of the anti-submarine squadrons … [and was] not prepared to talk about the matter at this time." Since he had had numerous discussions with the British, he felt this was their "attempt to get in through the back door in some fashion." Lovett responded that this was more likely an effort on the part of the British "to obtain reconsideration at a higher level of a matter which they consider vital and which from our own experience seemed to make a great deal of sense. This did nothing to reduce the Admiral's blood pressure." King finally agreed to have Major Jackson confer with one of his underlings, but he declined to accept Lovett's suggestion that he call on him for further discussion. "It obviously was not one of the Admiral's good days."[26]

10

Keep 'em Flying

There was no question that the primary aim of the United States military was to defeat Adolf Hitler and Nazi Germany before any other foe. On the ground the Germans were fought by the armies of the Soviet Union, trying to turn back the Nazi assault on Russia, and by the British in Egypt and Libya. For the early part of the war, there was no opportunity for the American army to fight Germany on the ground, which placed all the emphasis of the U.S. Army on the heavy bomber program Robert Lovett had done so much to endow. Lovett was constantly on top of the bomber program, what it was doing, what it was capable of doing, and what it could be made to do. Back in November 1941, he had checked on the army acceptance tests of the Douglas B-19 bomber and was happy to see that it had completed the tests with a 3½-hour flight over the Southern California coast, including speed runs and two shallow dives. He was glad to see by the following January that military airplanes were being produced at the rate of nearly 3,000 each month. With the development and production, however, there was the concomitant need for accomplishment.[1]

The mainstay of the air fleet at the start of the war—and for quite some time after that—was the Boeing B-17. While the B-24 Liberator was used as well, the B-17 was considered the AAF's best weapon. As Boeing Model 299 the plane made its first flight in Seattle on July 28, 1935, and was soon christened the B-17, "the Flying Fortress." The plane could operate at very high altitudes, as high as 36,000 feet, had a ferry range of 3,600 miles, and could go 292 miles per hour.[2] Douglas MacArthur had a fleet of B-17s on his Philippine base, but they were destroyed sitting on the ground by the Japanese air attack on December 8, an attack that should have been anticipated by MacArthur but was not. For those early days of the war, with Japanese plans unknown, Lovett, Stimson, and Arnold concentrated on getting aircraft to the West Coast to protect against air attacks there. When it was recognized that such attacks were not forthcoming, additional planes were sent to General Kenney's Fifth Air Force in Australia, where they were very useful, as noted, in the Bismarck Sea battle to come and the raid on the Philippines.

In the meantime the main attention of the air force civilian and military leaders was directed to Europe. Up until the entry of the U.S. into the war the focus was on the bombers provided to the British under Lend-Lease and their efforts across the Channel into occupied France. At the beginning of the war between Germany and Great Britain, both nations used their air fleets in limited operations, aiming at targets like ships and docks, making efforts to avoid the civilian population. It was soon apparent that the limited accuracy of such bombing brought about sizable losses of civilian lives. The Luftwaffe "Blitzkreig" of English cities soon removed restrictions on targets. The first raid of the British Royal Air Force (RAF) on Germany took place on May 11/12, 1940, on the town of Monchengladbach.

On May 15, RAF Bomber Command authorized targets in Germany east of the Rhine, and on May 17/18 the RAF made heavy attacks on Hamburg, Bremen, and Cologne. The poor accuracy of the bombing made it apparent that the civilian population was paying a great price in these raids, and on February 14, 1942, the RAF Area Bombing Directive "focused on the morale of the enemy civil population and in particular of the industrial workers."[3]

The American Air Force made its first appearance in England in the summer of 1942, with B-17s assigned to the VIII Bomber Command, led by Major General Ira C. Eaker. This group made its first real attack across the English Channel on August 17, with 12 planes led by Eaker hitting the marshaling yards of Rouen-Sotteville, in France, with no loss of planes. Eaker, back on the ground after the foray, said, "Why, I never got such a kick out of anything in my life!" America's AAF was now in the war against Nazi Germany.[4] It had taken quite an effort to get it there. In August 1941 the Air War Plans Division had put together, at the direction of the War Plans Division of the Army, what was called AWPD-1, a report of the requirements for the coming war of the United States Army Air Forces. Arnold and Lovett had declined to simply lend a few officers to the group putting together the army's over-all report as they had been requested to do, instead insisting that the air force prepare its own. A four-man team, led by Lt. Col. Harold L. George (who was called later "the prophet of Air Power" by Hansell) and including Lt. Col. Kenneth Walker, Major Laurence S. Kuter, and Major Haywood S. "Possum" Hansell, Jr., quickly got to work to prepare a report in the two weeks allotted for it. Not surprisingly, the four of them got together frequently with Arnold and Lovett, with Lovett helping particularly in putting it into a form that took account of possible political sensitivities.[5]

By the end of the month, AWPD-1 was complete, providing for five major air tasks. These were: first, and primarily, as Lovett had urged, to conduct a sustained strategic air offensive against Germany and Italy to destroy their will and capability to continue the war and to make an invasion possible if necessary; second, to provide air operations in defense of the Western Hemisphere; third, to provide air operations in Pacific defense; fourth, to provide large tactical air forces for close and direct support for the invasion of Europe and for land campaigns thereafter; and fifth, to determine the calculation of total air requirements to carry out all of the prior tasks, requirements that were projected to be immense. AWPD-1 was based on an 18-month lead time for putting together the necessary bombing strength required for the strategic air offensive, with two years for amassing an invasion force. The six months in between would be for the strategic bombing of Germany in order to assist with the invasion. That first task, as broken down, entailed the destruction of Germany's electric power grid, the transportation network, and the oil and petroleum industry, with 124 vital targets set forth, and it recognized that it would be necessary to neutralize the German air force, the Luftwaffe, by attacking its bases, the aircraft factories that built it up, and the light metal industries supporting those factories.[6]

AWPD-1, after an initial presentation to the G-3 of the War Department General Staff, came before Brig. General Carl Spaatz, chief of the air staff, Brig. General L.T. Gerow, assistant chief of staff, War Plans Division, and Robert Lovett. Lovett, of course, who had helped to write the plan and was "one of the real architects of American air power," was firmly in favor of it, as was, naturally, Spaatz. Gerow, somewhat surprisingly, also looked upon AWPD-1 with favor. Finally, on August 30, came the crucial presentation to General George Marshall, the army chief of staff, who could have shot the whole plan down with a few words. Instead, he said, "Gentlemen, I think the plan has merit. I would like for the Secretary and the Assistant Secretaries to hear it." With this, the AWPD-1 was on its way, and the air force began the year to year-and-a-half development the plan envisioned.[7]

Strategic bombing was a new factor in warfare; before the development of the long-range heavy bomber, it was impossible to carry out such attacks. Such a role of the air force in a war was unprecedented, and it encountered resistance from military figures unfamiliar with the possibilities of strategic bombing. Lovett was not only a major figure in creating the role of strategic bombing but also in the necessary concept of selling it to those at the top of the military ladder. After Pearl Harbor, Lovett wanted to warn Stimson and the War Department against the natural inclination to spread military strength around the globe. "Looking at the record so far," he said in a memorandum submitted in early March, "it is a tragic story of dispersing inadequate units of the Navy, Air and Ground troops all over the map." Pushing hard for the concept of strategic bombing, he wrote, "The quickest way to kill a man is to shoot him in the brain or in the heart.... [O]ur main job is to carry the war to the country of the people who are fighting us—to make their working conditions as intolerable as possible, to destroy their plants, their sources of electrical power, their communications systems and thereby soften them up for the inevitable engagement between ground troops and naval forces." Not surprisingly, Henry Stimson saw matters pretty much as Lovett did.[8]

Lovett's thinking in favor of strategic bombing was based on the logical conclusion that the best way to win a war was to destroy the enemy's means of resistance. He supported precision bombing of German military installations, factories, transportation systems, and oil and coal resources, rather than the RAF's procedure of mass bombing cities with the resultant death of large numbers of civilians. He did of course want to make Germany's civilians so aware of the horrors of war that they would never support another one. But he felt that his strategic bombing would accomplish that result quite well.

In addition, the image of the American air force to the public was a matter of concern. Lovett did not want the people of the United States to believe that their air force was massacring civilians, and he did not want to arouse congressional opposition in that manner, with the problems that might be caused for future appropriations. He knew that large numbers of American civilians, many of them Germanic in background, did not hate the German people, only their Nazi overlords. Finally, Lovett did not want to provide fodder for enemy propaganda. The British air leaders put some pressure on the AAF to join in area bombing, which involved civilians. Spaatz wrote of this to Arnold, telling of "pressure on the part of the Air Ministry to join hands with them in morale bombing. I discussed this matter ... with Lovett when he was here and have maintained a firm position that our bombing will continue to be precision bombing against military objective[s]."[9]

As things worked out, the army's Eighth Air Force was activated on January 2, 1942, at Savannah Air Base in Georgia, and three days later Carl Spaatz, now a major general, assumed command of it. Three days after that, on January 8, the order activating the "U.S. Air Forces in the British Isles" was promulgated, and on May 12 the air force personnel started to arrive in England. On June 15 Spaatz arrived there, at Bushy Park, to set up the headquarters of the Eighth Air Force. The principal component of the Eighth Air Force was VIII Bomber Command, designed to carry out strategic bombing with heavy four-engine bombers. This group, as noted, was headed by General Ira Eaker. The first combat group of this unit to get to England was the ground echelon of the 97th Bombardment Group, which arrived on June 9. The two other major components of Eighth Air Force were VIII Fighter Command, which would provide fighter escorts to the bombers on their missions, and the VIII Air Support Command, for reconnaissance, transport, and tactical bombardment as needed, with two-engine medium bombers. As described above, the first American air attack on German-occupied Europe was on August 17.

The British RAF, having suffered large losses to enemy fighters and antiaircraft fire during daylight raids, had shifted its bombing program to exclusively nighttime attacks. There was no way at night, with limited vision, to attack specific military targets, so the RAF bombing was on areas in which such military and industrial targets were located. Area bombing obviously had the effect of doing major damage to nearby neighborhoods, with damage to specific targets mostly a matter of chance. British leaders realized this fact, but they justified it on the basis that such attacks caused substantial damage to the morale of the German populace.

The American bombing program was considerably different from that of the RAF. The British leaders hoped to bring the Eighth Air Force bombers into their nighttime bombing fleets, but the Americans said "no." The Eighth Air Force, led by Carl Spaatz and then by Eaker, did daylight bombing of clearly targeted military, transportation, and industrial installations, aided to a considerable extent by the newly developed Norden bombsight, which helped the bombardiers immensely in getting a good fix on their targets. There was much danger in the attacks of the Luftwaffe fighters, the Messerschmitts and Focke-Wulfs, as well as in antiaircraft fire from the ground, but the well-armed B-17s and their accompanying fighter planes were able to resist the fighter attacks. The fighter escorts had a limited range, and they could not accompany the bombers all the way to the designated targets, leaving the bombers open to enemy fighter attacks.

The Eighth Air Force started delivering on its mission to destroy the German ability to continue the war. The air force leaders in England, Spaatz and Eaker, were longtime pals of Hap Arnold, the air force chief of staff. Through the years the three of them had often worked together, with Arnold always a bit superior in rank, on many Air Corps projects. Arnold had become friends with Bob Lovett at about the time Lovett arrived in Washington, and Lovett soon became good friends with both Carl Spaatz, known as "Tooey," and Ira Eaker. Years after the war Lovett spoke of Eaker as "one of my closest friends" for whom he had "a deep admiration and affection."[10]

Like Lovett, Eaker was a long-ago product of a small town in Texas. Eaker was born in 1896, six months after Lovett, in Field Creek, a tiny hamlet about 280 miles west of Huntsville. Young Ira did not go east, as Lovett had, growing up instead in Texas and Oklahoma. He went to school at what became Southeastern Oklahoma State University, and on the day the U.S. declared war on Germany in April 1917 Ira enlisted in the army. He signed up for officer training and soon became involved in flying. He did not get overseas or see any combat, but because he had a Regular Army commission he stayed in the military after the war. Stationed at Rockwell Field, near San Diego, it was here that Eaker made the acquaintance—and friendship—of Arnold and Spaatz. Years later Lovett recalled that Eaker was sometimes "over-awed" by Arnold, who was "often a bull in a china shop," but with Tooey Spaatz Eaker enjoyed a "true, relaxed friendship."[11]

Lovett had met Ira Eaker in the late twenties, when Trubee Davison, then assistant secretary of war for air, would return to his Long Island home for weekends, with Eaker as his pilot, and get together with the Lovetts. "We became very fond of him," Lovett said later. "Adele and I both thought that way about Ruth [Eaker's wife] and Ira almost instantaneously. It's unusual for me to make friends that way. It usually takes me a little time, but this was a complete capitulation almost on introduction."[12]

With Arnold and Spaatz, Eaker became a lifetime Air Corps flyer, with academic interludes in law at Columbia University and journalism at the University of Southern California, and he helped to develop the Air Corps as it evolved over the years. Though still small in size when World War II came, the Air Corps—as shaped by men like Arnold, Spaatz, and Eaker—was ready to expand into the great fighting machine it became. For this development, of course, there was also needed the guiding hand of Robert A. Lovett.

Two days after the raid on Rouen-Sotteville, Eaker was able to send nearly two dozen B-17s to attack airfields near Abbeville in France, home to a highly regarded Luftwaffe fighter wing. This mission took place as an effort to divert German air from the ill-fated landing raid on the French coastal town of Dieppe. Over the next couple of days, Eaker's bombers made additional attacks, much to the joy of Arnold and Lovett back in Washington. In August, Lovett, as was to occur regularly, traveled to the West Coast, "where he made," as Stimson recorded it, "a pretty thorough inspection of the facilities in southern California and Seattle." Throughout the war Lovett periodically checked up on both the factories producing needed airplanes and the Air Corps operations that utilized what was produced.[13]

This trip came shortly after President Roosevelt had sent Stimson a message that aircraft production had fallen below what had been estimated some months before. Stimson turned this over to Lovett, who crafted a proposed response that, as Stimson said, "pretty well disposes of the trouble." Lovett's position was that the estimates from the White House were always too high, that they actually presented targets for production, and that the heavy bombers that were most needed were a bit slower in completion than the lighter planes that made up a good part of the estimates.[14]

On September 2 Henry Stimson met with Eaker, who was recalled to Washington to report on the bombing missions. Eaker "made a very favorable impression" on the Secretary of War: "quiet, modest, but very determined." Eaker assured him that German air production had been reduced by a third and that the Germans were now mostly building obsolescent planes "because they have not the facilities to continue their present operation during the inevitable gap while they are tooling up for the new models." He told Stimson that the British airmen "had been entirely converted to the marvelous accuracy of our daylight bombing and believed that that daylight bombing can be indefinitely continued." All in all, the meeting was a productive one for both Eaker and Stimson, although Eaker's estimate of the British conversion to daylight bombing was somewhat premature.[15]

Through the fall and winter of 1942 VIII Command made every effort to send waves of B-17s on daylight bombing missions, but the weather over East Anglia from which they took off was so often heavily overcast that there were long inactive periods between missions. Only three times in December was the weather clear enough to send off the bombers. These frequent postponements were frustrating to Eaker and his airmen, but there was little they could do to overcome then. From mid–August on, the Eighth had flown 1,547 bombing sorties (individual bombers) in 1942, with a loss rate less than 2 percent. But Eaker knew he needed more bombers as well as fighters to accompany them.

Further disappointments came about with the transfer of a large number of planes (and Carl Spaatz) to the North Africa and Mediteranean areas, to support the TORCH operation and landing in Morocco, as well as further efforts in Tunisia, Sicily, and Italy. The heavy bombers in England for the strategic bombing of Germany fell from about 300 in early October to something like 200 in the following January. And more planes scheduled for the Eighth Air Force were sent off to the South Pacific. Eaker saw many of his best planes and crews leave for the south, and he realized that he would have to indoctrinate and train untested airmen sent over from the U.S. With Spaatz gone, Eaker took command of the Eighth Air Force. In England he became famous for a short speech given at a local dance when, called upon to speak, he reluctantly complied and said, "We won't do much talking until we've done more fighting. After we've gone, we hope you'll be glad we came."[16]

11

The Campaign for 1943

As 1943 got under way Bob Lovett and the leaders of the army air force could look back upon a successful year of production and even better things to come. The *New York Times* had on January 3 published a long article headlined "AIRCRAFT INDUSTRY IN FULL WAR STRIDE," that stated, "We are already producing the world's most deadly bombers ... and since last May have been building more aircraft than the entire Axis combined." With a 1943 production goal double that of 1942, "if the necessary materials and manpower are allotted to the aircraft industry, it has the know-how and the drive to make enough planes for all the needs of the United States and the United Nations on all the world's far-flung battlefronts."[1]

One of the first major occurrences in the new year took place in Casablanca, in Morocco, when Franklin Roosevelt and Winston Churchill—and their military staffs and advisors—met there January 14–24. The principal purpose of the gathering was to finalize Allied war plans for 1943. Josef Stalin, the Soviet leader, had been invited to attend, but he felt it best to stay home in light of the fighting taking place in Russia.

In his preparation for the meeting with Churchill, President Roosevelt met with Lovett and Henry Arnold on January 7. The two leaders of the air force presented FDR with statistics and evidence showing the effectiveness of high altitude daylight precision bombing. What they presented to the president proved to be quite influential in the decisions ultimately made at Casablanca. In addition, of course, Roosevelt spoke often with Stimson, Marshall, and his close buddy Harry Hopkins, and each of these three advisors was close to Bob Lovett and his way of thinking about and describing air power and its possibilities.

Plans were finalized for the concentration of forces in England for the cross-Channel invasion, although it was recognized that this would not take place in 1943. What was decided upon was the attack on Sicily and ultimately Italy to take Mussolini and the Italians out of the war. The strengthening of the strategic bombing campaign against Germany was seen as very important, and objections to the U.S. Air Forces' daylight bombing by the British were finally dropped. At the end, it was announced that "unconditional surrender" was to be the outcome of the war, unlike the armistice that terminated World War I.

Ira Eaker was called to Casablanca for a two-hour meeting with Churchill during which the prime minister argued with him in an effort to convert him to night bombing. Eaker held his own, with the support of Hap Arnold, and showed Churchill that American daylight-bombing methods were rapidly proving superior to those of the British at night. The result was that the AAF's continued use of daylight bombing was confirmed.[2] At Casablanca the overall objective of strategic bombing was set as the "destruction and dislocation of the German military, industrial, and economic system and the undermining of the morale of the German people to the point where their capacity for armed resistance is fatally weakened."[3]

And so the Eighth Air Force started off in 1943 with its ultimate goal established, although the means of accomplishing it were still somewhat limited. The raids of the B-17s into Germany were stepped up, although the losses were considerable due to the inability of the accompanying fighter planes to keep up with the bombers very far inland. The fighters, mainly the P-47s, engaged the German Focke-Wulf and Messerschmitt fighters over the Channel and the coastal regions of Europe and held their own in these battles. The P-47 was faster at altitude and in the dive but inferior in some other respects. Their range was limited, which left the bombers flying on to face German fighters and antiaircraft fire unprotected.

On April 17 the Eighth Air Force fleet of B-17s carried out a raid on the Focke-Wulf fighter plane factory in Bremen, one of the largest assembly lines for German fighters. While sixteen B-17s were lost, "hits were observed squarely on the target area" and more than fifty of the German defensive fighters were shot out of the air. Returning airmen estimated that more than 100 fighters attacked the bombers, "perhaps the largest force of enemy planes ever encountered by an American bomber group." It was just a sample, of course, of what was to come.[4]

In the meantime, however, the air force achieved a notable victory in the Pacific against a Japanese military to that point having its own way in most encounters, except for its losses at Midway. The Battle of the Bismarck Sea took place March 2–4, 1943, with the Japanese attempting to transport 6,900 troops from Rabaul to Lae on New Guinea. Their eight destroyers and eight troop transports set out from Rabaul on February 28 and were soon detected by the air force and attacked by General George C. Kenney's Fifth Air Force bombers and fighter planes of the Royal Australian Air Force, all land-based planes, on March 2 and 3. Follow-up attacks were made by PT boats and more planes on the 4th. The results were spectacular: 213 tons of bombs were dropped and all eight transports and four of the destroyers were sunk; 102 of the 150 Japanese fighters were downed; only about 1,200 Japanese troops made it to Lae; and no further efforts were made to reinforce Lae by ship. Robert Lovett described the battle as "the equivalent of a football coach's dream of a perfect play, in which every blocker succeeded and the man with the ball crossed the line." Citing it as the dream of General Kenney, "whose knees had been calloused from praying for the chance," Lovett said, "the results were superb.... It was a whale of a job." Henry Stimson called it "a very complete victory ... accomplished ... only by land-based planes—the kind of planes that [Navy Secretary] Knox is always saying are no good."[5]

In the meantime, Lovett had his staff analyze the arguments in the de Seversky and Michie books referred to earlier, and a number of factual errors were turned up. In addition, statistical evidence of Lovett's position to the contrary of what was in the two books was brought forth. Soon thereafter, Lovett met with columnist Walter Lippmann, who was following the controversy. Lippmann was impressed with Lovett's careful analysis of the facts in dispute. He told Lovett the get-together "was decisive for me on a very controversial business and I feel I have been saved from blundering into something that would probably in the end have wasted more of your time."[6]

Robert Lovett was steadfast in his feeling that good press relations were essential in achieving the maximum results for the air force and its strategic bombing campaign. He maintained good relationships with numerous leaders of the national press such as Charles Merz, editor of the *New York Times*, Cass Canfield of *Harper's*, Merrill Meigs of the Hearst papers, Eugene Meyer of the *Washington Post*, Henry Luce and Roy Larsen of *Time*, columnists Walter Lippmann and Arthur Krock, and of course his buddies Averell and Bunny Harriman, who controlled *Newsweek* financially. When he could, Lovett did favors for members of the media, and he was frequently rewarded with publicity favorable to his aim of building up the air force. When *Life* magazine wanted to do an article on complementary American and RAF bombing activities, Lovett had Eaker send photographs and information on the coordinated bombing of Hamburg. Eaker responded promptly and afterward sent Lovett much material for public release. "I was astonished and greatly moved by these reports," Lovett wrote, "and there is much in them which would be helpful to getting prompt action on some of our controversial problems."[7]

Later in February the War Department (and the government) had to deal with a potentially damaging labor problem. The AFL union in the Boeing plant in Seattle—the source of the B-17s—on February 25 announced that unless, through the War Labor Board, their members' wages were increased they would go on strike and that they would be followed by the workers at the Lockheed plant and then those at the Consolidated Company in San Diego. As Stimson put it, "it was a real gauntlet thrown down to the government." He and Lovett took the matter up with Jimmy Byrnes, "and by the end of the afternoon we had hammered out a plan of action: to have all of them reclassified by their draft boards and put up to them 'the alternative of either work or fight.'"[8] The potential strikers, however, "apparently terrified by the adverse reaction that their movement ... had met in the press," backtracked very quickly and said they had not intended to strike but had merely wanted "a succession of meetings without the stoppage of work." So the aircraft production went ahead with no interruption. Lovett and Stimson, in the meantime, were gratified at the outpouring of public support for the aircraft production program on the issue.[9]

Putting such matters behind him, Lovett continued his practice of visiting air bases and production facilities around the country. On one such visit, with Arnold, to the Technical Training Command in Miami Beach, he was quoted as saying, "The proof is in the box scores," with American planes downing the enemy at a rate of three to one (and in some theatres, six to one).[10]

In England, the Eighth Air Force and Ira Eaker were going to receive a distinguished and very welcome visitor. On May 7 Colonel George Brownell of Lovett's staff received a letter from the headquarters of the Air Transport Command (ATC) on the subject of "The Air Itinerary and Arrangements for Honorable Robert Lovett and Party." The trip was to originate in a C-54 plane at Washington National Airport on May 11 or 12. It covered the various steps in the journey, with the eventual way back "via the South Atlantic Route."[11] And in fact the C-54 was off from Washington at 9:50 a.m. on May 12. Lovett's party consisted of David Griggs of Lovett's office, Sir Richard Fairy of the RAF, one French officer, and five air force officers, including Col. John Sessums, whose diary of the trip was made available to Lovett many years later.[12]

After a stop in Gander, Newfoundland, for lunch, the plane flew on to Prestwick, Scotland, although its heater quit during the night and parkas were passed out to all aboard. After a special lunch for Lovett at Prestwick, the party departed by car to Glasgow. Here they caught a train to London, where General Eaker met them. After several days of gatherings in London, the group moved to East Anglia, the site of the Eighth Air Force bases, and Lovett, at Eaker's initiative, moved into the general's home at Castle Coombe. He and Eaker, already friends, were able to exchange all sorts of information, recommendations, and inside data on planes, personnel, Washington goings-on, and plans for bombing missions.

While in England, of course, Lovett visited British aircraft factories and all of the Eighth Air Force bases and spent as much time as he could talking with the personnel, flyers, ground crewmen, and anyone else he could find, as well as air force leaders of both the U.S. Army Air Force and the Royal Air Force. He spoke with many fighter pilots, and from them he learned first-hand one of the major problems facing the Eighth Air Force: while the P-47s could usually hold their own against German fighters, they had such limited range that they had to turn back long before the B-17s reached their targets in Germany, leaving the Flying Fortresses on their own against the enemy defenses. Long-range fighters, he soon understood, were a basic necessity now on the books for the strategic bombing of Germany. Lovett also had to give Ira Eaker the news that his old buddy and commander, Hap Arnold, had suffered a second heart attack and was currently indisposed.

On May 30 Lovett and his crew left by air for Scotland again, from whence they departed at 9:10 p.m., flying across Ireland and then out 400 miles to sea to avoid France and Spain and possible enemy aircraft. An engine broke down at about 3:00 a.m. and they briefly considered flying the short distance into Lisbon, Portugal. This idea was discarded when it was realized that they might be interned in neutral Portugal, so they flew on south. After close to six hours in the air—on three engines—the plane landed at Marrakesh in Morocco, their intended destination. After lunch in Morocco, the party boarded a B-17 Tooey Spaatz had sent over to fly them to Algiers for an overnight. Then on June 1 they went on on to the town of Constantine, where they were met by Spaatz and General Jimmy Doolittle. Spaatz was commanding the Northwest African Air Force, and Doolittle headed the Northwest African Strategic Air Force under Spaatz. The next day was set up for Lovett's business meeting with Spaatz, Doolittle, and General Hoyt Vandenberg, Doolittle's chief of staff, in the headquarters of the Strategic Air Force.

On June 3 the party flew to Tunis, where they could observe the results of the air forces' precision bombing, and they even drove on to Carthage for some historical views. They were advised to "stay away from Bizerte as the A.A. guns were very jumpy from frequent Jerry bombings," so they flew back to Constantine. Over the next week or so there were travels to necessary sites, conferences with Spaatz, Doolittle, and Vandenberg, and discussions with other officers on specific subjects. Doolittle and Vandenberg in particular had modifications in mind for the air forces in the Mediterranean area, and Lovett made careful note of them.

On June 13 the group flew to Algiers again, where Lovett was able to get together with RAF Air Marshal Arthur Tedder, and the next afternoon they flew back to Marrakesh, where they stayed overnight. It was on this flight that Lovett was able to indulge in one of his hobbies. As their B-17 soared over the Atlas Mountains, the plane's radioman tuned in on a BBC broadcast of Erskine Hawkins playing an obscure number. Lovett recognized it immediately, identified it to the radio operator, and then told him about the brass section of that particular band. A few minutes later, the radioman went up forward and said to the rest of the crew, "See that baldheaded ol' bird back there? He's the first fella outa Washington I ever met who knew anything about *anything*!"[13]

On the morning of the 15th they were off on the C-54 to Dakar, in French West Africa, flying over hundreds of miles of Sahara Desert. At Dakar ("the whole place was sort of a dump") they were taken to the PX for cold beer and had dinner at the officers' mess. After dinner they took off for the transatlantic crossing over 2,400 miles of water to Belem, Brazil, where they landed two hours early. After breakfast the group toured Belem. "Mr. Lovett looked for a semi-precious stone," noted Sessums, presumably for Adele. At 11:05 in the morning, they were off to Puerto Rico, where they had "a delicious dinner" before a 2:00 a.m. departure for Washington. Headwinds held the flight back slightly, but they arrived back in Washington on June 17.[14] Ira Eaker told Lovett, "You did this Air Force of ours, my Staff, and particularly myself, a great deal of good by your visit. You pointed to our weaknesses in a friendly, cooperative way and set us at greater energy to righting them. You gave us encouragement on some of our good points, which helped a lot too. We don't get much of this, and coming from you who have been through in the last war what we are now going through, it eased our burden."[15] When he got back home, Lovett assured Eaker that his meetings with front-line airmen would "be put to good use and pay dividends." The most important outcome of his trip was his call for quick development of longer-range fighters for the protection of the B-17s. One historian wrote that "the turning point in the drive for range extension came with the visit of Robert Lovett to England in mid–June."[16]

In a long memorandum he wrote to Arnold as soon as he got back to the War Department, Lovett insisted on the "immediate need for long range fighters" to supply *long range* protection for the B-17s. "This may be met by proper tanks for P-47s, but ultimately P-38s and P-51s will be needed." The P-47 Thunderbolts then in primary use needed additional fuel tanks in order to give them much longer range, but Lovett recognized that the newer fighters were what was ultimately needed. "Fighter escort will have to be provided for B-17s on as many missions as possible," he wrote, "in order particularly to get them through the first wave of the German fighter defense, which is now put up in depth so that the B-17s are forced to run the gauntlet both into the target and out from it." He felt that the "ideal plane … for long-range escort duty" was the P-38 then in production, and, he added, "high hopes are felt for the P-51 with wing tanks."[17]

Tommy Hitchcock, in prewar days famed as one of the world's greatest polo players, was serving as assistant air attaché to the U.S. Embassy in London. Hitchcock, who had been a flyer with the Lafayette Escadrille in World War I, was a good friend of Bob Lovett, and he worked with Lovett to push the USAAF into producing the P-51 Mustang as the long-range escort for the bombers.[18] As it turned out, the P-51 Mustang, which Lovett worked hard to get into high production and eventual transport to the Eighth in England, was the real deal—the fighter which could escort the B-17s far into Germany and back after bombing. But it did take some time. The P-51 was originally produced for the RAF, but the British were disappointed with it. When they replaced the Allison V-1710 engine with a far stronger Rolls Royce-Merlin 61, the plane did much better. The American aircraft people noted this, and when the Allison was replaced with a Packard-Merlin engine, the P-51 of the AAF soon outclassed all other planes of its type, though it was not sent over to the Eighth Air Force until the spring of 1944, when it proved to be a critical factor in the aerial victory over Germany.[19]

When Arnold returned to the Pentagon early in June, he kicked off a series of gruff messages to Eaker raising all sorts of questions about the bombing missions, personnel problems, even Eaker's command style. Arnold was beginning to doubt the daylight bombing operation. "Hap was having a hell of a time hanging on...," Lovett later recalled. "I think he was beginning to worry about it because the attrition rate was too high." Eaker, with Lovett's full support, answered Arnold's cables with bluntly stated responses of his own, and eventually the issues died down and the problems went away. Ira Eaker was left with the task of building up his bomber force and training the necessary crews and ground support for it to take on its appointed task of severely damaging Nazi Germany.[20] Years later, Robert Lovett considered Arnold's criticisms of Eaker and the Eighth. "It was clear from the start that Hap had been making wild statements about what the B-17 could do. It couldn't do everything. It needed a nose turret above everything. They put this chin on it. That helped. Another thing it needed was fighter escort in deep penetrations. I think Hap transferred some of his acrimony to Ira because of the failure of the B-17 to perform as he said it would," Lovett recalled. "There was some acrimony, but as far as Ira was concerned, it made no difference. It certainly never affected his loyalty to Hap.... I pushed hard on Hap.... He said our only need was Flying Fortresses, that's all; very few fighters could keep up with them.... The Messerschmidts had no difficulty at all." As it turned out, of course, the long-ranging P-51 eventually took care of the problem.[21]

Lovett, upon his return to Washington in mid–June, had calmed Hap Arnold down, assuring him that Ira Eaker was running things quite competently in England and that Eaker was well justified in pleading for "more replacement crews ... better trained crews ... delivery of operational equipment and ground echelons prior to, or concurrent with, the arrival of combat groups...." Eaker stated, "If these urgent needs are promptly met the operational efficiencies of the Eighth Air Force will, in my opinion, increase by at least 50 percent."[22] Interestingly, General Eaker wrote to Lovett several weeks after the latter's return from overseas that he had "noted a great change, all on the improvement side, in our relations with the 'Home Office.' This I attribute almost entirely as an aftermath of your visit here and to your very hard work on our behalf after your return." There had been numerous improvements in various areas in which Lovett, alerted to needs by Eaker and his airmen, had produced corrective actions, including Hap Arnold's disposition.[23]

Early in December, Lovett spoke publicly about the new fighters coming on line. Up to that year, he said, "it was generally agreed that the Army Air Forces had the best bombers, heavy, medium and light, in existence. This year we believe our fighters will gain the same verdict."[24] With the drop tanks attached to the P-51, its range could take it farther than Berlin, even as far as Vienna. The P-51 Mustang became a very important participant in the air war over Germany in the spring of 1944, although there were still a large number of P-47 Thunderbolts in action as well. Lovett was always ready to give credit to others. "Tommy Hitchcock was largely responsible for the P-51B, for pushing on that project until it got through," he said. "The only person who could have done this was someone who was both knowledgeable as a pilot and who had the qualities of leadership to take a group of disparate people and get them moving in a common direction." But, of course, it was Robert Lovett's constant push in the War Department that insured the major production of the P-51.[25]

On July 6 Stimson held a meeting to take up the matter of demobilization planning, for the end of the war. Lovett, Bundy, Patterson, and McCloy were all present as well as George L. Harrison, another Skull and Bonesman whom Stimson had assigned to get together with Marshall. Marshall had set up a special committee on this subject, and it was the general consensus of Stimson's group that Marshall's committee needed "some representatives from the Air Corps and from the ground services." After the meeting, Stimson headed home, where he and Mabel were to celebrate their golden wedding anniversary. Adele and Bob Lovett were on hand for the occasion as were John McCloy, the Bundys, and several others. "A most delightful dinner," Stimson recorded. "Everybody was in fine spirits and we had a wonderful evening together."[26]

But of course the war did not go away. In the summer of 1943, Operation POINT-BLANK was put into effect. A bombing plan drawn up largely by Carl Spaatz and RAF Air Marshall Arthur Harris, it called for the sustained strategic bombing of Germany. "With air power," Lovett explained, "we can accomplish the complete destruction of its [Germany's] means of war, and that's what we're going to do."[27] One unsuccessful effort, on August 1, was labeled Operation TIDAL WAVE, which consisted of a combined Ninth and Eighth air forces raid with 178 bombers on the oil refining center of Ploesti, Romania. The assault was a failure, with 53 planes and 660 crewmen lost, numerous bombers dropping their loads elsewhere than on the oil refineries, and little lasting damage being done. The raid failed to put much of a dent into the German military's major source of petroleum.

On August 17, the Eighth Air Force undertook a combined heavy raid on Regensberg, with its Messerschmitt aircraft plant, and Schweinfurt, the center of the Reich's ball-bearing industry. The plan was for the 4th Bombardment Wing of the Eighth Air Force to take off from England first for its attack on Regensberg and then fly on south to land in North Africa; the 1st Bombardment Wing would depart England shortly after the 4th while German fighters were still dealing with or returning from the first encounter, fly on for its raid on Schweinfurt, and then return back over the Channel. Unfortunately, while the 4th, under Colonel Curtis LeMay, took off on time, the 1st was kept on the ground by fog before finally taking off 3½ hours late, led by Brig. Gen. Robert B. Williams. With the timing of the operation—the gimmick that was to save the Schweinfurt B-17s from attack—set askew by the late departure, the Schweinfurt bombers met with heavy opposition, especially after their fighter escorts had to turn back around the Belgian border. Although both forces carried out their assigned bombing raids, with the Messerschmitt factory in Regensburg being knocked out for two or three months, the losses were very bad. Between the two wings, 60 of the total three hundred seventy-six B-17s were lost, with their crewmen. With the sizable losses suffered by the Eighth Air Force, General Arnold back in Washington was becoming more and more concerned. Looking back on it, Robert Lovett said, "Hap was having a hell of a time hanging on." He added, "I can't document it but I think he was beginning to worry about [the daylight bombing] because the attrition rate was too high." And so it would continue, until long-range fighter protection was provided.[28]

While the first raid reduced Schweinfurt's ball-bearing production by 34 percent, a good part of it was soon replaced by the Germans, particularly with the expedited purchase of ball bearings from neutral Sweden. This "had filled the gap which we had made from her manufactories," Stimson explained to Secretary of State Hull, whom he urged to take action in regard to Sweden. "I told him," Stimson related, "that there was no longer any excuse for Sweden to say that she was ... afraid of reprisals from Germany."[29] Because of the heavy air losses, though, a second attack on Schweinfurt was delayed until October 14. The two hundred ninety-one B-17s of the second raid carried out the attack on the plants, hitting them with precision, but 60 bombers were lost, 17 were damaged so much they had to be scrapped, and 121 suffered damage of some sort. Five hundred ninety-three crewmen, 22 percent of the total engaged, were lost, though it was estimated that half of them would be alive as prisoners of war. Hermann Goering, head of the Luftwaffe, looked at the American losses and reported to Hitler that the second Schweinfurt raid had ended in a great victory for his German flyers. Albert Speer, however, after checking with his production people in Schweinfurt, told Hitler that in fact the air attack had been very successful, that the damage to the ball-bearing plants was "far worse than after the first attack."[30] The Associated Press reported that "the American loss represented 600 American fliers killed or missing and perhaps 20 million dollars worth of precision bombing and fighting machinery." But it added "that the plant, whose products form key parts of the German war machine, was knocked out of production." It quoted one crewman as saying, "There ought to be ball bearings rolling all over Germany tonight."[31]

Henry Arnold called the Schweinfurt raid "a heart-damaging blow to the entire German war production and machinery maintenance program" and he "ranked the attack on the ball bearing plants in importance with the previous blasting of the Ploesti oil fields in Rumania by American bombers."[32] While the Schweinfurt raid did cause considerable damage to the German war production, later examination disclosed that the Germans were still able to restore production, although not to the prior level, more quickly than was anticipated by the Allies. Nevertheless, because of the great damage caused by German fighter defenses and antiaircraft fire, the long-distance raids were suspended and not resumed until the February 1944 initiation of what was called "Big Week," with the addition of the long-range P-51 fighters for protection. Still, Lovett, filling Henry Stimson in on the air battles, continued to be "very optimistic." Despite losing 60 Flying Fortresses in the second Schweinfurt raid, "whereas we had 947 of the Flying Fortresses just before the Schweinfurt raid, now we have 1035," even with the loss of those 60. Production of the heavy bombers was coming along at a superlative clip. By November Eaker's Eighth Air Force had 1,500 heavy bombers.[33] Many years later, Ira Eaker sent Bob Lovett a copy of Thomas Coffey's book, *Decision Over Schweinfurt*, noting that "your encouragement sustained our morale and your influence in the highest political levels insured that we got the chance to prove the case for daylight bombing, and the weapons with which to accomplish it. For this," he concluded, "every veteran of the 8th Air Force who is armed with the facts will always be indebted to you."[34]

In August, Bob Lovett even found that his office involved him acting as Cupid. A young Washington stenographer was trying unsuccessfully to get married by telephone to her lover, a corporal with the Air Transport Command in Brazil. Because of problems in putting telephone calls through from Brazil, the couple were becoming increasingly frustrated. Eventually Lovett was contacted for help at his Georgetown home, and he made several suggestions on how to get it done, going through General Cyrus Smith, head of the Air Transport Command. The message had to be certified as necessary to the conduct of the war, and Lovett was called back. "I'm getting a little old and bald to play Cupid," he said, "but I have asked Gen. Smith to see what he can do about getting this message through. If these young persons hate each other for the rest of their days, I'm going to feel guilty about it." The calls went through and the two were married. How the rest of their lives went is not known, but Bob Lovett had no reason to feel bad about it.[35]

The National Safety Congress heard from Lovett at its banquet at Chicago's Hotel Sherman on October 6. He told the diners that daily there are 98,000 airmen in training in this country. "In this country alone," Lovett said, "airmen flew more than three and one-third billion miles, or 134,000 trips around the world during the last year."[36] Finally, as the year's end was approaching, Robert Lovett, in a speech to the University Club in New York City, put together what the overall purpose of the strategic bombing campaign looked like:

> It has been an unhappy fact for the rest of the world that these gullible and warlike people [the Germans] should have developed a powerful industrial and technical organization to support a huge military machine. This machine depends on some 90-odd industrial centers of which perhaps 50 are of major importance. If these centers can be destroyed or seriously damaged it must be obvious that her means to make war will be reduced. And in the process of destroying them the people can be given their first searing lesson, in the heart of their hitherto untouched homeland, that crime doesn't pay. This should reduce their *will* to fight. If, therefore, we can reduce the *means* to fight and the *will* to fight, the tasking of overpowering her is made easier or the time shortened. That, very simply, is the contention of the Air Forces.[37]

Lovett, of course, with his strong belief in the power of strategic bombing, felt that the Eighth Air Force, stationed in England, was the ideal weapon for the bombing campaign against Nazi Germany This belief was behind his efforts to do all he could to build up Eaker's force. Even with the bad weather of December, the Eighth continued periodic raids on German towns. Eaker wrote to Lovett: "I think those who discount and discredit the effect that our overcast bombing on German cities is having on the enemy are unrealistic and unwise."[38] At the same time, Lovett reported to Henry Stimson's War Council "what the American Air Force is doing to Germany and the rate of its progress as compared with the estimates of two years ago. He felt that on the whole we would more than meet our estimates provided there were no further diversions."[39]

In addition to longer-range fighter protection, Lovett knew that the Eighth should be supplied with more and more of the heavy bombers being manufactured. One of the problems that had to be dealt with was the continuing pressure for more bombers in the Mediterranean Theatre. While coping with this demand, Lovett and the AAF had to contend as well with the ever-expanding scope of naval air activity and the competition this produced for those strategic airplanes available. Obviously, all this kept Bob Lovett a busy man, but the ultimate success of the strategic bombing of Germany's factories, transportation, and aircraft facilities demonstrated his competence.

12

The War Grinds On

During 1943 the German army on the ground had been retreating. It had been pushed back in Russia, in North Africa, in Sicily, and in Italy. In each of these instances, the Allied army moving forward had recently established air superiority, which was essential for the advance. How did this happen? The Luftwaffe had been forced to pull its air power away from the front lines and back into Germany, where it was needed to attempt to give protection to the industrial plants being attacked by the U.S. and British strategic bombing runs. These runs, of course, worked to diminish German aircraft production, which further enhanced Allied air superiority. The reliance on strategic long-range bombing, pushed hard by Lovett, Arnold, and the AAF leaders, was showing a very beneficial effect to the entire Allied war effort.

On November 30, 1943, the leaders of the Combined Bomber Offensive devised a plan they called Operation ARGUMENT as a part of Operation POINTBLANK to deliver a stunning series of blows to the Luftwaffe and German industry through a round-the-clock bomber offensive. Weather in December and January prevented the immediate implementation of Operation ARGUMENT, but the necessary build-up of bombers, fighters, and crews was carried out. A few American planes were equipped with the new H2X radar system, but even this did not do a complete job in piercing cloud cover.

Along the way Lt. General Carl Spaatz was appointed commander of the United States Strategic Air Forces (USSTAF), Ira Eaker was moved to Africa to take charge of the Mediterranean Allied Air Forces there, and General Jimmy Doolittle was sent to England to command the Eighth Air Force. The Ninth Air Force, reestablished in England, was run by General Lewis Brereton. In addition, the Fifteenth Air Force, based in Bari, Italy, would also participate in the operation, under its commander, General Nathan F. Twining. The RAF would contribute what it could as well. The USSTAF listed for President Roosevelt the targets: 11 fighter plane factories, 15 bomber factories, 17 airplane engine plants, 20 submarine yards, 38 locomotive building shops, 37 electric plants, 14 aluminum plants, two synthetic rubber plants, and 23 oil plants.

While the adjustments in the Air Force commands were being made, Bob Lovett was pleased to see his wife, Adele, given the honors in cracking a bottle of champagne to christen a troopship, the *General George M. Randall*, in Kearny, New Jersey, on January 30, 1944.[1]

Finally, on February 19, 1944, the weathermen at USSTAF predicted an extended period of clear weather over central Europe, and Spaatz ordered Operation ARGUMENT to commence the next day. That evening, in fact, the RAF sent 823 bombers to Leipzig, setting the stage for the American attacks of the next days. The bombing operations carried out from February 20 to February 25 became known as "Big Week." They were aimed at the

German aircraft industry, and the American daylight runs were supported by the RAF Bomber Command going after the same targets at night. The B-17 and B-24 bombers of the Eighth and Fifteenth air forces were protected on their runs into Germany by the P-51 Mustang fighters, which had finally arrived in quantity in Europe, with their far longer range than the P-47s of the past, though the P-47s and P-38s were still used.

With the P-51s protecting the B-17 bombers as well as inviting opposition from German fighter planes, the German fighter losses mounted substantially, with 3,450 Luftwaffe fighters going down along with many of their most experienced pilots in the first three months of 1944. After the war "German air generals responsible for operations in France stated under interrogation that on D-Day the Luftwaffe had only 80 operational planes with which to oppose the invasion."[2]

In the six days of Big Week, German aircraft factories in Leipzig, Brunswick, Gotha, Regensburg, Schweinfurt, Augsburg, Stuttgart, and Steyr were attacked by the Eighth flying more than 3,000 sorties and the Fifteenth more than 500. Between them the two forces dropped roughly 10,000 tons of bombs on or around their targets. The Eighth lost ninety-seven B-17s and forty B-24s, with twenty more scrapped because of damage. The Fifteenth lost ninety bombers, and fighter plane losses were twenty-eight. While these numbers look high, the number of bombers in their sorties was far higher than previously and the losses were smaller, percentage-wise, than in earlier missions. In addition, replacements for those lost came over from the United States in a steady stream. Nearly 300 German fighters were downed, with the loss of pilots who could hardly be replaced, and of course there was considerable damage to the airplane production plants. As a result of Big Week, and the irreplaceable losses suffered by the Luftwaffe, air superiority over Germany passed irrevocably to the Allies. One German historian wrote of the Big Week: "Nothing in war history up to that time was even remotely comparable to the annihilating capacity of those hordes in the sky."[3]

Shortly thereafter, on March 4, the USSTAF launched 730 bombers with 800 fighter escorts in its first raid against Berlin. Although sixty-nine B-17s were shot down, these American losses could be, and were, quickly replaced. The Luftwaffe lost 160 planes in defense; their losses could not be made good. Robert Lovett was not able to enjoy all of this, due to what Stimson called "a couple of weeks' absence partly on business and partly on recuperation. He isn't yet feeling right and I am a little worried about him." Lovett's continual health problems were interfering once again.[4]

In April, American bombers returned to Ploesti, the oil refining center in Romania. In August the year before, an attack on Ploesti had done very little to damage Hitler's primary source of oil. This time, though, nine groups of B-24s and four groups of B-17s hit Ploesti on April 5 and dropped almost 1.2 million pounds of bombs on the refineries. Over the next month additional raids on Ploesti reduced it to an almost worthless pile of rubble.[5] Back in Washington, Henry Stimson, Robert Lovett, and Henry Arnold could look upon the news coming in from Europe with great satisfaction. Lovett and Arnold particularly, the leaders who had pushed the strategic bombing campaign as a major factor in the war to defeat Germany, knew that Allied air superiority was essential to an invasion of Europe and that invasion planning was now something that could move forward, as the Luftwaffe was under control. Indeed, on April 1 the combined bomber offensive officially ended and control of the strategic air forces was turned over to Dwight Eisenhower for use in the coming invasion. While some strategic bombing continued, most of the army air force's efforts through April, May, and into June were tactical flights in support of the upcoming Normandy invasion.

One new feature that would help in the coming invasion had been developed early in the year. One day late in January, Colonel George W. Goddard was brought into Lovett's office by General Hoyt Vandenberg. Goddard, who had been involved with aerial photography (and flying) since joining the army in 1917, was an enthusiastic advocate and developer of the continuously open-shutter strip camera, which he pushed as a great advance over standard aerial photography, as it synchronized its film speed to the speed of the aircraft in which it was mounted. The new camera was being produced by the Chicago Aerial Survey Company, which had worked with Goddard in putting it together. Goddard was unable to get the army air force interested in it because Henry Arnold was firmly opposed to the strip camera, as he was to Goddard as well. Goddard, however, had gotten the navy to make good use of the strip camera, so he felt he should try the army once again. Walking down a corridor at the Pentagon, he encountered Vandenberg, whom he had known for some time; after Goddard explained what he was hoping to do, Vandenberg got on the phone and soon had him in Bob Lovett's office. Lovett was not particularly pleased to hear of Goddard's work with the navy, but he was quickly taken by the underwater test data Goddard showed him.

"We need this kind of camera for amphibious landings in every theatre of operations," Lovett said. "Goddard, how many do you think we should buy for the Air Force?" The reply: "At least two hundred, sir." Lovett picked up his phone and summoned Maj. Gen. Oliver P. Echols, at the time chief of Air Force Material; when Echols appeared Lovett told him he wanted the strip cameras purchased immediately. Then he thanked Vandenberg and Goddard for bringing such a valuable item to his attention. As Goddard started across the room, "walking on air," as he recalled, Lovett said, "Where are you going, Colonel?" "Why, back to the Navy, sir," Goddard replied. "You're doing nothing of the sort," Lovett exclaimed. "I want you to go home and pack your bags. I'll have an airplane at National tonight at ten o'clock to pick you up. You're flying to England. Come back here in half an hour so I can give you a letter I want you to personally deliver to Elliott Roosevelt." Roosevelt, the president's son, was working with military aerial photography in England.[6] Goddard reported to young Roosevelt on February 1, 1944, and, after overcoming some initial cynicism about his camera's usefulness, was able to demonstrate the value of the strip camera, which was ultimately of considerable good use in preparing for the landings of D-Day.[7]

Well after the war, Goddard wrote to Lovett expressing his appreciation for Lovett's help in pushing the strip camera "for determining water depth and beach gradients during the War. Without your help it would never have been used in Europe and the Pacific in connection with the preparation of timely coastal maps for amphibious landings." Lovett quickly responded: "I recall very vividly my introduction to advanced aerial photography under your guidance and I know how much our successful war effort depended upon your imaginative inventiveness."[8]

On another front, radar use in air force planes was developed in the spring of 1944. On March 7 David Griggs, a technical specialist in the office of Dr. Bowles, did a memo for Lovett in which he noted that the major problem holding up the use of radar was "trained personnel." He quoted Maj. General Fred Anderson saying that if the radar navigator-bombardiers were given as much training with their equipment as regular bombardiers were with theirs "the H2X equipment would be capable of as accurate bombing as we can do with the Norden bombsight on our critical targets in Germany." Still, as Griggs noted, the H2X program had moved very quickly in the prior three months, and steps were taken to improve personnel training.[9]

The new B-29 Superfortress bombers were coming on line in the Pacific, planes that were considerably larger than the mighty B-17s. The B-29s were 99 feet in length, and the B-17s were 74 feet. The B-29 wingspan was 141 feet, contrasted with the 103-foot B-17 span. The B-29s had a range of 5,830 miles and a top speed of 365 miles per hour and could attain altitudes up to 31,850 feet. On April 10 Lovett reported to Stimson on their worth and how they were to be used. The first B-29 combat mission, bombing Bangkok, followed on June 5, and on June 15 a B-29 raid on the town of Yahata was the first attack on Japan since Doolittle's in April 1942.[10] That the B-29s were being involved in the fighting was owing to a gamble taken by Lovett and Arnold. The AAF entered into a contract for production of the B-29 long before the plane's model had been flight-tested; indeed contracts had been let in September 1942 for 1,644 planes. Under normal routines, it was very possible that the B-29 would not have seen combat in the war at all.[11]

There was a concern with self-sealing gasoline tanks on air transports, which had resulted in questioning from Senator Kilgore of the Truman Committee. Lovett worked with Stimson on a letter to the senator "so that it would show my own personal investigation and interest in the airborne troops." Stimson also agreed with Lovett "that we should send over to the European theatre a lot of self-sealing bags ready to go into tanks so that the theatre commanders there" could equip planes with them. "That," Stimson wrote, "would show our critics better than anything else that our minds were open and we were trying to do what we could without weakening the range and the speed and the carrying power of the planes."[12] On June 1 Stimson and Lovett had a long talk on the self-sealing tanks issue. Stimson recorded, "Bob has been very judicial and fair-minded in it and he proved so today." And so the self-sealing tanks problem was taken care of, with multiple tanks being shipped over to England.[13]

With the attainment of the air superiority for which he and the leaders of the air force had striven, Lovett was able to consider and take actions upon several issues that looked to the postwar period. After the D-Day invasion of June 6, the AAF in Europe was occupied primarily in support of the ground forces, although strategic bombing of German aircraft factories, transportation systems, and other areas of assistance to the Reich's war effort was continued at a lesser rate. The Eighth Air Force from England and the Fifteenth Air Force from Italy were now fully equipped to carry on these efforts. An example of the sort of postwar items that forced themselves upon Robert Lovett was proposed funding for the development of a new airport in the northeast section of Philadelphia. Lovett wrote to Philadelphia congressman Hugh D. Scott that "neither War Department lawyers or those of the Civil Aeronautics Administration have been able to devise any lawful means of making funds from either department available." He added that "the only courses of action open to the city are those which we have discussed," such as special legislation, city or air carrier financing, or some combination.[14]

One of the matters Bob Lovett kept in mind was the question of unification of the

American armed forces—primarily the creation of a single department for all of the American military and, what should necessarily be a part of that, elevation of the air force to an equal status with the navy and army. With the granting of autonomy to the air force earlier in the war it had been assumed that the total revamping of the American military could not be done during the war for fear of unnecessarily complicating the war effort. In 1944, however, an end to the war somewhere down the line could be foreseen, and the postwar unification question became an issue to be discussed. Stimson and Marshall, while allowing for private discussion of unification, still felt that the question should be kept off the board until after the war, but Lovett no longer agreed with that position.

In early November 1943 Marshall had submitted a memorandum to the Joint Chiefs of Staff asking their "agreement in principle" on a unified war department, a suggestion that drew immediate rejection by Admirals King and Leahy. A special committee to consider reorganization was created, but Lovett, in a letter to Tooey Spaatz, anticipated that the committee would come to a position "by a mixture of vested interests and compromise rather than on the basis of lessons learned and errors corrected." He said he would take an active role in the debate he anticipated, "regardless of the consequences." Lovett continued: "Feeling as strongly as I do about the subject, I expect to be in more or less continuous hot water from now on as I am going to battle for a unified Air Force from here on out."[15]

It did not take long to get Henry Stimson on his side. Stimson believed that a future unification would be wise, and he asked Lovett to prepare a letter to be sent to Frank Knox, the navy secretary, on the issue. "Our experience of the past two years," Lovett's draft opened, "has led me to the firm conclusion that modern warfare requires a more closely unified command of our armed forces than exists at this time." After discussing the problems of supply and procurement that should no longer be handled by competing services, the letter as drafted by Lovett wound up with "the task of fitting" the air arm "into the structure so that it will with the least duplication and the greatest efficiency be operated in conjunction with our ground and sea forces."[16]

Shortly thereafter, Congressman James H. Wadsworth introduced in the House a resolution creating a "Select Committee on Postwar Military Policy." With the approval of President Roosevelt, the leadership of the House set up a special committee to look into the questions involved, the committee to be chaired by Congressman Clifton A. Woodrum, a progressive Democratic congressman from Virginia who had been a member of the House since 1923. On April 25, 1944, Stimson testified before the committee, speaking as briefly and as broadly as possible, leaving specifics to later discussion. He was followed by General Joseph T. McNarney, Marshall's deputy chief of staff, who also spoke as broadly as he could.

The following day, though, April 26, Lovett testified to the Woodrum Committee. He got into quite a few specifics. "It is my conviction," he told his listeners, "that the present system of two independent departments charged with national defense is not designed to translate the tremendous war effort of the nation into maximum effectiveness and efficiency in waging modern war." The nation had been lucky in the ongoing war to have had "the personal qualities and abilities of our military leaders" who had to set up "what is in effect another department of national defense consisting of a great number of joint Army, Navy and civilian committees." Obviously, we were unlikely to be that fortunate the next time around. "At irregular intervals in history," Lovett went on, "some new development has altered the art of warfare and changed the fate of peoples and the world" like gunpowder and steam-driven warships. "Today that development is the airplane, and particularly the fast bombing plane. It annihilates distance ... a striking force undreamed of a few years ago." "But," he added, "to be effective it must be used by an organization as modern as the instrument itself, trained to think in terms of shrinking distances." He mentioned the "visible line of demarcation between Ground and Sea force functions," the shoreline. "No such boundary exists in the air," and airplanes fly over the land and the sea. "The lessons of the war to date point clearly" to the fact that future wars will be "a series of combined operations in each of which Ground, Sea and Air Forces must be employed together and coordinated under one directing Staff and under one over-all command."

Lovett summed up his belief "that the single Department of Armed Forces offers the best means, of which I am aware, of providing for intelligent progress in the air arm and of obtaining unity of planning and of operations and most effective and economical use of the nation's manpower, material and monetary resources." Reminding the committee that he was not stating the War Department position but was drawing on his own experience in the last war and the present one, he went on to give numerous examples of situations in which a unified and consolidated department would clearly function more efficiently than the present setup. There were many areas of duplication that could be eliminated. He went on to note that many army officers with whom he had discussed the question "feel that the unification of the Services operating in three elements into a single department will improve combat effectiveness, promote efficiency and thereby better enable the taxpayers of the country to support a modern establishment designed to insure national security."[17]

When the representatives of the navy appeared before the committee, it became clear that their position was sharply counter to that of the army, as expressed by Stimson, McNarney, and Lovett. Rather than engage in a public controversy, which could be damaging to the war effort, Stimson on May 5 met with James Forrestal (acting navy secretary after the April 28 death of Frank Knox), Woodrum, and members of the committee, and an agreement was reached to wind matters up with no endorsement at that time of the principle of unification. The whole issue would await the end of the present war.

Lovett expressed his thoughts on the matter in a letter to his friend, Ira Eaker. "Much to everyone's surprise," he wrote, "the Navy, who had previously indicated a general concurrence at the Secretarial level, reverted to the old Army-Navy game frame of mind. The bureau chiefs in solemn procession said that everything was daisy and there wasn't any point in changing the organization." They said "that duplication is not duplication but is 'paralleling.' This fancy bit of semantics hasn't fooled anybody although it has clouded the issue somewhat." Lovett felt that "the public reaction has been about 80% in favor of the Army's suggestion, but there are indications that the White House does not want the matter considered further at this time." So there it would remain.[18] Lovett of course took a slight risk in setting forth his position as clearly as he did to the Woodrum Committee. He knew that he was going beyond where Stimson and Marshall wanted him to go, but he was aware too that he was not going too far beyond the actual though unstated thoughts of his superiors, and he wanted very much to get his position into the open—for whatever value it would have in future, even postwar, considerations.

Another major area of postwar planning involved the question of national security. Marshall for the War Department and Arnold for the Air Force each put together committees to think about and plan for national security in the years following the defeat of Germany and Japan. These committees had to think of (a) another war with (b) a totalitarian power, a contest between (c) good and evil. Their results were necessarily based on reactions to the experiences of the '30s and '40s rather than thoughtful analysis of how strategic needs would be met. Arnold's committee initially came up with a plan for a postwar air force of 105 groups, which Marshall rejected because he felt that a postwar Congress would not authorize an army of the size that such a proposition required. Lovett too felt that the postwar American public would not tolerate an adequate strategic bombing force. He believed that future security could be provided for with the maintenance of a standby air capacity through civilian aviation.

As long as there were several strong aircraft companies competing for domestic and international business, Lovett felt, such a competitive industry would sustain what had been developed in wartime in airframe and engine manufacture. Such competition would also inspire technological innovation and improvement, which would surely have military applications. He felt that surplus property should be disposed of after the war in a way that would encourage trials of new airframe, engine, and weapon designs. An aircraft industry so developed would surely be available for speedy conversion to military usages in the event of another war or even the threat of one.

As far back as December 1942, Lovett had been instrumental in having Secretary of State Cordell Hull and Assistant Secretary of State Adolf Berle create an advisory body to look to postwar aviation policies that would adequately safeguard national security. This body, designated by FDR as the Interdepartmental Committee on Civilian Aviation, was made up of Berle, Lovett, Civil Aeronautics Board chairman L. Welch Pogue, Assistant Secretary of the Navy Ralph A. Bard (later replaced by Di Gates). and representatives named by the Commerce Department and the Bureau of the Budget.

Starting with meetings of the group in January 1943, Lovett made it his task to convince its members of the ties between international aviation and national security. He stressed that "air power will be a dominant military weapon after the war." Freedom of the air, he emphasized, "will be meaningless unless there is one power"—which should be the United States—"which can and will see that the rules are obeyed."[19]

Lovett was a strong believer in having overseas air bases; bases located in the continental U.S. could not guarantee security in other continents. "I cannot over-emphasize the importance that I place on this entire base problem," he wrote to Arnold and Eaker. He felt that American rights should be asserted for commercial use of airline facilities built with Lend-Lease assistance, and this insured access to an international air route system would promote world peace and safety.[20] He also wrote to Harold George: "We have a heavy responsibility to protect American interests and to see that the lives which have been lost and the money which has been spent in developing these world-wide airways have not been wasted." And these airfield rights should be secured while the war was going on and American strength was relied on: "We must make the trades while we still have something to trade with and not rely on the good faith and gratitude of the recipients of American help." Accordingly, George was to examine closely the terms of U.S. participation in the construction of numerous important airfields around the world.[21]

On Lovett's suggestion, Berle set up a staff subcommittee for the Interdepartmental Committee to put together information and make recommendations on air bases built under Lend-Lease that could have strategic significance postwar. When he read a draft of the subcommittee's report, Lovett was unhappy that national security considerations were largely neglected. "It is," he wrote, "absolutely necessary for this Government to make up its mind promptly … in order to reach an intelligent conclusion" about the treaties on air rights still to be negotiated.[22]

On November 11, 1943, President Roosevelt met with Lovett, Berle, Pogue, Undersecretary of State Edward Stettinius, and Harry Hopkins, to discuss postwar international aviation. After setting forth his view that Germany, Italy, and Japan should be totally denied any aviation facilities whatever, the president said that allied countries should control their own internal aviation developments and American international aviation should be handled by several airlines, with no single company having a monopoly as Pan American was reported to be seeking. Roosevelt also, as to landing rights, "wanted a very free interchange … arrangements by which planes in one country could enter any other country for the purpose of discharging traffic of foreign origin," with liberal arrangements for the right of free transit. When Berle suggested an international conference to set up ground rules for postwar civil aviation, Lovett objected that such a gathering should be deferred until after the U.S. had secured such commercial landing rights as reflected considerations of national security. FDR agreed on the idea of such a conference, but he agreed with Lovett that it was premature and suggested possible preparations for it to be held late in 1944. In his later review of this meeting, Lovett felt that national security issues involved with postwar aviation were not much involved in the president's thinking.[23]

Along the way, Cordell Hull dissolved the Interdepartmental Committee on Civil Aviation and replaced it with a study group within the State Department. At the same time, Hap Arnold's War Plans Division was working on a paper showing the relationship of international civilian aviation to national security, so Bob Lovett got very much involved with that. The result, naturally, was that the final product of Arnold's Air Force group—the War Department Statement of Policy on Civil Aviation—was essentially a restatement of Lovett's position. As he was espousing his general position in favor of vigorous airline competition after the war, Lovett quickly learned that this position was in conflict with that of the British government, which was in favor of restricted access to key areas limited to the government-owned British Overseas Air Corporation, as well as with that of Pan American Airlines, which, under its president Juan Trippe, was pushing for designation as the only American carrier in international air service.

Trippe had gone so far as to recruit senators friendly to his airline to frame a bill in Congress to replace the Civil Aeronautics Act of 1938. The bill, entitled the Civil Aeronautics Act of 1944, provided for a single American carrier in international civil aviation, on the theory that competition from government-owned or goverenment-financed foreign airlines required the U.S. to be represented by one airline alone (and presumably this would be Pan American). Lovett opposed this bill because of his conclusion that an aeronautic monopoly would hold back the development of worldwide routes and modern aircraft equipment, but he opposed it as well because of the probability that Pan Am would get the nod as the American airline.

From his experiences with Pan American and Juan Trippe during the war up to that point, Lovett was totally opposed to Pan American's interests in the bill. As the prime contractor for the Air Transport Service, Pan American had frustrated both the navy and the War Department with its inefficiencies and drawbacks. Lovett wrote to Harry Hopkins:

"All this difficulty has arisen from the fact that the company too frequently seems to be unable to subordinate its own interests to those of the national war efforts." He went on, "Of all the companies in the United States, none had a greater opportunity to render a real public service to the common cause. To say that they have been slow in taking advantage of their opportunity is to put the situation mildly."[24]

During 1944, Lovett helped to form a coalition of major airlines (not Pan American, obviously), the Civil Aviation Board, and the War Department to oppose and ultimately defeat the bill providing for the Civil Aeronautics Act of 1944. With that legislative threat out of the way, Lovett got to work helping to prepare for the Chicago International Civil Aviation Conference scheduled for December 1944. He felt strongly that a unified U.S. position in support of overseas airlines operations was necessary, with continuing arguments here enabling "foreign competitors to take advantage of vacillation and uncertainty on our part while driving ahead with orderly plans for their own national aviation." In his letter to FDR's advisor Bernard Baruch, Lovett said, "There has ... been a popular idea that the United States holds all the cards in international negotiations," which he found "false and, therefore, dangerous."[25]

On October 11 Lovett warned Henry Stimson of what might take place at the Chicago gathering, telling him that the conference should avoid specific route negotiations, and that the United States should move ahead with bilateral negotiations for landing rights in key places. Stimson asked Lovett to prepare a letter for him to send to Hull setting forth what should be America's objections. Lovett did so, and Stimson's letter went on to Hull. Hull turned Stimson's letter over to Adolf Berle, who had chaired his group on civil aviation. Berle chose to consult, of all people, Robert Lovett (who had of course been on his interdepartmental committee) for preparing a response to Stimson's letter. Lovett suggested language for Hull's reply that put the State Department in line with the War Department position, which was of course his own. Berle followed through as directed, and the two departments became united in recognizing, as Lovett reported to Di Gates (who for the Navy Department concurred with the War Department position), "the over-riding importance of ... national security," stood for "the acquisition of the widest possible system of air routes," and assured that the Chicago proceedings would be "conducted on the basis of multiple operations rather than a monopoly."[26]

As it turned out, the 55-nation Chicago Conference, designed to set up agreements on how international commercial aviation was to be conducted in the postwar years, was somewhat of a disappointment. Both the U.S. and Great Britain felt that it was somewhat premature, and the settlement of major issues was put off while the two major powers could secure their own bilateral agreements. The conference did see some moderate issues decided, and it provided a forum for its members to express their hopes and ambitions for the future, but that was about it. Robert Lovett was satisfied with the way the Chicago meeting worked out.

13

Moving Onward

In June of 1944 Robert Lovett made another trip to England, a trip by which, as he had the year before, he would endeavor to learn from those in the midst of the action what improvements or corrections could be made in air force equipment and practices. He did not on this trip meet with Ira Eaker, who was now commander of the Mediterranean Air Force in Italy (though Eaker did suggest unsuccessfully a diversion to Italy for Lovett) but instead met with Jimmy Doolittle, who now led the Eighth. Lovett also met with Carl Spaatz on June 9, at which time he warned Spaatz that negative feelings in Congress and around the country had arisen about the inhumanity of indiscriminate area bombing and that such should not become the announced policy of the air force. He urged Spaatz to respect such feelings in carrying out his bombing program. Even Bob Lovett, though, could on occasion harbor feelings of satisfaction with such bombing. After seeing reports and photos of an RAF obliteration raid on Essen in 1943, he told RAF Marshal W.L. Welsh that he had "studied the pictures with great interest and, I confess, some of that sadistic barbarism that I was joking about the other night."[1]

There was an unhappy diversion for Lovett on June 21, when Maj. Gen. J. Lawton Collins, leading the American troops attempting to capture Cherbourg, the port of the Cotentin Peninsula to the west of the Normandy beach landings, ordered saturation bombing of the town when the German commander refused his demand for surrender. Spaatz and Lovett were flown over to witness the operation, which helped to lead to Cherbourg's surrender in a week, though such a massive air raid was not one that Lovett could sanction, especially since it was a French town rather than a German one being destroyed.[2]

Back in England, in Lovett's discussions with Doolittle after checking out the B-17 and fighter crews and combat units, their needs and their recommendations, he went over a number of suggestions, including the following: "Among other things some armor plate for engines; the possibility of obtaining water injection for emergency power, or any other method of increasing performance; the need for additional H2X [radar] test equipment; the automatic gyro leveling device for the Norden bombsight; and increased allotments of electrically heated gloves and shoes." Lovett reported to Doolittle some two weeks after his return to Washington: "I have been riding herd on these and other similar points and I believe some progress has been made since my messages from England dealing with such matters." He set forth in his letter some of the improvements that had been brought about. He concluded his lengthy letter to Doolittle with "how much I enjoyed being with you and how warmly I appreciate your many courtesies to me during my stay."[3] A couple of days later, Lovett sent Doolittle a second letter, giving the Eighth Air Force commander further information on the procurement and production of the automatic gyro leveling devices coming to the Eighth. Doolittle sent off his appreciation for all that Lovett was doing and added how pleasant it was to have him visit: "I only regret that we didn't have more time together."[4]

The war moved on, centered now in Normandy, where the invading Allies were moving slowly, stymied by hedgerows and enemy resistance. On July 18 Lovett held a press conference, at which he emphasized that the lull in strategic bombing, brought about by the diversion of much of the Eighth Air Force to tactical support of the invasion in Normandy, was giving the German aircraft factories an opportunity to rebuild the Luftwaffe. He pointed out that the enemy could replace major factories in five or six months, so that the Eighth Air Force would have to return soon to destroy these plants. Lovett also said he found it hard to understand "the unreasoning optimism" on the home front that the war was nearly over.[5] On July 25 Lovett wrote to Spaatz about the concern that was growing at home over the lack of progress in Normandy: "People over here were beginning to wonder why in the heck the Ground Armies didn't get rolling." At the press conference where this came up, he said, "I naturally avoided the question, mumbling into my beard about the difficult terrain, the ditches and hedgerow character of the countryside, etc." One change he suggested to Stimson was that Eisenhower should "get his advance headquarters into France at once and let the American armies know that he is the Commander-in-Chief," which Marshall quickly took care of.[6]

Once back from Europe, of course, Lovett, with McCloy, Harrison, and Bundy, resumed his regular civilian staff meetings with Secretary Stimson. On September 18 their meeting was occupied with a discussion of what was to be done with Germany after the war. At the recent (September 16) conference in Quebec of Roosevelt, Churchill, and Canada's prime minister, Mackenzie King, the president had brought up and gotten partial approval (soon to be reversed) of the Morgenthau Plan, by which Germany was to be stripped of its industries and turned back to an agricultural and pastoral country. Stimson and his staff were not in favor of any such program, and Roosevelt soon dropped his support of it.[7]

Several days later Bob Lovett was happy to be one of those present in General Marshall's room to celebrate Henry Stimson's 77th birthday. Born in New York City on September 21, 1867, Stimson had served his country well over those many years, and his staffers were glad to recognize that.

As the war ground on through 1944, Lovett and Hap Arnold discussed the creation of an agency to go over all the information available on the results—good, bad, or indifferent—of the strategic bombing efforts of the army air force. They recognized that there had been contentious arguments following World War I about who had won the war and how, and Lovett and Arnold wanted to avoid such disputes at the end of World War II. An "accurate, unbiased analysis of the effects of our bombing on the enemy's economy, on his military operations, and on the termination of hostilities," as Arnold put it in his memoir, would throw great light on the value of strategic bombing to the overall war effort.[8]

From this discussion came the creation of the United States Strategic Bombing Survey, which issued its "Summary Report" on September 30, 1945. Arnold's original presentation of the project was rather limited in scope, to gather experiences in Germany for target selection in the developing attack on Japan. Lovett felt that appointment by the president was desirable to attract high-level civilian membership for the survey and that its aim should include post-war planning rather than just the war on the Japanese. Lovett tried James Conant, the president of **Harvard**, but Conant turned him down, and Lovett was unsuccessful in going after academics to chair the survey. He tried to enlist Donald K. David, dean of the Harvard Business School, with a letter early in September, in which he stated two important uses of the proposed study in addition to planning the attacks on Japan. First, he said, was "the influence which a factual study will exert on the formation of our national defense policy, with particular reference to the size of the military establishment and its makeup," and second was "the bearing that such a study will have on the future layout and plans of factories and industrial establishments." "With the age of jet-propelled and rocket aircraft at hand," Lovett said, "ought we to begin to build vital facilities part underground or baffled with blast walls, or … in more distant suburbs in order to remove the targets from the congested housing areas?" Unfortunately, the letter to David failed to produce any volunteers.[9]

Lovett wrote later to Spaatz on ways to make such a survey particularly valuable: "We have a great opportunity right now if we act intelligently. We can photograph and measure bomb damage until we are blue in the face but nothing is as persuasive as the statement of the German leaders as to what did them the most harm…. We need a lot of such statements from military leaders as well as plant managers to offset the inevitable claims that will be made by the proponents of other arms."[10]

With the college presidents and professors he solicited for the chairmanship turning him down, Lovett turned to the business community. He and Hap Arnold met on October 21 with Franklin D'Olier, president of Prudential Insurance Company and, in 1919, the very first national commander of the American Legion before he got into the insurance business. D'Olier agreed to take on the job.[11] Lovett was then able to get his "old and close friend" Henry C. Alexander as vice chairman. Alexander had been general counsel to Brown Brothers Harriman before becoming vice president of J.P. Morgan. Lovett knew Alexander "to be of complete integrity with the courage to state the facts that a trained lawyer is able to dig out," and his personality too "was an invaluable asset." Alexander turned out to be a very useful member of the survey.[12] In addition to D'Olier and Alexander, the survey board had nine other members, including economist John Kenneth Galbraith, Chicago attorney George W. Ball, investment banker and head of the Foreign Economic Administration Paul H. Nitze, aeronautical engineer Theodore P. Wright, and Rensis Likert, from the Department of Agriculture. The secretary to the survey board was Judge Charles C. Cabot of the Supreme Court of Massachusetts.

The United States Strategic Bombing Survey was officially formed by Henry Stimson on November 3, 1944, as directed by President Roosevelt, in order to produce an impartial report on the effects of the strategic bombing of Germany. The organization for the survey brought on board 300 civilians, 350 officers, and 500 enlisted men, working out of headquarters in London, along with forward and regional headquarters following the advance of the Allied armies into Germany. As Lovett had recommended from the start, testimony was extracted from German officers, mayors, and public works officials, as well as from higher-up military and political leaders. The survey "made a close examination and inspection of several hundred German plants, cities and areas, amassed volumes of statistical and documentary material, including top German government documents; and conducted interviews and interrogations of thousands of Germans, including virtually all of the surviving political and military leaders." Key among the latter efforts was Nitze's several days of interrogation of Albert Speer, Reich minister of Weapons, Munitions, and Armaments.[13]

November 7 was the presidential election, but, as Stimson noted, "there was no sign of it in the Pentagon." Franklin D. Roosevelt was elected to a fourth term, defeating New York governor Thomas E. Dewey. And the war against Germany and Japan ground on.

Hap Arnold and his staffers came up with a program, dubbed Operation CLARION, to send American fighters and bombers all over Germany to attack industrial, military, and transportation facilities in small towns. While not specifically aimed at civilians, CLARION would inevitably produce huge civilian casualties. Ira Eaker protested vehemently, reminding Spaatz that this operation was completely opposed to what Lovett had said about sticking to military targets. "I personally," he said, "have become completely convinced that you and Bob Lovett are right and we should never allow the history of this war to convict us of throwing the strategic bomber at the man in the street."[14] Nevertheless, CLARION had the support of Stimson, McCloy, Marshall and, ultimately, Robert Lovett, who up to that time had been resolutely opposed to strategic bombing of civilians. "If the power of the German people to resist is to be further reduced," Lovett wrote to Arnold, "it seems likely that we must spread the destruction of industry into the smaller cities and towns now being used for production under the German system of dispersal." So CLARION was carried out on February 22–23, 1945, with 9,000 fighters, fighter-bombers, and medium bombers hitting railroad stations in hundreds of towns and villages that had theretofore been spared such bombing.[15]

Earlier, just after Christmas, Lovett spoke to the Bond Club in New York City, where he discussed the Battle of the Bulge (which was underway) and the use of weather by the Germans. Later he told Stimson "of his trip to New York and the devilish time he had coming back on the train where he finally got a seat with a colored woman on one side of him holding a baby who called him 'Dada,' and a fat Army nurse on the other side sitting on the arm of his chair." Such were the perils of wartime travel.[16] As 1944 came to a close, Germany and Japan were still at war, but the leaders of the American military could reasonably presume that the war was drawing nearer to a victorious end. Bob Lovett could look back on the year—his testimony to the Woodrum Committee, his constant activity in bringing about the necessary aircraft production for the war effort, his work in bringing into existence the Strategic Bombing Survey, his participation in planning for postwar airline and Air Force activities—and see that what he had done was important in setting forth not only the present capacity of the force but also the future role of air power in the realm of national security.

14

To the End

New Year's Day in 1945 fell on a Monday, so that was just another working day for Bob Lovett and his colleagues at the Pentagon. The war was going well—they all recognized that—but there could be no letup. The German attack through the Ardennes in December—the Battle of the Bulge, which was continuing—had shown that there could be no military relaxation until the war was actually over.

In mid–January 1945 Hap Arnold suffered a massive heart attack while working at his desk. It was his fourth coronary since the war had begun, and he began a convalescence in Coral Gables, Florida. During that period, the army air force "was run, for all intents and purposes, not by Deputy Commanding General Barney Giles, but by Robert Lovett." Marshall, who had developed a close relationship with Lovett, ignored Giles and consulted Lovett on most things relating to the AAF.[1] Lovett, in a chatty letter to Eaker, discussed Arnold's problem:

> I have tried ever since I have been here to impress on Hap the necessity of delegating more and more responsibility and emulating the example of General Marshall in avoiding unnecessary speeches, dinners, and the vast number of exhausting engagements which could so easily be declined. In his penitent mood Hap agrees fully but when he begins to feel well again he hops into a plane, makes an inspection at Indianapolis, Louisville, Richmond, a speech that night before the United Bustle and Whistle Manufacturers convention, gets back here at night and then tries to clean up his desk the next day, while attending during the evenings a dinner to a visiting Mexican General, a party for three movie actresses who have come to inaugurate the March of Dimes, a session with the National Geographic Society, and a hearing on the conservation of automobile tires. Worthy as these organizations may be, General Marshall is able to avoid them and I feel that Hap can too.[2]

Arnold returned to Washington late in March but soon fell ill again. By this time, Ira Eaker had been brought back to the Pentagon as deputy commanding general, and of course he always worked well with Lovett.

Various new items of warfare needed to be dealt with. Lovett became involved with the proposed use of the JB-2, a United States copy of the German V-1 flying bomb. Through 1944 work was done on the JB-2 by Republic Aviation, with a Ford-produced pulsejet powerplant, and launch testing was carried on at Eglin Air Field in Florida and at Wendover Field in Utah. In March of 1945 Lovett suggested that Landing Ship Tanks (LSTs) might well be used as mobile launches for the JB-2s. Brig. Gen. Grandison Gardner wrote to Lovett on March 14, advising that inspection of an LST confirmed that his suggested launching use was "very feasible and would not require more than very minor modifications of the vessel."[3] Lovett thanked Gardner for the good news and told him that plans were moving ahead for coordination with the navy on mounting launching ramps on the LST. In April

Lovett was involved in meetings regarding the JB-2. In fact Lovett's suggested program with the navy was agreed upon, and the navy prepared to test the launchings. As it turned out, however, the war ended before any JB-2s were actually launched against the enemy.[4]

As the fourth year of the American war opened, the Germans, Lovett felt, showed no signs of giving in, and the forces of the Reich continued to fight with the "skill and fanaticism" that might produce "a type of dug-in, trench warfare which will be slow, costly in lives and difficult to synchronize with the increased demands of accelerated Pacific operations." The best method of overcoming such resistance was continuing, even increasing, air power.[5]

As German resistance continued, however, Eisenhower's infantry ranks were being depleted through 1944 by the increase of casualties in France. Starting in the summer, the army was transferring what was considered excess ground personnel for retraining as infantrymen. The losses during the Battle of the Bulge made an increase in such transfers even more necessary. It was not long before such transfers were being taken out of the air force as well. Lovett complained of this new struggle to Tooey Spaatz: "The battle for manpower is still continuing and the Air Forces over here (in the U.S.) have so far given up 101,000 men to the ground troops. I think we have made our last contribution but I cannot be certain of it." In the newest draft call, engineers working on the air forces' first jet plane, the P-80, were soon to be drafted, this at a time when Lovett, Arnold, Spaatz, and the rest of the USAAF high command feared that the ongoing development of the German jet program might severely compromise Allied air superiority.[6] This transfer of air force personnel continued on into March, with some of those not physically up to fighting work in the infantry being retrained for ground support positions to replace those who were fit for combat. Spaatz gave Lovett the details of what was happening in Europe: 4,000 men in January taken for infantry training, 15,000 more to be taken by March 20. He concluded, "You are undoubtedly well aware that this contribution cuts our manpower resources to the bone."[7]

Meanwhile, as the air force was losing men to the infantry, and the infantry was pushing hard to get into Germany to bring that part of the war to a close, combat against Japan continued in the Pacific. The resounding defeat of the Japanese at the October battle of Leyte Gulf had seemingly insured that the Allies would triumph in the Far East, but no one was quite sure what it would take to bring it to an end. Robert Lovett, while overseeing all of the air force activity, did not become involved in the infighting that took place in the Pacific war, which featured such disparate characters as Hap Arnold, Douglas MacArthur, Chiang Kai-Shek, Claire Chennault, Chester Nimitz, and Joseph Stilwell. In September 1944 Arnold had transferred Curtis LeMay from Europe to run XX Bomber Command in China, but even LeMay could not originally generate the desired bombing success of Japan from Chennault's bases in China. As 1945 developed, however, the Japanese recognized that their sources of coal and iron ore in China and Manchuria, relied upon for steel manufacture, had been reduced to one-third of their 1941 level by American bombing from China. In the spring of '45 the Japanese abandoned their drive into China and pulled back so that they could defend Manchuria, Korea, and Hong Kong.

Early in 1945 military leaders determined that all of the available B-29s in China, in India, and in the Philippines, should be taken to the Mariana Islands (Guam, Saipan, and Tinian) and concentrated there for the steady and continuous bombing of the home islands of Japan. This step was taken after it was recognized that attacks from the Marianas could be carried out much more efficiently than those from the Asian mainland. In January Arnold named LeMay chief of staff of the Twentieth Air Force. On February 25 LeMay's one hundred seventy-two B-29s hit Tokyo with incendiaries that enflamed one square mile of the city. With further training, the incendiary attacks with napalm turned deadly. On March 9 LeMay sent three hundred thirty-four B-29s to Tokyo in a raid that reduced to ashes sixteen square miles of Japan's capital, killed 85,000 people, and left another million homeless. From then on, the B-29s carried out incendiary attacks on most of Japan's major cities.

Germany, too, was suffering intensive bombing. On the night of February 13, seven hundred fifty RAF Lancaster bombers had dropped 1,400 tons of high-explosive bombs and 1,175 tons of incendiaries on Dresden, the medieval capital of Saxony, and the next day three hundred eleven B-17s pounded the city with 700 tons of bombs, half of them incendiaries. On the following day two hundred eleven B-17s hit Dresden once again with nearly 500 tons of high explosives in the city center. Some 30,000 civilians died, while some 500,000 lost their homes. The ancient city of Dresden was destroyed.

On April 12 Lovett, the air force staff, and the people of America were stunned to learn of the death, in Warm Springs, Georgia, of Franklin Roosevelt, who had served as the country's president since March 4, 1933. Bob Lovett had not supported FDR politically, but he was able to work well with him in the nonpolitical war effort. Roosevelt was succeeded by Vice President Harry S. Truman, who had, as a senator, supervised the work of the Truman Committee, which had done a good and serviceable job making sure that America's armaments and military were in proper shape to fight a global war. Robert Lovett, though he had had little more than fleeting personal contacts with Senator Truman, had worked well with the committee and had been pleased to note its accomplishments, both in aviation and in other military fields. It would become the function of President Truman to see to the proper termination of the war, both in Europe and in the Pacific.

Henry Stimson was not a great fan of Harry Truman. Early in 1944 Stimson, annoyed by some of the actions of the Truman Committee, had written, "Truman is a nuisance and a pretty untrustworthy man. He talks smoothly but he acts meanly." Truman felt uneasy about Stimson, too, but he respected him for his ability and the advice he gave. As it developed, the two of them got along surprisingly well during the remainder of the war.[8]

On May 6 Lovett wrote to Carl Spaatz, reporting a front-page story that had appeared in the *Washington Post* of an interview with German General Gerd von Rundstedt in which he said he "regarded air power as the most decisive factor in the Reich's military failure." The main factors were, first, lack of fuel—oil and gasoline—followed by destruction of the railway system, then Germany's loss of raw material areas, and finally smashing of the home industrial sections like Silesia and Saxony by air attacks. Asked about D-Day, when he was in command, von Rundstedt said his "reserves were so dispersed and placed that I could have met the D-Day landing, even though it surprised us, except for the fact that we had no mobility, and could not bring up our reserves … [and] the unheard of superiority of your air force made all movement in daytime impossible." Lovett told Spaatz, "I am sure you must realize how terribly proud and gratified all of us are with the results of the combined bomber offensive and the magnificent job turned in by the Air Forces under your command."[9]

Less than a month after Truman took office, Hitler committed suicide in his bunker in Berlin while the Russian army was overrunning the city. Soon the German army surrendered to Eisenhower, on May 8. The war in Europe was over, and questions immediately came up about the treatment of defeated Germany. The Soviets planned to strip German industry in their claims for reparations. American leaders were not agreeable to that. Robert Lovett, for one, "argued that plants, equipment and other industrial treasure should not be taken from Germany," as the people of the country would still need to be supported and fed.[10]

With Germany (and Italy) defeated in Europe, attention was now shifted to the war against the Japanese, with great concern felt for the potentially bloody task of overcoming the enemy army on its home islands. One area that was not much in the minds of the American leaders was Indochina. Long under the colonial rule of the French, during the war Vichy France officials had worked together with the Japanese to run the country, although there was minor military opposition from native groups such as the Viet Minh. Roosevelt was not in favor of aid to the French, as he looked forward to an Indochina liberated from its colonial bonds after the war. But he kept the United States from taking any particular position in regard to the country, although a Japanese coup to take over Indochina in March 1945 led to more serious American military involvement. On April 13, 1945, the day after FDR's death, Robert Lovett told the State, War, and Navy Coordinating Committee that Roosevelt's ban on formulating a definite policy toward Indochina prior to war's end should be reconsidered. Having no definite policy, he said, was "a source of serious embarrassment to the military."[11] The request of the State, War, and Navy Coordinating Committee for an actual policy on Indochina eventually produced a State Department paper recommending that the U.S. not oppose the restoration of French sovereignty but seek French assurances of a trend toward self-government and local autonomy. Obviously, the United States would hear more of Indochina and Vietnam as time passed.

While the heavy bombing of Japan continued in 1945, Lovett still had to deal with questions of postwar policy and the issues with the navy so many of them raised. Among these were reconversion, civilian aviation and its relations with the government, reparations, postwar budgets, and, of course, unification of the military services. Robert Lovett had firm views on these issues, but he was uncomfortable with the debates discussion of them would stir up while the war itself was still on. In mid–May he took a four-week trip to Europe to handle the reorganization of the air force there in order to make it ready for participation in the campaign against Japan. Accompanying Lovett on his journey were Harry Hopkins and his wife and Charles "Chip" Bohlen.

The war in the Pacific was moving along quite well, with the heavy bombing of Japanese cities, the destruction of most of the Japanese navy, and the isolation of numerous enemy army units on Pacific islands. On April 27 Lovett sent a memo to General Lauris Norstad, acknowledging "with thanks receipt of the Report of Operations, Twentieth Air Force, Volume 1, through 15 April 1945. It is a superb record and I am delighted to have it." Numerous other memos came in to Lovett, detailing the increasingly destructive actions against the Japanese.[12]

In the meantime, the development of the atomic bomb was also proceeding at a good pace, and the American leadership hoped that an invasion of the Japanese home islands could be avoided. The estimates for an invasion and land campaign in Japan ran from

500,000 to 750,000 likely deaths. When the atomic bombs were in fact dropped in early August, first on Hiroshima and then on Nagasaki, they resulted, to the great relief of all, in the Japanese surrender and the end of the war. Henry Stimson recorded Lovett coming in to tell him "that the Jap radio announced that military operations had ceased."[13] Carl Spaatz was quoted as saying that air power had done the job—that the atomic bomb made armies unnecessary in the future. While Lovett did not agree that armies were done for, he agreed otherwise with his friend Tooey. "The decisive factor in the sudden collapse," he wrote to Spaatz, "seems to have been air power, and the old myth of not being able to defeat a major country with its armies intact except by invasion seems to have been shattered once and for all."[14]

With the termination of the war, the leaders of the War Department planned their departures from public office. Henry Stimson submitted his resignation to President Truman on September 4 and arranged for his leave-taking on September 20, but Harry Truman asked him to stay on until Friday, the 21st, which just happened to be Stimson's seventy-eighth birthday. At 10:30 that morning Lovett, Patterson, McCloy, Bundy, and other members of the civilian staff came into Stimson's office "to make their formal goodbye," as the secretary recorded it, "and presented me with a very pretty antique silver tray with the names of those present engraved on it." At eleven o'clock, George Marshall came in for an hour's talk with Stimson, "a very deep emotional experience for me and I think also for him."[15] Then, after a lively lunch in the general officers' mess, featuring a very large birthday cake, Stimson and his wife were off to the White House, where Truman presented him with the Distinguished Service Medal and then had him give his views on the control of nuclear energy to a meeting of the cabinet, his final act as a member of the government.

Earlier, on September 7, Lovett and McCloy had offered Stimson their letters of resignation, to be sent on to the White House. "They are resigning with me from the Department," Stimson noted, "but we are all submitting to the President the choice of the time when each one shall leave." They did tell Stimson they were "evidently now anxious to get out as soon as they can without inconveniencing the President," but Truman took his time releasing these valuable members of his team.[16] Finally, on September 18, before a considerable assemblage of War Department personnel, generals, and wives, including Adele, Stimson presented Distinguished Service Medals to Patterson, McCloy, Lovett, and Bundy, reading the citations and pinning the medals on the recipients. As he noted, "the spirit was very cheerful and cordial." The citation he had written up for Robert Lovett read as follows:

> The Honorable Robert A. Lovett has served as Assistant Secretary of War for Air matters since April 22, 1941. He has been a trusted representative of the Secretary of War in the development of the largest, most extraordinary and efficient Air Force in the world. He early envisaged the vast possibilities of air power and by diplomatic tact and wise counsel solved the major issue of the organic relationship in the War Department between the Ground and Air Forces. He thoroughly appreciated the concept of Air Force strategy as employed by our allies in the Battle of Britain, but boldly sponsored a more flexible organization aimed to provide coordination and unity of command in the great combined air and ground offensive strikes which he foresaw would be launched in the later phases of the war. His sound principles based on the decisive employment of all arms in mutually supporting, single-headed efforts contributed signally to the destruction of our enemies. He successfully supervised the procurement of airplanes and the development of new types with the required combat characteristics. He participated largely in perfecting the means and methods which made our bombardment of the war industries of Germany devastatingly successful. He has truly been the eyes, ears and hands of the Secretary of War

in respect to the growth of that enormous American air power which has astonished the world and played such a large part in bringing the war to a speedy and successful conclusion.[17]

With those words ringing in his ears, Bob Lovett was hoping to head off to civilian life, which he did late in November. On September 30, however, he was intrigued to read the Summary Report that Frederick D'Olier and the other members of the Strategic Bombing Survey had prepared for publication. While parts of the report indicated that some of the bombing attacks had not had the continuing impact on certain parts of the German economy that many of the air force generals thought they had, it indicated that the bombing impact on transportation, railways and waterways, oil production, and coal production had been immense and most damaging to the Germans. The report concluded as follows:

> Allied air power was decisive in the war on Western Europe. Hindsight inevitably suggests that it might have been employed differently or better in some respects. Nevertheless, it was decisive. In the air, its victory was complete. At sea, its contribution, combined with naval power, brought an end to the enemy's greatest naval threat—the U-boat; on land, it helped turn the tide overwhelmingly in favor of Allied ground forces. Its power and superiority made possible the success of the invasion. It brought the economy which sustained the enemy's armed forces to virtual collapse, although the full effects of this collapse had not reached the enemy's front lines when they were overrun by Allied forces. It brought home to the German people the full impact of modern war with all its horror and suffering. Its imprint on the German nation will be lasting.[18]

Reading that of course brought satisfaction to Bob Lovett as he prepared for leaving the War Department, which he would do in a couple of months. Before that, however, he received one last assignment. On October 22 Bob Patterson, now secretary of war with Stimson's retirement, created a special committee of five generals and a colonel to advise, among others, on the question of following up the Office of Strategic Services [OSS], which was going out of existence with the war's end, with a new organization, possibly to be called the Central Intelligence Agency (CIA). To pull this committee together, he named Bob Lovett as chairman. Lovett's committee got quickly to work and gathered the views and recommendations of those connected with intelligence describing the functions of those units during the war, appraisals of how they worked, and what could have been done better.[19]

Lovett's committee held nine meetings in the short period of its existence. On November 3 Lovett submitted a lengthy report to Secretary Patterson, restricting its coverage to the question of the establishment of the Central Intelligence Agency and the future of the army's Strategic Services Unit. The report set forth what the Central Intelligence Agency should do, how it should do it, and with whom. "Except for its responsibility to the National Intelligence Authority," the report said, "the Central Intelligence Agency should be independent."[20]

This submission was followed by a meeting on November 14 comprising Secretary of State Byrnes, Secretary of War Patterson, Secretary of the Navy Forrestal, and four lesser officials, of whom Lovett was one. In the discussion that followed, regarding a Central Intelligence Agency Lovett's voice was predominant, presenting a summary of his committee's report as well as downplaying a separate plan presented by the Bureau of the Budget. Lovett and the others agreed that the FBI should be kept out of intelligence; he felt that when both intelligence and police powers were put "in the hands of a single agency the result is a 'gestapo.'"

With all present in favor of a central agency, Byrnes and Patterson suggested the appointment of a working committee "to get at the problem as quickly as possible since the existing organization is rapidly disintegrating." With two representatives from each department to be on that committee, Patterson named Lovett and George Brownell as the War Department members. As a final touch, Patterson asked whether anyone knew of a good man for the important position of director of intelligence. Bob Lovett said the only name he had heard mentioned was that of Allen Dulles, "generally regarded as highly competent in that field."[21] Allen Dulles, who had spent most of the war years in Bern, Switzerland, working for the OSS with both Allied and Nazi figures, was indeed to be the first civilian head (named in 1953 as the third director overall) of the Central Intelligence Agency, for a lengthy period of postwar time and with many controversial results.[22]

The Lovett Committee put together final recommendations on the subject of a Central Intelligence Agency that, after being approved by Patterson, went off to the State and Navy departments. No final conclusions were reached at that time, and Lovett left the committee as he left public service, with Brownell submitting the committee's final report on December 17. It was just one final job that Bob Lovett did for the government.[23] Lovett really was leaving the government. For one thing, his gallbladder and ulcers were giving him trouble, and he needed a period of rest. He wrote a letter to the president of the Carnegie Corporation in which he said, "My present program is to go away for a couple of months and try to get back into physical and mental shape. After more than five years in Washington I find it very hard to bring reasonable judgment to bear on personal matters and I am, therefore, trying to take two months off without reaching any decision as to where to pick up my life as a private citizen."[24] Lovett wrote to one friend that he would try to meet him at Delray Beach in Florida "so that we can fight the war on the only type of beachhead for which I now have any use."[25]

In the meantime, there were numerous tributes coming in to the departing assistant secretary for air. Stuart Symington, future secretary of the air force and, at the time, surplus property administrator, said, "Nobody knows more than I how much you will be missed in the trying days to come." Lovett's old friend Roland Harriman wrote, "I don't know of anyone connected with the waging of this war who has had so much of the admiration and respect and—yes—gratitude from so many of his fellow Americans as you have." Donald Douglas, of Douglas Aircraft, said, "All of us whose privilege it was during the last few eventful years to work with you in the dramatic drive for war production and supremacy in the air, know how much you personally have contributed to the victory, which at one time seemed so doubtful and remote.... No one served our nation better or more effectively and no one deserves a rest and relief from great responsibilities anymore than you do."[26]

A week and a half later, Bob Patterson, who had more opportunities to observe Lovett's service than anyone except perhaps Stimson, wrote him: "My mind goes back to the time when you got the President to give top priority to the heavy bomber program. You won the point over heavy opposition. That move did as much to decide the outcome of the war as anything I know. My mind goes back, too, to many other times when you saw clearly what needed to be done and you put in the push required. The result of all these pushes was the building up of the greatest Air Force the world has ever seen."[27] Finally, at the farewell party organized to see Bob Lovett on his way, Brigadier General George Brownell, who had served as Lovett's executive officer throughout the war, took the "opportunity to tell our late Assistant Secretary of War for Air what we think of him and of the job he has done." He noted that "all this oratory about himself" was making Lovett very uncomfortable, "but for once we have him where he can't stop us." After quoting Hap Arnold's conclusion that he would "not forget the inspiration and guidance you gave me in the arduous war years," Brownell described the grand merger of the 1 percent of professionals with the 99 percent of amateurs in the U.S. Army Air Force during the war and how much Lovett had to do with that:

> He has preached and practiced the doctrine that our air power as it exists today ... springs from no one group alone, but from the American people as a whole. Those of us who have had the privilege of working on his personal staff know in how many countless ways he has pushed and pulled, cajoled, threatened and begged, to keep all of those elements pulling steadily in the same direction. And that is all, Mr. Secretary. We shall miss you, professionals and amateurs alike. You may step down from the important office you have filled so well, secure in the knowledge that your patriotic and unselfish labors will never be forgotten by your old colleagues, or by your countrymen.[28]

Looking back on his wartime service some years later, Lovett said, "I think the period under General Marshall and Colonel Stimson was one of the happiest times of my life and I have an enormous feeling of thankfulness for the good fortune that gave me the opportunity to work with people I admired, respected and came to love."[29]

15

On to the State Department

The War Department behind them, Robert and Adele Lovett left Washington, moved their belongings home to Long Island, and then headed south for four months of loosening up at Hobe Sound, Florida. Besides the tiresome day-to-day routine that Lovett had gone through in the Pentagon as the war was drawing to a close, he had his usual stomach suffering, which he had to watch out for all the time.

In Florida they took in the beaches, the waters, the sun, and the warm weather, and Lovett did some of the painting he enjoyed. A number of their friends—Prescott Bush, Philip Barry, Archibald MacLeish, and others—dropped in for visits. Soon enough, though, the Florida time ended, and the Lovetts headed back up north to their home on Long Island and to Brown Brothers Harriman on Wall Street. It had been more than five years earlier that he had said good-bye to his partners, and Bob Lovett was happy to be received by them once again. He returned officially to Brown Brothers on June 1, 1946, once again as a full partner, and he took up some of the other connections he had given up in 1940 such as membership on the board of the Columbia Broadcasting System and, what was of particular interest to Lovett, the Union Pacific Railroad. Unfortunately his health continued to give Bob Lovett problems. In June 1946 he developed a severe cold and during a coughing attack had a sudden attack of typical gallstone cholic. That November his gallbladder was found to be full of faceted stones and was removed.[1]

As he worked his way back into the financial world, Lovett was given reminders from time to time of the governmental life he had left behind. On November 13, 1946, he journeyed down to central Jersey to give a talk at a conference held by Princeton University. The conference was headed "University Education and the Public Service," and Lovett's contribution was a lecture entitled "A Top Management View of the Federal Service."[2] While Lovett was back at Brown Brothers, the postwar world was developing in a way that some had foreseen but few desired, with the Soviet Union's belligerent and noncooperative actions sparking what eventually became known as the Cold War. There were numerous efforts to recruit Lovett back into government service, efforts he turned down.

George C. Marshall on January 21, 1947, had replaced Jimmy Byrnes as Harry Truman's secretary of state, and at that point it had been agreed that Lovett's friend Dean Acheson, who had been serving in the State Department since 1941 and as undersecretary since 1945, would be allowed to return to his private practice of the law. The date for his leaving was generally agreed upon as July 1, although he resigned on May 12. Marshall soon decided that he wanted Bob Lovett as the man to replace Acheson, as Marshall and Lovett had worked closely together during the war and entertained considerable respect one for the other. He asked Acheson what he thought of Lovett as undersecretary. Acheson noted that he and Lovett "had known each other since Yale days. He had all the necessary requirements of mind, character, and Washington experience. Most importantly, that experience included years of working with General Marshall under the severe pressures of wartime. He knew Europe well. I thought it an excellent idea."[3]

On February 6, 1947, Marshall wrote Lovett, asking him to succeed Acheson as undersecretary at the end of June. "Under the present regime," he wrote, "Acheson is, to use Army terminology, my Deputy Chief of Staff, and coordinates and manages all administrative and operational affairs of the Department. This was not the case when I took over, but is now and will continue to be." After briefly describing affairs in the department, he said, "I hope that you can give favorable consideration to my proposition. The President was very enthusiastic over it. But as for me, it would mean a great deal to feel that I could look to a man with your character and ability to take over the job of Under Secretary."[4]

Lovett down through the years often said, "There are three people to whom I can never say no—my wife, Henry Stimson, and George Marshall." Naturally, when Marshall asked him to take on the position of undersecretary of state, Lovett agreed, although in his letter of acceptance he pointed out that his gall bladder—his "glass insides," as he called it—had been removed late in October. "Minor post-operative difficulties put me back in the hospital for a week in December, and, much to my chagrin, I was hustled in again last week. As far as I know, there is nothing radically wrong but it seems clear that I have not licked this affair yet, and I am told that I must allow a further ninety day period for internal readjustment." His doctors, he said, wanted him to take six weeks to convalesce, "mainly to regain some weight and get used to having fewer gadgets inside me." So he and Adele planned to go the following week to their cottage at Hobe Sound. So if, he said, "responsibility need not be undertaken for a couple of months," as Marshall had mentioned in his letter, "I would be proud to serve under you again."[5] Marshall wrote back on February 18: "I cannot tell you what a relief it is to me to feel that I will have your strong support during the difficult days ahead. I contemplated with almost fear the departure of Acheson with no assurance of just who I would have to assist me in his stead. Now that I know you are willing to take on the chore, my whole point of view has changed and my spirits are lightened accordingly."[6]

While the Lovetts were at Hobe Sound, Acheson called. Lovett missed the call but wrote back, "I'm sticking to that darned health-building regime and, somewhat to my surprise, it seems to be working. I've gained a little weight & am beginning to feel almost human."[7] So, it was once again getting rid of his business connections and investments, saying good-bye to his partners at Brown Brothers Harriman, and heading back to Washington. His son Robin wrote him: "Mommy says she doesn't think you are very happy to come, but it is about time somebody forced you into it."[8] Lovett stipulated that he needed two more months to recover from his gall bladder operation—which he would do in Hobe Sound—and one month of overlap with Acheson, so that he could get a firm grip on State Department activities before becoming responsible for them. It was openly recognized that there would be overlap: "While Lovett will not take over his post until July 1, it is understood that he will work with Acheson in advance of that time to acquaint himself with many problems with which Acheson has dealt."[9]

President Truman formally nominated Lovett on May 14, 1947, and, after Acheson introduced him to the Foreign Relations Committee, he was quickly confirmed unanimously by the Senate (it helped that he was a Republican), and he was sworn in as undersecretary on the first of July. Among Marshall's goals in the State Department were enhancing inter-departmental cooperation, reconciling economic and geopolitical views, and mitigating suspicion between defense officials and foreign service officers. Lovett, a close friend of Forrestal, the defense secretary, Harriman, the secretary of commerce, and Stuart Syming-ton, head of the air force, was an inspired choice for achieving these goals.[10]

In the meantime, after his return from Florida, Bob Lovett worked side by side with Acheson, read all the papers Acheson got, attended all the meetings, and took a shadowy part in all the decisions. Acheson introduced him around town; one of the key introduc-tions, with the Republicans in control of Congress after the 1946 elections, was to Senator Arthur Vandenberg of Michigan, the chairman of the Senate Foreign Relations Committee. Acheson told the senator, "I've known Bob since Yale and I hope you will be agreeable to accept his service." Vandenberg welcomed Lovett, saying, "God have mercy on your soul." As it developed, Vandenberg was to be a key figure in Lovett's State Department career.[11]

As part of his learning process, Bob Lovett had a discussion of almost five hours on May 12 with a small group of knowledgeable associates at the Council on Foreign Relations in New York. They tried to go over everything—U.S. interests in Latin America and the Pacific, occupation duties in Germany and Japan, goings-on in Iceland, England, and the Middle East. They talked over the future prospects for France and Spain and the expan-sionist tendencies of the Soviet Union. They discussed the immensity of American interests compared with the scarcity of available resources as well as U.S. priorities. When it was over, almost five hours later, Bob Lovett had a clearer sense of the great responsibilities of the position he would soon be assuming.[12]

On June 13 Lovett had lunch with his friend Jim Forrestal, and he talked about the difficulties of getting the State Department organized. As Forrestal recorded it, "He said that the preceding Secretaries of State had made almost no progress in the creation of a rational organization. With the result that while there were many good men in the Depart-ment, the means for using their abilities were extremely limited."[13] Some time later, after he had been involved for a while, Lovett was heard to compare the operations of the State Department to the love life of elephants: "The analogy is simple, but astonishingly true. It falls into three phases of comparisons; the first, that all important business is done at a very high level; secondly, that any developments are accompanied by tremendous trumpeting; and thirdly, that if any results are accomplished, the period required is from eighteen months to two years."[14] However, one historian noted, "In terms both of staff talent and staff use, Marshall's years began a State Department 'golden age' that lasted until the era of McCarthy. Moreover, as his undersecretary, Marshall had, successively, Dean Acheson and Robert Lovett, men who commanded the respect of the professionals and the regard of congressmen."[15]

While Bob Lovett was learning his way around the State Department under Acheson's tutelage, there took place a major event that would tend to dominate much of Lovett's career at Foggy Bottom, the Washington neighborhood where the department's offices were located. On June 5, in Cambridge, Massachusetts, Secretary of State Marshall delivered an address at Harvard's commencement in which he discussed in broad terms the necessity for the United States to look after the increasingly dire economic needs of the countries of Europe, with their almost nonexistent recovery from the devastations of World War II.

From this talk came what was soon called the Marshall Plan, the great relief effort of the U.S. government, the implementation of which would occupy much of Lovett's time and effort as Marshall's undersecretary of state.

On July 1 Lovett "merely moved to the chair at the desk, thoroughly familiar with what was going on across it." Robert A. Lovett became George Marshall's undersecretary of state. He was sworn in by department chief of protocol Stanley Woodward (who happened to be a Skull and Bones man) at 11:45 a.m. as Adele, General Marshall, Dean Acheson and his wife, and Norman Armour (sworn in as assistant secretary) and his wife looked on. He had lunch with his old buddy Averell Harriman, then secretary of commerce, and meetings during the day with his friend Jim Forrestal, Paul Nitze, British minister Sir John Balfour, and Charles Fahy, as well as a 5:25 phone conversation with Senator Vandenberg.[16]

One commentator, after going over Lovett's close relations with the likes of Forrestal, Harriman, and Symington, said, "Lovett was an inspired choice, if Marshall's goals were to enhance interagency cooperation, reconcile economic and geopolitical views, and mitigate suspicion between defense officials and foreign service officers." Columnist Marquis Childs, noting that Lovett was a "Wall Street banker," remarked on the frequent use of that term as a smear phrase. "There are various kinds of bankers on Wall Street and on Main Street. Lovett is one ... who looks realistically at America's responsibilities in a swiftly changing world. He knows that we cannot impose our will and our ideas on the rest of the world either by dollars or by arms.... Lovett is an enlightened capitalist. He has a strong sense of the responsibility which goes with wealth and power."[17]

Clark Clifford, Harry Truman's right-hand man, was happy to work with Lovett, "a Republican who served Democrats with loyalty and skill." Clifford wrote as follows:

> I was pleased President Truman had asked Lovett to become Undersecretary of State, replacing Dean Acheson.... I respected Acheson greatly for his achievements, his intellect, and his conceptual abilities; but ... he did not possess Lovett's ability—unsurpassed in my entire Washington experience—to get people to work together with a minimum of friction. Where Acheson was decisive and impatient, Lovett was thoughtful and conciliatory. In informal settings, he was witty and charming, with a fine sense of detachment and irony—he was one of the best raconteurs I have ever met. But these charming qualities would have been of interest only to hostesses if they had not skillfully covered an immensely tough interior.[18]

The next day, July 2, Lovett started with a meeting with Kenneth Royall, the secretary of the army, on a rubber situation and followed that up very shortly with a phone call from Robert Garner, of the International Bank, who was concerned with the shaky situation of the French government. What were the prospects, they discussed, of giving the French the encouragement of possibly getting $250 million in October? Garner would check with John McCloy, then president of the World Bank, and advise.

Ten minutes after his conversation with Garner, Lovett had his first staff meeting; among those present were Armour, Fahy, George Kennan, Charles Bohlen, Dean Rusk, John Hilldring, Loy Henderson, Willard Thorp, Freeman Matthews, and several others. Most of the matters of State Department business were hashed over during the following two hours, as Lovett absorbed the opinions and positions of the top assistants in the department. Later, John Vorys, one of the Yale Unit fliers from World War I, now a Republican congressman from Ohio, called to invite Lovett to lunch with him and other members of the House Foreign Affairs Committee a week later at the Army-Navy Club.

Late in the morning of July 3 Lovett met with Marshall, who had just come from a meeting with the president, and then the two of them sat down with General Pat Carter (Marshall's personal assistant), Kennan, and Freeman Matthews to work out a proposed draft on European aid for Marshall to take to Truman. When Truman had approved it, the message, as basically prepared by Lovett, was sent off to Paris for delivery there to Ernest Bevin and Georges Bidault, the British and French foreign ministers, following their meeting with Russia's Molotov, during which the refusal of the Soviet Union to participate in the Marshall Plan was made clear:

> I have followed with complete understanding the course of your patient efforts to find agreement with the Soviet Government on a broad and constructive approach to the problems of European recovery. We realize the gravity of the problem with which you have been confronted and the difficulty of the decisions which you have been forced to make. At least the Soviet attitudes in these questions have been clarified at this stage and will not continue to represent an uncertainty in the working out of a recovery program for other countries. We here are prepared to do all in our power to support any genuine and constructive efforts toward restoration of economic health and prosperity in the countries of Europe.[19]

Lovett's days were filled with meetings, telephone conversations, periodic press conferences, reports to or talks with the secretary, and the frequent intervention of major issues and problems. It was the business of the Department of State. There was even one day, September 26, when Lovett was advised that a cholera epidemic had broken out in Egypt; he quickly arranged to ship $9,000 worth of cholera vaccine and plasma to Cairo.

Bob and Adele Lovett were occasional participants in what became informally known as the Georgetown Sunday Night Supper Club, which started as Sunday night gatherings at the 3327 P Street home of CIA official Frank Wisner and his wife, Polly. The Wisners furnished a hot dish for supper, while the other guests brought salads, side dishes, and desserts. The group was initially mainly CIA members and their wives, but it soon included others like the Achesons, Justice Felix Frankfurter and his wife, the Scotty Restons, the Kennans, the McCloys, the Averell Harrimans, the Alsop brothers, the Lovetts, and others. These dinners "were loud, informal, combative affairs with an abundance of smoking, drinking and shrieking about the role America should play as a postwar world power," sometimes going until 3:00 or 4:00 in the morning. Given Bob Lovett's intestinal conditions as well as his reserved temperament, these gatherings could hardly have been favorites of his.[20] Philip and Katherine Graham of the *Washington Post* became good friends at the same time with the Lovetts, Avis and Chip Bohlen, the McCloys, David Bruce and his wife, Jane and Bob Joyce (he was in the State Department), columnist Joe Alsop and his wife, and Frank and Polly Wisner. These folks, wrote Katherine Graham, "made a group of which we gradually became a part," presumably a bit less raucous than the Sunday Night Supper Club.[21]

Lovett periodically had lunches or dinners with friends from the press like Joe Alsop, Hanson Baldwin, James Reston, and Arthur Krock, colleagues in the government like Marshall, Harriman, Forrestal, Stuart Symington, Clark Clifford, John Snyder, Chip Bohlen, Adlai Stevenson, and Henry Cabot Lodge, and old friends like Carl Spaatz, John McCloy, Sir John Balfour, and Di Gates. Many of the lunches were at the popular 1925 F Street Club, to which Lovett belonged.[22] He frequently got together socially with visiting representatives of foreign governments, and from time to time he hosted socials recognizing certain persons, accomplishments, or causes. Lovett was constantly getting invitations for speeches and attendance at various functions, most of which he turned down, citing time conflicts or other reasons, although many of the turndowns were really because of his always-shaky health.

There were, of course, cabinet lunches on just about a weekly basis, most of which Lovett attended, either because Marshall was away or because Marshall wanted company. Some of these lunches were at the White House, many were at the Pentagon in Forrestal's offices, some were at other cabinet locations, and some were at Foggy Bottom. In addition to these lunches, there were regular meetings of the National Security Council (NSC) that Lovett attended. Created by the National Security Act on July 26, 1947, the NSC was supposed to be chaired by the president, with the secretaries of state, defense, army, navy, and air as members. Truman somewhat resented the action of Congress in creating such a body to advise him of the integration of domestic, foreign, and military policies relating to national security, so he mostly avoided going to its meetings. On September 25, 1947, Bob Lovett attended a preliminary gathering to the first formal meeting in Jim Forrestal's office in the Pentagon, along with Kenneth Royall, Stuart Symington, navy secretary John L. Sullivan, Sidney Souers (named by Truman as executive secretary of the new council), Admiral Chester Nimitz, and Generals Eisenhower, Spaatz, and Alfred Gruenther. The next day was the first actual meeting of the National Security Council, with the president, Royall, Sullivan, Symington, Forrestal, Souers, CIA director Roscoe Hillenkoetter, and Lovett in attendance. At Forrestal's suggestion, Lovett presented a review of the kind of subject on which the advice of the NSC would be useful to the State Department, and that was on the struggle in Italy between the Communists, the extreme right, and the current government in the middle, Lovett laid out several situations that might develop, where the U.S. failure to act could have an extremely negative impact, and where the NSC could work out possible reactions in advance.[23]

During Robert Lovett's tour as undersecretary of state, George Marshall had lengthy stays at foreign ministers' meetings and other such gatherings in Paris and elsewhere as well as several hospitalizations, during which times Lovett served as acting secretary of state. In addition, as Marshall noted in a message to Henry Stimson in July 1948, he regularly assigned the "principal burden" of the office to Lovett, whom he knew was quite capable of handling the job, so that he (Marshall) could avoid the day-to-day minutiae of his position.[24] Lovett, as undersecretary, was considered Acheson's equal in ability "and by far his superior in political tact." Lovett was "sober and cautious in his approach to foreign policy commitments, but convivial and effective in selling them to a doubting Congress." Harry Truman, though never as close personally with Lovett as he was with Acheson, very much understood Lovett's value.[25]

Lovett and Forrestal had a meeting on Sunday, November 16, 1947, with Senators Vandenberg and Bourke B. Hickenlooper (a Republican from Iowa and still quite isolationist) concerning their opposition to the wartime atomic energy arrangements made between Roosevelt and Churchill providing for the sharing of information on atomic developments and for Britain to have to agree before the atomic bomb could be used against any other country. Lovett told the senators that the information exchange was to cover certain scientific fields but not everything; he mentioned that the British were getting restless at not receiving a complete exchange of information. Vandenberg said he thought the wartime agreements were "astounding" and "unthinkable," and that they had to be revamped before congressional consideration of the Marshall Plan. In January 1948 an agreement was reached with Britain (and Canada) removing the restrictions on American use of the bomb.[26]

From the time he took on the post in the State Department Lovett was greatly involved in the construction of the Marshall Plan with the European nations and getting it affirmed by Congress as well as in procuring from Congress not only interim emergency aid funding but also the permanent European Recovery Program funding. Although there were no State Department studies leading up to Marshall's talk, it had followed months of attempting to resolve the economic problems of Western Europe, whose recovery from the war was proving far slower than anticipated. Europe was in sad financial shape, the result of the devastation caused by the war, labor strife, and a lack of gold and dollar reserves necessary to import raw materials, manufactured goods, and even food. Its economies were producing very little, with a tough winter weather-wise having added to the problems. The question of providing adequate food and fuel for the continent's people was turning out to be a major issue. The Soviets looked forward to the economic collapse of the western European nations, with their Communist parties ready to seize control when this happened.

Germany's coal, it soon became clear, was essential to a proper functioning of the various European countries, and this question soon ran into the Russian intransigence on any question of aid to the defeated nations. Marshall had attended Four Power meetings in Moscow, hoping for answers to his questions, but cooperation from the Soviets was not forthcoming. As a result, the United States and Britain had combined their occupational zones of Germany economically in Bizonia, a move which was bitterly resented by the Russians.

On March 12, 1947, Harry Truman had given a speech calling the nation's attention to the dangers Greece and Turkey faced after Ernest Bevin had advised that Great Britain was no longer able to support the Greeks, who were embroiled with Communist revolutionaries. Marshall had prepared the basic outline of what became known as "the Truman Doctrine," and Congress passed the bill to provide aid to Greece and Turkey—the Senate on April 12 and the House on May 8. Though the specifics of what Truman requested in his speech were funds and military assistance to Greece and Turkey, the overall effect of the president's position, as he put it, was "that it must be the policy of the United States to support free peoples who are resisting attempted subjugation by armed minorities or by outside pressures."[27]

On August 31 Robert Lovett visited Forrestal to describe to him a State Department paper Forrestal would be getting in the next week or so dealing with courses of action in the event of a Communist seizure of power in Greece. The coming paper would set up steps to be taken at the present time to prepare for a withdrawal if the Communists took power. He and Forrestal had a lively discussion on the Greek business and particularly on keeping the Communists out.[28]

In the meantime, Marshall had gone to Moscow for the highly anticipated meeting of the Council of Foreign Ministers. The conclave, opening on March 10, featured Bevin, Soviet minister Molotov, Georges Bidault of the French Foreign Ministry, and Marshall. There were 43 sessions from early March until near the end of April, mainly dealing with Germany and how it was to be handled by the occupying powers, The French, based on their fear of regenerating a Germany that could threaten France once again, did not always go along with the British and American plans for rebuilding the conquered nation, while the Russians claimed the right to $10 billion worth of reparations from Germany. (Indeed, General Lucius Clay, in charge of the American occupation zone, regularly blamed the French even more than the Soviets for obstructing programs for Germany.) The conference came to no agreement. It indicated that there was little hope of postwar cooperation with the Soviet Union, the same conclusion that had been reached earlier in George Kennan's famous "long telegram."

The failed Moscow conference, then, was the background for Marshall's talk at the Harvard commencement, although first he gave a nationwide radio address on April 28 in which he went over the failures of the meetings in Moscow. The secretary did not speak of any irreconcilable breakup with the Soviet Union, but he did emphasize the terrible economic difficulties Europe was facing and for which they needed solutions, with ongoing and growing shortages of food and basic necessities. In the meantime, Kennan and the newly created Policy Planning Staff (activated May 5) were working within the State Department on what needed to be done to provide aid to needy parts of Europe, primarily Britain, France, Italy, and the western zones of Germany and Austria.

After several messages back and forth, Marshall at last told Harvard president James B. Conant that he would be able to receive an honorary degree on June 5 and would make a short speech. Along with Omar Bradley, J. Robert Oppenheimer, the poet T.S. Eliot, and several others, Marshall received his doctor-of-laws degree at the commencement, was served lunch, and at two o'clock went out to the alumni gathering on the lawn. After a couple of other speakers, George Marshall was introduced, and he gave his short talk, making clear that Western Europe was in need of much assistance from the United States and would need outside aid for three or four years. "Our policy," he noted, "is directed not against any country or doctrine but against hunger, poverty, despotism, and chaos." He went on: "Any country that is willing to assist in the task of recovery will find full cooperation, I am sure, on the part of the United States Government." He added, "The initiative, I think, must come from Europe…. The program should be a joint one, agreed to by a number of if not all European nations."[29]

Marshall's Harvard address was greeted warmly, especially in Europe—British foreign minister Ernest Bevin called it "one of the greatest speeches in world history"—and in the American press, but it was quickly noted that it had not proposed any structure for the policy. That would have to be developed by those in the State Department, the leaders of Congress, the Foreign Service, and particularly by the European nations involved. And of course there was much curiosity as to the reaction of Russia and her satellites regarding participation in the plan. In late June and early July, Molotov, Bevin, and Bidault had met in Paris to determine the Soviet reaction, which was clearly one of nonparticipation. It was following this conclave that Marshall sent off the July 3 message quoted earlier.[30]

George Kennan's Policy Planning Staff was studying Europe's economic problems and early in June had produced a memorandum entitled "Increase of European Coal Production." Later, at the request of Robert Lovett (not yet the undersecretary), Kennan's group examined the probable effect of foreign aid on the American domestic economy and natural resources. Lovett had been urged to ask for this by Senator Vandenberg. Kennan recognized that such a study required much further work, so he put together a recommendation for this and gave it Lovett on June 19. Lovett accepted it and passed it on to the president.

Three days later Truman announced the formation of three committees to provide guidance with European aid; the first was to examine the state of the country's resources, the second to check the impact on the national economy of aid to other nations, and the third to "determine the facts with respect to the character and quantities of United States resources available for economic assistance to foreign countries." It was to be explicitly nonpartisan and was chaired by Averell Harriman (and bore his name). The Harriman Committee, which ultimately included representatives of business, agriculture, labor, and academia, played a prime role in selling the Marshall Plan to Congress and the American public.[31]

As those in Washington looked across the Atlantic to the economic crisis threatening to consume Western Europe, the need for something like the Marshall Plan seemed clearer and clearer. Bob Lovett wrote on July 31, "At no time in my recollection have I ever seen a world situation which was moving so rapidly toward real trouble, and I have a feeling that this is the last clear shot that we will have in finding a solution."[32]

16

Working on the Marshall Plan

Even before officially assuming his job in the State Department, Robert Lovett was involved in Marshall Plan preparations. On June 26 he asked for a meeting with treasury secretary John Snyder and Jim Forrestal at which he said that there had been "much too much loose talk about the vast sums to be advanced by the U.S. to European countries." Lovett wanted to keep Marshall from being pushed too far out on a limb, with a few supporters talking about $5 billion a year as a necessary figure. Snyder agreed, feeling that reference to any such high sums could freeze sentiment in Congress against any further American attempts to aid Europe.[1]

Lovett, though, clearly recognized the compelling need for something like what Secretary Marshall had suggested. In a letter to Thomas Lamont, head of the Morgan bank, Lovett said, "We can no longer nibble at the problem and then nag the American people on the basis of recurring crises." He went on: "It is equally apparent that the Congress will not make funds available unless there is some reasonable expectation that the expenditure of these funds will produce more visible results; or alternatively, unless it can be shown that the failure to expend these funds will produce calamitous circumstances affecting our national security and our economic and social welfare."[2]

The secretary, in his Harvard speech, had made it clear that the initial response must come from the needy nations of Europe. On July 12 the sixteen European nations who were invited to participate in the plan, without the Soviet Union and its Eastern European satellites (some of whom would have liked to be involved but were forbidden by Russia from participating), gathered in Paris as the Committee of European Economic Cooperation (CEEC) to work out an appropriate response. The French had agreed that the executive committee of the conference (consisting of Britain, France, the Netherlands, Italy, and Norway) would be headed by Britain's Bevin and would be responsible for setting general policies for the conference. Below that would be a "working committee" to set up ad hoc subcommittees for such areas as agriculture, labor, steel, and others. The chairman of the working committee was the French diplomat Herve Alphand.

The sixteen nations, and all the ad hoc committees, were soon hard at work. Sir Oliver Franks, Bevin's man who actually served in his place as head of the conference, was an Oxford philosopher who had led Britain's supply service during the war. He set forth the three broad areas he felt needed clear conclusions: (1) measures to increase European production generally, (2) programs to stabilize the finances of the participating countries, both internally, within each nation's own economy, and externally, in the balance of trade among nations, and (3) measures to ease and stimulate European trade. Each country's home government was sent questionnaires so they could make honest appraisals of their needs.[3]

It was not long before the conference was up to its collective neck in what looked mostly like "shopping lists" of the individual nations' needs. The French, of course, were very much interested in getting their hands on the German coal mines in the Ruhr and as much else of Germany's industry as they could manage. The Franco-German issue would be a factor throughout the conference. France's government, of course, was trying to steer a difficult course internally between a sizable Communist bloc on the left and the followers of Charles de Gaulle on the right.

As the conference dragged on, the United States was represented informally (the U.S. was obviously not a member of the conference) by three State Department functionaries who felt free to observe the goings-on, to criticize, and to make suggestions from time to time. The three were Will Clayton, undersecretary of state for economic affairs, Jefferson Caffery, a career diplomat at that time ambassador to France, and Lewis Douglas, ambassador to Great Britain, as he had succeeded Averell Harriman in 1947. Clayton, Caffery, and Douglas had hoped to take a part in shaping the European response to come out of the conference, but Washington had instructed them not to interfere—let the Europeans do their own planning. When Bob Lovett reviewed reports Clayton sent home of his discussions, he suggested that Clayton had "developed some points further than we have taken them," and there were a number of issues and questions for which no policies had yet been adopted by the department.[4]

Lovett, in the meantime, was going over a much longer report from the Policy Planning Staff, entitled "Certain Aspects of the European Recovery Program from the U.S. Standpoint," which George Kennan presented to him on July 23. Despite its length and detail, it did not pretend to make up a blueprint for aiding the European countries; they themselves still had to take the responsibility for this as Marshall had called upon them to do.[5] Another serious problem cropped up when Secretary of the Army Kenneth Royall, prompted by General Lucius Clay, commanding in Berlin, who was fed up with French obstruction to German rebuilding, held a press conference in Berlin on August 1 saying there was "no agreement by the War Department or the State Department to consult with France before promulgation of the plan to raise the level of industry in Western Germany."[6] Needless to say, Bidault and the French were infuriated by Royall's talk, since Marshall and Bevin had both assured Bidault in July that France would be given the opportunity to present its views for full consideration concerning the bizonal level of industry.

On the evening of August 2 French ambassador Henri Bonnet called Bob Lovett at home and went on for about forty minutes on the "renewed crisis" in France arising out of Royall's press conference. Lovett tried to calm Bonnet, telling him that the U.S. and Britain would certainly give a full hearing to the French on German industrialization. The next morning Lovett looked over his files and felt that Bonnet's concern arose partly out of a misunderstanding as to the form the discussions were to take. He went to the French embassy at noon and spent an hour and a half with Bonnet, finally calming him down, in part because Bonnet took the personal visit as a "friendly and considerate act." Lovett further urged Bonnet not to attach too much importance to Royall's press conference. Finally, Lovett conducted a teletype conversation with Clayton in Paris and urged him to calm Bidault and assure him that French views would be given full consideration.[7]

On August 5 Bonnet called on Marshall to pass on to the secretary a message from Bidault, assuring Marshall that the French government was convinced that an agreement on German industry and German production was possible but that it should be the result of understanding among the U.S., the UK, and France. Marshall replied that he had been informed of Bonnet's recent conversations with Lovett "and he wished to confirm what Mr. Lovett had told the Ambassador." With this, with a meeting with Bidault, Caffrey, and Clayton in Paris, and with Marshall admonishing Royall about the primary role of the State Department in foreign relations, the affair passed over. On August 9 Lovett got a call from Ambassador Bonnet thanking him for the pleasing note sent to Paris the evening before and mentioning that Bidault had called that morning to express his thanks to General Marshall.[8]

As Secretary Marshall was leaving for a conference in South America, Lovett was in charge of the State Department and it was his task to keep a rein on Clayton, Caffery, and Douglas and to maintain the posture that the initiatives must come from the European nations. If the American representatives suggested specific programs, Lovett warned, this might lead the Europeans to think that accepting them would then commit the U.S. to give whatever aid was requested. The stress must be on what the European countries could do to help themselves turn around their economies. Lovett wrote the following on August 14: "We gain the impression that too little attention is being paid by the participants to the elements of self-help and mutual aid which constituted an integral part of the suggestions made by the Secretary in his Harvard speech.... The program should provide for the greatest possible European self-help, should provide for action on the part of the participating countries which they will in fact be able to carry out, and should be such as to assure the maintenance of the European economy without continued support from the U.S."[9] As Lovett stressed to the American representatives in Paris, the CEEC should concentrate on increasing production, reforming finances, slowing down inflation, and bringing down bilateral barriers to intra-European trade. Just as much, there should be preserved the appearance of European responsibility for what was proposed and no impression of America's dictating to the CEEC.[10]

French ambassador Bonnet met with Lovett on August 21 as he was ready to return to Paris, and Lovett told him "that time was running short and that he was disturbed lest the conference of the 16 nations in Paris should produce little more than 16 'shopping lists' for which the United States would be expected to pay the bill." Lovett read to Bonnet the telegram he had sent Caffery quoted above and urged him "to impress on his government the necessity for bringing home to the governments of the smaller countries at Paris this basic conception of ours."[11]

As the conferees in Paris were putting together their numbers, however, they came up with the total figure of $29 billion in American aid, an amount they still did not figure would make Europe self-supporting by the time the Marshall Plan ran out. This number, of course, was not the basis of a final report, but it was getting close to one. When this news was sent on to Washington, Lovett promptly sent off a telegram to Marshall, who was at the moment at the Inter-American Conference for the Maintenance of Peace and Security, near Petropolis, Brazil. "Seven days from now," Lovett wrote, "the Paris Conference is scheduled to produce a plan. Progress so far is disappointing in that all that has come out so far is sixteen shopping lists." The grand total of the shopping-list approach, he said, was "unreasonable, not solely because of its size but because on its face it indicates that even these huge sums will not accomplish the rehabilitation over a four-year period, still leaving a deficit at the end of that time amounting to about four billion dollars annually (mostly a food deficit according to their experts)."[12]

Summarizing some of the problems, Lovett went on: "In these circumstances and against the background of our promise to lend friendly aid in drafting, I am convinced that the time has now arrived for us to give some indications that the present plan is not acceptable and to do so promptly." He recommended a message to Clayton and Caffery reiterating "our object to obtain from the Europeans a plan which will enable them to improve production to the point where they can become self-supporting at whatever minimum scale is tolerable through the principle of self-help and mutual help rather than have them lean on us to rebuild, on a long term basis, their entire production machine." He also said he would like to send both George Kennan and Charles Bonesteel to Paris to make sure that Clayton and Caffery were brought up to date on the thinking in Washington. And he would notify Sir Oliver Franks, the chairman of the executive committee, that there would be no problem with extending the closing date of the CEEC in order to give time for putting forth a proper constructive program rather than a shopping list. "While the present outlook seems gloomy," Lovett concluded, "I am not one bit discouraged, as we are only now coming up to the point where we have something concrete to work on and where we can point out the unsatisfactory measures so far taken. If we can keep the conferees from getting crystallized into a bad plan, perhaps we can swing them into a good one, or at least a better one." Marshall wired back: "I concur completely in your views and action proposed."[13]

Accordingly, at 8:00 that evening, telegrams went off to Caffery and to Clayton, setting forth what Lovett had proposed to Marshall, with the "view here that there must be major changes in both content and conclusions of CEEC report prior to completion. Realistic and workable program more important than meeting predetermined deadline for completion of report."[14] The next afternoon Clayton sat down with Franks for a discussion of a couple of hours, during which Franks casually knocked $5 billion dollars from the earlier figure. To go below that, though, he indicated that the European governments could not agree on their own (for political reasons at home), and the United States would have to tell them what to do. With Kennan and Bonesteel on the way, Lovett shipped off a long telegram on August 26 to Clayton and Caffery setting forth basic American policy and concept of the program, the basic objective of which, he said, was "to move entire area progressively from present condition to working economy independent of abnormal outside support."[15] Lovett then went on with several pages of specifics, of the possible forms of U.S. assistance, of relations with Eastern European countries, the place of Germany in the program, the possible role of the UN, and the procedures the conference should follow, with its first draft to be reviewed informally by the U.S. representatives in Paris, for the completed report to be transmitted to Secretary Marshall, and finally for CEEC representatives, presumably the executive committee, to come to Washington to discuss it.[16]

In the meantime, Kennan and Bonesteel arrived in Paris, to consult first with Clayton, Caffery, and Douglas, which they did for a couple of days, and then to sit down with Franks, Herve Alphand, and the other members of the CEEC Executive Committee. The basic aims and assumptions of the Marshall Plan were laid out by Kennan and Bonesteel, so that the Europeans got a realistic view of what was expected: to provide the groundwork for a workable European economy for a period of four years, able thereafter to sustain itself without outside help. The dollars that the U.S. would provide to push it along would gradually diminish and eventually disappear. After the necessary repartee with the executive com-mittee members, who now had a good idea of what the United States was expecting, Kennan then sent his message back to Lovett, who passed it on to Marshall: "We both feel that visit thus far has been highly illuminating and worthwhile … [and the] time has come to present our views to governments directly." Lovett added, to the secretary, "Decision involved in quoted portion above can safely await your return and report of Kennan and Bonesteeel."[17]

Another serious matter came up at about the beginning of September—a very serious grain shortage in France due to bad crop conditions—this at a time when the Soviets were boasting of their large crops of exportable grain. The State Department feared that the Rus-sians would make some sort of offer of grain to the French in a way that would bolster the growing French Communist party. Lovett on September 3 sent off a telegram to the embassy in Paris, setting forth how they were planning to handle the matter. He said that he or Mar-shall would make a statement to the press "of our grave concern at natural disaster which has made French harvest worst in recent history and of efforts which we are making and will continue to make to alleviate to the greatest degree possible its consequences" with exportable grain surpluses from the U.S. In the press conference hope would be expressed "that in this emergency USSR will share with us burden of feeding western Europe." Lovett noted the "belief here that if in face this campaign USSR does not offer (or refuses possible French request for) grain, French Communists position will be weakened. If on the contrary Russian grain is offered, US will be in position to take credit for forcing this grain into open while comparative figures for USSR-US contributions will weigh heavily in our favor, whether Russian offer is large or small." In this way, the U.S. would come out ahead of Russia in this crisis.[18]

Lovett did speak to the press that day, stressing that the economic crisis in Europe was developing much faster than expected. He told reporters that appropriate steps to solve Europe's problems would have to be taken in a matter of months rather than sometime the next year—both temporary devices such as financial assistance and what he called perma-nent measures, obviously referring to the Marshall Plan. Two major reasons, Lovett said, were the contagious effects of the British financial crisis and the necessity for many Euro-pean countries to divert their resources from productive uses such as the purchase of machinery for new plants to nonproductive uses such as the purchase of food.[19] The British problem, Lovett felt, was due in part to what he called a deterioration in the ability and quality of the British governmental staffs and the recklessness shown by the present Labor government in dealing with their monetary crisis. At a September 10 lunch with Marshall, Forrestal, Harriman, Bernard Baruch, and Kennan, Lovett went on at some length about the problems caused by their goal of establishing a pattern of life for the British people based on Labor Party philosophy. And he concluded that even if Britain's economy collapsed it did not mean that the collapse of the rest of Europe would necessarily follow.[20]

In the meantime, Kennan had flown back to Washington and wrote a lengthy mem-orandum entitled "Situation with Respect to European Recovery Program" for the edifica-tion of Marshall, Lovett, and the rest of the State Department. "We must not look," Kennan wrote, "to the people in Paris to accomplish the impossible." They had scaled down their preliminary figures, and a further scaling down would come from U.S. pressure. "Perhaps a gesture or two will be made toward a reduction of the barriers to intra-European trade," and an appeal could be included "to the participating governments to put their financial houses in order." But "glaring deficiencies will remain. No bold or original approach to Europe's problems will be forthcoming. "[21] In summary Kennan said, "The long-term problem before us [is] a deeper, more far-reaching, and more complex one than any of us have realized. We cannot deal successfully with a program of this nature on the spur of the moment or under the abnormal pressure which would be caused by a further deterioration of conditions in Europe. [So] we must undertake at once an interim aid program with which to buy time. If we do this, then both problems—the short-term one and the long-term one—may still be solved. If we do not do it, we shall solve neither the one nor the other."[22]

Lovett, after reading Kennan's memorandum and discussing it with him, shipped off a 1:00 a.m. September 7 telegram "to certain American diplomatic officers," those accredited to the CEEC countries (and the U.S. political adviser for Germany, Robert Murphy), directing them to tell the foreign minister of their country that the presently proposed report of the CEEC "has numerous deficiencies which if publicized as final report by Europeans in response SecState's Harvard speech would make it unacceptable to State Dept, would undoubtedly evoke strong criticism in US and consequently endanger US support of any more reasonable or more realistic European aid program." Lovett concluded with three crucial matters to stress that (1) "CEEC to date has perhaps been too much on technical level with delegates unable to cut through instructions so as to concert on and actually apply principles of maximum production and cooperative self-help"; (2) "opponents of program in U.S. will magnify any indication aid is being requested from U.S. to take up slackness by Europeans"; (3) "the real chance for success of the European Recovery Program rests on a popular European desire to make it work."[23]

Lovett was doing what he could otherwise to get the CEEC straightened out. Early in September he met with Lord Inverchapel, the British ambassador, who cabled home the following message: "I saw Lovett yesterday and he expressed to me his despondency at the probable outcome of the Paris Conference. He referred repeatedly to what he called the 'shopping lists' ... and said that the report ... could not in its present form meet with a favorable reception here or be supported by the representatives of the United States Government." He went on: "I asked him whether the visit of Mr. Kennan, together with representations made by Mr. Clayton, had done anything to meet United States criticisms." Lovett "replied that small improvements had resulted but the report was still unsatisfactory."[24]

Following this, there were more meetings in Paris, with Clayton, Caffery and Douglas sitting down with members of the executive committee but with little give on the part of the CEEC. Then, though, Secretary Marshall himself sent off cables to Paris suggesting what the executive committee should be doing, and these seemed to have some effect. In addition, Lovett's instructions to talk with the home governments had been useful, and representatives in Paris were being told by their leaders to make some adjustments. In Paris, the CEEC Executive Committee put together its report, which they carefully called a first report, and Clayton, Caffery, and Douglas duly shipped it back to Washington with a sense of pride in what had been done with their assistance. Lovett looked at the finished product and responded coolly: "For your info we believe it will become clear from discussions in Washington that further substantial work by Committees in Paris will be necessary."[25]

Another development in the growing Cold War took place in late September, when the Soviets called a meeting in Warsaw of East European, French, and Italian Communists. With all Europe now divided into "socialist" and "capitalist" camps, what had been called the Comintern—Communist International—which had been abolished during the late war, was now to be revived and called the Communist Information Bureau, or Cominform. A couple of days later Lovett made the first official comment of the American government on the organization of the Cominform. He told a press conference that the department had "taken careful note of the terms of the manifesto issued by this conference, which maligned the aims of the American and British people in the recent war and carried to new lengths the distortions of United States policy with which the Communist press everywhere has recently been replete." He went on: "The documents issued by the Warsaw conference speak for themselves. The parties and governments associated with this program have made clear their intention to prevent, if they can, the economic recovery of Europe.... [T]here could be no possibility of avoiding economic disaster in Europe if the concepts of the Warsaw conference were to prevail." Americans, he said, "must not allow ourselves to be deflected from the course we have chosen; and we must continue to study with sympathy but with calm realism the problem of how Europe can be assisted to regain its proper place in a stable and peaceful world."[26]

In Washington, Marshall and Lovett had been convinced that a program of immediate interim aid was necessary, along with the major European Recovery Program (ERP), which could not be finalized until the following year's session of Congress. In mid–October, with Marshall off at a UN meeting in New York, Lovett sent a message to the President stressing the need for interim aid:

> There are many uncertain factors, both economic and political, which may affect the financial positions of the western European countries during the coming winter months. It is most likely ... that, pending the appropriation of funds under a general recovery program, interim aid will be needed by some of those countries if their positions are not to deteriorate even more dangerously. Unless these crises are met as they arise, there is little hope that the economic and political foundation on which to build a recovery program will be preserved. In the case of both France and Italy a serious crisis already exists and its dimensions are discernible.[27]

After setting forth the specific numbers anticipated for France's and Italy's economic emergencies, Lovett asked that a special session of Congress be called to authorize appropriations adequate to cover food and fuel necessities in France and Italy through June 1948, with additional credits allocated for essential items to be imported to Europe until Congress could pass the Marshall Plan. President Truman—convinced by Lovett, Marshall, and Will Clayton that Europe could not wait for the Marshall Plan—on October 23 called the special session of Congress for November 17 to consider the proposal for appropriations to cover needed food and fuel requirements in France and Italy.[28]

On September 29 President Truman had called a meeting in the White House to discuss the report from Paris and to determine "what action we should now take." Present at Truman's gathering were Marshall and Lovett, the aecretaries of agriculture and commerce, five senators including Vandenberg and Connally (each party's leader on the Foreign Relations Committee), and six House members. First Lovett and then Marshall spoke and answered questions. "After everyone had had his say," Truman continued, "I stated the case categorically and told them what we faced and what in my opinion we had to do." It appeared that it would require $580 million "to take care of immediate European needs until March

31 of the following year, the earliest date on which the proposed plan could be made effective." He asked the Senate and House committee chairmen "to give earnest consideration to the need for speedy aid to western Europe." The upcoming special session of Congress was also discussed.[29]

It was soon recognized that the initial report of the executive committee of the CEEC, the one Truman had discussed with the Congressional leaders, would need considerable reworking, and the executive committee members were invited to Washington to meet with the State Department for such reworking. The mission arrived in the American capital on October 9, and Sir Oliver Franks quickly began informal talks. In addition, other members of the executive committee got together with lesser figures in the U.S. government to iron out passages in the report that could be improved. On the evening of October 22 Franks sat down with Bob Lovett for a conversation on the report of the CEEC and what might be done with it. Franks left with Lovett a lengthy paper entitled "Unofficial Aide-Memoire," summing up his position. He felt that the Paris Conference had made the people in Europe feel that they had responded successfully to the initiative of the United States and "they are now looking to these discussions in Washington as the next step in the fulfillment of this common endeavour." What was most important, of course, was that "the programme is a *recovery* program and not a programme of temporary relief."[30]

Lovett had an hour-long gathering with Franks and the other executive committee members on October 24 at which he could see noticeable improvements in the report. He indicated that the State Department would try to secure congressional adoption of the general outline of the Paris Report and would seek an appropriation for 1948.[31] Following this meeting Lovett prepared an "Informal Aide-Memoire," which he gave Franks on November 3, prior to a meeting of the State Department's Advisory Steering Committee with the CEEC delegation the next day. In the aide-memoire, Lovett stressed that the program must be "designed to achieve genuine recovery ... not ... a mere program of temporary relief." He added that the report from Paris "is a well reasoned analysis of the problem and presents fundamental lines of action for the achievement of genuine European recovery." He recognized that the recovery problem had "both a commodity aspect and a financial aspect," and he hoped that the program of American aid could be worked out to be successful "from either point of view." And he mentioned "the controlling voice the Congress will exercise in these matters," a feature to be kept in the Europeans' minds at all times.[32]

The meeting on November 4, at 3:30 p.m. in the Department of State, brought together the members of the Advisory Steering Committee, which Lovett had helped to establish, with Lovett and Harriman present and including Willard Thorp, Bohlen, and Bonesteel from State, and Representatives from Commerce, Labor, Treasury, the Army, and Interior, with Sir Oliver Franks, six other CEEC delegates, and five additional aides.

Lovett opened the meeting by stating that "agreement must be reached on certain basic policy decisions," most of which "cannot be decided on the basis of present information" or that showed "alternative courses of action" that required "extremely delicate evaluation before decisions are made." The gathering then got into discussions of prospective U.S. actions with respect to various items. Lovett stated that "in so far as possible, procurement and trade should follow normal channels of trade." Congress, he said, "will be requested to appropriate funds to the U.S. agency administering the program and an effort will be made to provide for wide flexibility in the allocation and administration of such funds"—though "such an arrangement is dependent entirely upon Congressional action." Lovett added that the thinking at the present time was "that U.S. assistance would be partly in the form of loans and partly in the form of grants-in-aid." By this time, the dollar amount had been whittled down by the CEEC members to $17 billion, considerably below their earliest number. While "various segments of the U.S. Government and the U.S. public might advance extreme suggestions" for dealing with problems that might arise, the members of the CEEC delegation should bear in mind "that they should take their cue on this matter from the U.S. Administration." Lovett emphasized once again Marshall's statement that some countries' national approaches needed to be set aside in favor of a joint effort geared toward the overall recovery.[33]

After further discussion on various points at issue, Franks, speaking for his delegation, expressed appreciation for information on the basic lines of American thinking, stating further that the CEEC delegation was encouraged by the expression of U.S. views. After this, the CEEC gentlemen returned to Europe, with guidance on specific areas of their report and the understanding that the United States was totally involved in the program under discussion but that the Europeans would have to broaden their contributions and lay aside national approaches in favor of a multinational effort directed toward achieving recovery.

17

Getting It All Done

The first order of business in regard to the Marshall Plan was the passage of a bill providing interim aid to the suffering European states, before the actual European Recovery Program could be considered and enacted. Harry Truman had stated this in his October 23 notice of the special session of Congress he was calling, and it then became the work of the American senators and representatives to take this first and very necessary step to stave off the crisis that was close to swallowing up Europe before anything else could be done. In both France and Italy, the principal subjects of the interim aid provisions, Communism was a threat to take over each country's government in the event of the collapse of its economy and its basic need for food and fuel. The proposal of the president to Congress as it convened in special session was that $597 million be provided for short-term aid to cover needs until the end of the following March. On November 11 Lovett testified before the Senate Foreign Relations Committee (Arthur Krock phoned him at 5:10 p.m. to tell him how good his presentation was), and the next day Marshall and Lovett appeared before the House Committee on Foreign Affairs. Congressman John Vorys (Lovett's old Yale Unit flying buddy) asked why could they not simply move on to the long-range recovery program. Marshall responded that there would be too much delay; without the interim aid, he said, there was "not much hope for the long-range plan because the situation will so deteriorate that its prospects for success would be too poor."[1]

The next afternoon Vorys called Lovett to discuss "questions he didn't ask yesterday," questions raised by agricultural people, and said that if Lovett would send him the answers to these questions that afternoon Vorys would show them to his agriculture people. If there was a wide difference of opinion he would get back in touch with Lovett before they were put on the record. Apparently Lovett's answers were adequate for the time being. On another day Lovett recalled "having a rough ride" before the House Foreign Affairs Committee from Vorys: "Now John Vorys was a classmate of mine at Yale and a clubmate of mine in Bones, and he just started to peel the skin off me, so much so that the other members of the Committee came to my defense. Then when I was excused from further testimony John handed me a little note and said, 'How about having lunch?'" In the cafeteria upstairs, Lovett said to Vorys, "What in hell got into you today?" Vorys replied, "Well, after all, when I left Yale I went out to Yale in China … and I wanted to get you on the subject of China, and you just refused to talk on it." Lovett said, "Yes, because that's General Marshall's specialty." "You see," Lovett recalled, "he was just putting on a show."[2]

Marshall was off to London in late November for a Council of Foreign Ministers meeting, so the basic necessity for dealing with Congress fell, as usual, on Robert Lovett. On November 25 Lovett got a call from Congressman Walter Judd (R–Minn), who wanted to add an amendment to the interim aid bill giving China $60 million for the first three months of the next year. Lovett pointed out that aid to China would be entirely different from the proposed aid to Europe, that for China it would be for maintaining the status quo rather than the relief provided for Europe, and that China would not be able to meet the requirements that had been set for the recipient countries in the current bill.

Lovett sent off to Marshall on December 4 a "hasty report on present situation regarding interim aid." The Senate, he said, "has reported the bill out in full amount and in acceptable form." The House Foreign Affairs Committee, however, had reported the bill out at $590 million but had injected China as a recipient of $60 million of that (Judd had gone ahead despite Lovett's rejection of his proposal), meaning that the intended initial recipients of the aid would receive $67 million less than the president had proposed. "The bill is now on the floor and is being heavily attacked by many members," mostly right-wing isolationists.[3] In addition, the Senate Appropriations Committee had been holding hearings all week, with appearances by the secretaries of agriculture and commerce as well as farm groups and others. "Session," Lovett noted, "devoted almost entirely to attacks on lend-lease shipments to Russia, Communism, grain shortage, past relief abuses, German plant dismantling and reparations deliveries, and German currency system. While no direct attack was made on sin, I judge the Committee omitted that feeling that the Department of State was an adequate substitute."[4] "While the ride was rough," Lovett continued, "it could have been worse and probably will be when I go back tomorrow."

The principal contention of any note seemed to be "protection to this country against the continuance of relief aid where the recipient country falls under the control of Communists." Lovett pointed out a provision in the act for the president to terminate promptly aid to any country whenever he finds "by reason of changed conditions, that the provision of assistance authorized by this act is no longer necessary or desirable." Senator Styles Bridges (R-NH) was particularly persistent on this question because he felt the State Department "could not be relied on in such matters." He asked on the record for a "direct answer" on our policy if these countries should "fall under Communist control." Lovett again pointed out the section under which the president could promptly cut off aid. Bridges then said he wanted an answer as to what the State Department would do. Lovett replied, "I am not in a position to speak for the Secretary of State. In his absence, if I must give a direct answer, it is that I would recommend to the President and his advisers that aid to such countries be stopped if those countries fell under Communist control." Lovett told Marshall that he would have preferred to have avoided the question, but "it seemed absolutely necessary to meet the situation frankly and the result in the Committee was to stop that line of questioning."[5]

Lovett then reported to Marshall that House Appropriations Committee hearings were scheduled for the following Monday, and that he had had a "long work-out" with Chairman John Taber (R-NY) the day before, and that Taber, who just happened to be a Yale grad, was hopeful to have the bill through his committee by the next night. Lovett also said the legislation for the ERP was being completed, with Truman's message nearly ready in draft form. He concluded, "We are still in business. Best regards."[6] On December 9 Lovett sent off another message to Marshall in London with the news that the basic ERP program was complete and the president's message should be in final draft form shortly. Because of the violent debate in the House on the interim aid, he felt there would not be action on that bill before the following week, which would delay the submission of the president's message on ERP.

On the 13th Lovett had another conversation with Senator Connally, the minority leader of the Senate Foreign Relations Committee, on the matter of aid to China in the interim aid bill. Lovett told him the entire amount proposed was needed for France, Italy, and Austria, and that any amount for China out of this sum would be detrimental to the requirements for the three European countries. The aid to China would be scaled down in the final working of the bill, but it would not be eliminated. The interim aid bill was finally passed by Congress on December 15 and signed by President Truman on December 17 as the Foreign Aid Act of 1947, with funds provided by the act approved December 23, 1947. As Congress finalized it, there was $522 million for Italy, France, and Austria, and $18 million for China.

With the interim aid problem out of the way, Harry Truman proceeded into the major part of the recovery program. There had been some dispute over the timing of the president's message to Congress on the Marshall Plan. On November 25 Clark Clifford brought up the question at a staff conference, saying the message was set for the following Monday. Lovett, though, said that Senator Vandenberg thought it should be delayed. Vandenberg feared what might happen to the interim aid bill if the whole Marshall Plan program should come before Congress while the interim bill was still being kicked around. Truman was opposed to delaying the message, but ultimately he went along with Lovett's and Vandenberg's position.[7] On December 19 Truman submitted to Congress his special message on the European Recovery Program, arising from what the president now referred to as the "Marshall Plan." Truman knew not to become too closely identified with the plan and relied on the great prestige of George Marshall. When there had been a suggestion earlier to call the program the "Truman Plan," the president told Clifford, "Can you imagine its chances of passage in an election year in a Republican congress if it is named for Truman and not Marshall?"[8]

Charles Bohlen was designated the head of the State Department's congressional liaison, but realistically, for winning the consent of Congress to the programs of the Marshall Plan and the sums of money that would be involved, George Marshall and the department relied most heavily on Robert Lovett and the close relationship he had developed with Senator Vandenberg. The two met frequently during the day and spoke often on the telephone. In addition, Lovett on numerous occasions stopped by Vandenberg's apartment in the Wardman Park Hotel on his way home from work. The two quite often put their heads together to figure out how best to sell their foreign aid program to a hesitant and sometimes-suspicious 80th Congress. Sometimes Lovett would bring along with him to show the senator classified State Department cables about the activities of the Communists in western Europe. Lovett, as instructed by the president, "was always completely frank" with Vandenberg. He would stop by the senator's apartment "on the way home with a sheaf of telegrams in my hand and go over what had happened during the day with him if it was a thing in which he was interested. Some things he'd never talk with me about at all—China. 'No,' he said, 'that's not up to you, that's Secretary Marshall, the China problem. But everything else,' he said, 'you're in charge here and I'd just like to know what's going on.'"[9]

Vandenberg had been a leading isolationist in the Senate. When World War II broke out, however, he switched his views on foreign policy and became an internationalist and, indeed, one who believed that the formulation of America's foreign policy could and should be above the level of partisan politics. It was to the great advantage of Harry Truman, George Marshall, and Robert Lovett—and the American people—that a bipartisan foreign policy was advocated by the chairman of the Senate Foreign Relations Committee. Lovett said later, "I do not think any appraisal of ERP could be complete without recognizing the extraordinary role which Senator Vandenberg played in it and the extremely close cooperation that existed between the Congressional committees and the Department of State."[10]

Opposition to the proposed legislation was formidable, with isolationism adding to frugality and fear of inflation. There was, in the Congress (and in the country at large), a widespread desire to economize, to cut back on government spending, and shipping money overseas seemed to many people the very opposite of what should be done. Marshall and Lovett reiterated over and over that the ERP would be in effect self-liquidating, stressing the benefits the U.S. would derive from a prosperous Europe, but this all seemed too far down the road for some to grasp. Fortunately, the bulk of the Republicans in the Senate listened—some with reluctance—to Vandenberg, while Charles Eaton (R–NJ), chairman of the House Committee on Foreign Relations, worked hard at keeping the House majority in line.

The country was given great amounts of propaganda in favor of the Marshall Plan as it came before Congress, not just from the Truman administration but also from civic groups, charitable organizations, veterans groups, university professors—from anyone who favored the program and could conjure up a means of getting the message out. Of course, there was also much talk from groups or interests that did not find the Marshall Plan to be what was needed. As to the process of preparing the sale to Congress, Lovett recalled the followig:

> The preparation for the Congressional hearings was ... unprecedented.... In order to make the presentation lucid and persuasive, I borrowed six outstanding officers from the military services, with whom I had previously worked ... and, as I recall it, we used all of the IBM machines in the Census Bureau and finally ended by borrowing those of the Prudential Insurance Company in Newark in order to make our calculations. The sheer mechanical figuring of the so-called "country needs" and pricing these items was beyond anything we had anticipated and far exceeded any similar effort made in the government. Our main purpose in the presentation to Congress was to develop the facts in such form as to indicate that the Marshall Plan was designed to get the European economy in motion so that there would not be an economic vacuum which would attract Communism.[11]

The lead for the administration before Congress was, naturally, George Marshall, who appeared before Vandenberg's Senate committee on January 8, 1948. Marshall was placid and relaxed, assuming that the committee accepted the need for aid. He would work to make the program effective, while he opposed placing requirements on receiving countries that would impinge on their sovereign rights. Most of the questions he got concerned what kind of an organization would run the ERP for the United States.[12] Four days later Marshall appeared before the House committee, making most of the same points again, stressing the "hunger, poverty, desperation, and resulting chaos" threatening the people of Europe, and explaining how the economic distress would be exploited for political purposes by Soviet Russia and the Communist parties in the states in question. There was, again, considerable interest in how the organization was to be set up to run things and who would head that organization. Marshall was a little vague in this area, but he did say that there could not be two secretaries of state. With Lovett, Lew Douglas, Chip Bohlen, and Willard Thorp sitting behind him and filling him in with specific items of information when needed,

Marshall's appearance went well. After his congressional appearances, Marshall took to the road to sell his plan to the American people, particularly to the Middle West, where the *Chicago Tribune* was, not unexpectedly, giving it a hard time.

It soon became clear that sentiment in Congress was opposed to the State Department's operating the ERP. Lovett appointed a special committee headed by Lincoln Gordon to put together the body to administer the program—one that would attract outside managerial talent and furnish a businesslike administration to the aid program. Members of the Bureau of the Budget were doubtful of the Gordon plan and secured Truman's tentative support for State Department administration. Lovett met with the president at the White House on November 28 and convinced him that the State Department's prestige as worldwide policy-maker should not be endangered by direct operational responsibility for the particulars of the aid program. He persuaded Truman to reverse his position and won presidential approval for an administrative scheme like that proposed by the Gordon committee. With the aid of the Gordon committee's report, Vandenberg was able to amend the bill to provide for an independent director to operate the Economic Cooperation Administration (ECA) as well as a special representative with ambassadorial rank to handle specific matters in Europe.[13]

In mid–February Vandenberg (after frequently calling upon Bob Lovett for help when any part was questioned) was able to have his committee give the ERP legislation unanimous approval and send it to the Senate floor for debate. Very soon thereafter, the Communists took over the government of Czechoslovakia and threatened that of Finland, and the fate of economically endangered European countries became even more of an issue. With the Czech coup staring them in the face, opponents of the ERP bill in the Senate—including Republican leaders like Robert Taft of Ohio and Kenneth Wherry of Nebraska—lost much of their argument. Vandenberg stressed the Soviet menace was a very realistic threat, with possible economic failure in western Europe. He eased some opposition by cutting the cost down from $17 billion over four years as proposed in the legislation submitted to Congress to $5.3 billion over a twelve-month period, with a new figure to be voted for each year. With this change, Vandenberg was able to repulse all efforts to cut back or restrict the program, with the aid of Marshall, Lovett, numerous well-placed industrialists, and even former president Herbert Hoover. The bill was passed by the Senate on March 14 by a 69–17 vote, with 38 Democrats joining 31 Republicans in favor.

On it went to the House of Representatives. Eaton's Foreign Relations Committee worked on the program's basic structure, while John Taber's House Appropriations Committee looked at the funding. Paul Nitze, a specialist in international trade in the State Department, was assigned to testify on the particulars of the funding to Taber's committee following opening remarks by Lovett and Paul Hoffman, who had been designated to head the program. Taber permitted no experts to sit with NItze, who was required to justify the entire appropriations request in great detail. Taber demanded that Nitze start alphabetically, with Austria. Down the list they went, until they came to pulses, a type of bean. Why ship pulses to Austria, Taber demanded—they can grow them there. Then tractors. Nitze struggled for answers with no experts to help him. Suddenly Taber got up and went into an office next to the hearing room to use the phone. Nothing was heard from him for half an hour. Then Taber returned and startled everyone by saying, "Mr. Nitze, you can call your experts. We'll adjourn the hearing now and you'll have them here tomorrow morning."

Back at the State Department, Nitze spoke with Bob Lovett and was startled to learn what had happened. "John Taber called me," Lovett said, "and described the full horrors of your presentation, particularly your inability to justify the need for pulses, the fact that you'd never grown them, and that you had not been to Austria to learn whether they could grow there." Bob said he listened to Taber until he had completed his full catalog of horrors. Then Lovett said to Taber, "You know, I could ask you a question that you couldn't answer. For example, 'How many rivets are there in a B-29 wing?'" To this Taber replied, "You would know that better than I because you were assistant secretary of war for air in World War Two." "Well," Bob said, "that's just the point. Some people are more knowledgeable about certain matters than other people. So why don't you let Nitze have his experts there to answer these technical questions?" Before Taber could answer, Bob asked him another question: "If it takes eight yards of pink crepe paper to go around an elephant's leg, how long does it take him to kill a fly with a flyswatter?" Taber said, "That's a nonsensical question." Bob told him, "Of course. Now why don't you stop asking Nitze nonsensical questions?" And Taber agreed. Nitze went on:

> That exchange between Taber and Lovett over the phone saved the Marshall Plan. Bob Lovett understood Taber's mentality. They had worked together many times before and over the course of their dealings Bob had learned how to handle him, how to present a problem to get around Taber's prejudices. A conservative with isolationist leanings, Taber was deeply skeptical of the Marshall Plan; his line of questioning was designed to find any legitimate excuse to block action on the program. He knew that if and when the bill cleared his committee, he would be the one who would have to lead the fight in the House for its passage. If he finally decided to support the bill, he wanted to be able to demonstrate to his colleagues that having taken the bill apart piece by piece, he knew it thoroughly; he wanted to anticipate and be able to answer any criticism. Though I came to understand Taber's position and what he was trying to do, I found his methods tedious and time consuming. I had lost fifteen pounds by the time those hearings ended some forty sessions later![14]

With Eaton's committee reporting the bill favorably to the floor and with the approval of John Taber and his Appropriations Committee, the bill was approved in the House by a vote of 329–74 on March 31. A compromise between the two versions of the bill was quickly reached and passed by both houses, and the president signed the European Recovery Program into law on April 3. When it came to securing an administrator for the program, Lovett had prepared a list of suggested names for the position, all well-regarded businessmen. He favored Paul G. Hoffman, president of the Studebaker-Packard Corporation, who was supported by both business leaders and Washington insiders. Other names popped up as suggestions for this post. When Will Clayton's name was mentioned, Vandenberg quickly sent Marshall a letter opposing that. "This is no reflection on Mr. Clayton," he said. "It is simply a reflection of the overriding Congressional desire that the ERP administrator shall come from the outside business world with strong industrial credentials and *not* via the State Department." For those "strong industrial credentials" it was soon decided that the job should go to Hoffman, who had some years earlier pulled Studebaker back from financial failure.[15]

On the morning of April 7, Hoffman appeared before the Senate Foreign Relations Committee, accompanied by Robert Lovett. Hoffman did very well in his testimony to Senator Vandenberg and his committee, and there was no trouble whatever in getting him approved and onto the job. Paul Hoffman became the administrator of the Economic Cooperation Administration (ECA) and was sworn in on April 9, 1948. He did a fine job of running it. There was to be an appointive post of special representative who would direct operations in Europe on problems such as trade restrictions, competing currencies, and even national rivalries. It was agreed that Truman should give this position to an identifiable Democrat, and Hoffman asked for either Averell Harriman or Lewis Douglas. Douglas did not want to give up his position as ambassador in London, and Truman at first wanted to keep Harriman in his cabinet. Hoffman wanted Harriman. Lovett was for Harriman's appointment and he wired Marshall: "I have kept strictly out of this in order to avoid embarrassment to Harriman, to Department, and to myself because of personal relationships, but I think Hoffman's recommendation is right." Harriman, too, was reluctant, but Truman insisted and Averell took the job on April 21; as Harriman usually did, he performed well in the position.[16] Over the four years of the program's operation, the United States expended $12.4 billion. By 1952, when American funding ended, the economy of every participating nation had surpassed prewar levels. Economic output in 1951 was 38 percent higher than in 1938. Harry Truman, George Marshall, Bob Lovett, Arthur Vandenberg, and numerous others could look back with pride and satisfaction on what they had worked out.

Robert Lovett, looking back in later years, felt that a major factor in the Marshall Plan's success was "that the organization of the European Recovery Program contained a system of having the claimants for help screen each other's request so that the group in Washington would not be faced with a series of letters to Santa Claus since each beneficiary would cautiously look at what his neighbor got and thereby impose a reasonable discipline before the matter came to the decision stage." And he felt "the ability and personality" of Paul Hoffman helped greatly in "working matters through the Congress." He also said the Marshall Plan "was one of the very few large undertakings in which the estimates of total funding were reasonably accurate and which was terminated on the date promised when it was started."[17]

18

The Issue of Palestine

While so much effort in the high levels of the State Department was being given to the creation and development of the European Recovery Program, another combustible issue was arising in another part of the overseas world, one that held much importance to the United States. The story of the population and control of Palestine, the Holy Land, was one that could be traced back to biblical times and later to the Crusades. Contending numbers of Arabs and Hebrews had made it a struggle for lengthy periods of years, and these contentions were to become a major problem for Harry Truman, George Marshall, Robert Lovett, and their State Department.

Over the centuries Palestine's population had become more and more Arabic and less and less Hebraic, but Jews from all over Europe and the Middle East always seemed to have a longing within their hearts and minds for the ancient homeland. After World War I Great Britain was granted a mandate over the whole of Palestine—one they handled rather clumsily—and after World War II the Brits announced that they would terminate their mandate, in May 1948. In addition, the Anglo-American Committee of Inquiry in April 1946 announced its recommendation for the immediate immigration of 100,000 Jewish refugees from Europe to Palestine and that there be no Arab or Jewish state, neither side being dominant there. President Harry Truman issued a statement supporting the acceptance of 100,000 refugees but refusing the balance of the committee's recommendation. The British then placed the question of Palestine before the United Nations.

Where Truman stood on the issues involved with Palestine, Zionism, the Jews, and the Arabs was at times a bit difficult to ascertain. As a senator, he had voted with the majority in support of the Zionist goals of opening Palestine to unrestricted Jewish immigration and ownership of land. He felt that the British should establish (or permit) a Jewish homeland. A week after assuming the presidency, Truman met with Rabbi Stephen S. Wise, assuring Wise that he was in sympathy with the plight of the Jewish refugees in Europe and that he would carry out Roosevelt's policy in that regard. Since FDR's policy on Palestine had held basically that no change should be made without the full agreement of both Jews and Arabs, this did not encourage Wise greatly. The State Department under Stettinius and Byrnes tried to keep the president from taking any position that would offend the Arabs, while numerous American politicians were pushing him hard to support the Zionist cause of substantial immigration of the displaced Jews of Europe.

In the meantime, tension and violence were growing in Palestine. The stream of mostly illegal Jewish immigrants had become sizable since Hitler's accession in Germany and was creating, whether accepted or not, a state within a state. It was estimated that by the end of the war there were some 600,000 Jews in Palestine, and they had their own schools, public services, and even an army of their own, called Haganah. On July 22, 1946, the Irgun, a Jewish terrorist group, bombed and partially destroyed the King David Hotel in Jerusalem, a British army headquarters, killing 91 persons.

Truman's reaction in April 1946 to the Anglo-American Committee of Inquiry report accepting 100,000 Jewish immigrants but declining to sign off on the reservation of neither an Arabic nor a Jewish state caused dissatisfaction among the Arabs (and the British). At this point, with greater violence looming ever nearer, Truman consulted his Joint Chiefs of Staff, who told him that the U.S. should commit no armed forces to problems in Palestine, that sufficiently offended Arab states might move closer to Moscow and have the Soviet Union replace America as a substantial power in the Middle East, shifting to Russia control of the area's vast oil reserves. The Palestine question continued to harass President Truman, with political pressures coming at him from all sides—Republicans as well as Democrats but most particularly the Jewish partisans. On Yom Kippur, October 4, 1946, Truman issued a statement in which he cited Jewish suggestions of a viable Jewish state in a part of Palestine, rather than all of the mandate, and said, "To such a solution our Government could give its support." The most pro–Zionist statement a president had ever made put the U.S. on record in favor of partition for the first time.[1]

On May 15, 1947, the UN created the United Nations Special Committee on Palestine (UNSCOP), a group made up of representatives from eleven countries. After hearings and a survey of the situation, UNSCOP issued a report on August 31, with seven of its members recommending the creation of separate Arab and Jewish states, with Jerusalem under an international trusteeship. Three members wanted a single federal state containing both Arab and Jewish constituent states, while one member, Australia, abstained. The Jews were very much in favor of such a partition, while Arabs opposed it bitterly. The White House supported it, while the State Department was opposed, fearing a realignment of the Arab nations with Russia. Secretary Marshall, meeting with the U.S. delegation at the opening of the September 1947 session of the UN General Assembly, took a neutral stand on partition but was most concerned that the United States would likely have to supply troops to enforce such a procedure.

Truman had a short talk with Marshall on October 5, instructing him to make public American support for the partition plan. Several days later Truman met at the White House with Clark Clifford, David Niles, and Bob Lovett to review a proposed statement prepared by the State Department supporting partition and a Jewish state. John Hilldring, placed in the State Department by the White House to support pro–Jewish positions, spoke with Lovett on the phone a few minutes later and Lovett told him "that the President approved the statement and in view of the shortness of time, did not ask for any change in the language." But Truman told Lovett to be sure the U.S. delegation understood clearly "that with respect to financial and economic aid to Palestine ... the United States would contribute its part only under the auspices of the United Nations and that no direct United States contribution should be looked for and ... that any contribution we might make toward the preservation of law and order in Palestine" as part of a UN "constabulary" would also be only as a contribution under the UN obligation. Lovett then sent off a 4:00 p.m. telegram to the delegation in New York, emphasizing the gist of the paragraphs Truman had stressed.[2] In any event, the United States delegation supported the majority report of the UNSCOP. What arose as a serious issue was the partition's granting of the Negev, the sizable desert area in the south of the mandate, to the Jewish state. The Arabs, who were practically the only inhabitants of the Negev, were furious that this was to be taken from them.

On November 10, 1947, Loy Henderson, director of the Office of Near Eastern and African Affairs, presented a memorandum to the secretary of state, which was concurred in by Lovett and others and marked "OK" by Marshall, suspending immediately "authorization for the export from the United States of arms, ammunition and other war material intended for use in Palestine or in neighboring countries, until the situation in that area has become somewhat more clarified." Of course, despite a United States arms embargo, there was a continuing flow of military might into Palestine from Great Britain, Czechoslovakia, and other sources, to both the Arabs and the Jews.[3]

On November 19 at noon, President Truman met with Chaim Weizmann, one of the principal Jewish leaders, who gave him a broad and convincing description of the manifold ways in which Jewish settlers would make use of the Negev. Truman promised Weizmann that he would get in touch with the delegation at once. However, at just about the time Weizmann was leaving the White House, at 1:00 p.m., Lovett was sending off a wire to the delegation "that facts regarding Negeb [*sic*] warrant its inclusion in Arab State."[4] When Truman called New York, Hilldring told him of Lovett's instructions for the Negev to go to the Arabs. The president made it clear that the U.S. was to go along with the majority report giving the Negev to the Jews. With these conflicting directions, Hilldring and Acting Ambassador Herschel Johnson decided the U.S. would take no position on the Negev at the time. Around 6:00 p.m., Lovett phoned Truman, who told him he had not changed Lovett's instructions but had merely tried to keep the U.S. from taking a useless minority position on the question. Lovett subsequently changed his instructions, telling Johnson and Hilldring they should not let the U.S. be placed in the position of a lone dissenter on the Negev question.[5] Three days later the American proposal to award the Negev to the Arabs was withdrawn, but Johnson introduced a proposal that Beersheba and a strip of land along the border with Egypt be awarded to the Arabs, and this was successfully carried.

On the morning of November 24 Bob Lovett went to the White House to determine Truman's views on an issue raised that morning by the UN delegation "on whether or not the United States should participate in a Commission to implement partition in Palestine." Truman said "he would be most reluctant to see the United States on such a Commission," and only if the USSR were being placed on such a commission would he agree to the U.S. accepting a similar post. The president went on to emphasize that the U.S. would participate in enforcing a plan for Palestine "only as a Member of the United Nations and jointly with other Members. It would not be a protagonist." In addition, Truman did not want the U.S. delegation using threats or improper pressure of any kind on other delegations to vote for the report favoring partition. At 2:20 that afternoon Lovett telephoned Johnson and Hilldring at Lake Success and passed on to them what Truman had told him.[6]

Nevertheless, there was considerable pressure laid on various delegations regarding the upcoming vote on partition, some by U.S. diplomats (present and former), some by industrialists threatening withdrawal of American aid to countries voting "no," and much by Jewish agencies of one kind or another. Lovett at one point called Matt Connelly at the White House to say that the cause was being impeded by pressures put on by Jewish agencies. Lovett tried to make it crystal clear to the American delegates: "The president did not wish the United States delegation to use threats or improper pressure of any kind on other delegations to vote for the majority report favoring partition of Palestine."[7] At a luncheon with Truman and Forrestal after the UN vote, Lovett told them "he had never in his life been subject to as much pressure as he had been from Jews in the three days beginning Thursday morning and ending Saturday night." At one point he told Truman that he had received several threatening telephone calls and numerous pressuring telegrams, and the president promptly offered him special Secret Service protection. Lovett thought about that but declined Truman's offer. He said his study was on the first floor of his house at 2425 Kalorama Road, which made it easy for any determined terrorist "to ride by on a bicycle any evening, and lob a grenade through the front window." He doubted whether a Secret Service detail could be effective.[8]

In any event, the report of the UNSCOP proposing partition, with the lines slightly amended, came up for a vote in the UN General Assembly on November 29, with two-thirds needed for approval. When the voting was done, the report was approved by a tally of 33 to 13, with ten abstentions. The partition, as voted, was to take effect upon the termination of the British Mandate, at 6:00 P.M (Washington time) on May 14, 1948, or 12 midnight, May 15, in Palestine. Not unexpectedly, Arab violence increased markedly after the partition vote, and concerns arose over the question of who was going to enforce whatever the UN ultimately decided to do in Palestine. Truman was adamant that American troops were not to do it, except only as a portion of a UN force. And within the State Department and the Pentagon it was firmly believed that war in the Middle East and the resulting loss of Arab friendship (and oil) was far too high a price to pay for a Jewish state in Palestine. Forrestal, Marshall, and Lovett felt the danger of risking Arab antagonism, while Truman's advisers believed that the Jews could defend their own interests, provided that the arms embargo then in place could be lifted.

Early in January 1948 Lovett had meetings with the presidents of oil companies, Socony-Vacuum and Arabian-American Oil, to discuss at some length the possible impact on the oil situation in the Arabic countries of partition in Palestine. Bob Lovett had numerous off-the-record conversations about the situation in Palestine with people such as Jim Forrestal, Dean Rusk, Rabbi Stephen Wise, Admiral Sidney Souers (of naval intelligence), New Jersey Senator H. Alexander Smith, Congressman Jacob Javits, and others. The constant strife between the Arabs and the Jews made the implementation of partition look riskier as time moved on. On January 21 Lovett showed Jim Forrestal a memorandum recently done by the Policy Planning Staff of the State Department, setting forth the position that U.S. support of partition was based on the assumption that it could be carried out without conflict, and since it was now clear that peaceful implementation of partition was unworkable the U.S. delegation should propose that the United Nations withdraw its partition plan.[9] One prominent member of the UN delegation had very little time for Lovett— Eleanor Roosevelt. As her son Elliott wrote, "The State of Israel was all that counted with her. One State Department sympathizer with the Arabs' cause was Robert Lovett—Yale, Harvard, and a background in banking. Mother rated him 'dangerous' and prayed that he would either quit or be fired."[10]

On the morning of February 16 Lovett received a call from Charlie Ross, the president's press secretary, telling him that Truman was upset at Drew Pearson's broadcast in which he had sent personal appeals to King Ibn Saud of Saudi Arabia and to the leaders of Iraq, asking them to go easy in Palestine. Truman had no objection to the facts being known but disliked being prodded into it by Pearson. Lovett called Ross back shortly with a statement that he had prepared for him: "In an effort to prevent the spread of disorder in the Middle East this Government has ... addressed appeals to certain interested governments stressing the importance ... of the exercise of restraint in dealing with the Palestine situation. Some of these appeals were made directly by the President." Ross thought this sounded fine, and Lovett told him that Pearson was right about a message to Ibn Saud but wrong about Iraq.[11]

As partition seemed more and more questionable, the idea of a UN trusteeship over Palestine received more support. Ambassador Warren Austin, the head of the UN delegation of the United States, prepared to make a speech to the Security Council on February 24, 1948, to set forth the American understanding of the legal situation in the General Assembly. Several days earlier Lovett had spoken on the phone with Clark Clifford, telling him it would be a good idea for the president to make a statement after Austin's speech to the UN so that the people would be aware that the president had something to do with it—to the effect that the position had been thoroughly studied, conferences held, and the policy reached to sustain the UN, and that Austin had stated the position correctly. Clifford agreed, and Truman, cruising in the Virgin Islands, did in fact issue a statement approving the speech.

Austin in his speech said the council, though empowered to deal with threats to the peace in Palestine, did not have the power to enforce partition. He had cleared his speech with a message to Truman on February 21, a message that also contained the idea that if Arab intransigence continued beyond the Security Council's control, the whole matter should go back to the General Assembly where some form of trusteeship for a time should be considered. This latter point was not in the February 24 speech, but it showed which way the State Department was moving.

On the same day on which Austin made his speech, Bob Lovett attended a luncheon at the Statler for the American press at which he gave the reporters as much as he could of a background for the American position on the issues in Palestine and the Middle East. Late in the afternoon reports came in that the press representatives had much appreciated Lovett's talk. Also, Joseph Alsop (who had not been at the luncheon) called Lovett to tell him that he was "fascinated with our solution" to the Palestine problem. Lovett said "it was not a solution" and that if Alsop came right over he would brief him. Alsop duly showed up twenty minutes later, and he and Bob Lovett hashed matters out for an hour.

On February 25 Lovett was advised that Francis B. Sayre, longtime State Department man and former Harvard Law School professor, had been mentioned as a possibility for governor of Jerusalem by the UN Trusteeship Council. Lovett felt that that position should not be filled by an American, and he advised that the United States did not want any member of the Big Five named as governor of Jerusalem.

On March 6 and again two days later Clark Clifford submitted memos to the president presenting the arguments in favor of partition. Delay, he said, would result in more worldwide instability. On the question of offending the Arabs, he said they "must have oil royalties or go broke." Failure to implement the partition decision, Clifford felt, would damage the reputations of both the United Nations and the United States.[12] On March 12 Bob and Adele Lovett took off for Hobe Sound for a couple of weeks, ordered by George Marshall for a much-needed rest, but all sorts of things broke loose before their return on the 26th.

Marshall, on March 16, directed Austin to make his speech supporting trusteeship as soon as possible "as Austin believes appropriate," with no word that the president was to be informed when Austin was to make his speech. As another Clifford memo, describing these developments, set forth, "Text of Austin's speech was not submitted to President for his approval." But, of course, "it was the same substance as the draft previously submitted to President."[13] On March 18 Truman met with Chaim Weizmann and discussed Palestine and where things were headed. Weizmann left with an understanding that the United States supported partition. The next day Truman was astounded when Austin arose in the UN Security Council, said that efforts to put into effect the partition plan were unsuccessful and should be suspended and that instead Palestine should be put under a temporary United Nations trusteeship. Truman felt that he had been double-crossed by Austin and the State Department, and he had no hesitation in letting his feelings be known. He wrote in his diary that "the State Department pulled the rug from under me today." He went on: "This morning I find the State Department has reversed my Palestine policy. The first I know about it is what I see in the papers…. I am now in the position of a liar and a double-crosser." He blamed "people on the third and fourth levels of the State Department who have always wanted to cut my throat."[14]

Truman felt that Weizmann would think he had lied to him; he told Clark Clifford Weizmann must think him a "shitass," and asked Clifford to find out "how this could have happened." His opinion of his State Department was at a very low level, even though he had been shown earlier, and approved, the gist of Austin's speech.[15] Clifford, unlike Truman, felt that Marshall was to blame. "Marshall," he said later, "didn't know his ass from a hole in the ground. Marshall left every one of those who had done this thing to the President in power. Not a hair singed…. But every Jew thought that Truman was a no good son-of-a-bitch."[16] Dean Rusk, one of the State Department members of the UN delegation in New York, said that he "was the hapless official who met with the press to represent the administration" after Austin's speech "exploded like a bomb and raised hell with the Zionists." At Rusk's press conference, "the atmosphere was so thick you could cut it with a knife. I have never seen such an emotionally charged press conference."[17]

On March 22, however, a couple of days later, Bob Lovett prepared and sent up from Florida a statement to be passed on to Marshall. In the statement, Lovett said that Clark Clifford had just called him in Hobe Sound and said the president "had never approved " Austin's speech. Lovett was surprised; he pointed out that Austin's speech, with the recommendation for trusteeship, had been given to Clifford on March 6 to be turned over to the president, and that same day Truman had told Lovett that he had received it and would read it. Marshall and Lovett then met with the president on the morning of March 8, with Lovett telling him that a March 5 resolution Austin had presented to the Security Council calling for acceptance of the partition recommendation had been rejected. Lovett went on: "I said that we would have to have an alternative and that was the trusteeship proposal contained in the latter part of [Austin's] draft statement. The president said we were to go through and attempt to get approval of the [partition] resolution but if we did not get it we could take the alternative step." Lovett continued, "*That was perfectly clear. He said it to General Marshall and to me…. There is absolutely no question but what the President approved it. There was a definite clearance there.*"[18]

On that same March 22 Truman met with George Marshall and "said that the reason he was so much exercised in the matter was the fact that Austin made his statement without the President having been advised that he was going to make it at that particular time." Truman allowed that "he had agreed to the statement but said that if he had known when it was going to be made he could have taken certain measures to have avoided the political blast of the press." On March 25 the president put forth a statement supporting Austin's speech, not as a substitution for partition but to fill the vacuum to be created by the ending of the mandate.[19] On March 29 Lovett had been much pleased to find his face (the work of artist Ernest Hamlin Baker) once more on the cover of *Time* magazine, with a lengthy article inside, "New Policy, New Broom," detailing Lovett's work in the State Department. It ended with these words: "The prospects for success that Bob Lovett could see were neither completely reassuring nor completely depressing. They would be considerably more reassuring when U.S. policy had matured beyond the stage of crisis statesmanship. They would also be more reassuring when the U.S. Government had more men like Lovett himself to keep it clicking."[20]

In Palestine efforts were afoot to negotiate a truce—to shut down the increasing violence between Arabs and Jews (and Britons)—but a truce had little possibility of succeeding, as both Jews and Arabs were against it. This effort was partially inspired by the fact that the Jews appeared to be failing in the fighting and the fear that American armed intervention to save the Jews would be called for, a possibility that Truman and the State Department were heartily against.

Through April there were various discussions and proposals going on at the United Nations relative to possible trusteeship or other options in Palestine, but mostly they appeared to be maneuvering for positions relative to one side or the other. Dean Rusk took the lead position for the American delegation, which held its own along with the Brits and the Soviets. Of course, at the same time, there was continued fighting between the Jews and Arabs in Palestine itself. And Bob Lovett had a series of appointments to take care of a dental problem, while Secretary Marshall was at a lengthy conference of Inter-American states in Bogotá, Colombia. In the meantime, the days were passing away until the May 15 date the British had set as the termination of their mandate of Palestine. Just what was going to happen at that time was still undetermined, and it was a subject of dispute between Harry Truman and the State Department.

Loy Henderson in the State Department suggested, and Lovett approved, that Judah Magnes, head of a small group called Ihud, be invited to visit the United States. Magnes's group was committed to a binational Palestine, and he had supported the plan for a truce and a trusteeship. He was considered one of the few Jews in Palestine with whom the Arab leaders would deal. Henderson and Lovett both wrote letters to Magnes, who was old and in ill health (with but seven months to live) but agreed to come. Accompanied by his wife and his physician, Magnes arrived in New York on April 26. A call was made to Lovett, who said he would like to see Magnes but in his state of health he should talk with Rusk up there. Then a decision could be made if Magnes could make it to Washington.

On April 27–28, there was some good news—the Jews and Arabs had agreed to accept a truce in the Walled City of Jerusalem, where a number of holy places were situated. Later on the 28th, Lovett got a phone call from Senator Millard Tydings (D–Md), who asked if the State Department was trying to do something to meet the situation that would prevail when the British withdrew from Palestine. Lovett said, "We were beating our brains out on it." Tydings said he personally would be willing, assuming there was an Arab serving as boss in Palestine, to offer a bill to the Senate that the U.S. would buy a part of the territory for the Jews. Lovett said "whoa," as there had already come into being a trusteeship of the Walled City and it was important that U.S. hold off on any further statements that could only disturb the situation.[21]

On May 3, as instructed by Bob Lovett, Dean Rusk proposed at the UN, as an emergency measure, a ten-day cease-fire order and truce to begin May 5, with a party to fly from New York to undertake negotiations on the spot in Palestine. It was hoped, as Lovett directed, the cease-fire "will permit the parties to agree upon a truce for a further period during which the fighting can be stopped and negotiations for final political settlement can take place under conditions of greater calm."[22] Initially, Rusk said, it was favorably received by both Jews and Arabs—in New York. The next morning, though, Rusk called Lovett with the word that Moshe Shertok, head of the Jewish Agency's political department, had turned down the ten-day offer because it was "too spectacular" and it would throw on them a moral responsibility they were not prepared to accept (Lovett told Rusk he thought "we should let them stew in their own juice for a while"). Meanwhile, Judah Magnes met with President Truman for a half-hour on May 6. Nothing came of the meeting. As time ran down to the end of the British mandate, Harry Truman was having difficulty with his secretary of state. On May 7 Clark Clifford met with the president and delivered a draft of a statement he thought Truman might read at his next scheduled press conference on the 13th of May. Clifford had already set forth his basic argument on May 4, as follows:

1. Recognition is consistent with U.S. policy from the beginning.
2. A separate Jewish state is inevitable. It will be set up shortly.
3. As far as Russia is concerned we would do better to indicate recognition.
4. We must recognize inevitably. Why not now.
5. State Department resolution doesn't stop partition.[23]

Clifford's draft said that the U.S. would recognize the Jewish state as soon as it came into existence (at the termination of the mandate). The president agreed with that position but said he would speak to Secretary Marshall first. He phoned Marshall, and the secretary strenuously opposed recognition. Truman told Marshall he wanted to have a meeting to discuss the subject, a meeting he scheduled for May 12, three days before the expiration of the mandate. After hanging up the phone, the president told Clifford he would be called upon in that meeting to argue the case for recognition. "You know how I feel," Truman said. "I want you to present it just as though you were making an argument before the Supreme Court of the United States. Consider it carefully, Clark, organize it logically. I want you to be as persuasive as you possibly can be."[24]

And so, at 4 o'clock on May 12, the gathering Truman had mentioned to Marshall a few days earlier took place. Those present from the State Department on a hot and sweltering afternoon were Marshall and Lovett to the president's left, and two others, Fraser Wilkins of the Near East Agency and Robert McClintock from the UN office behind them. Just before the meeting, Lovett had decided that the presence of Dean Rusk and Loy Henderson, both of whom had been involved in the Palestine maneuverings all along and were considered pro–Arab, might be too inflammatory, so he had Wilkins and McClintock in their place. The president had sitting to his right Clifford, David Niles, a White House aide strongly committed to the Jewish cause, and Matthew Connelly, his appointments secretary. Truman said he had called the meeting because he was seriously concerned as to what might happen in Palestine after May 15.[25] Clifford later called this "of all the meetings I ever had with Presidents ... the most vivid," pitting him "against a legendary war hero whom President Truman revered but ... over an issue of fundamental and enduring national security importance—Israel and the Mideast."[26]

Marshall and Lovett presented a "Memorandum for the President," a two-page document setting forth the basics of the State Department position attempting to obtain a truce in Palestine, secure a UN commissioner for the territory, establish a Temporary United Nations Trusteeship for Jerusalem, and support the November 29, 1947, resolution.[27] Robert Lovett started things off with "a lengthy exposition of recent events bearing on the Palestine problem," including well-armed Arab Legion forces ready to strike and a meager Haganah army for the Jewish forces. He described a meeting the previous Saturday that he and Marshall had attended with Moshe Shertok of the Jewish Agency in which Shertok said that King Abdullah of Transjordan might enter the Arab portions of Palestine but would not seek to penetrate the Jewish areas. Shertok said also that a deal might be possible between Abdullah and the Jewish Agency whereby the king would take over the Arab portion of Palestine and leave the Jews in possession of the rest. This intelligence, Lovett went on, had caused an abrupt shift in the position of the Jewish Agency, and they were now confident "on the basis of recent military successes and the prospect of a 'behind the barn' deal with Abdullah, that they could establish their sovereign state without any necessity for a truce with the Arabs of Palestine."

At this point Marshall intervened to recall that he had then told Shertok "it was extremely dangerous to base long-range policy on temporary military success." Marshall told Shertok "that they were taking a gamble." Should the tide turn against them "and they came running to us for help they should be placed clearly on notice now that there was no warrant to expect help from the United States, which had warned them of the grave risk which they were running."[28] Lovett then resumed his summary, reading a telegram just received from New York stating that while the British were prepared to support the proposed U.S. resolution on a truce they hoped we would give further consideration to the possibility of a commission being set up by the UN "to deal with the administration of Palestine, this commission to be made up of Belgium, France and the United States." It was generally agreed by the group that the Brits had played "a lamentable, if not altogether duplicitous, role in the Palestine situation" and that their last-minute "indications of a change of heart could have no effect upon our policy." Marshall then concluded the State Department presentation by saying "the United States ... should continue supporting U.N. trusteeship resolutions and defer any decision on recognition."[29]

Truman then called upon Clark Clifford "to make a statement." Clifford started off his twenty-minute talk with his objection to the U.S. support of the continued efforts of the UN Security Council to secure a truce in Palestine. "He said this reference was unrealistic since there had been no truce and probably would not be one," despite efforts since March. Instead, he said, the actual partition of Palestine had taken place "without the use of outside force." Clifford went on to urge the president "to give prompt recognition to the Jewish State immediately after the termination of the mandate on May 15," a move that should be taken quickly, before the Soviets could recognize the new state. "It would have distinct value in restoring the President's position for support of the partition of Palestine." Finally, Clifford went on, the president at his May 13 press conference should state his intention to recognize the Jewish State and his direction to the secretary of state to have our UN delegation urge early recognition of the new state by other members of the UN.[30]

"I had noticed Marshall's face reddening with suppressed anger as I talked," Clifford recalled. "When I finished, he exploded. 'Mr. President, I thought this meeting was called to consider an important and complicated problem in foreign policy. I don't even know why Clifford is here. He is a domestic adviser, and this is a foreign-policy matter." Truman calmly replied, "Well, General, he's here because I asked him to be here." Marshall angrily shot back, "These considerations have nothing to do with the issue. I fear that the only reason Clifford is here is that he is pressing a political consideration with regard to this issue. I don't think politics should play any part in this."[31]

Lovett came back with the rebuttal to Clifford's points. First, the United States and the Security Council were still working on a truce and it would be most unbecoming for the U.S. by its unilateral action to get the Security Council to drop this matter. Upon recognition, Lovett said "that it would be highly injurious to the United Nations to announce the recognition of the Jewish State even before it had come into existence and while the General Assembly … was still considering the question of the future government of Palestine." He believed "such a move would be injurious to the prestige of the President. It was a very transparent attempt to win the Jewish vote but, in Mr. Lovett's opinion, it would lose more votes than it would gain." And finally, Lovett said, "To recognize the Jewish State prematurely would be buying a pig in a poke. How did we know what kind of Jewish State would be set up?" He then read excerpts from intelligence telegrams and reports regarding Russian activity in sending Jews and Communist agents into Palestine. He also failed to see any particular urgency in rushing to recognize the Jewish State ahead of the Soviets. Clifford later said "no evidence ever turned up to support" Soviet activity in the area. "In fact, Jews were fleeing communism throughout Eastern Europe at that very moment."[32]

George Marshall, in what Clifford called "a righteous, goddamned Baptist tone," then told Truman that he believed "the suggestions made by Mr. Clifford were wrong" and adopting "these suggestions would have precisely the opposite effect from that intended by Mr. Clifford. The transparent dodge to win a few votes would not in fact achieve this purpose. The great dignity of the office of the President would be seriously diminished. The counsel offered by Mr. Clifford was based on domestic political considerations, while the problem which confronted us was international. I said bluntly that if the President were to follow Mr. Clifford's advice and if in the elections I were to vote, I would vote against the President."[33] As the shock of Marshall's statement swept the room, stunning everyone there, the president abruptly called the meeting to a close, saying, "I understand your position, General, and I'm inclined to side with you in this matter." Marshall, Clifford noted, "did not even glance at me as he and Lovett left." After the others had left, Truman told Clifford, "Well, that was rough as a cob. That was about as tough as it gets. But you did your best."[34]

For Truman, of course, the danger contained in Marshall's statement was immense. His chances of reelection that November, already considered scant, would almost certainly disappear altogether were Marshall, the most highly regarded member of Truman's team, to resign with a public statement of disagreement. In addition, such a development might endanger the then-forming Western Alliance. Bob Lovett, too, realized that Marshall's threat, if carried out and combined with a resignation, could be extremely damaging. He took it upon himself to call Clifford later, saying, "I have been deeply disturbed ever since the meeting in the President's office this afternoon. It would be a great tragedy if these two men were to break over this issue." Lovett asked Clifford to stop by his house for a drink on the way home "to talk … more about this." Clifford stopped at the Lovetts' house in the Kalorama area, went into the library with him, and had a bourbon and branch water, while Bob Lovett, always worried about his innards, had a sherry.[35]

Lovett opened by saying that a break between Truman and Marshall at that point would be catastrophic, given the state of the Cold War. "Do you think," he went on, "that if you were to present some modification of State's views to the President as something he could live with, he might be persuaded to modify his position and work something out with General Marshall that would get us past this crisis—at least past the next two days?" Clifford responded: "Bob, there is no chance whatsoever that the President will change his mind on the basic issue…. He wants to recognize the new state. So all I can say is that if anyone is going to give, it is going to have to be General Marshall, because—I can tell you now—the President is not going to give an inch." It was essential, Clifford thought, to turn the pressure back on Marshall, "and Lovett was the only channel through which to do it." "Well, then," said Lovett, thoughtfully, "let's see what can be done at State."[36]

Clifford reported to Truman the next morning, and the president said, "Okay, this is part of the process of letting the dust settle. Keep encouraging Lovett to work on the General." When Truman was asked at his press conference on May 13 what he planned to do about the new Jewish state, he answered simply, "I will cross that bridge when I get to it."[37] Over the next couple of days, Lovett and Clifford worked together toward the creation of agreement between the White House and the State Department on the recognition question after Clifford had made it clear this was the course on which Truman had settled. When Lovett suggested de facto rather than de jure recognition, Clifford felt that this was an area where a compromise could be made. Lovett took it upon himself to convince Marshall that recognition had been decided upon and that the secretary should not oppose it in any public manner. Clifford felt "Lovett was the moving force that caused the change toward the White House position. I believe he persuaded Marshall to alter his attitude." Lovett later denied that he was the "moving force" but just one of a number of advisors consulted by Marshall, although this seems to be just a bit of modesty on Lovett's part.[38]

On Friday, May 14, Clifford and Lovett lunched together at the 1925 F Street Club, after which Clifford told him "the President was under unbearable pressure to recognize the Jewish state promptly." He reviewed the arguments Lovett and Marshall had made at the May 12 meeting and said both the President and he were impressed by the facts set forth. But, he went on, "at six o'clock Friday night there would be no government or authority of any kind in Palestine. Title would be lying about for anybody to seize and a number of people had advised the President that this should not be permitted. The President had decided to do something about recognizing the new state if it was set up but that he would agree to wait until the request had been made and until there was some definition of boundaries." What Lovett did not know, of course, was that at ten o'clock that morning Clifford had arranged with a representative of the Jewish Agency to submit to Truman a request for recognition as soon as the British mandate expired, at 6:00 p.m. Washington time. Clifford went on to ask Lovett to have the State Department "recommend language to put into effect recognition in the event the President decided upon it." He said they had been informed that an appeal would be made for immediate recognition by the new state, which proposed to live within the conditions (and borders) of the General Assembly resolution.

Lovett told him there was no legal bar to recognition, but "indecent haste in recognizing the state would be very unfortunate for some of the reasons I had mentioned on Wednesday. I therefore urged the President to delay action for a day or so until we could confirm the details of the proclamation." Clifford said he was sure there would be adequate details of the provisional government, and the timing of the recognition was "of the greatest possible importance to the President from a domestic point of view." Lovett "emphasized especially the tremendous reaction which would take place in the Arab world ... [and said] that we might lose the effects of many years of hard work in the Middle East with the Arabs." They then discussed notifications to Senator Austin at the UN and the British, French, and Belgian governments in advance.[39] Clifford marveled that, "with time literally slipping away, Lovett and I functioned in a kind of never-never land; while we calmly and professionally discussed technical aspects of the decision, we continued to disagree profoundly as to whether or not the decision should be made at all. Lovett's ability to function effectively on such murky terrain was one reason I respected him so much."[40]

Lovett and Clifford continued telephone conversations during the rest of the afternoon. At about 4 o'clock, Lovett called and said, "Clark, I think we have something we can work with. I have talked with the General. He cannot support the President's position, but he has agreed that he will not oppose it." Clifford was thrilled, thanked Lovett for his efforts, and asked him to get Marshall to call the president. Lovett himself confirmed Marshall's position directly with Truman a few minutes later.[41] The language to be used in the White House release was arrived at in the middle of the afternoon. At about 5:30 Lovett called Clifford and told him the UN General Assembly was in session and would probably work until around ten o'clock that night. Could the announcement of recognition be delayed until after the General Assembly closed down? Clifford said again that "time was terribly important" but he would discuss it with the president. At about 5:40 Clifford told him that Truman would make his announcement shortly after six o'clock and that it was all right to call Senator Austin and fill him in, which Dean Rusk promptly did. Austin had to leave the floor of the assembly to take Rusk's call, and "he made a personal decision not to return to the Assembly or to inform other members of our Delegation—he simply went home," to indicate to the General Assembly that this was an act of the president the U.S. delegation had nothing to do with.[42]

Robert Lovett, in his memorandum of the afternoon with Clifford, left out the long arguments back and forth. "My protests against the precipitate action and warnings as to consequences with the Arab world appear to have been outweighed by considerations unknown to me." "I can only conclude," he summed up, "that the President's political advisers, having failed last Wednesday afternoon to make the President a father of the new state, have determined at least to make him the midwife."[43] At 6:11 p.m. on May 14 Harry Truman made his announcement. "This Government has been informed that a Jewish state has been proclaimed in Palestine, and recognition has been requested by the provisional government thereof," Truman's statement read. "The United States recognizes the provisional government as the *de facto* authority of the new State of Israel."[44]

Lovett, Clifford later wrote, "never told me exactly what had passed between him and

Marshall in those last two days. From his general comments I concluded that Lovett had finally sat down alone with Marshall on Friday and said, in effect, that, having argued their position, they had an obligation to accept the President's policy or resign." Clifford went on: "These events did nothing to impair my relations with Lovett. In fact, the curious combination of disagreement over substance and collaboration to solve the crisis had forged stronger and closer bonds between us. At the beginning of 1949, just before he left the government and returned to New York, we exchanged personal letters. In his, he wrote, 'One of the happiest recollections of my tour of duty down here is the basis on which we worked on our common problems, and I am grateful to you beyond words for the understanding and help you always gave me.'" Clifford added, "I certainly felt the same way."[45]

At 6:30 that day, Lovett called Forrestal to advise him of the recognition of the new state of Israel. Lovett "said he expected severe fighting would ensue but that the Jewish Army ... could probably take care of themselves"—and they did.[46] Truman was careful, in his workings on the Palestine problem, to keep on good terms with Marshall, "whom he so admired," and Lovett, "who had been as successful in cultivating the president as he had with members of Congress." Indeed, Truman "found the prospect of conflict with either man politically and emotionally intolerable." His relations with other State Department personnel were not so satisfactory. Later, when Bob Lovett had a chance to talk with the president after the recognition, he referred to the second or third echelon of the State Department and said, "They almost put it over on you."[47]

Two days after recognition of Israel, Senator Austin reported to the State Department the general feeling at the UN that the United States, by its immediate recognition of Israel, had endorsed the Jewish undermining of the truce efforts and violated the terms of the Security Council truce resolution—just as Lovett had said immediate recognition would do. Those delegations that had collaborated most closely with the American delegation felt deeply offended—"double-crossed." Austin said the action had "deeply undermined the confidence of other delegations in our integrity."[48] Rusk later wrote the following in a letter: "I cannot vouch for this, but there was a story later that some of Secretary Marshall's friends had told him that he ought to resign because of this incident. He ... replied, 'No, gentlemen, you do not accept a post of this sort and then resign when the man who has the Constitutional authority to make a decision makes one. You may resign at any time for any other reason but not that one.'"[49]

Nevertheless, the United States had duly recognized the new state of Israel, with whatever consequences this action should result in over the years ahead.

19

On to Berlin ... By Air

With recognition of the new state of Israel now behind them, the officials of the State Department showed up for work on May 15. Not unexpectedly, most of what confronted them that morning was concerned with what had happened the day before. At 8:55 a.m. Clark Clifford phoned Robert Lovett to tell him of the disagreeable reception at the United Nations of the American recognition announcement. Lovett said "we would just have to get thru it." Later that day Lovett had discussions with Clifford, Eliahu Epstein (formerly of the Jewish Agency, now representing the State of Israel), and Chip Bohlen, about UN hearings on Palestine, the arms embargo, and the exchange of diplomatic representatives. Lovett called Charlie Ross, the president's press representative, about a press report on the arms embargo. Ross had said the question was under study; Lovett said he thought Ross should say that it had been under continuing study for a long time and that there was nothing new. Ross agreed with that.

On the morning of May 17. 1948, Lovett spoke with General Alfred M. Gruenther, director of the Joint Chiefs of Staff. Lovett was to go before the Senate Foreign Relations Committee the following day to discuss the Western European Union, its importance from the point of view of national security, and the ongoing London Conference on Germany. The union was a result of the Treaty of Brussels, signed March 17 by Great Britain, France, Belgium, the Netherlands, and Luxembourg. Gruenther agreed to put something military together for Lovett to use, which he did.

The French, however, were not pleased with the workings of the London Conference, in which talk of a government for West Germany was moving ahead. Lewis Douglas reported to Bob Lovett from London on the French reaction. Lovett got together with French Ambassador Henri Bonnet, to set him straight. France, he said, was unlikely to get any American help if she wrecked the talks in London. Congress was not happy with paying more than a billion dollars for the support of British and French troops in Germany when that money could be better spent on British and French economic recovery. "The German burden," he went on, "must be taken off our backs and the Germans made self-supporting. We were determined that Germany should not again become a menace but felt that if it did not become self-supporting it would become a cesspool into which all the evil of Europe could flow and which the Russians could easily take over," which the French surely did not want.[1]

Lovett heard that afternoon, and passed on to Epstein, the word that an Egyptian plane had been shot down bombing Tel Aviv, with the Egyptian officer being captured. With Egypt, Transjordan, Syria, Lebanon, and Iraq all invading Israel with their armies upon the end of the British mandate, the war had broken out for real in the Middle East. The

Secretary-General of the Arab League, Azzam Pasha, declared, "It will be a war of annihilation. It will be a momentous massacre in history that will be talked about like the massacres of the Mongols or the Crusades." Unfortunately for Azzam Pasha, the Israelis made sure that it came out nothing like that.

Another matter in which Robert Lovett was slightly involved was called Operation Bloodstone. Truman and Marshall by the summer of 1948 had assigned responsibility for oversight of all peacetime clandestine operations to George Kennan. Kennan and his Policy Planning Staff had come up with a framework for such operations against the Soviets, a program that utilized former relatively high-level Nazis and Nazi collaborators to work undercover behind the Iron Curtain. Lovett gathered together political warfare specialists in Kennan's PPS and the Office of the Assistant Secretary of State for Occupied Areas to organize things, and Frank Wisner (former head of the OSS in southeastern Europe and at this time high in the CIA) won approval of the program by the National Security Council and the State, Army, Navy, Air Force Coordinating Committee (SANACC). SANACC formally approved the operation on June 10, 1948, and in the same month the NSC had given it the go-ahead. Lovett directed Chip Bohlen to discuss Bloodstone secretly with influential congressmen so that they would be forewarned should the entry of an undesirable alien be revealed. Otherwise, Lovett's participation in the Bloodstone program, which was carried on in the State Department until 1950, appears to have been minimal.[2]

On a totally different subject, on May 18, columnist Dorothy Thompson called Lovett from New York, saying she was disturbed about Henry Wallace's "open letter" to Josef Stalin, a letter Wallace had read during a Madison Square Garden speech on the night of May 11 as a part of his third-party campaign for the presidency, announced the prior December 29. Wallace in his letter called for a series of "definite, decisive steps" to end the Cold War. He also added a few lines about an exchange during the previous few days between Soviet foreign minister Molotov and U.S. ambassador Walter Bedell Smith in Moscow. Ms. Thompson felt that the inclusion of Molotov's very recent response indicated that Wallace was in communication and collusion with the Soviets in preparation of his "open letter." It all seemed to boil down to when the letter was printed for 20,000 handouts for the Madison Square Garden crowd.[3]

A few minutes later Lovett talked with Attorney General Tom Clark, urging him to get J. Edgar Hoover and the FBI into the matter to find out when the copies of the speech were printed; if they were printed prior to Molotov's answer to Smith in Moscow, that could put an end to the whole Wallace business. Clark said that Truman had asked him to look into it as well. Unfortunately for Dorothy Thompson and Harry Truman, the State Department's investigation turned up very little, because the FBI said that 20,000 papers could be printed in three to four hours. It was, of course, not to be the last involvement of Bob Lovett and the State Department in the 1948 presidential election.

Another Israeli problem soon cropped up when the president invited Dr. Chaim Weizmann, Israel's chief of state, to dinner. The day before Weizmann was to arrive, on May 24, Marshall sat down with Truman and went over the risks inherent in the situation, given the lack of de jure recognition of Israel. Marshall "emphasized the tragic results which might well follow any action not carefully considered, its devastating results to him, not to mention the situation in the Middle East." He felt "the only protection" he could see against such unconsidered acts "was a very careful maintenance of a relationship" between Clifford and Lovett, "so that no action be taken that had not been either cleared by the State Department or the conditions implied explained for the President's information." Truman agreed.[4]

Marshall notified Lovett of the problems, and Lovett called Clifford and told him the invitation had gotten the U.S. into trouble. If Truman had invited Weizmann as a personal friend, that would be one thing, but if he invited him as head of state then Truman had recognized the state de jure and "we have made asses of ourselves." Lovett asked Clifford to get the exact facts, because State did not choose at that time to recognize Israel de jure. Matt Connelly called back and said Truman had instructed David Niles to get in touch with Weizmann to see if he would like to come down to Washington (from New York) before he headed home. Weizmann said it would be a great honor. Lovett told Connelly that it was necessary that Truman put it on a personal basis and that Weizmann be put up overnight at Blair House, not the White House. When Weizmann arrived in Washington he saw Pennsylvania Avenue adorned with flags of both the United States and Israel as he headed toward his "personal meeting" with Truman. As Lovett noted, the White House had gotten into a mess over the question because no one had checked with the State Department.

At the same time, Paul Hoffman got in touch with Lovett, because he had heard that Congressman Taber and his House Appropriations Committee were to cut a billion dollars from the ECA budget. Lovett told him to see Taber, after which Hoffman told him Taber had said a 20 percent cut would be made. Lovett said a fight against such a cut must be made on the floor of the House: "If such a cut goes into effect it would ruin a lot of hard-won territory we have fought for for over a year, would play right into the hands of the Soviets, who have claimed all along that this would happen."[5] The next day Bob Lovett called Congressman Charles Eaton, alerting him to the disastrous cuts Taber was pushing. Eaton assured him that he would do everything he could to fight off the ERP cut in the House.

On June 4 Lovett called Arthur Vandenberg and discussed at length the proposed cuts in the funds for Europe; he said they had gotten many press and radio reports from abroad about the cuts, which might be helpful in fighting them. Vandenberg suggested sending them over to Everett Dirksen (R–Ill) in the House. A couple of days later Lovett passed on to Vandenberg's office messages that had come in first from London and then from Paris indicating that the British and French leaders were severely shaken by the House action in reducing ERP funding, predicting that far-reaching social and political repercussions would result. On June 9 Vandenberg appeared before the Senate Appropriations Committee, made what was termed "a terrific appearance," and ultimately had the Senate approve the original appropriation. Speaker Joe Martin was also upset about the ECA funds cut, and he went to work on it in the House. In the conference the House Appropriations Committee held firm briefly but eventually agreed to the Senate version.[6]

Another issue came up, that being the selection of a special representative to Israel. Lovett and Forrestal kicked some names around, with Lovett suggesting that someone with a background in intelligence would be a good choice or a career foreign service officer. While the two of them were discussing the matter, in mid-afternoon of June 22 Lovett got a phone call from Clark Clifford that the president had selected James Grover McDonald for the job and wanted the announcement made that day. An astonished Bob Lovett asked whether Mr. Truman had considered the fact that McDonald was a confirmed Zionist "and the repercussions which this would have on the Truce Commission's work." Clifford said he was sure Truman had considered it, and he wanted action on it at once.[7] Lovett pointed out that it would be difficult to make the announcement that day because the Israeli government had to agree to it. The president said to contact Epstein in Washington on behalf of Israel. When Epstein responded that he had the authority to accept the appointment for his government the matter was concluded and the announcement made. In the meantime, Marshall had written a personal letter to the president, objecting strongly to the way the McDonald appointment had been made, without his "having an opportunity to investigate the fellow or at least talk to the President about it." Lovett delayed delivery of the letter, went to see the secretary in the hospital on the 24th, and found him "pretty hot about it"— not about the individual "but only the principle involved" in the appointment process. With an hour's conversation Lovett managed to talk Marshall out of sending the letter; the secretary agreed to talk it over with Truman at his upcoming regular appointment. With that problem resolved, Lovett, as acting secretary of state, made sure to meet with McDonald on the afternoon of June 25, before the new appointee headed off to Israel.[8]

In the meantime, another and far more dangerous problem had arisen. As noted previously, the British and American zones in occupied Germany had been combined into what was called Bizonia, and this had been finally joined by the French in what was to become Trizonia. The Russians, of course, were not pleased by these developments. On the 25th of March they had imposed restrictions on railroad and highway imports into West Berlin (the three Allied-occupied sectors), to begin on April 1. On the following day, General Lucius Clay, the American military commander, directed that West Berlin be supplied by air. Clay also wired Omar Bradley, the army chief of staff, that he would "instruct our guards to open fire if Soviet soldiers attempt to enter our trains." Bradley's reaction to this message was that "had I enough hair on my head to react, this cable would probably have stood it on end." A series of hasty, informal meetings of Forrestal, Lovett, army secretary Royall, Dwight Eisenhower, and the Joint Chiefs resulted in a cable to Clay ordering him to use restraint, "and under no circumstances to fire on the Russians unless they fired first." The crisis was gathering steam, though the Soviets relaxed some restrictions in response to tough U.S. diplomatic notes.[9]

The Reichsmark, Germany's currency, had been systematically debased by the Soviets, and so on June 18 the United States and the British announced a new Deutsche Mark to be introduced on June 21. The Russians refused to allow it as legal tender in Berlin, but the Allies had already brought 250,000,000 Deutsche Marks into the city and it was soon the accepted currency throughout Berlin. The Soviets continually took steps or issued statements that were designed to make the Western allies' occupation of three-quarters of Berlin questionable, but there was on the part of the Allies no thought of leaving. As far back as mid–January Lovett had made it clear at a press conference that "the American policy is to remain in Berlin in charge of our obligations." This was in response to what a reporter described as "the recent Soviet press campaign against continued four-Power occupation of the former German capital."[10] The Russians all along felt that they were entitled to Berlin. They had captured the city on May 2, 1945, the American army not arriving until July 3. Of course, it was estimated that there had been one million rapes in the city committed by the Soviet troopers before the Americans got there, and the Russians had removed some 3,500 factories and 1,115,000 pieces of industrial equipment for shipment to the USSR. It was their idea to keep Germany weak, having been engaged in two wars with the Germans in 31 years.

The day after the announcement of the new Deutsche Mark, June 19, the Soviets began again a gradual stoppage of train and auto traffic into Berlin, and on the 21st they halted an American military supply train and forced it back to western Germany. On the 24th the Russians cut off all land and water connections from the non–Soviet zones of Germany to Berlin. Soon, the air corridors to Berlin were the only routes open, despite the Allies' protests. That morning, with the news in from Berlin, Charles Bohlen presided over a lengthy conference between army and State Department officials to consider the situation. They agreed that, for the time being, inquiries from the press should be answered with the phrase "no comment." Bohlen then checked this out with Bob Lovett, who confirmed this view and felt that the army should also be advised of it.

At this time, the sectors of West Berlin had on hand about 36 days' worth of food and some 45 days' worth of coal, with over 2.1 million people to feed and keep warm. There was no possibility of a military response to the Soviet moves: against the one-and-a-half million Soviet troops in the sector surrounding the city the U.S. had approximately 31,000 combat troops in West Germany. The three Allied countries had in western Berlin about 22,000 troops. As Robert Lovett said, "all the Russians need" to overrun American forces in Germany "is shoes." As Lovett put it at the time, the heads of the Soviet leaders were "full of bubbles," and American firmness had to be coupled with caution.[11] When General Clay suggested pushing either an armored train or an armored column through to Berlin, Lovett reacted immediately, using "strong adjectives in telling Secretary Marshall that the idea was absurd," as he later related to Philip Jessup of the State Department. "As an experienced railroad man … Lovett pointed out that if you sent an armored train, all the Russians had to do was to pull up a stretch of track in front of the train and then make a similar gap behind the train," Jessup wrote in notes for a book that was never completed. "If you sent an armored column down the autobahn," Lovett went on for Jessup, "it would undoubtedly come to a spot where, as Bedell Smith suggested, the Russians would have quickly put up red flags and signs announcing that this was an artillery range; their guns would be firing across the road and if the American column started to force its way through, it meant war. Lovett would have none of it and Marshall agreed with him."[12]

There were, as had been agreed in November 1945, three 20-mile-wide air corridors, from the three West Germany zones, providing aviation access to Berlin. It came time for General Clay to work out with General Curtis LeMay, commander of U.S. Air Forces in Europe, how to support the sizable population of West Berlin. Bob Lovett was happy to work with Lucius Clay, whom he had gotten to know well during the war. "I was very much impressed by him, not only his ability but his character," Lovett remembered. "He was a very straightforward, upright man." As to Berlin, Clay "was one of the first people who came to my mind when we were talking about putting someone in charge of Berlin, because he had, I thought, and I think most people thought, the ideal qualities to deal with both the Russians and the Germans. He was sure of himself, he was politic, he was very correct in his treatment of them and just as hard as nickel steel when he reached a conclusion."[13]

It was soon calculated that a minimum daily ration of 1,990 calories was needed from flour and wheat, cereal, fats, meat and fish, potatoes, sugar, coffee, both powdered and whole milk, yeast for baking, dehydrated vegetables, salt, and cheeses. This would come to

1,534 tons each day, along with 3,475 tons of coal and gasoline. American and British planes, it was calculated, could haul in about 700 tons a day, not nearly enough to start out, but it was expected that a substantial increase in available aircraft would take place quickly. Lovett later recalled, in regard to the establishment of an airlift, that "we also had the corridor.... Now, the first question that came up was whether or not we had enough airlift, whether we could lift stuff in, and that was my dish right there, because we had run the China-Burma-India thing [during World War II] by airlifting over the Himalayas." So, on June 25, Clay gave the orders to launch the airlift (presumed to last about three weeks).[14]

Sunday, June 27, saw what General Bradley called "the most important" of "a series of hastily arranged emergency meetings," this one held in Secretary Royall's office from 2:45 in the afternoon to 7:00 in the evening, with Forrestal, Lovett, Bradley, General Lauris Norstad (deputy chief of staff of the air force), navy secretary Sullivan, and a few others from the Pentagon and the State Department. The choices for formulating a national policy on Berlin, as Bradley saw them, were three: "get out; fight; or try to stand on quicksand, hoping for a diplomatic solution or another sudden change in Soviet policy." Clay's policy to "shoot our way into Berlin" was discussed but not approved, but nothing could be settled without decisions and guidance from the president A meeting the next day with Truman was set, as well as the possibility of dispatching additional B-29 squadrons to Germany and England.[15] On Monday, the 28th, Lovett, Forrestal, and Royall met with the president at the White House in an off-the-record discussion of the Berlin situation. When Forrestal asked what the policy was to be—"were we to stay in Berlin or not?"—Lovett began to list various options, one of which included leaving the city. Truman interrupted to say there was "no discussion on that point, we were going to stay period." It was a position the president would hold unchanged throughout the Berlin crisis.[16] Royall asked the president if the consequences had been thought through. "We will have to deal with the situation as it develops," Truman replied. "We are in Berlin by the terms of the [Potsdam] agreement, and the Russians have no right to get us out by either direct or indirect pressure." He also approved the provision to Europe of the B-29s, which of course was an unspoken threat, as the B-29 was the plane to deliver atomic bombs. Accordingly, Lovett cabled to Ambassador Douglas in London that night: "We stay in Berlin."[17]

Later that afternoon Lovett met at Vandenberg's request with the senator to bring him up to date on Berlin. And that evening a telegram was sent off to Douglas in London, setting forth the department's policies. The next day Lovett had a long talk with General Norstad of the air force, going over some questions about the British portion of the airlift as well as the provision of ground crews and where additional aircraft would be coming from. There was some confusion at the moment about air groups, but Lovett believed an airlift was possible and might very well be the best way to answer the Russian blockade.[18] With an airlift in mind, Lovett spoke with General Hoyt Vandenberg, the air chief of staff, and with Royall, "warning them that every type of available load-carrying plane would have to be assembled from all areas of the world and concentrated on the job of supplying Berlin."[19]

On June 30 Lovett had a call from Dwight Eisenhower, who said he was under pressure in New York, where he was now serving as president of Columbia University, to comment to the press about China, Russia, Germany, and practically everything else. He wanted to be sure that what he might say would be helpful rather than harmful. Lovett, who was always on an "Ike and Bob" relationship with the general, said that he would send to him any statements Secretary Marshall had made as well as the general outline of the various situations as expressed by the State Department.

The airlift to Berlin was underway by July 1. With C-54 Skymasters and C-47 Skytrain planes arriving in substantial numbers, the Rhein-Main Air Base outside of Frankfurt and the base at Wiesbaden became the major bases for the flights into Tempelhof Airport in Berlin. A complex timetable for flights was put into effect, with a "ladder" system instituted for planes to fly one thousand feet higher than the flight in front of them, which had taken off four minutes earlier. On July 6 Secretary Marshall met with the Soviet ambassador Alexander Panyushkin and handed him a note setting forth the United States' reaction to the Berlin blockade. The note, which detailed the "extremely serious international situation" the Russians had created, called the move a "clear violation of existing agreements." It stated that "in order that there should be no misunderstanding whatsoever on this point, the United States Government categorically asserts that it is in occupation of its sector of Berlin with free access thereto as a matter of established right deriving from the defeat and surrender of Germany and confirmed by formal agreements among the principal Allies." The note stated that the U.S. "will not be induced by threats, pressures or other actions to abandon these rights," and "hoped that the Soviet Government entertains no doubts whatsoever on this point." Finally, it demanded that "the movement of freight and passenger traffic between the western zones and Berlin be fully restored ... since the needs of the civilian population in the Berlin area are imperative." Marshall's note had been written largely by Senator Vandenberg and Robert Lovett. Vandenberg noted, "Undersecretary Lovett came to my apartment five times in connection with this note." On one final visit, Lovett, the senator wrote in his diary, "brought me an original and partial draft. After much consideration I drew the final form on my own Corona one midnight." There were still a few changes made, but it was presented to the Soviets largely as Vandenberg and Lovett had written it.[20]

On July 22 Truman called a White House meeting of the National Security Council, with Marshall, Lovett, Lucius Clay, Robert Murphy, Chip Bohlen, the Joint Chiefs of Staff, and several Defense Department officials. The question at issue was whether to increase the airlift to circumvent the blockade. The Joint Chiefs raised some objections, noting the limited supply of military transport aircraft and pointing out that "if all of it was assigned to an airlift there would be little left for regular military use and virtually none in the event of war." Bob Lovett was concerned, saying, "It is obvious that the Soviets know that flying weather will be too bad for this operation to continue beyond October.... We should clearly recognize that the airlift is a temporary expedient." Some discussion followed, until the president made his decision to proceed "with the airlift and ordered the Joint Chiefs to provide the planes necessary to make the operation a success," expressing "his absolute determination to stay in Berlin and not be driven out by any form of pressure."[21] At one point in the meeting Lovett asked General Clay "if he thought the Russians might try to block our airplanes with fighter patrols or by other methods." Clay said "the Russians would not attack our planes unless they had made the decision to go to war."[22]

August 13, 1948, became known as "Black Friday," with bad weather, stacking, and pilot mistakes causing the Tempelhof tower to lose control of the situation and endanger all of the flights, several of which crashed. As a result, new rules were put in place that eliminated stacking and improved pilot safety. Maj. Gen. William H. Tunner, commander of the entire American operation, noted that it was from that date that the success of the airlift was worked out. The C-47s were reduced once it was realized it took no longer to unload a 10-ton C-54 than it did a 3.5 ton C-47. And of course the number of available airplanes was increased substantially. At the Berlin airport, the problem Allied air crews faced—lack of ground manpower—was resolved by the replacement of Allied crews with crews made up wholly of local Berliners.

Secretary Marshall set up an informal organization called the Berlin Group, composed of various State Department officials concerned with the crisis in Germany, a group headed by Chip Bohlen. Bohlen "was responsible for instructing our ambassadors overseas and officers in the department on the execution of policy. I reported," Bohlen wrote, "to Under Secretary Lovett and Secretary Marshall." He noted that he frequently "went to the Pentagon in the evenings for teletype exchanges with Berlin." In those long days and nights, Bohlen recalled, "the irrepressible Lovett provided us with welcome breaks in tension. One night, when the subject of Berlin sewers came up, Lovett said with a grin, 'I wish General Clay would realize that our policy is open sewers, openly arrived at.'"[23]

On June 24, the day the Russians halted all rail traffic into Berlin, the Republican Party, meeting in convention in Philadelphia and very confident of a victory in the fall, nominated New York governor Thomas E. Dewey as its candidate for president. Senator Vandenberg, who had himself made a half-hearted effort for the nomination, urged the administration to keep John Foster Dulles, Dewey's chief foreign affairs advisor, fully informed of current foreign policy happenings and developments in an effort to influence Dewey and keep foreign affairs from becoming a nasty part of the campaign. Secretary Marshall considered this to be good advice, and he assigned Bob Lovett, who was of course a Republican though not a politician, the task of briefing Dulles from time to time on the Berlin crisis.[24]

In mid–July Lovett spoke with Sir Oliver Franks, the British ambassador in Washington, telling him that Truman and his administration felt the way to maintain bipartisan support for their policies was to keep up a thoroughly firm attitude toward the Soviets, although they were still anxious to find a peaceful solution to the present impasse. Franks also passed on a message from Bevin in London, considering the arrival of B-29s in England (and their capacity to deliver atomic bombs) to be "highly important."[25]

Meanwhile, Lovett kept up his policy of informing Dulles of what was happening around Berlin and even seeking his advice, as well as keeping in close touch with Senator Vandenberg. And Governor Dewey, though tempted to attack the Democratic foreign policy, decided that such attacks would cause the Russians to feel that the nation was too divided to stand firm in a crisis. After a meeting with Dulles and Vandenberg, Dewey issued a statement: "The present duty of Americans is not to be divided by past lapses, but to unite to surmount present dangers." Harry Truman saw that foreign policy was not to be an issue in the presidential campaign; he could stand firm on Berlin and attack the "Do-Nothing 80th Congress" on domestic issues.[26]

On Labor Day, September 6, Lovett stopped by Jim Forrestal's office, along with generals Bradley and Gruenther, to review the Berlin situation and the hopeless-looking negotiations, especially in light of discussions there with Marshal Sokolovsky, the Russian representative in the city, who had backed away a couple of days before from a position it appeared he had taken earlier. Lovett said that the Soviets, in aiming for the control of Berlin and Germany, had made three errors of judgment: underestimating the determination of the American people, the capacity of the airlift, and the temper of the people of Western Europe. Lovett said he had a "hunch" (Forrestal noted, "He reiterates that it was only a hunch") that the Soviets wanted no agreement, that they would break off negotiations unless the Allies would agree to their terms, which changed frequently.[27]

On September 9 a meeting of the National Security Council discussed at length the failure of negotiations with the Russians on the blockade issues. Marshall and Lovett went over the diplomatic events of the prior month and concluded "that apparently we would have no alternative but to put the case before the United Nations." Lovett noted that the Soviets had stated their intention to hold air maneuvers "in a general area that included the air lanes used by our airlift." To that, "we informed the Russians that we would not halt our air operations."[28]

On September 14 there was a dinner meeting at the home of Philip Graham, publisher of the *Washington Post*, attended by Marshall, Lovett, Bohlen, Forrestal, Dulles, and others, as well as a large group of newspaper publishers and editors, to bring them up to date on the Berlin crisis and the Allied reactions to it. Marshall, Lovett, and Bohlen set forth at some length what had been happening in Berlin (and Moscow) in the previous six weeks, and Forrestal even brought up the question of the A-bomb. The newspapermen were just about unanimous that in the event of a war developing out of the situation the American public would expect the bomb to be used. The next morning publisher Arthur Hays Sulzberger of the *New York Times* called Lovett to tell him that his presentation at Graham's, on what happened to be Lovett's 53rd birthday, was magnificent.[29]

The allies made it clear that they would stay in Berlin and supply the city by air, with no negotiations on any matters until the blockade was lifted and no party was negotiating under duress. West Germany, it was made clear, would not be sacrificed in order to win a settlement for Berlin. As Lovett put it, the Western powers would not yield even if they risked war.[30] In October, as General Clay was requesting more airplanes in order that the airlift could be sustained through the autumn and winter, the Joint Chiefs of Staff prepared papers urging, if the decision to stay in Berlin was to be maintained, that it be determined "whether or not the added risk of war inherent in the Berlin airlift is acceptable" and if so, that "full-out preparations for the early eventuality of war be inaugurated immediately." At a special session of the National Security Council on October 14 the position of the Joint Chiefs was firmly rebutted, with Ken Royall and Bob Lovett leading the way. Lovett pointed out that the July 22 decision of the NSC to stay in Berlin "in any event" had been made with full recognition of all the facts; the Joint Chiefs, Lovett said, seemed to have "a case of the jitters." The Joint Chiefs agreed to withdraw their papers questioning the assignment of the additional aircraft Clay was seeking.[31] Accordingly, on October 22, the president submitted a memorandum to the NSC authorizing (1) up to 66 additional C-54s for the airlift; (2) actions to assure sufficient aviation petroleum to support the airlift; and (3) steps to be taken to ensure adequate personnel and financial support for the operation.[32]

Over the course of the airlift's existence there were occasional efforts to discuss matters with the Soviets, but these efforts always came to an end when the Soviet leaders sought to impose conditions on the ending of the blockade. When the matter of the Berlin blockade was taken up by the United Nations, as submitted by the Western allies, efforts to have the Security Council proceed on positions taken by the General Assembly were naturally met with a Russian veto.

As the airlift continued into the fall, it was ascertained that, with additional coal to be flown in, the total daily amount of cargo had to be increased by about 6,000 tons. The system had to be expanded substantially, and a serious lack of runways became a problem. There were two at Tempelhof and one at Gatow, an airport in the British sector, and these runways were starting to deteriorate from overuse. Additional runways were constructed at both sites, the existing runways were substantially upgraded, and the French, using primarily female laborers, built an airport in its sector, on the shores of Lake Tegel, which was called the Berlin-Tegel Airport. A Ground Controlled Approach radar system was installed at Tempelhof, and, with this in place, all-weather operations were assured. Weather did create problems in November and December, but with improvements in the skies more than 171,000 tons were flown to Berlin in January 1949, 152,000 tons in February, and 196,000 tons in March. The Soviet blockade was thwarted, and the Berlin Airlift was a success. In May of 1949 (well after Robert Lovett was gone from the State Department), the blockade was lifted.

20

More Problems

Although the Berlin blockade and airlift would keep Robert Lovett and his associates at the State Department occupied while they continued, there were other issues that arose from time to time demanding answers and actions, among them the hostilities in Palestine as well as the creation of the North Atlantic Treaty Organization (NATO). All the while, too, the hard-to-imagine campaign for the 1948 presidential election was carried on, with four candidates: Harry Truman, Thomas E. Dewey, Henry Wallace, and Strom Thurmond.

With Dewey's pledge to support a bipartisan foreign policy, it was hoped that the State Department would have little part to play in the election, but there was always a chance for some partisan issue to arise. Indeed, on June 24 Lovett explained to Clark Clifford that he and Chip Bohlen were going over the items on foreign affairs to be included in the platform plank to be adopted by the upcoming Democratic convention in Philadelphia. The Republican platform, Lovett said, stated that a GOP administration would extend prompt, full recognition to the State of Israel. Lovett said he would like to say in the Democratic plank, "This country takes pride in the fact that it was the first to give the State of Israel full recognition and to recognize the Provisional Government as the de facto authority." Clifford agreed that such a sentence would be fine. On July 7 Lovett attended an off-the-record meeting with Harry Truman to help draft the foreign policy plank of the Democratic platform.

It may be noted, as this chapter rolls along, that a recent book about the 1948 election alleges that Robert Lovett met secretly with Republican strategists, giving away bits of knowledge about the Democratic campaign, and even schemed to gain a place in the Republican cabinet to follow. It called him an "inveterate leaker of information to Dewey's foreign-policy brain trust."[1] These allegations ignore the fact that Lovett was directly ordered by the White House and Secretary Marshall to consult with John Foster Dulles and Arthur Vandenberg on foreign affairs for two purposes: first, to maintain the bipartisan nature for both party campaigns to follow, thus keeping foreign policy out of the electoral struggle, and second, as a good-government measure, to keep the Republicans knowledgeable about current foreign policies in the event (considered probable) they should take over the government in January. As to looking for a post in a Dewey administration, Lovett was prepared, if not eager, to go back to Wall Street at the end of Truman's term and not to take on another job in Washington.

There were other problems that arose, problems considered minor compared to those in Berlin and the Near East but that had to be handled before they became major. One such was that of the Netherlands East Indies, also known as Indonesia, which under the leadership of Sukarno was seeking independence after being freed from Japanese occupation.

In October 1947 Frank Graham, the former president of the University of North Carolina, arrived in Indonesia on behalf of a United Nations committee, studied the situation there, and upon returning to the U.S. informed the State Department the Indonesians were demanding unqualified independence and the Dutch were resistant but sure to lose in the long run. Lovett reminded Graham that support by the United States for the Indonesian separatists would undermine the Netherlands government, which the U.S. at that point was trying to bolster, and would weaken our position in Europe.[2]

As time passed, however, and it became clear that the Indonesian separatists would most likely succeed, Lovett reflected the modified American approach when, in a meeting in Washington on September 17, 1948, he informed the Dutch that "Indonesian nationalism must be accommodated in a just and practical way as a condition precedent to dealing with communism in that area." With the changed American position (and threats from members of Congress to cut off Marshall Plan aid), the Dutch ultimately awarded independence to Indonesia in late 1949.[3]

A continuing issue for the State Department was the armed strife in Palestine after the recognition of the State of Israel. On May 15, as the mandate ended and the state of Israel appeared, Egyptian troops invaded the new state from the south, while armies of Iraq and Transjordan from the east and Syria from the north marched in as well. Also involved were the Arab Liberation Army and corps of volunteers from other Arab nations, Saudi Arabia, Lebanon, and Yemen. Coordination among the varied Arabic forces was virtually nonexistent, and progress was limited.

A truce was declared by the United Nations on May 29, to begin on June 11 and to be supervised and overseen by Count Folke Bernadotte, a diplomat and president of the Swedish Red Cross, named on May 20 as a mediator by the UN General Assembly and directed to "assure the safety of the holy places, to safeguard the wellbeing of the population, and to promote a 'peaceful adjustment of the future situation of Palestine,'" a considerable charge, to say the least. The British foreign office felt that the appointment of a mediator meant he was to seek some solution for the conflict other than the partition earlier approved by the UN, and Bernadotte was inclined to accept such an interpretation as well. The initial truce was to last until July 8, the ceasefire to be overseen by army officers from France, Sweden, Belgium, and the United States. Both sides violated the ceasefire, reinforcing their positions and increasing their weaponry despite the arms embargo imposed.

As the truce in Palestine was coming to an end, the Lovetts, along with their son Robin, had a fine dinner on July 10 with Katherine and George Marshall at the Marshalls' home in Leesburg, Virginia. The family dinner was a symbol of the closeness Marshall shared with Bob Lovett, a closeness Marshall's biographer said was "similar to the mental processes of identical twins." Lovett said later, "I was his alter ego. We worked together almost as brothers." Marshall, he said, "never called me anything but Lovett. He would call my wife by her first name, but I never heard him call any of his close friends by their first names. He was military right straight through." It was a relationship that certainly aided the functioning of the State Department—and later the Defense Department.[4]

Late in the afternoon of July 9 Clifford called Lovett to tell him he had heard that Governor Dewey was going to make a statement the following day about the lifting of the arms embargo on Israel. Was there any basic objection to the president's issuing a statement that, subject to the approval of the UN, the U.S. favored the lifting of the arms embargo?

Lovett thought there would be, that the U.S. was trying to have the truce extended and there was some possibility of success because King Abdullah of Transjordan might be broken loose from the rest of the Arab states. The administration could, Lovett suggested, charge Dewey with upsetting the applecart, but the president should not be put in that position. A half-hour later, Lovett, getting back to Clifford, thought a statement could be prepared blistering Dewey for jeopardizing the UN approach, casting it into discord at a most critical time, and acting in a reckless and ill-advised manner. Clifford asked who might release such a statement and suggested Marshall, but Lovett said it would have to be the president or Senator J. Howard McGrath, the Democratic national chairman. Clifford also said it might be a good time to explain to the public just what the arms embargo was, as he found that few people knew much about it. Lovett thought this an excellent suggestion.

On both July 13 and 14, Robert Lovett was consulted on proposed planks in the Democratic platform, particularly the one on the arms embargo as well as one pledging continued economic cooperation with the countries of Latin America.[5] On July 27 he got a call from former commerce secretary Jesse Jones in Houston, telling him that ex-governor Coke R. Stevenson of Texas, who was running for the U.S. Senate, was coming to Washington, and Jones would like to have him briefed on foreign affairs. Could Lovett see him? Lovett said to have Stevenson call when he arrived. On the 29th, Attorney General Tom Clark (a Texan) called Lovett to tell him Stevenson was in town and was coming to see Lovett. He said Stevenson needed the appointment for political purposes, so he could later tell the newspapers that he was up to date on world conditions. Lovett said he had already made the appointment and would carry it through.

That afternoon, Stevenson came and met with Lovett, then told the Texas press that he had done so and went on to the runoff election in the Democratic primary for the Texas Senate seat. A couple of days later, Congressman Lyndon Johnson called, told Lovett he was the one running against Stevenson in Texas, and said Stevenson had made a long public statement about his talk with Lovett for use in his campaign. Johnson wanted to state publicly that he had often talked with both Lovett and Secretary Marshall and had consistently supported their foreign policy. He wanted to say something of that sort to counter Stevenson's talk. Lovett said that was fine and he could do so; he then summarized for Johnson his talk with Stevenson. As matters turned out, Johnson defeated Stevenson by 78 votes in a hotly contested runoff, earning a nickname of "Landslide Lyndon," and going on to a distinguished career in the Senate and later becoming president.

On August 6 Bob Lovett had a phone call with Senator Carl A. Hatch (D-NM), who had written him asking him to make political speeches. Lovett told him he would not, and Hatch agreed that he was absolutely right in refusing. When Lovett mentioned it to the president, Truman told him, "I don't care who telephones you and says that I want you to go out and help Mr. so and so. I will not have the Department of Defense or the Department of State campaigning or taking part in this campaign, and if anybody calls you, refer them to me. Don't answer them yourself, just say, 'I refer you to the President.'"[6]

There was another event in August that attracted much press coverage. A 52-year-old Russian schoolteacher, Oksana Kosenkina, who had been working in the Russian consulate in New York teaching the children of Soviet UN delegates, was desperate to avoid her scheduled return to Russia. She had managed to escape to a farm in upstate New York, run as a haven for White Russian (anti–Communist) refugees by the daughter of the great Russian novelist Count Leo Tolstoy. Unfortunately for Ms. Kosenkina, Consul General Jacob M. Lomakin, in a "cloak-and-dagger" operation, had kidnapped her at the farm and dragged her back to the Russian consulate. At that point, Alexander S. Panyushkin, the Soviet ambassador to the U.S., went to the consulate, on August 7, to urge Ms. Kosenkina to sign an affidavit that she was there of her own free will, was being well treated, and would face no harm upon her return to Russia. She refused to do so. Several days later, on August 12, Ms. Kosenkina managed to reach a window in the consulate and jump out, landing on Sixty-first Street, where she was picked up by New York police and taken to Roosevelt Hospital for treatment of her injuries. The Soviet vice consul had then gone to Ms. Kosenkina's hospital room, but when she saw him she refused to talk to him and he was forced to leave.

On August 14 Panyushkin and an aide arrived for an hour and forty minute meeting with Robert Lovett (the longest that any Russian envoy had spoken to anyone at the State Department since the war). Lovett was joined by Chip Bohlen, who spoke Russian and could help with translation, and Ernest Gross of the department's legal staff. Panyushkin demanded that the woman be turned over forthwith to the Soviets for "protection," that the consul general Lomakin could visit her hospital room (although she did not want to talk to him), and that they could place a 24-hour Soviet guard on her and move her "to whatever place" they chose. Lovett promptly said the United States would not permit any such thing, which would be an infraction of the personal liberty enjoyed in this country. Lovett made it clear to Panyushkin that in this country a person was free to do or go wherever that person wished, within the law, in contrast to the Russian system where every person was at all times under exclusive Soviet order. Ms. Kosenkina, he said, is free to see whomever she wished to see, but the U.S. "has not the right to force her to see anybody, or to put herself under the control of anybody against her will." As a reporter noted, "The mood of the conference was polite, although anything but pleasant." But Oksana Kosenkina was free and remained so, a heroine of a story that received great coverage in the American press.[7]

Back in Palestine, at the close of the ceasefire on July 8, Israel launched a renewed offensive on all three fronts, capturing Nazareth and the lower Galilee area, and thousands of Arab residents fled for their lives. After ten days the UN declared a second truce, on July 18. The Egyptians regularly violated its terms, blocking the passage of supply convoys to Israeli settlements in the northern Negev. When another Egyptian attack began on October 15 it was countered by a planned Israeli action that successfully shattered the Egyptian army and forced it to retreat. On October 22 another truce went into effect.

In the meantime, Count Bernadotte had proposed on June 27 his plan for working out the problems of Palestine, a plan that in almost every regard followed Arab proposals. While George Marshall felt the plan offered a basis for a settlement (and Harry Truman approved this view with a notation on the message the secretary sent him), Israel rejected nearly every part of Bernadotte's proposal. On September 17 Bernadotte was assassinated in Jerusalem by Jewish terrorists, just as the United Nations General Assembly was preparing to examine his plan. Naturally, there were speakers at the UN who felt Bernadotte's plan should be adopted as a memorial to him and recognition for his work. Acting mediator Ralph Bunche (an American) endorsed the plan. On September 21 Secretary Marshall, in Paris, released a statement saying, "The U.S. considers that the conclusions contained in the final report of Count Bernadotte offer a generally fair basis for settlement of the Palestine question."[8] Marshall had cabled his statement to the White House for Truman to see on September 18, but the president was off on his whistle-stop campaigning and most likely never saw it. It is doubtful Truman would have approved it in its entirety, but the statement was now out there and the reactions were fast in arriving. The Jews in the United States were outraged by Marshall's statement, particularly since it approved the transfer of the Negev back to the Arabs, a particularly sore point with Israel.

Eddie Jacobson, Truman's old business partner and a fervent advocate of Israel, joined the campaign train in Oklahoma to talk again with the president. As Jacobson noted, "H.S.T. told us he would not budge from the U.N. decision of November 29th, regardless of what Marshall-Lovett or anyone else said." Truman wrote out a telegraph message to Marshall, pointing out that he, the U.S. government, and the Democratic platform had all endorsed the November 29 partition boundaries.[9] On September 29 Clark Clifford phoned Lovett in Washington from the train in Tulsa and told him of the mounting pressure on Truman from Jewish groups, "that the position taken in Paris by this Government [Marshall's statement] was contrary to that of the Democratic National Platform." Lovett, though, told Clifford that Truman had approved in writing Marshall's earlier suggestion of the boundary change, and for Truman to send his message to Marshall now "would put the Secretary in an intolerable position and, because of the agreements made with other countries in the light of the agreed policy, would label this country as violating its agreements and as completely untrustworthy in international matters." After Lovett read to Clifford the memorandum "specifically approved by the President on September 1 which set out in detail the possibility of a swap of Western Galilee for portions of the Negeb," Clifford agreed to see that the telegram to Marshall would not be sent.[10]

As things worked out, after Dewey, on October 22, accused the administration of vacillating on Palestine and Israel, Truman on the 24th stated, "I stand squarely on the provisions covering Israel in the Democratic platform." This differed from Marshall's earlier statement, and on October 28, in a speech at Madison Square Garden, after stating that "the subject of Israel ... must not be resolved as a matter of politics in a political campaign," Truman said he had "never changed my position on Palestine or Israel," a statement that could confound quite a few historians following U.S. policy on Palestine over the years. According to Lovett, Marshall was not consulted before the speech but was told afterwards.[11]

On October 29 Truman sent a message to the State Department and its delegation in Paris directing that he be advised of any U.S. statement on the issues before it was made, especially in the closing days of the electoral campaign. Marshall was not pleased with this restriction on his discussions, and he asked Lovett about it. Lovett felt that the restrictions on the department and its delegates would continue a bit longer, "until the silly season terminates." The next day he told Marshall, "I can imagine what you have been through in Paris. It has been absolute hell here."[12] The warfare in Palestine continued off and on, with Israel holding its own for most of the fighting, until armistices were signed with the Arab countries in 1949. In regard to these future developments, Lovett had little further participation.

On October 20 Bob Lovett made some news in a different way. A reporter wrote that Lovett, "a man who leans to conservative elegance in dress, showed up at a news conference today wearing a hula girl tie." It turned out that Walter Bedell Smith "had read in the papers that Lovett always wore a single color pale cravat" and accordingly asked him "if he would wear a brighter tie if Smith bought him one. In an unguarded moment, Lovett said yes." Lovett wore the tie at his press conference "but told friends never again. He said the row of dancing girls under his chin distracts him from his work."[13]

Another matter in which Lovett participated to a considerable extent was what came to be called the "Vinson mission." As October got underway, Harry Truman was more and more concerned about his chances for victory in the following month's election, as the press and pollsters were almost universally predicting a big Republican victory and Governor Dewey was campaigning in a manner that showed he was totally confident of winning. Truman was of course equally concerned about the Berlin crisis and the looming shadow of Russian aggression. The president found during his campaigning that occasional references to peace seemed to bring out the warmest applause from his audiences. Thus, when two of his speechwriters, David Noyes and A.Z. Carr, suggested sending Dwight Eisenhower to Moscow on a goodwill mission to talk with Stalin and assure him of America's peaceful intentions, Truman jumped at the idea. The mission might avert any impending movement toward war, and it might, if successful, improve his chances of electoral victory.

Instead of Eisenhower, however, the president decided the man to send to talk to Stalin was his old friend Fred Vinson, who was at the time chief justice of the Supreme Court. On October 3 he summoned Vinson to the White House to tell him of his decision. Vinson, who had no experience in diplomacy or foreign affairs, declined at first, but when Truman insisted Vinson agreed to do it. Later that evening, Truman told the chief justice that he was not to negotiate on any specific foreign policy issues but simply to clear the air with Stalin about America's peaceful aims and to improve the now-alarming Soviet-American relations.

On the morning of October 5 Charlie Ross, the president's press secretary, advised representatives of the four major radio networks that the president needed a half-hour time for a nonpolitical speech. The network men were suspicious of what this could all be about, well into the campaign, so Ross, after swearing them to secrecy, told them of the proposed Vinson mission. Later in the morning Lovett, at the State Department, saw a copy from the code room come across his desk of Truman's notification of the mission to Ambassador Walter Bedell Smith in Moscow. Astounded at such a development, Lovett at once phoned the White House and asked for an immediate conference with the president. Lovett ordered his official car and directed that he be driven speedily to the White House, with lights flashing and sirens blaring. When he got together with Truman, Lovett told him bluntly that the plan was utterly unacceptable and should be cancelled without delay. When Truman demanded to know why, Lovett explained that in addition to the mission's being an impractical scheme—involving an amateur diplomat with little knowledge of what he was supposed to be doing—it would without doubt result in the resignation of George Marshall, who was then in Paris engaged in an interminable foreign ministers' conference.

Truman, fearing the electoral repercussions of an abrupt Marshall resignation, accordingly cancelled Vinson's mission. Lovett promptly called Marshall in Paris to tell him of the mission and its cancellation. Marshall and his chief aide, General Pat Carter, started drafting a reply to the White House. Carter's opening sentence—"Never in the history of diplomatic bungling"—was one that Marshall said would never do in a message addressed to the president. Shortly Truman spoke on the phone with Marshall, who firmly opposed the idea of an emissary to Moscow, noting that such a unilateral approach to Stalin and the Russians would upset our allies in Europe and jeopardize the gathering Western Union alliance. Truman agreed and suggested that the secretary should fly home for a conference.[14]

On October 9 the story about the cancelled Vinson mission inevitably made a big-time splash in newspapers across America, leaked by one of the radio executives. At 10:00 a.m. Lovett and the president met Marshall at the airport and the three of them went to the White House for a lengthy conference. Late in the day Truman publicly announced the cancellation of the Vinson mission, based on Marshall's advice, and Marshall stated there was "no foundation" for rumors of dissension between him and the president. The next day Marshall flew back to Paris, denying that he had threatened to resign.[15]

While the political press had a high old time with the now-defunct Vinson mission, the Republicans mostly let it go by, assuming that Truman would suffer greatly from it without their having to say much. Dewey hardly mentioned it. As it turned out, Harry Truman probably profited from it. He had shown that he cared deeply about the danger to the world of possible warfare; he would do whatever it took to keep the peace, even with a strange mission like the one he had thought up. The unusual effort to achieve a peaceful settlement undoubtedly appealed to quite a few of the Wallace supporters and probably won back some of their votes. And the whole affair demonstrated once again that Robert A. Lovett, sitting in his chair in the undersecretary of state's office, continued to have a substantial influence over the affairs of the Department of State and the United States government.

As matters developed, the 1948 election resulted in a totally unexpected outcome, Harry Truman defeating Thomas E. Dewey with 303 electoral votes to Dewey's 189. (Strom Thurmond, the Dixiecrat candidate, won 39 electoral votes, while Henry Wallace carried no states.) When Truman returned to Washington with Vice President-elect Alben Barkley on November 5, Lovett was there to watch and report to George Marshall: "The President returned to Washington Friday to receive one of the most genuinely enthusiastic receptions I've ever seen. The crowds lined the streets solidly from the station to the White House.... The police estimated there were about 750,000 people." He noted a large banner over the *Washington Post* (a newspaper that had of course predicted a Truman defeat) building showing a large black crow lying on its back dead as a doornail, and the message reading, "Welcome Home, Mr. President, from the Crow Eaters."[16]

Back at the White House, Truman interrupted the celebration to call Lovett over to ask him about the rumors that Marshall wanted to resign. He hoped Marshall would wait until the president had a chance to talk with him. Truman also thanked Lovett for holding the fort in Washington while he had been out campaigning and he hoped Lovett was not also thinking of resigning. Lovett should ignore press reports that Truman was thinking of replacing him; Truman suggested that both Marshall and Lovett should sit tight and say nothing.

In the same message that described Truman's return to Washington, Lovett counseled Marshall against any early withdrawal of American forces from South Korea, which had been the scene of a Communist uprising on October 28 The question of the withdrawal of outside forces from North and South Korea had been an issue between the United States and Russia going back to 1947. The following couple of months, of course, would see how things were to work out. In the meantime, there was still State Department business to take care of.

21

Setting Up NATO

One other major project with which Robert Lovett was much involved but was completed after he had left the State Department was the North Atlantic Treaty, which led to the North Atlantic Treaty Organization, familiarly known as NATO.

The United States, of course, had helped to unify much of Europe with the Marshall Plan and its requirement of participation by the countries included. The Brussels Treaty, signed March 17, 1948, after an initial push in the direction of mutual defense by Ernest Bevin of Great Britain, had united five European nations into a fifty-year military defense group—Great Britain, France, Belgium, the Netherlands, and Luxembourg. For military defense, obviously against a Soviet or communist threat, the assistance of the United States was certainly considered necessary. And that is where discussions with the State Department about U.S. involvement got their start. In addition, of course, the seizure of the Czechoslovakian government by the Communists in February had underlined Europe's insecurity as it stood.

Earlier, in January, Bevin had communicated to George Marshall his thoughts on such an alliance, with the hope that the United States might consider participation, and Marshall on January 19 had indicated to Lord Inverchapel, the British ambassador, that the U.S. might indeed consider such a move. Inverchapel met on the 27th with Robert Lovett to discuss the same, and Lovett cautiously informed him "that this proposal raised questions of the highest importance" and a definite response at this time was premature.[1]

On February 2, following up on the meeting of the 27th, Lovett wrote to Lord Inverchapel, stating that "European initiative is of first importance" and "the injection of the United States into the matter" before completion of a European union "would be unwise." But—"when there is evidence of unity with a firm determination to effect an arrangement under which the various European countries are prepared to act in concert to defend themselves, the United States will carefully consider the part it might appropriately play in support of such a Western European Union." Inverchapel responded four days later with Bevin's hopes for informal talks in Washington.[2]

The next day Inverchapel sat down with Bob Lovett and Jack Hickerson, director of the State Department's Office of European Affairs, to discuss the ambassador's letter of the day before. Lovett pointed out that Congress was at that time considering the Marshall Plan, to help Europe economically. If it became known in Congress that new military commitments were also being requested, "it might well adversely affect the prospects for the approval of Congress of the European Recovery Program." Besides, he went on, the U.S. did not have a very clear picture of what Bevin's proposals really were. "You are in effect asking us to pour concrete before we see the blueprints," Lovett said. He felt that it was not advisable at the moment to undertake the discussions in Washington Bevin had suggested. Inverchapel expressed his appreciation for Lovett's frank comments and said he would pass them on to London.[3]

Bevin and the European leaders did move ahead with their discussions, even with no more than hope of American support, and the Brussels Treaty was signed on March 17, 1948, creating the Western Union while the Lovetts were on a two-week vacation at Hobe Sound. On the same day, Harry Truman spoke to Congress about it, suggesting that the determination of the European countries to protect themselves should be matched by an American determination to protect them as well. The five-nation agreement, Truman said, "deserves our full support. And I am confident that the United States will, by appropriate means, extend to the free nations the support which the situation deserves."[4]

On March 22 Hickerson, who felt there was no real alternative to American commitment, began secret discussions with British and Canadian representatives concerning associating the U.S. and Canada with the Brussels Treaty nations. On April 5 Prime Minister Paul Henri Spaak of Belgium met in Washington with Lovett and Hickerson to discuss what the U.S. thought of the Brussels Treaty. Lovett told Spaak "that we considered it very satisfactory indeed" and were "actively studying how it [the U.S.] could best support and reinforce the Treaty." Lovett and Spaak went over the varied problems in Europe, such as countries like Italy, Norway, and Denmark, which were not part of the Brussels group, and the necessity of considering the continent as a whole. In conclusion, Lovett assured Spaak "that the President's statement left no question whatever as to our determination to support the Parties to the Five Power Treaty; the only question was how this could best be done."[5]

On April 7, four days after Congress had approved the Marshall Plan, Bob Lovett took Policy Planning Staff/27 (completed March 23, 1948, stating that Europe needed assurances of military support from the United States in case of Soviet aggression) to President Truman to acquaint him with the possible outlines of a proposed North Atlantic treaty, linking the military security of Western Europe formally to that of the United States. This was the first serious consultation with the White House about the proposed treaty. The next day Lovett met again with Truman, asking for permission to meet with key congressional leaders to lay the foundations for eventual consideration by the Senate of a possible treaty. The president gave him the "green light" to move ahead.

On April 11 Lovett—described by fellow State Department fixture George Kennan as "personally one of the most charming of men, a seasoned financier and a very smooth, capable operator"—sat down with Arthur Vandenberg to get his thinking on several major issues, such as the type of aid Congress would approve, the form of an arrangement the Senate might approve, the role of the United Nations in collective security plans, and the legislative preparations that would be needed for a European security agreement. Kennan agreed with Marshall and Lovett that close liaison with the influential foreign policy leaders of the Senate was important, but he "sometimes felt that it went so far as to assume on the part of the Senators a wisdom greater than was actually there" when they "might better have attempted to educate its protagonists to a more enlightened and effective view."[6] Some years later, Lovett wrote that "Kennan's comment is absolutely wrong when he suggests, at least by implication, that we should have tried to bully the Senate in some fashion. I had the most contact with Senator Vandenberg and our relationship could not have been closer or, indeed, more fruitful."[7] Margaret Truman wrote the following in her biography of her father: "Bob Lovett, another outstanding American who made a great contribution wherever he served, from Under Secretary of State to Secretary of Defense, had won the senator's friendship and confidence. With extraordinary patience he worked through draft after draft of what eventually became the Vandenberg Resolution."[8]

Lovett was of course all too familiar with the deep prejudice against "entangling alliances" George Washington had expressed long ago but was still present in many congressional minds, although Truman and Marshall had tried from time to time to show that the world had now become too small for such a prejudice. Also to be considered was the constitutional prerogative of Congress to declare war, a limitation on any commitment that might automatically propel the U.S. into a conflict. Lovett remarked at one point that dealing with Congress was "like getting a shave and having your appendix taken out at the same time."[9]

A week later, following up on their lengthy discussions, Lovett and Vandenberg got together again to consider timing and procedures, to figure out how the House of Representatives could be partially involved, and to finish up the wording of a resolution Vandenberg could present to furnish the legislative groundwork for a long-term alliance. The two of them met several times in the evening at Vandenberg's dwelling in Georgetown to prepare the appropriate document.[10] Lovett recalled, "I had made it a rule to stop by and see him every night with the day's cables and everything that the Senate Committee was going to be acting on." Vandenberg "lived just across Rock Creek Park from us, and on my way home to dinner around 7 o'clock I'd stop by and go over these things with him." "I took him a three page of legal size paper that we drafted in the Department on this Senate 239—what became Senate 239—and he said, 'I'll tell you one thing, Bob, it's much too long. You've got so many whereases in there you forget what you are going to resolve.'" Lovett said, "I think you are right. I've been apprehensive about that." Vandenberg said, "Give it to me. I'll take a crack at it. You go talk to my wife, Helen, who is in the living room." Lovett began to chat with Helen as directed, the Senator disappeared, "and in about twenty minutes he came back with one sheet of paper, and that one sheet of paper is 239. But he got everything in it. And it went through like a breeze."[11] As Harry Truman put it, Vandenberg "was thoroughly familiar with the workings of the Senate and knew how to get results. He could take ideas conceived by others—many in this case came from the State Department—and then include an element or two that would add his legislative trademark without changing anything basic."[12]

On April 23 Lovett met with President Truman, showing him a secret wire from Ernest Bevin outlining the possible risks involved in a formal North Atlantic treaty but advising that his governmental leaders had agreed that a conference with the U.S. to discuss defense arrangements was the best present move to make. Truman told Lovett to circulate this message to the National Security Council members. This, of course, was to lead to the establishment of a series of serious discussions.[13]

On May 11 Arthur Vandenberg and Robert Lovett completed their work, and the Senator from Michigan presented to the Senate Foreign Relations Committee (with Lovett present to show the administration's blessing on it) the resolution that he and Lovett had drafted. It resolved that the Senate reaffirm the commitment of the U.S. "to achieve international peace and security through the United Nations so that armed force shall not be used except in the common interest," and it then set forth seven objectives to be pursued by the U.S. "within the United Nations Charter." Among them were efforts to remove the UN veto from certain areas, to review the UN charter, and to provide the UN with armed forces "as provided by the Charter." Also included were the following purposeful objectives:

2. Progressive development of regional and other collective arrangements for individual and collective self-defense....

3. Association of the United States, by Constitutional process, with such regional and other collective arrangements as are based on continuous and effective self-help and mutual aid, and as affects its national security.

4. Contributing to the maintenance of peace by making clear its determination to exercise the right of individual or collective self-defense under Article 51 should any armed attack occur affecting its national security.[14]

Executive session hearings on the resolution got underway, and on May 12 and 19 Robert Lovett was the only witness called to testify. Vandenberg, as committee chairman, gave Lovett some help in explaining the background and the aims of the resolution. The Foreign Relations Committee on May 19 unanimously approved what was to be called the Vandenberg Resolution.

The National Security Council met the next day, May 20, and Bob Lovett pointed out that the resolution "would put us in a stronger position to discuss with the countries of western Europe measures to strengthen our national security as well as theirs." Two basic factors were involved in our planning, he said: "First, we wanted to get away from the one-way arrangements in which we did something for foreign countries without receiving anything in return; second, we did not want any automatic, unlimited engagements under our constitutional system. We could not agree upon anything amounting to a guarantee. But we had to give assurances sufficient enough to inspire the confidence and bolster the faith of the countries of Europe who felt themselves under constant and heavy Soviet pressure." The NSC then recommended to the president that the line of action proposed by Lovett should generally be followed.[15]

On June 11 Vandenberg introduced the resolution he and Lovett had crafted into the full Senate, which considered it for eight hours of a single day of debate and then passed it by a vote of 64 to 4. Although the House of Representatives did not take simultaneous action on the resolution, the way was now open to the negotiation by the State Department of the North Atlantic Treaty.[16] Many years later Robert Lovett wrote, "I have consistently felt that Senator Vandenberg has never received adequate credit for the important part he played in making the State Department's efforts effective in a Republican controlled Congress under a Democratic Administration."[17]

On June 23 Robert Lovett held a news conference at which he disclosed the private talks with Britain and Canada and said they would be expanded to include other European countries. "These discussions," it was reported, "will be based on the Vandenberg resolution, adopted by the Senate, which proposes strengthening the United Nations and developing regional defense organizations within the world organization, and includes the possibility of military support by the United States."[18]

With the Vandenberg Resolution now in place, the earlier Anglo-American-Canadian talks were accordingly opened up to secret discussions now including France and the

Benelux nations, with Lovett leading the way. The opening meeting of what were called "the Washington Exploratory Talks on Security" was held at 11:30 a.m. on July 6, with Lovett, Bohlen, Hickerson, and a couple of others in the U.S. delegation, and representatives (including the ambassador of each to the U.S.) of five other countries, Britain, France, the Netherlands, Belgium, and Canada.[19]

Lovett, starting the meeting, "referred to the Vandenberg Resolution as being the basis of the United States approach to the problems of mutual security and defense in Western Europe." He reviewed the resolution and the thinking behind it and went on to say the meetings should be completely informal, "with frank exchanges of view." The State Department felt "that there should be a preliminary canter over the questions which had been tentatively put forward as an agenda, following which there would be a breakdown into a working party or working parties to discuss details." The talks in Washington were to cover the political field, with military problems dealt with by the group meeting in London. As it developed, this first meeting was pretty much monopolized by Bob Lovett.[20]

Over the next three days there were four more meetings of the Washington Exploratory Talks, all presided over by Lovett, who took the minutes of each meeting to Harry Truman. In the second meeting, still on July 6 but at 4:00 p.m., Lovett said that the United States in the past "had sought peace through weakness but that after many heartbreaks it had reversed its policy and was seeking to deter aggression by proof of determination. The only question was how its determination should be implemented." That question, of course, was what that meeting and the subsequent ones were to answer, as well as the arrangements being developed by the Brussels Pact nations and which other countries ought to be involved.[21] At one point, Lovett noted "that the present discussions would be justified if they brought out what was necessary and possible on the Eastern side of the Atlantic and what was requisite and desirable for the Western Hemisphere nations; any recommendation to the Congress would have to take account of both elements." Referring to past wars in Europe that had ultimately involved the United States, he "reiterated that ... now the people of the United States desired to avoid mistakes of the past and make a constructive contribution to world security."[22]

Over the five meetings of the high-level representatives of the countries involved there was much lucid discussion of all the problems in the possible expansion of the Brussels Treaty into an arrangement that would contain both the United States and Canada, although no definite setup was reached. As the final meeting was winding up, Baron Silvercruys, the Belgian ambassador, noted that despite the "most useful exchange of views" he had not yet "a very clear picture as to the sort of association which the United States and Canada were prepared to contemplate." Lovett responded "that an effort had been made to find the form of organization and the method of association necessary to bring the United States into some form of collective security enterprise as a member." With the task now to be turned over to "working parties," Jack Hickerson suggested that the working parties should go over the agenda of the meetings being concluded and "examine some of the items in much more detail against the background of these discussions." Everyone agreed with this, and a meeting of the working group was to be called by Hickerson and Chip Bohlen.[23] The "International Working Group" duly got under way on July 12, its first meeting directed by Bohlen, who, with Kennan, Hickerson, and several others made up the American participants in the group. Six other nations were included in the fifteen meetings of the group held between July 12 and September 9, principally directed by Hickerson, to develop papers on the general security needs of Western civilization, geographical limits of any such arrangements, and the differing needs of the countries involved.

As all this was transpiring, Italy's ambassador Alberto Tarchiani cornered Bob Lovett at the State Department to express his country's concern that it had not been invited to join the Western Union. "It would not seem worthwhile," he said, "to build up Italy economically and not take appropriate steps to prevent her from being overrun by the Soviets." Lovett suggested that the Italian government should address itself to the Western Union countries; the U.S. could consider Italy in this regard only if the Western Union powers brought it up.[24]

On Friday, August 20, an informal, off-the-record meeting was held at the Lovetts' home at 2425 Kalorama Road, attended by the French, Belgian, and Dutch ambassadors, the British minister, and two Canadian officials, one of whom was secretary of state for external affairs (and future prime minister) Lester Pearson. The purpose of the get-together was for everyone to become fully aware of the U.S. and Canadian positions relative to North Atlantic defense, and the discussion certainly helped that. Lovett emphasized that whatever was entered into must contribute to American security. There was a diversion when French ambassador Henri Bonnet sounded off with a prepared speech on France's immediate need for military equipment. Bonnet occupied about an hour in doing so. Other than this, the conversations, which lasted more than two and a half hours, were useful in setting forth the possible forms an agreement might take.[25]

This gathering was followed on September 3 by the Sixth Meeting of the Washington Exploratory Talks on Security to discuss a paper prepared by the working group. The thoughts expressed were forwarded to the working group, which came up with a slightly revised version on September 9. Lovett's Seventh Meeting of the ambassadors followed on September 10, and it was agreed that the September 9 document adequately reflected "the sense of the last meeting" and that it should be forwarded to each member's government for further consideration. The crucial compromise, put forward by Canada, was that, while an attack on one member nation would be considered an attack upon all, each nation would then be expected to lend aid in accordance with its own constitutional processes. As Truman later put it, "in plain language this means there is an obligation to give all aid possible, but subject to the constitutional procedures of each country." Without such a provision, no treaty could get through the United States Congress.[26] As the final Exploratory Talk ended, Baron Silvercruys of Belgium "paid tribute to the admirable manner in which Mr. Lovett had conducted these discussions and wished to convey the gratitude of the other representatives for the help that he had given them all." As a final word, Robert Lovett thanked all those present.[27] While the product of the working group was duly forwarded to all of the governments involved, nothing further transpired while the American government awaited the result of the November presidential election.

On November 24 Kennan, still not happy with the proposed treaty, submitted a lengthy memorandum to Marshall, warning that a formal security arrangement as contemplated would not be the answer to a Soviet attempt to dominate Europe, and he then expanded on his argument in terms with which both Marshall and Lovett were familiar. Marshall left a response up to Lovett, who wrote that "a North Atlantic Security Pact is an essential supplement to the Marshall Plan … designed to contribute to restoring a sense of security in the area, development of defensive power throughout the area, and act as a deterrent to outside aggressive forces."[28]

The next step was a reopening of the Washington Exploratory Talks on Security, over which Bob Lovett presided on December 10. His position now was that it was desirable to make rapid progress on concluding the pact. He suggested that the procedure should be established in light of whatever suggestions might have been received from the home governments abroad following up the adjournment of September 10. The discussion of the ambassadors demonstrated that there was still not a firm outline of a treaty, so Lovett suggested preparing a "summary of suggestions," since "the present type of exploratory discussion had gone far enough and that there was a need for greater definition." The suggestions, he said, should be given to the working group on the following day, with the next meeting of the Exploratory Talks to be held on December 13.[29]

At the next meeting, after the Canadian ambassador presented the views of his government in some depth, Lovett emphasized that "from the American point of view, it was desirable that the Pact be completed as rapidly as possible. If there was a ... failure to settle upon a target date, the driving force of the new Congress and the favorable tide of opinion might be lost." He suggested February 1 as a target date for concluding a treaty.[30]

The next meeting of Lovett's group took place on December 22, at which a December 21 draft treaty prepared by the International Working Group (headed ironically by George Kennan, who, though not in favor of the treaty, performed in good order his duties with the working group) was discussed and opinions expressed. The result was the finalized Report of the International Working Group, dated December 24, which demonstrated "agreement on practically all the articles of a possible Pact." The Working Group, as Lovett had suggested, asked that the ambassadors "forward a copy of this report to their governments with the request that the latter furnish as soon as possible their comments on the text of the Treaty" as well as views on certain unresolved points such as the area to be covered, whether French North Africa was to be included, and the duration of the treaty.[31]

On January 14, 1949, Lovett presided over a final meeting of the Washington Exploratory Talks, called to discuss three remaining important questions: (1) Italy and its wish to be included, (2) the departments of Algeria that, though geographically in North Africa, were politically part of France, and (3) the duration of the treaty. After these issues were kicked around and the meeting was headed to a close, Lovett said "that in view of his resignation [from the State Department] he would probably not be present at the next meeting; and expressed his appreciation for the cooperation of the other representatives," who then "expressed gratitude for the great contribution which Mr. Lovett had made to the talks."[32]

From that point on, Dean Acheson, the newly appointed secretary of state following George Marshall's resignation, handled negotiations on the North Atlantic Treaty. The treaty was ultimately completed and signed on April 4, 1949. There were issues raised in the Senate, with Senators Vandenberg, Connally, Donnell, and others that Acheson had to handle. On April 1 Acheson wrote to General Marshall asking for him and Lovett to appear at the hearings on the treaty before the Senate Committee on Foreign Relations. Marshall wrote back to Acheson, saying it would be a burden but he would do what he could. Acheson responded on April 6, saying that Marshall's presence was not essential, since "we are expecting Bob Lovett to help us and I do not anticipate any substantial difficulties." Lovett, in his testimony, assured the Senate committee that in the course of drafting the NATO treaty the United States had given to its European allies no firm promises about what military assistance it would provide them. With that final contribution to NATO by Lovett, the Senate approved the treaty by a vote of 82 to 13, and it took effect on August 24, 1949.[33] Dean Acheson later wrote, "Senator Vandenberg, the Vandenberg-Lovett-Marshall collaboration, and its product, the Vandenberg Resolution, made possible the North Atlantic Treaty."[34]

On April 13, 1950, Robert Lovett received from the minister of Luxembourg "on behalf of his colleagues" a silver cigarette box bearing the signatures of the participants in the NATO negotiations, followed shortly by a letter from Baron Robert Silvercruys of Belgium, saying, "We all wished to honor your contribution to the Pact. You presided over our labors and you guided our efforts. You were a tower of strength in the negotiations."[35]

One historian has written that 1948 and 1949 were probably the most dangerous times of the Cold War, what with the Communist takeover of Czechoslovakia, the Berlin blockade and airlift, the formation of NATO, and the first Russian atom bomb. For a good part of this period, Robert A. Lovett was one of the most important members of the United States government.[36] Clark Clifford summarized Bob Lovett's service in the State Department:

> Because Lovett did not leave behind policies or theories in the manner of Acheson and Kennan, later historians would find it hard to understand his great value to any Administration fortunate enough to have him. I respected Acheson greatly for his achievements, his intellect, and his conceptual abilities; but despite his great stature, he did not possess Lovett's ability—unsurpassed in my entire Washington experience—to get people to work together with a minimum of friction. Where Acheson was decisive and impatient, Lovett was thoughtful and conciliatory. In informal settings, he was witty and charming, with a fine sense of detachment and irony—he was one of the best raconteurs I have ever met. But these charming qualities would have been of interest only to hostesses if they had not skillfully covered an immensely tough interior.[37]

22

Back to Wall Street ... for a While

As the days passed following the 1948 election and as the nation suddenly began to accommodate the idea of four more years of Harry Truman's presidency, Robert Lovett worked at his desk in the State Department, dealing with such problems—great or small— as came across it. At the same time, he was preparing for his departure from Washington and the return to Brown Brothers Harriman.

One issue that arose in mid–November was who was to head the U.S. delegation to the United Nations for the continuing session of the General Assembly in Paris. Secretary Marshall was returning to the United States, and Warren Austin, the U.S. ambassador to the United Nations, was not well (also, Marshall felt that Austin was no longer up to the job). On November 16 Bob Lovett called Clark Clifford, who was in Key West with the president, to tell him of a message from Marshall "requesting decision by President on successor to Austin, and recommending [John Foster] Dulles for post, subject to clearance with Dulles that he will carry out President's instructions fully." Truman, however, did not want Dulles, a close advisor to his late opponent Tom Dewey, to be chairman; he wanted Philip Jessup in the job, and Jessup was named as acting chairman of the United Nations delegation, with Dulles in a contingent position in light of Jessup's questionable health.[1]

On November 19 Bunny Harriman stopped by for lunch with Lovett to discuss Lovett's rejoining Brown Brothers Harriman. Later that afternoon, Lovett got a phone call from Bernard Baruch telling him what a good job he had been doing—a hell of a tough one, Baruch said. He added that if Lovett's daddy, with whom Baruch had worked in World War I, were alive he would be very proud of his son.

When General Marshall went into Walter Reed Hospital on December 29 for removal of his right kidney, Lovett once again became acting secretary of state during the secretary's lengthy recuperation. It might be noted that at this point, with George Marshall's overseas meetings and his hospitalizations, Robert Lovett estimated he was acting secretary of state 73 percent of the time after he took his job in the State Department.[2]

All sorts of issues came up for Lovett, many of them familiar—Palestine, Berlin, the UN delegation, NATO, China, Paul Hoffman and the ECA, admission of Israel to the United Nations, Indonesia—and he dealt with them with his usual competence. There were a lot of phone talks with Clark Clifford, numerous calls to those who were concerned about Marshall's condition, and discussions about the president's upcoming inaugural address. At one point, Joe Alsop called to say good-bye before leaving for Europe. Lovett offered to send telegrams to London, Paris, Rome, Trieste, Belgrade, and Berlin to facilitate his trip, and Alsop said he would appreciate that very much.

On December 21 Lovett got a call from the president asking if there was any objection to his sending a birthday greeting to Josef Stalin on his 69th birthday, since Stalin had sent him one on his birthday. Lovett checked it out and got back to Truman, telling him that the personal angle bothered some in the department; they would prefer that it be sent through the embassy rather than directly. President Truman said that was fine, and he asked Bob Lovett to take care of it.

Several days later Clifford told him of a lunch discussion with Senator Vandenberg, who felt if Marshall were unable to resume his duties a successor had to be found. "That did not bother him so much as the President's ability to find a successor for Lovett." What Clifford declined to tell the senator at that point was that Dean Acheson had already been selected for secretary of state and that Budget Director James E. Webb was to be moved over to Lovett's position. Later that day, Vandenberg called Lovett, who told him that Marshall was definitely not coming back. Vandenberg asked if the likeliest ones to be named in Marshall's place were Harriman or Acheson, and Lovett was happy to say yes.

On the afternoon of the 28th Lovett took Marshall, discharged from the hospital, to the airport for his trip to Pinehurst; they were both pleased that there were no reporters present to begin speculation about future plans. On the 31st Lovett and Clifford talked over the work they had been doing on the inaugural address, but Clifford said he would be busy for a couple of days on the State of the Union talk. On January 5, in the new year, Lovett was pleased to visit the capitol for the president's State of the Union address, after which he had lunch at the Pentagon with his friend Jim Forrestal. At Harry Truman's press conference of January 7 he announced the resignations of Marshall and Lovett as well as the nominations of Acheson and Webb to succeed them. For Bob Lovett, this set off rounds of regrets that he was leaving and congratulations on the job he had done. He also made plans with Jim Webb to bring Webb up to date on the work of the department. On the 11th Lovett appeared before an executive session of the Senate Foreign Relations Committee to report on the North Atlantic pact and to bring the committee up to date generally on foreign affairs. He was also trying to win the members of the committee over to Dean Acheson, whose appointment was leading to some controversy but was ultimately confirmed.

Several days after that, Lovett cabled the U.S. embassy in Paris to alert the French that the State Department was hoping the French would reach an amicable agreement in Vietnam with Bao Dai "or any truly nationalist group which has reasonable chance winning over preponderance of Vietnamese." Bao Dai had been emperor of Annam since 1932 but had abdicated after World War II. In 1947 the French had begun negotiations with him as a possible counterweight to the incipient Vietnamese Communist revolution under Ho Chi Minh. Lovett warned, though, that "we cannot at this time irretrievably commit US to support of native govt which by failing develop appeal among Vietnamese might become virtually puppet govt, separated from people and existing only by presence French military forces." Vietnam was looming on the horizon of the future for the State Department and the U.S. military.[3]

Robert Lovett was engaged in one last issue—a curious matter, as it had to do with Harry Truman's inaugural address. After the election Clark Clifford sent a memo to the State Department asking to be provided with some ideas for the address. A young public affairs man in the department named Benjamin Hardy acted upon Clifford's request. During the war Hardy had served in Brazil and had observed a backward economy that might benefit from the application of modern technologies. So he sent a message to his boss in the department, Francis Russell, proposing that technical assistance be made a major component of American foreign policy—"a dramatic large-scale program that would capture the imagination of the peoples of other countries ... and create a decent life for the earth's millions."[4]

Hardy's proposal made its way to Bob Lovett's desk, and Lovett looked at it and promptly sent it back to Russell with a memo that the proposal needed more study. Hardy, saddened to learn the fate of his idea, decided to take a bold and risky course of action. He called George Elsey, Clifford's top assistant, arranged a meeting with him, and gave Elsey his thoughts on technical assistance being included in foreign policy. Elsey took the matter to Clifford, who felt "it was the right idea at the right time." To protect Hardy, who had gone far out of official channels, a message was sent to the State Department that Truman wanted to include in his speech a proposal to expand scientific and technical aid to the poorer countries.[5] At the State Department, Lovett referred the message to Paul Nitze and Chip Bohlen, who agreed that it was not a bad idea, "but because the executive branch had not yet had time to think through and flesh out the details of a program of the indicated magnitude" it should not be in the inaugural speech. So Lovett sent this message back to the president.[6]

Clifford heard nothing more for ten days, until Hardy showed up in his office carrying a memorandum of his idea, saying that it had been blocked by Lovett and Nitze, who said that there had been insufficient preparation for the idea and that further study was needed—just what Lovett had said earlier. Clifford told Elsey to prepare drafting the speech to include four major points. The first three were not surprising: continued support for the United Nations, full support to the Marshall Plan, and continued work on what was to become NATO. The fourth point was to be a description of Benjamin Hardy's proposal. The work on the speech took up a goodly amount of time, even with Hardy working as a clandestine member of the speechwriting team. Finally, less than 48 hours before the inauguration, the final version of the speech was sent to the State Department, where Lovett and Nitze once again objected to the inclusion in it of the fourth point. Nevertheless, President Truman, learning of it, was enthusiastic about the idea, and it remained in the address as given on January 20, 1949, soon christened Point Four as a major new proposal.

The Point Four program needed some study and preparation (as Lovett, Nitze, and Bohlen had insisted), and it was not until late October1950 that the Technical Cooperation Administration was set up within the State Department to run the Point Four program and provide technical and agricultural aid to countries that concluded agreements with the United States for the program. Robert Lovett took some heat for trying to block Point Four from the inaugural address, but he was not against the idea of it; he simply felt the timing was inappropriate.

As Truman's second term was about to start, Lovett was preparing to depart Washington. On the morning of January 18 the staff in the department presented Lovett with a silver cigarette box as a farewell gift, and later that day Knight Woolley of Brown Brothers Harriman made arrangements to meet Lovett at the Brook in New York on Monday the 24th. On the 19th Lovett held his final press conference as acting secretary of state, and that evening he and Adele held a farewell reception at the Carlton Hotel for all their friends in the capital. The next day, Inauguration Day, Bob Lovett, with other members of the cabinet and the president, attended a morning prayer service at St. John's Episcopal Church before preparing for the big goings-on. With Adele, Bob Lovett watched as President Truman was sworn in as president once again, and Kentucky's Alben Barkley was inaugurated as vice president. Then they rode in the inaugural parade (Lovett as a cabinet member; Acheson was not confirmed until the next day) to the reviewing stand in front of the White House and watched the rest of the parade, later attending a reception at the National Gallery of Art. On January 21 Lovett and Adele visited the White House to observe Dean Acheson being sworn in as secretary of state, and at 4:00 o'clock they attended a reception given by Snyder and his wife in honor of Harry and Bess Truman.

On Monday the 24th Lovett took the train to New York for his four o'clock meeting with Knight Woolley to discuss his upcoming return to Brown Brothers Harriman. Not much of note took place on the 26th, but the next morning Arthur Krock called Lovett to ask about the identity of the originator of Point Four in the president's address. Lovett held back a bit on the real story, telling Krock that it had a long history, that a number of people had worked on it, that it probably came originally from the State Department and was later merged with the views of several others. Nothing untrue there, but it obviously left Bob Lovett out of the picture. After a noon dental appointment and a pose for a formal portrait at three o'clock, Lovett was the guest of honor at a five o'clock reception of the State Department Press Correspondents Association at the National Press Club. His service in the State Department for the past twenty months was over. Bob Lovett had cleaned out his office and was no longer an employee of the government.

One of those with whom Lovett had worked closely in the department was Paul Nitze, who would write later his impressions of Robert Lovett, "whom I had known from my days on Wall Street":

> He was widely admired for his wit and negotiating skill…. As Marshall's deputy in the State Department, he concentrated his efforts on relations with Congress and on dealing with the European ambassadors in Washington. He was wise, skillful, and knowledgeable in his dealings with them. I considered his abilities to be more in the direction of tactical skill than profound analysis. But I thought him to be one of the great men of that age. I still have his picture hanging on my office wall….[7]
> As Lovett prepared to leave, he sent off a note to Arthur Vandenberg:
> "If a man is very lucky he has an opportunity once in his life to serve a good cause with men of singleness of purpose, integrity and complete understanding, and with friends whom he both admires and loves. I have had that experience with you and the General [Marshall]."[8]

After a brief return to Locust Valley and several trips to Wall Street, Bob Lovett chose to take a much-needed vacation. He and Adele headed down South to their beach cottage in Hobe Sound, Florida. Here, Lovett was to be subjected to one of the worst experiences of his life, which involved his close friend Jim Forrestal.

Forrestal had been increasingly troubled by the pressures of life, and unfortunately they got into his head. During the presidential campaign it was rumored that Forrestal had met with Dewey to see if he could remain in the cabinet of Dewey's upcoming administration, which of course strained considerably his relations with the members of the Truman administration. The departure of Bob Lovett, Forrestal's most trusted friend in Washington, from the capital late in January was a grievous loss for Forrestal. "In Lovett," it was written, "he would lose one of his closest friends and most valuable collaborators." Associates in Washington heard Forrestal on occasion talking wildly. Clearly something was going wrong.[9]

Harry Truman had lost all faith in Forrestal—his perceived lack of loyalty added to what was becoming an obvious mental problem as well as differences on defense policies—and on March 1, 1949, Forrestal was called to the White House and asked to resign as secretary of defense. Truman had decided to give the position to Louis Johnson, who had been one of his top fundraisers in the recent presidential campaign. Forrestal, shattered by this development, worked late into the evening drafting his letter of resignation, to take effect March 31. Once again, on March 29, he was invited to the White House, where he was presented the Distinguished Service Medal by the president. Forrestal was unable to respond at all. As Clark Clifford noted, "It was suddenly clear to everyone that something was very wrong."[10]

After a special meeting on the same day that the House Armed Services Committee honored Forrestal for his many contributions to the nation's defense, it was obvious something had to be done. His friend and former business partner Ferd Eberstadt met with him and was shocked by Forrestal's appearance and agitated conduct. Forrestal told him "that he was a complete failure and that he was considering suicide ... that a number of individuals—Communists, Jews, and certain persons in the White House—had formed a conspiracy to 'get' him and had finally succeeded." Eberstadt contacted Secretary Johnson and arranged to have Forrestal flown to Florida that evening in an air force plane to Hobe Sound, where both his wife, Jo, and the Lovetts were staying. Eberstadt then called Bob Lovett on the phone, telling him of Forrestal's condition and asking him to meet the plane.[11]

The plane arrived at a private airfield near the Jupiter Island Club, putting down in the early evening hours of the same day that its sole passenger had been honored by both the president and the House Armed Services Committee. At the airfield to meet the plane were his wife, the Lovetts, and several other friends. Robert Lovett hardly recognized his longtime friend, now "a wizened, shrunken man, uncertain of movement," his eyes searching the faces of those who had gathered to meet him, hostile and suspicious. He almost fell off the narrow ladder by which he was leaving the plane, then Lovett reached up to grab him and prevented a tumble. Lovett tried to humor him. "I'm glad you brought your golf clubs," he said, "because I'm going to take every dollar you've got." Forrestal stared at him and mumbled, "Bob, they're after me," citing the Russians, the FBI, and the Zionists.[12]

In the house where he would be lodged, Forrestal searched under the beds and in the closets for hidden microphones. Later, as he and Lovett went walking on the beach, Forrestal gestured at the metal sockets placed in the sand to hold up beach umbrellas. "We had better not discuss anything here," he said. "Those things are wired, and everything we say is being recorded." Very soon the eminent psychiatrist William Menninger was summoned to examine his friend Jim, and the doctor concluded that he desperately needed hospitalization.

"On one occasion" during the few days Forrestal was at Hobe Sound, Lovett recalled, "when Jim lunched alone with Adele and me on the terrace of our little beach house, he seemed to both of us to be normal, and we resumed the old kidding and arguing about books and plays of our friends which had played so large a part in our association." That evening, though, was the time of Forrestal's first suicide attempt, even though Lovett called it "half-hearted" and "never intended to succeed." It was soon decided to fly Forrestal to the naval hospital at Bethesda, Maryland, for much-needed treatment. Lovett "drove over with Jim to the airport at Stuart, and he seemed calm but depressed. I [Lovett] recall particularly that he thanked me for 'standing by him.' And when I said that was nonsense and that we had been through a lot worse things together than just being tired out, he didn't smile or kid me about my golf game or any of the usual things I would have expected him to do. That is the last personal conversation I had with Jim, as the hospital would not allow me to speak to him on the phone when I called subsequently."[13]

On April 2 Forrestal was flown back to Washington and admitted that night to the hospital at Bethesda for treatment. A couple of weeks later, on April 20, Lovett was able to talk with the head psychiatrist, who "said that Jim was progressing very satisfactorily but there was still a long road ahead. It was a serious nervous breakdown and a strong persecution complex coupled with a feeling of baseless guilt." Treatment continued for several more weeks, but on the morning of May 22 Forrestal's room on the sixteenth floor of the hospital was found empty, the window open, and his lifeless body on the third-floor roof far below. Robert Lovett's longtime friend Jim Forrestal was gone and Lovett was devastated.[14]

From Hobe Sound, of course, the Lovetts returned to Long Island, and Robert headed back to Wall Street, where he resumed his partnership at Brown Brothers Harriman, officially on April 1, 1949, although he did not get there physically until several days later than that. He was welcomed back most heartily; the partners even threw a cocktail party in his honor on June 23, although Lovett, as always, had little more than a single old-fashioned to protect his always-sensitive insides.

Hardly had Lovett checked back into Brown Brothers Harriman, though, than he was offered the position of president of the International Bank for Reconstruction and Development (IBRD, a major part of the World Bank), a job his buddy Jack McCloy was giving up. Truman, McCloy, and the bank's executive directors had all settled upon Lovett for the position, to head an institution established at the Bretton Woods conference of 1944 with the mission of financing the reconstruction of war-torn Europe. While the Marshall Plan had stepped in with the same goals, the IBRD was working hard, financing projects to dam rivers, generate electricity, and improve sanitation across Europe. Truman and the IBRD's directors felt that a legal education and an extensive financial background were necessary for the bank's head, and "Mr. Lovett was considered admirably qualified in both respects." Lovett, however, having just completed his second tour of government duty, declined the offer. He was back to stay with Brown Brothers Harriman—or so he thought.[15]

Lovett was happy to get back into the banking business, and he was always glad to hook up once again with his friends and partners like Bunny Harriman, Knight Woolley, Elbridge Gerry, Pres Bush, Ellery James, and quite a few others. He was pleased that as usual there was a majority of Yale men on the partnership rolls and that quite a few of them were Skull and Bonesmen. It took a while, obviously, for him to pick up on all that he needed to be aware of as a banking partner, but he had done it several years earlier, coming back from the War Department, and he had a very good idea of what had to be done.

Bob and Adele were also happy to return to living in Locust Valley on the northern side of Long Island. While Robert was working hard at his job at 59 Wall Street, Adele was working on a job of her own—supervising the construction of their new house on the east side of Birch Hill Lane, which she called "Pleasance," defined as "a small house or pavilion in the midst of gardens laid out for delight." The house had two master bedrooms with baths, a guest room with a bath, a library, living room, entry hall, flower room, and servants wing. "When we sold our old house at the top of the hill," Judge Lovett's Woodfold, Adele later wrote, "we kept two and a half acres at the foot of the hill to build a small one-story house for our old age. It was a big square of lawn under very beautiful old trees." Adele listed herself as the architect.[16]

A state building structure form, prepared in July 1978, described Pleasance as a "1 storey flat roofed stucco structure." It went on to say, "This interesting contemporary structure sits among excellent gardens. It was built by the Lovetts on part of his father's estate."[17] Adele Lovett, in the paper just described, notes that before they could live in Pleasance they returned to Washington, to the Defense Department. "But before we left," she writes, "I was able to start the first plantings." She describes in great detail the "flowering trees and shrubs and evergreens to screen out our neighbors on the northeast and south borders and the road on the west," "dogwood, hollies, sorrel, tree lilacs, cornus mas, benzoin, clethra, hornbeam, the viburnum and sixty-eight varieties of rhododendron and azaleas underplanted with wildflower, bulbs, ferns and various kinds of ground covers." There was also "a small picking garden ... a tiny herb garden at the kitchen door with about fifty essential herbs for cooking and fragrance, and a border of blue and white flowering trees, shrubs, perennials and annuals and ground covers edging the lawn to the east."[18]

Adele Lovett was always an avid gardener, and the opportunity to embellish the outdoor surroundings of a new and elegant little house appealed to her greatly and obviously kept her quite busy. She did so well that later she said, "We have had to chop out, dig out, prune out and give away much of what we over-planted!" When the Lovetts moved back from Washington in 1954 Adele asked her husband what he wanted for Christmas. "A machete," Bob said. "Whatever for?" she asked. He answered, "To hack my way through to the garage from the front door!"[19]

We now return to 1949, when Robert Lovett found himself testifying before the Senate Foreign Relations Committee, on May 3, as that body was considering the North Atlantic pact. He stated that the pact gave the president no inherent powers to send troops to Europe to resist aggression, that such action would require a declaration of war by Congress. Opponents of the treaty indicated by continued questioning that they remained unconvinced, although the same position had earlier been taken before them by both Dean Acheson and Averell Harriman. Senator Arthur V. Watkins (R–Utah), an opponent of NATO, asked Lovett whether an attack on London or Paris would not be regarded in the same light as one on Washington or New York. Lovett said the answer was "no," that it would be up to the president and Congress to decide on steps to be taken. The pact, he said, "leaves it to the Congress to determine whether or not the facts require a state of war. Lovett concluded that the treaty was "essential" to American security and world peace and urged prompt Senate ratification, even if Russia suddenly eased up on the cold war and started talking "honeyed words."[20]

At the same time, Bob Lovett was quite fully occupied. On the second of July 1949, the Honorable Robert A. Lovett was awarded a citation in Chicago from the Air Force Association, honoring the outstanding work he had done for the air force. In addition to the fulltime banking work at Brown Brothers, he resumed directorial duties with the Union Pacific and a number of other corporations such as the New York Life Insurance Company.

He wrote to Pat Carter (George Marshall's former military aide), "The prospect of 'plenty of time to myself,' which I so fondly cherished, has not materialized largely as a result of my being stupid about taking on too many extra-curricular activities." These included such things as a speech at the annual managers' meeting of the New York Life Insurance Company, which he delivered on February 2, 1950.[21]

Another notable speech he gave was on November 17, 1949, to the national dinner of the railway-oriented Newcomen Society (of which he was a member), at the Hotel Pierre in New York. Lovett was introduced by his old friend Bunny Harriman, and he then gave his speech, entitled "Forty Years After: An Appreciation of the Genius of Edward Henry Harriman (1848–1909)." He described E.H. Harriman as "Financier, Railroad Rebuilder and Strategist, Industrial Statesman of One Epoch and Prophet of a New." Lovett gave a finely structured talk on the ways in which Harriman thought and acted, his many accomplishments in the railway business, and his policies and beliefs. He concluded his speech thus: "Many years have gone by, and yet the perspective of time has not lessened Harriman's accomplishments, nor his stature. His profound belief in the future of the West, his convictions about the vital role that cheap and dependable transportation must play in this Country's development, his principles of public service by private corporations, and his policies of management and finance have stood the test of time. E.H. Harriman remains, *after forty years*, a proven industrial statesman of the past and a prophet of a new epoch."[22] There were many other requests made of Robert Lovett in 1949 for speeches, almost all of which he turned down. There were invitations from the U.S. Naval Academy, Yale, Harvard Business School alumni, Common Cause, the Canadian Institute of International Affairs, the University of Pennsylvania, the ninth grade of Locust Valley Public School, the Massachusetts Building Congress, Lafayette College, the Special Staff School of the Air Force, and the Pratt Institute, among numerous others.[23]

Without the pressures of government service, Bob Lovett had turned to art as a pastime. He called upon Louis Bouche, a well-known Paris-educated artist and muralist, to train him in the fundamentals of painting. With Bouche's assistance he was soon turning out landscape paintings and other still-life works that he found very satisfying. Unfortunately, Lovett's upcoming return to Washington would cut short his artistic career for several more years.

His old friend Dean Acheson, now serving as Truman's secretary of state, got himself into terrible hot water on January 25, 1950, when he told a press conference, "I do not intend to turn my back on Alger Hiss." While Acheson was blasted both in and out of Congress and in and out of the press, Robert Lovett offered Acheson the use of his house in Hobe Sound to rest up in. Lovett wrote him: "I pray for you—quite literally."[24]

In April 1950 Lovett was advised by his old friend Dwight Eisenhower that Columbia University, of which Eisenhower was then president, wished to confer an honorary doctorate of laws degree upon him. Lovett expressed much appreciation for the honor, writing back to his old friend Ike: "Your decision has given me the greatest pleasure, and I want you to know personally of the special gratification I feel over this honor because of your association with it." And indeed, Bob Lovett felt a special shiver of delight when the degree was conferred upon him on June 8, 1950, the first of many honorary degrees he would receive.[25] September 11, 1950, was the date on which Robert A. Lovett was awarded the Grand Cross of the Order of Leopold II, by Belgium, most likely at the urging of his friend Baron Robert

Silvercruys in the Belgian embassy. The Chancery Document pertaining to the award was presented to Lovett in Washington on September 29, 1950—a fine tribute to his World War II work as well as to his contributions to Belgium and Europe while in the State Department. On October 9, 1950, James P. Baxter, president of Williams College, wrote Lovett asking him to accept an honorary doctorate at the June 17, 1951, commencement in Williamstown. Lovett, after first checking that the centennial address he was to give at the Hill School on June 9, 1951, would not conflict, accepted the honor from Williams.[26]

Soon enough, though, Robert Lovett would once again leave Brown Brothers Harriman and move back to Washington. Harry Truman was having serious problems with Louis Johnson, whom he had installed in the Defense Department to succeed Forrestal. Johnson had developed a considerable hostility between the Defense and State departments. Secretary of State Dean Acheson wrote about relations between the two departments: "At the time of the General's [Marshall's] return, relations were at their lowest ebb."[27] At the time, there was serious discussion in the White House about a successor to Johnson should he be let go. According to Eben Ayres, the assistant White House press secretary, at a meeting on August 26 including himself, George Elsey, and Charlie Ross, after considerable talk Elsey suggested Lovett, "a name that," as Ayres himself said, "was in my mind."[28]

Harry Truman had it in his mind to see if 69-year-old George Marshall was fit for the job. After meeting the general for a pleasant lunch, Truman asked Marshall if he would return to the government as secretary of defense. Marshall had been serving as chairman of the American Red Cross since leaving the State Department, and he was perfectly content to keep on doing so. However, on September 6, 1950, Marshall met with the president at Blair House and, subject to a couple of conditions, agreed to take the position, yielding to his never-ending commitment to the well-being of the American nation. First he wanted Truman to agree that his term would be limited to six months or at most a year, and second he wanted to have Robert Lovett appointed as his deputy secretary so that Lovett would be able to succeed Marshall when he stepped down. Truman was able to accept the two stipulations, particularly since he already had a high opinion of Lovett, so Marshall said, "Mr. President, I'll do it." There was another problem to be taken care of, the provision in the National Security Act that barred a military man from being secretary of defense. Truman assured him that he would take care of that, which he did.

At 6:45 a.m. on September 28, as Bob Lovett was eating breakfast in his Locust Valley home, the old superintendent's cottage on his father's place they had lived in before moving into Pleasance, the phone rang and Adele answered it. She called down to him, saying, "Bob, Washington is calling." He picked up the extension, and a voice said, "Bob?" Lovett said, "Yes." The voice said, "This is the president." Lovett snapped, "Now listen, this isn't at all funny. It's 6:45 in the morning. I'm right in the middle of breakfast, I'm trying to get the early commuter train to New York and for God's sake this is no time for jokes!" The voice then said, "This is really the president." Lovett said, "Well, I beg your pardon, sir. I didn't realize that." The voice of Harry Truman then told him that he was being asked to serve as deputy secretary of defense, as Marshall had insisted. Lovett quickly accepted the offer, despite what it had done to his breakfast.[29] When he got to his office on Wall Street, Lovett "said he expected to go to Washington 'just as soon as I can resign and get my desk clear here.' Another phone call brought him wishes of good luck; Lovett 'laughed and said: "I guess I'm going to need it. It looks like a hot seat."'[30]

Lovett once again went through the now-familiar business of selling his securities, stepping down from his Brown Brothers Harriman partnership, and resigning from the various boards of which he was a member. "Every time I went down there," he said, "I had to resign from every board and had to sell everything I had that related to anything in which there was a possible conflict of interest. When you work for the Army or the Air Force you have dealings with almost every corporation in the country. So it was a horrendous problem to take care of, legally and otherwise." It was the same procedure he had gone through in 1940 and 1947, but he wanted to make sure that there could be no conflicts of interest affecting his government service.[31]

So Robert Lovett was to return to Washington, to a Defense Department that had been busy getting reoriented after the Unification Act, which created it, and was now fully occupied with the war in Korea, which had begun on June 25 and had not worked well for the South Koreans and the U.S. Army in the time since, until the daring invasion at Inchon in mid–September. Lovett knew he was going to be sitting in "a hot seat."

23

On to the Defense Department

As the word got out about Robert Lovett's appointment to the Defense Department he was gratified to receive numerous notes and letters of congratulation. One of the earliest, a wire on September 28, 1950, came from General Marshall: "I cannot begin to tell you how grateful I am that you are willing to make the sacrifice that I know this appointment imposes." Justice Felix Frankfurter said, "As the right arm of the General you will fortify his strength and thereby the Nation's." Bernard Baruch wired, "Once more into the breach, dear friends, once more." Congressman John Vorys, his old Yale Unit buddy, said, "It is a comfort to know that you are in harness again. You certainly are a bear for punishment." David Lilienthal, of the Atomic Energy Commission, said, "You have the great good sense and the salt of humor that a tight pinch calls for."

Stewart Alsop said he had received a cable for Lovett from brother Joe: "News you are back in harness gives more hope the coach will get over the rise than anything I have heard since you left Washington and having you back is an immeasurable pleasure. Dear love to Adele who I am sure is furious." Stewart then added his own thought: " I feel just the way Joe does about your return to the snake pit." And from Columbia University came a message from Dwight Eisenhower: "Every person to whom I have spoken has expressed sentiments of the deepest satisfaction because of your willingness to enter the Defense Department— a satisfaction that I share to the full."[1]

During his tenure in the Defense Department Robert Lovett did not have the ups and downs of famous issues that he had in the State Department—things like the Marshall Plan, recognition of Israel, the Berlin Crisis, and NATO. With the war going on in Korea, what was of the greatest concern to Lovett was something at which he was very accomplished: keeping everything working right and the guns and tanks and planes coming as scheduled for use by the troops—that, and the ultimate issue of providing for the long-term defense establishment of the country and getting the Defense Department functioning efficiently.

Asked later about his taking over the job in defense, Lovett said, "The transition of going back as Deputy Secretary of Defense in 1950 and then Secretary of Defense in 1951 was very simple because I had been all through it, both from the point of view of the Air Force and the War Department. I knew all the men, I knew them well, great friends. It was a very simple thing to step in, it was like going home." What he and Marshall "wanted to do was to try to get the whole machine of Defense reduced in scale and increased in efficiency so that it would be viable in peacetime."[2]

As he had done in the State Department, Robert Lovett worked hard. He customarily arrived at his office by 8:00 a.m. daily and usually was home around 6:30 p.m.—although his homecoming arrivals had often been later when he was stopping off to see Senator Vandenberg. He generally worked in the office for part of Saturday and was frequently there for three or four hours on Sundays as well.

Among things to criticize, Lovett recalled, were "disruption of the Department and, in general, a low state of morale." He also noted "it was a period in which we had to take an economy which had already been blown up extravagantly in size as a result of the cold war recently and the amount of stuff we were doing in aid around the world. Now we had to superimpose on that another war, a small one but with strong logistic problems."[3]

The presence of George Marshall in the Pentagon resulted in what Truman had hoped for. Marshall obviously did not have the vigor of his younger years; and, as with the State Department earlier, he left much of the detail of running the department to Bob Lovett. With Omar Bradley as head of the Joint Chiefs and J. Lawton Collins as his deputy as army chief of staff, Marshall had just the right kind of military help. His commanding presence restored order after the disorder of Louis Johnson, and it boosted morale throughout the Pentagon and repaired relations with the State Department.

Shortly after bringing Lovett on board, Marshall appointed Anna M. Rosenberg as assistant secretary for manpower. It was a most controversial choice. Rosenberg was a liberal, Jewish, female, and, as the right-wingers in the Senate soon proclaimed, a suspected Communist. She was excellently qualified for the position; she had served on the War Manpower Commission during World War II and had been sent to Europe by both Roosevelt and Truman to check out military manpower problems. With Senate confirmation required, Anna was subjected to all sorts of bullying and harassment The McCarthyites, however, were dismayed to learn that there was another Anna Rosenberg the FBI eventually found was the Communist on the West Coast: Marshall's nominee was not the same one. Anna Rosenberg was eventually confirmed by the Senate, and she went on to do a fine job in the manpower position for both George Marshall and Robert Lovett.

Indeed, years later, at the Eleanor Roosevelt Political Award Dinner in New York on April 16, 1974, Bob Lovett gave a speech in honor of Anna Rosenberg, then bearing the married name Hoffman. He related how "Anna, exhausted by wretched days and sleepless nights, dashed to General Marshall's office" once she had been confirmed. Marshall, meeting with the Joint Chiefs of Staff, "heard the news with grave delight, walked over to Anna, leaned down, kissed her on the cheek and said, 'That's wonderful, Anna. I know you've been through hell. Now go home and get a facial. That's an order.'" Lovett went on: "From my own experience with General Marshall, I'm inclined to believe that this was the first and only time that our great architect of victory ever kissed a subordinate before issuing an order." Lovett described Anna Rosenberg: "It has long been our habit to think of the virtues of courage, fortitude, loyalty, devotion to duty and acceptance of arduous responsibility as the 'soldierly virtues.' And properly so. Since these are among the most important criteria of a soldier, then Anna Rosenberg Hoffman—visual evidence to the contrary notwithstanding—is one of the finest soldiers I have ever seen. For she has these virtues in full measure."[4]

The war in Korea had taken a strong swing in America's favor with the amphibious invasion of Inchon, far to the northwest in South Korea, on September 15, 1950, days before Lovett's entry into the department. The victory at Inchon cut off many North Korean troops way down in the south of Korea, and those who escaped were forced far to the north. On October 1 Republic of Korea troops passed over the 38th parallel border, with Douglas MacArthur's UN troops following shortly thereafter and heading north. On October 19 Pyongyang, the North Korean capital, was captured. The war was suddenly going very well for MacArthur and his troops as they surged farther north toward Manchuria. On October 15 President Truman and MacArthur met at Wake Island in the Pacific, where MacArthur, summoned to the meeting against his wishes, assured the president that there was little chance of Chinese intervention in the fighting. American commanders felt that the war was almost over, and there were visions of a Thanksgiving Day parade in Tokyo. On October 25, however, 250,000 Chinese troops crossed into Korea, and the shape of the war changed irrevocably with the first confrontation of Chinese and American troops on November 1.

Robert Lovett did not oversee military matters as such; these were attended to by generals and admirals. The civilian leadership of the Defense Department watched to make sure that the military operations were being carried out in accordance with the law and as efficiently as possible. But there were times that the civilian heads became involved with what was going on out in the field. Douglas MacArthur made sure of that. Early in November MacArthur and his air force commander, Lieutenant General George Stratemeyer, planned an extensive bombing program, to destroy the "Korean end" of all the bridges across the Yalu River into Manchuria. One key target was the North Korean city of Sinuiju, the temporary location of troops, officials, and the fleeing government of North Korea's premier, Kim Il Sung. It was just across the river from Antung, Manchuria.

Stratemeyer chose to inform Hoyt Vandenberg in Washington of the planned attack, and word of it reached Bob Lovett. Noting that the attack was scheduled to begin in three-and-a-half hours, Lovett, along with Dean Rusk, State Department aide for the Far East, charged over to Acheson's office. Because of the shallowness of the Yalu, destroying the bridges would not necessarily stop troop movements, and the risk of stray bombs hitting Antung or other Manchurian points was "very great." Rusk agreed with Lovett; Acheson agreed that the mission should be postponed; and Truman was then contacted in Kansas City to get his agreement. An hour and 20 minutes before 90 B-29 bombers were to take off on Stratemeyer's mission, Lovett passed on to MacArthur the orders of the Joint Chiefs: not to bomb any targets within five miles of the Manchurian border. He also requested specific information from MacArthur on the necessity for the planned bombings. MacArthur of course was outraged. It was a close call.[5] When the American forces were suddenly overwhelmed by Chinese troops late in November MacArthur wrote, "This command has done everything humanly possible within its capabilities but is now faced with conditions beyond its control and strength." Lovett scornfully said MacArthur was "issuing posterity papers."[6]

Lovett was confirmed as deputy secretary of defense by the Senate on November 29, 1950, after serving under a recess appointment for a couple of months. On December 1 he participated in a meeting at the Pentagon in which leaders of the government tried to make some sense out of the mess in Korea. Acheson, Bradley, Marshall, Joe Collins, Paul Nitze, Admiral Forrest Sherman, Averell Harriman, Dean Rusk, Walter Bedell Smith, and a host of other State and Defense leaders were present. There were suggestions of forming a strong defensive line across the Korean peninsula or of forming firm positions on both the east and west coasts. Smith, then serving as director of the CIA, took the position that the U.S.

should get out of Korea. "The Russians," he said, "could bleed us to death in Asia while defeating the armament effort in Europe."

Lovett responded, saying he understood there was a consensus on two points, "first, that Korea is not a decisive area for us; and second, that while the loss of Korea might jeopardize Japan and perhaps bring about its eventual loss, Western Europe was our prime concern and we would rather see that result than lose in Western Europe." It was best, nevertheless, to hold on in Korea for political moves; "we should regroup our troops and stall for time," then try to obtain a cease-fire or truce in Korea along the model used in Palestine. "We should deliberately admit to ourselves," he said, "that part of the condition would be that the Chinese withdraw while we do too, [which] might involve the abandonment of Korea."[7] The conversation went on and on as the generals and Admiral Sherman kicked around the risks of generating Soviet bombing raids from Vladivostok, possible Russian involvement, and perhaps even the use of the A-bomb. It was finally concluded, as suggested by Acheson, that the best choice might be to accept a cease-fire and go back to the 38th parallel (without knowing that by January the UN troops would be pushed back more than 75 miles below the 38th parallel).

Over the next few days, more bad news kept coming from Korea, with statements emanating from MacArthur opposite to Washington's positions. On December 5 Truman ordered that speeches, press releases, or other public statements dealing with foreign or military policy or affairs were to be cleared by the departments back home before issuance. While the directive did not mention MacArthur by name, it was very clearly aimed, if not exactly at him then certainly toward him.

In Korea, General Walton Walker, who was with some difficulty commanding the Eighth Army, was killed in a jeep collision on December 23 and replaced by General Matthew Ridgway, who was to do a far superior job on the ground in Korea (while MacArthur supervised and issued statements from his palace in Japan). As Ridgway brought the UN forces up once again to the 38th parallel, President Truman prepared to issue a statement, designed for him by Acheson, Marshall, Lovett, and the Joint Chiefs of Staff, calling upon the Chinese to agree to an immediate end of hostilities and the commencement of serious talks to settle the issues of Korea. He submitted this to the other countries that had troops in the UN force in Korea to get their approval. MacArthur, however, when apprised of this intended proposal, took matters into his own hands and on March 24 set forth a statement asserting that Red China had been shown to be militarily impotent, that it had "shown its complete inability to accomplish by force of arms the conquest of Korea," and that it "must by now be painfully aware that a decision of the United Nations to depart from its tolerant effort to contain the war to the areas of Korea, through an expansion of our military operations to his coastal areas and interior bases, would doom Red China to the risk of imminent military collapse." Toward the end of his statement, MacArthur offered to meet with the commander of the Chinese army to discuss surrender.[8] MacArthur and his staff considered the statement a "routine" bulletin, but this outrageous issuance, of course, totally forestalled Truman's proposed effort to seek a cease-fire.[9]

Late on the evening of March 23 (MacArthur's statement came on the other side of the international date line) Lovett, Rusk, and several others gathered at Acheson's home to react to it. Acheson noted that Lovett, "usually imperturbable and given to ironic humor under pressure, was angrier than I had ever seen him. The General, he said, must be removed and removed at once." Acheson shared Lovett's outrage at "insubordination of the grossest sort to his Commander in Chief," and the discussion of what should be done with MacArthur continued until 1:00 a.m.[10] The next day Truman met at noon with Acheson, Lovett, and Rusk. He was "deeply shocked" at MacArthur's statement, which was "totally disregarding all directives to abstain from any declarations on foreign policy." "By this act," the president decided, "MacArthur left me no choice—I could no longer tolerate his insubordination."[11] The president had Lovett send MacArthur a message reminding him of the December 5 message about clearing all statements, "for the main thing to do now was to prevent further statements by the general." The message went off to Tokyo, while Truman wrestled with the problem of getting rid of MacArthur. Soon the general took care of that problem for him.[12]

On April 5 Representative Joseph Martin, the Republican minority leader of the House, rose in Congress and read a letter MacArthur had written to him on March 20 in response to a note Martin had sent to him earlier: "It seems strangely difficult for some to realize that here in Asia is where the Communist conspirators have elected to make their play for global conquest, and that we have joined the issue thus raised on the battlefield; that here we fight Europe's war with arms while the diplomats there still fight it with words; that if we lose this war to Communism in Asia the fall of Europe is inevitable, win it and Europe most probably would avoid war and yet preserve freedom. As you point out, we must win. There is no substitute for victory."[13] With this statement, the MacArthur situation came to a conclusion. Acheson had a late-night conversation on April 5 with Bob Lovett about the issue, and then he, Marshall, Bradley, and Harriman met with the president the next day, agreeing that MacArthur had to be dismissed. Bradley procured the unanimous agreement of the Joint Chiefs, and on April 9, at 3:15 in the afternoon, Truman signed the orders relieving MacArthur of his several commands and replacing him with Matthew Ridgway.

Transmission of the orders was messed up somewhat. Secretary of the Army Frank Pace was in Korea, and it was decided to transmit the orders to Pace, who would then go to Tokyo and personally hand them to MacArthur. There were mechanical difficulties in reaching Pace, however, and MacArthur actually learned of his dismissal on a news broadcast, which caused President Truman embarrassment. Following this, of course, came the massive criticisms of Truman for the dismissal, MacArthur's return to Washington for speeches to Congress, and parades and salutations. Nevertheless, the deed was done. Douglas MacArthur's military career was over, and Matthew Ridgway would take over and do a fine job of the supervision of the war in Korea, which would continue for some time.

Although Harry Truman had to deal with the repercussions of the MacArthur firing, for the Defense Department the deed was done, and from that point on one of the major priorities was the continuing supply of arms and equipment to the Eighth Army in Korea, the helm of which was taken over by General James Van Fleet following Ridgway's promotion. In addition, though, to make up for the sharp demobilization that had followed the end of World War II, there was the project of expanding the American armed forces over and above what was needed in Korea, to place them on a peacetime level that could be rapidly expanded when necessary.. This effort involved a considerable bite into the American economy.

The defense budget initially prepared for fiscal year 1952, the first one after the start of the Korean War, came to about $103 billion. Robert Lovett was required to give his personal attention to more than six weeks of budget hearings and to get these figures reduced to a level the nation's economy could maintain, around $60 billion. Thereafter it fell to the civilians in the Defense Department rather than to the Joint Chiefs of Staff to keep the defense budget under control and in line while the war in Korea was being carried on. Even with the budget cut down to $60 billion, many members of Congress were concerned, as columnist Marquis Childs put it, "that this vast infusion of Government spending will either wreck the economy or alter it so completely that freedom of enterprise will be destroyed." When Lovett was before the House Armed Services Committee, a member pointed out a request in the army's budget for 68,000,000 can openers. What would any army do with 68,000,000 can openers—fire them at the enemy? Lovett explained that "these were not actually can openers but small keys ... used to open sardine cans ... to be attached to 68,000,000 cans of the new and improved C ration." As Childs described it, "Lovett took some good-natured kidding when this was brought out. With his rigorous, precise, dedicated approach to the job of administering the huge program, he considered it an unfortunate minor lapse in budgeting." Lovett was "certain that one reason Congress is willing to accept the $60 billion is because the budget under his supervision has been so thoroughly and carefully prepared."[14]

As the year went on, George Marshall prepared to retire from government service, for personal reasons, he said; he was concerned about his wife's health as well as his own health. When Acheson argued against his stepping down, Marshall said he "was worried about his performance of his duties." He did not permit himself weaknesses, he told Acheson; they did not comport with his duty.[15] The general had told Harry Truman that he would take the position as secretary of defense for just six months, or perhaps up to a year, and on September 12, 1951, he stepped down, effective a week later. He had essentially let Lovett run the department for the year, and Lovett had done it very well. In what was regarded as a simple changing of the guard, Lovett succeeded Marshall as head of the Defense Department, as Marshall had intended when he had taken the job. The press reported: "Lovett, a tall, bald, hard-working and high-strung man, can take over without any difficulties at the Pentagon. He has handled much of the organization work of the defense preparedness and other problems." Marshall, it was said, "who has been at his desk only infrequently for nearly two months, said of Lovett: 'No other man in the United States has his ability and competence to take complete charge.'"[16] Marshall, as his biographer wrote, "had restored confidence in the armed forces, had ended open warfare between Foggy Bottom and the Pentagon, had increased the size of the services, had helped the President through a possible crisis over the MacArthur firing. Lovett was assuming more and more of the workload." It was a fine time for the retirement of a great American soldier and statesman.[17]

Asked about General Marshall's greatest contribution during his year in the Defense Department, Bob Lovett said, "He was of such a towering prestige and so much respected, properly so, in the Congress and generally by the public, that he supplied one of the fundamentals that you cannot operate this country without, and that is complete trust. If General Marshall said something was something, it was. If he said something would be done, it was done."[18]

On September 13 the Senate Armed Services Committee unanimously approved Lovett for his new position, and on the 14th, Lovett's fifty-sixth birthday, the whole Senate unanimously confirmed his appointment in four minutes. Lovett was then sworn in on September 17, with his salary going from $20,000 a year to $22,500.[19] On September 22 *Business Week* put Bob Lovett on its cover, with an article inside headed "'Scrawny, Ill-Fed Eagle' Takes Over the Pentagon," and *Life* carried an article headed "A Good Man Gets a Big Job." The *Business Week* article, which took its title from a description of Lovett by a coworker— a description Lovett enjoyed, claimed that government service was good for Lovett: "In private life … Lovett from time to time has been plagued by stomach trouble. Every time Lovett has come to Washington to take a job, his ailment has left him. There is no simple medical explanation; it seems that crisis assignments are good for Bob Lovett." It went on to point out that "by temperament and training, Lovett is ideally suited for the job he has held, and for the job ahead. He isn't bothered by his 12-hour, seven-day week. His principal asset is an ability to digest a complicated matter quickly.… Around the Pentagon, Lovett is considered a man of razor sharpness, tempered by a dry sense of humor and complete absence of self-importance."[20] Looking ahead to the man in his new position, the article stated, "Lovett is no war monger. But he wasn't impressed with Russia's intentions of peace when he was Undersecretary of State, and he isn't impressed today. Lovett is uncompromising with the Soviets, in his thoughts and actions. His emergence as secretary will tend to hurry up the rearmament program. His incisive mind enables him to make decisions more quickly than could Marshall, who was tired when Truman called him back from retirement.[21]"

The article in *Life* said Lovett was "the unfortunately rare good man and great public servant who does his duty and is the despair of biographers who depend on colorful anecdotes to make their subjects attractive to the public.… His devotion to work—he has hardly any hobbies and no social life—has preserved the essential privacy of his personal life." The story went on to say, "The man is respected in Washington for qualities of mind highly prized but seldom found there—incisiveness and independence of judgment." It concluded with Marshall's description: "There is no man … like him for stepping in and taking charge."[22]

As Bob Lovett prepared to settle into his new position, Adele prepared herself for a stay in Washington. She had completed her dream house, Pleasance, in Locust Valley and filled it with all the proper pieces of furniture. From then on she would be by her husband's side in their handsome apartment at the Shoreham Hotel. Asked whether she planned a lot of entertaining, Adele replied, "Of course there will be some entertaining, but I hope all of us will keep the entertaining down as much as possible in these times." She added that she was "so proud and pleased for my husband, and I hope to stay right here and help him all I can, but I want to stay very much in the background."[23]

24

In Truman's Cabinet

George Marshall succinctly summed up what the days ahead would require: "The pre-eminent job before Mr. Lovett is this: to keep the boat steady against emotional reactions on one side, and letdowns in defense alertness on the other. I leave this post with the very satisfactory feeling of complete confidence that he will splendidly perform his task. He not only understands the job and the personnel; he commands the respect of all the departments." An Associated Press reporter called Lovett "an old hand in the government with a reputation for getting things done quickly with little fuss."[1]

Lovett's primary responsibility was the overall movement toward national security, up from the general disarmament that followed the end of World War II, and which had especially been pushed by Louis Johnson as Defense Secretary, a movement Lovett and Marshall had been working on for the past year. He also had to watch for the decisions concerning day-to-day and month-to-month efforts in the ongoing conflict in Korea. "Autumn," one writer pointed out, "is budget-making time in the Federal Government and, in the Department of Defense, military planning precedes all budget preparation. Thus the time is at hand when, with the Joint Chiefs of Staff to advise him, Secretary Lovett must decide and recommend to the President the size and shape and character of our defense forces—Air Force, Army, Navy and Marines—to be established in the fiscal year 1953. To do this he must redetermine the defense force balance."[2]

Lovett would be looking at strategic bombing, guided missiles, the navy's air, surface, and submarine strength, and the ground forces, and make decisions as to where the department's energy and money should be directed. To all of this Lovett brought "a rich store of experience, both military and civilian, a tremendous capacity for work, a reputation for smooth, effective administration, and a rich, native wit denoting the complete absence of stuffiness."[3] Hanson Baldwin, the military editor of the *New York Times*, called Lovett, as he took command in the Defense Department "an old Washington hand with very considerable acumen, much wisdom, great ability, infinite patience and quick understanding, but withal a capacity for righteous wrath…. His will be a firm hand on the tiller; a better appointment could not have been made."[4]

Asked later if there "were strong people in your shop on whom you could really depend?" Lovett answered "Oh, yes…. Bradley, of course, Joe Collins, Matt Ridgway. Matt Ridgway was one of the finest soldiers we ever produced, as were Bradley and Collins. They were all there then."[5] Lovett described meeting with the three service secretaries—Frank Pace of the army, Francis Matthews of the navy, and Thomas Finletter of the air force—"every Wednesday in a room to the left of the Secretary's room…. Anna Rosenberg was there, she was first class too. We would go in there and we would have about an hour and a half of bringing up the problems which were immediately of their concern."[6]

Lovett sworn in as defense secretary, September 17, 1951; (left to right) George Marshall; son, Robin; Lovett; daughter Evelyn Brown; wife, Adele; Ralph Stohl of the Defense Department (Associated Press).

On September 25 Robert Lovett held his first news conference as secretary, dealing in large part with overblown expectations of fancy new atomic weapons. He cautioned Americans against thinking that the day of easy victory in war with atomic weapons was near. "We must rely," he said, "on the proven, tested and available models to win today's battles with men presently trained to use them." But, he added, there was "enough truth" in stories about new weapons to "encourage a very optimistic outlook" for improved weapons somewhere off in the times ahead.[7]

Several weeks later Lovett spoke about the atomic weapons program in a speech to the American Legion convention in Miami on October 15. He warned that the U.S. did not yet have atomic weapons that could win a quick and easy wartime victory. "The plain fact is," he said, "that, until new weapons and new military applications of atomic energy have proved their reliability and are available for field use, our national safety in the face of attack will have to depend upon improved orthodox weapons in ample quantity and with sufficient trained and equipped ground, naval and air forces to use them effectively." But he assured the American Legion that "there is nothing impossible about the tasks that face us today. We have the resources and we have the skills and we have the industrial capacity and the confidence and faith to make them work."[8]

In November Lovett, along with Adele, had the opportunity to visit Germany on the way to the NATO Council gathering in Rome. Before leaving, he sent a memo to his secretary that "we will need cash, not only for our expenses, a portion of which will be reimbursed, but also for Christmas presents which I am sure Mrs. Lovett will not be able to resist." He drew out $3,000.[9] Lovett's initial stop on the journey was in Berlin, where he met at a dinner party with his old buddy Jack McCloy, then serving as the U.S. high commissioner for Germany, and with West German chancellor Konrad Adenauer. After several other stops in Germany he and Adele flew to Naples and then on to Rome on the 24th for the NATO gathering.[10]

As the new year worked its way in, Washington was treated to a visit from Winston Churchill, now in his late seventies but recently returned to the office of prime minister of the United Kingdom. Churchill and Anthony Eden, his foreign secretary, arrived on January 5, 1952, and were treated to welcoming ceremonies at the airport and an official lunch at Blair House. Following these, the visitors and their hosts met for a cruise on the presidential yacht down the Potomac, with Bob Lovett enjoying the boat ride. The evening following dinner was occupied by much discussion of the various tasks to be taken up in Europe, and Lovett was a valued participant in this talk. The next evening was consumed by a great deal more discussion at the British embassy with a smaller group, the Americans being Lovett, Bradley, and Acheson, with Churchill, Eden, and Ambassador Oliver Franks. These talks, which went on past one o'clock in the morning, centered on Far Eastern and Middle Eastern problems.

Meanwhile, following the stalemate in the war in Korea, which had begun in May of 1951, the talks looking for an armistice were carried on, as the UN side tried to reach some kind of a settlement with the Chinese Communists. The armistice talks had opened on July 10, 1951, in Kaesong, and were soon transferred to Panmunjon. They would continue until the final agreement of an armistice on July 27, 1953. Lovett did not have much to do with those talks—always viewing them from a distance but making sure that the U.S. Army's troops, armaments, and equipment were up to the high standards required. There were numerous battles along the way. Americans became familiar with names like Bloody Ridge, Heartbreak Ridge, Triangle Hill, and Porkchop Hill, although these fights, while costing more lives and damage, did not do much to change the line between the two sides.

The major issue blocking the agreement on an armistice was the exchange of prisoners of war. Many of the thousands of POWs held by the UN forces were prisoners who were unwilling to be sent back to North Korea, many of whom were South Koreans forced into the North Korean army. Many were simply unhappy with the resumption of life in the north, and many feared that they would be put to death if they were turned back over to North Korea. The Communist negotiators, however, were adamant that *all* POWs be sent back, no matter what their wishes might be. The American position was that prisoners would not be forcibly sent back, probably to their execution, to the Communists against their will; only voluntary repatriation would be approved.

On February 4 a draft memorandum, signed by Acheson and Lovett, set forth for the president the American position on POW repatriation, the reasons for it, and the disadvantages it produced. On February 8 this was slightly reduced to a like memorandum signed by Acheson and delivered to the president. On the same day, following a cabinet meeting, Acheson and Lovett met with the president to discuss the matter.[11] The memorandum stated that requiring U.S. troops "to use force to turn over to the Communists prisoners who believe they would face death if returned, would be repugnant to our most fundamental moral and humanitarian principles ... and would seriously jeopardize the psychological warfare position of the United States in its opposition to Communist tyranny." However, it recognized that "maintenance of this principle will inevitably present risks to prisoners held by the Communists and to the achievement of an armistice." The recommendation to the president was that the present position be approved, while possible means to get around the problem should be sought.[12] Lovett told Mr. Truman "that he did not oppose the President's approval of this memorandum," but "he asked that the memorandum should not be regarded as 'definitive,' by which he meant, as indicated by his remarks, final and irrevocable." Lovett thought "that we could go ahead at once in implementing the memorandum." When Lovett finished, the president stated his approval.[13]

The major problem this position created was clearly set forth in a letter Senator Francis Case (R-SD) wrote to the president on October 1, describing a letter he had received from a South Dakota lady whose husband had been a prisoner of the North Koreans since 1950. She quoted from a radio talk she had heard "that we are willing to sacrifice the lives of our own prisoners, if necessary, to protect the freedom and the liberty of Asiatics ... the first time that the white man has ever done anything like that." The talk cited the "tremendous propaganda effect" this had produced in Asia. Case's correspondent then wrote, "My husband is worth more than 500 Communist prisoners of war." Case concluded: "How long must her husband and thousands more like him stay in the prisoner of war camps?"[14] Truman's secretary, Matt Connelly, sent Case's letter off to Bob Lovett with the request that he answer it. On October 30 Lovett did:

> The exchange of prisoners of war, particularly the question of forcible repatriation of some Communist prisoners now being held by the United Nations forces in Korea, is the most difficult problem confronting the United Nations in the Korean armistice negotiations. The decision of the United States Government not to forcibly return Communist prisoners, and to be firm in this decision, is based on fundamental moral principles and on practical military considerations.... [N]umbers of prisoners now held by the United Nations Command have sworn to die rather than be returned to Communist control, and others have so compromised themselves that there is little doubt but that they would be liquidated en masse if turned over to their former masters. [As Truman has said] ... [t]o return these prisoners of war ... by force would result in misery and bloodshed to the eternal dishonor of the United States and the United Nations. We will not buy an armistice by turning over human beings for slaughter or slavery.

Lovett went on:

> [T]he hope of refuge and asylum from Communist tyranny is an important cause of defection and surrender by soldiers of the Communist states. If enemy soldiers who laid down their arms in hope of refuge from Communism were returned ruthlessly for punishment by their former masters, the fact would be exploited fully by the Communists to deter surrender by their troops in the future. This would be a military factor of considerable importance to any resumption of hostilities. This stand was reached only after the most serious evaluation of all aspects of the problem. The Department of Defense is convinced that this decision was a wise one.

This stand, Lovett continued, "undoubtedly taxes the patience and forbearance of those whose loved ones are in Communist hands. Yet, an objective appraisal of over-all national interest leaves us no useful alternative than to follow the policy of no forced repatriation."[15] When the Korean armistice was finally settled, in July 1953, it included a Neutral Nations Repatriation Commission, which handled the repatriation question in a somewhat confusing manner but finally managed to get it taken care of.

On another subject, Robert Lovett spoke about U.S. and Russian airpower in testimony before the Senate Appropriations Committee on February 4, 1952. In "a crisp exchange with senators over relative Russian and U.S. air strength," Lovett called for approval of the proposed $52,100,000,000 military budget for 1952–53. Any cut in this spending program, which had already been cut back, would, Lovett said, "increase beyond the realms of prudence, the calculated risks already taken" in putting together the budget. Asked by Sen. Joseph O'Mahoney (D–Wyo), presiding over the meeting, about the comparative air-power issue, Lovett said that after World War II the U.S. "went to sleep" on its defenses, while the Russians pushed ahead. "We did not demobilize—in my opinion we disintegrated," he said. So, "we have to run faster now for several years to make up a deficit in aircraft." He pointed out, though, that the F-86, "in test," was a superior plane to the Russians' MIG-15.[16]

After doing his bit to get the budget passed successfully, Lovett was off to Lisbon, Portugal, where he, Treasury Secretary Snyder, Averell Harriman, and Dean Acheson made up the American team for the Ninth Meeting of the NATO Council. The Lisbon meetings were important, for they worked out German participation in NATO, overcoming French hesitation and possible opposition, and providing for increased American aid. France's Robert Schuman and Germany's Konrad Adenauer were important participants in the extensive discussions and negotiations. "The Lisbon conference," Acheson said, "was brought dramatically to a successful finish. At last the collective defense force for Europe under unified command was agreed on and on the way."[17]

Arriving back in Washington, Robert Lovett issued a statement at a Pentagon news conference regarding the goals established at Lisbon. The United States, he said, would add no more army divisions to its ground force in Europe in the coming year. But it would send considerably more air power, building up to an air force in Western Europe of about 4,000 planes from a current force of about one-fourth of that. The U.S. contribution would emphasize tactical aircraft, fighters, fighter-bombers, and transports needed to provide air aid for ground troops and help to move them rapidly from place to place. General Eisenhower commanded NATO, and his ground forces, Lovett said, would consist of 25 to 30 fully combat-ready divisions, with another 20 or so in reserve, with major combat equipment, transportation, and supply systems ready but without the manpower necessary for combat, manpower he said that can often in Europe be called to active duty quickly.[18]

A couple of weeks later, in a semi-annual report to the president and Congress on Defense Department activities, Lovett said that military manpower requirements would go up substantially, as "a large number of new recruits will be needed to replace reservists who were called to active duty after June, 1950, and to make up losses due to expiration of enlistments and other attrition factors." He also predicted that the military security budget would require a larger percentage of the gross national product in the coming year.[19] "So far as budget work went, Lovett was considered a master. One staffer said: "'Uncle Bob'" had a built-in calculator for knowing just what he was committing himself to. He had been in the banking system so long he could add up in his head what kind of expenditures he had approved; and his figure would be within one-half a per cent of the correct total even though it might take his staff two days to add it up precisely to see if he was right.'" And his deputy secretary, William Foster, added, "In development and control of the budget, Lovett was superlative."[20]

As March turned into April a major national crisis loomed. As of the final day of 1951 the labor contract between the United Steelworkers of America and the major steel-producing companies came to an end. The steel industry indicated that it did not want to discuss the demands of the union for increased wages and better working conditions, and the union, led by Philip Murray, who was also the national head of the CIO, announced a strike, to begin December 31. Robert Lovett had for several months been pointing out to the president "that the national defense program would be endangered if a strike was allowed to halt production," and the other members of the cabinet agreed with Lovett. So on December 22 Truman referred the dispute to the Wage Stabilization Board (WSB) for solution, with the Steelworkers Union agreeing to postpone the strike.[21]

Over the next several months, while steel production continued, there were various findings, recommendations, conferences, and consultations involving the WSB, the Office of Defense Mobilization (ODM), Congress, and other agencies, but the union and the steel companies were unable to come to an agreement. The principal conflict was in the steel companies' requirement of an increase in the government-regulated cost of steel in response to an increase in their workers' wages (a requirement that of course put the government in the midst of the negotiations). Robert Lovett had a strong feeling of unease, one that government officials feel when trouble is brewing. He warned ODM of the apparent stalemate in the steel negotiations "and of the impact of a steel strike on United States military requirements in Korea and throughout the world. Lovett's feelings on this score were strong, and he was capable of forceful statement."[22]

On April 3 much-delayed negotiations took place once again between the union and the steel companies. The companies offered a total of 14.4 cents in increased pay and "fringe benefits," the first offer made by the steel companies since the start of negotiations the previous November but well under what the Wage Stabilization Board had recommended. The union rejected the offer and announced that the much-feared strike would commence on Wednesday, April 9, at 12:01 a.m. At this point, the White House knew swift action had to be taken. Harry Truman called in his principal advisors. For the Defense Department, Lovett "said emphatically that any stoppage of steel production, for even a short time, would increase the risk we had taken in the 'stretch-out' of the armament program." He pointed out "that our entire combat technique in all three services depended on the fullest use of our industrial facilities." Finally, referring to Korea, he said "that 'we are holding the line with ammunition, and not with the lives of our troops.' Any curtailment of steel production, he warned, would endanger the lives of our fighting men."[23]

Faced with four choices—(1) seizure under Section 18 of the Universal Military Training and Service Act of 1948, (2) sending a seizure bill to Congress with little hope of a quick passage, (3) use of the Taft-Hartley Act, or (4) seizure under the "inherent powers of the President"—it was determined that acting under any of the first three choices would be complicated and uncertain. While there were possible constitutional issues in the "inherent powers" action, it was soon decided by the president that such action was the best way to move forward.

Accordingly, on April 5 a draft of the seizure order arrived at the White House from the Justice Department, a draft that left blank the designation of the department of the government assigned to carry out the seizure. Lovett had already objected to the Defense Department's being so designated, arguing that administrative manpower in his department should be conserved for military tasks. He had requested a meeting with the president before any such assignment was made, and in fact Truman ultimately chose the Department of Commerce, with its business-like secretary Charles W. Sawyer, to oversee the seizure.

On Tuesday evening, April 8, President Truman sat down at 10:30 before his microphone and announced to the nation that the secretary of commerce was to take control of the steel mills at midnight that night, one minute before the Steelworkers' Union's scheduled strike. The president had discussed the possibility of seizure with his close friend, Chief Justice Vinson, and had been told by Vinson that he thought a majority of the Supreme Court would agree that it could be done. Truman, in his speech, went on to lay most of the blame for the stalemated talks upon the steel industry, stating that the recommendations of the Wage Stabilization Board were fair and reasonable despite the refusal of the steel companies to accept them. "The plain fact of the matter," Truman told the country, "is that the steel companies are recklessly forcing a shutdown."[24]

Executive Order 10340, "Directing the Secretary of Commerce to Take Possession of and Operate the Plants and Facilities of Certain Steel Companies," had been signed by the president earlier that day, April 8. Secretary Sawyer issued an order to the managers of the industry to stay on their jobs while the workers returned to theirs and to keep separate books for the seizure period. The only indication of the takeover was the flying of American flags over the steel mills. The steel industry continued at work, while the industry leaders and newspaper editorials across the country condemned Truman for the seizure and for the government's handling of the labor dispute.

On April 9 three steel companies went to court, asking for a temporary injunction against the seizure. District court Judge Alexander Holtzoff refused on the ground that the companies had failed to show they would suffer "irreparable damage," the judge also doubting that he had the power to issue an injunction against the president. In the meantime, while Truman had sent a brief message to Congress suggesting that it might pass some legislation to deal with the problem, the members of Congress reacted strongly against him and soon four separate congressional investigations were under way.[25]

On April 24 Robert Lovett appeared before the Senate Committee on Labor and Public Welfare, answering questions from Senators Wayne Morse (R–Ore) and Hubert Humphrey (D–Minn). Referring to the stretched-out period imposed on military spending, Humphrey asked, "So current production is even more important with the stretched-out period than if you would have had, let us say, the more compact production program in terms of time." "That is correct, sir," responded Lovett, "and it is even more important because we are now in a period of maximum acceleration." Asked by Humphrey whether there were any stored surpluses of specific items like carbon steel, stainless steel, and superalloy steel that could have tided over a period of cessation of steel production, Lovett answered that such materials are given through the "controlled materials plan" several months in advance on certificates, "although they do not go into the work in process stage, we will say, until 6 months after the authority is given. Not that we would run out of steel the day after the strike or the week after the strike," he went on, "but with the mills shut down we would, after some period of time, which is a matter of guesswork, largely run out."

Later in his testimony, Lovett brought up the problems of stop-and-go in the steel business. "Our feeling," he said, "is that there is no such thing as a short stoppage, because of the peculiarity of the industry, and notably the extraordinarily long time it takes to reheat a furnace once it is cooled. It is a very long process, and of course a costly one. So that even if the strike existed only two days, that in itself would mean something over three weeks before we got back in production." Asked by Humphrey whether a shutdown of such duration would impair the operations of other defense-related industries, Lovett said, "Very seriously; yes, sir."[26]

While further futile efforts to settle the dispute were taking place, and the possibility arose of putting into effect the wage recommendations of the Wage Stabilization Board, the steel companies were back in court, seeking a restraining order against Secretary Sawyer. On April 23 Assistant Attorney General Holmes Baldridge appeared for the government before Judge David A. Pine. When the judge asked if the executive had unlimited power in an emergency, Baldridge answered that he had whatever power was necessary to protect the country in an emergency, adding, "I suppose if you carry it to its logical conclusion, that's what it is." Baldridge argued that an unlimited executive was "expediency backed by power."[27] Baldridge's assertion of unlimited power caused much astonishment in the White House, where the brief prepared by the Justice Department had not been seen ahead of time, and a statement was issued asserting that the powers of the president were of course limited by the Constitution. Nevertheless, Judge Pine on April 29 issued a 14-page opinion in which he declared the seizure of the steel mills illegal.

Pine's opinion came out at 3:45 in the afternoon, and at 5:00 p.m. Philip Murray of the Steelworkers ordered an immediate strike. The next day the government lawyers gained a stay of Judge Pine's order by the circuit court of appeals on the condition that a petition for review by the Supreme Court be made promptly. With a cost-of-living increase going into effect shortly, Murray agreed to end the strike on May 2. At 5:00 p.m. on May 3 the Supreme Court announced, by a 7–2 vote, that it would hold a hearing on May 12, and, in the interim, the Court ordered, no wage increase should be made. In the meantime, there were rumors coming to Washington from Korea indicating that the Communists might be near to breaking off armistice negotiations and resuming full-scale war.

The Supreme Court heard the case on May 12 and 13, with the justices pressing mostly on statutory bases for seizure, the lack of a formal declaration of war, and the president's failure to utilize the procedures of the Taft-Hartley Act. Among the documents presented to the court was Defense Secretary Lovett's affidavit relative to the danger to our military posture to be caused by a steel strike, which had originally been presented to Judge Pine. The Supreme Court handed down its decision on Monday, June 2, ruling 6–3 that the seizure of the steel mills was unconstitutional, upsetting Vinson's assurance to Truman that the court would uphold the seizure. The court's opinion was given by Justice Hugo Black. Two hours after the court's decision was announced, the steelworkers went out again on strike.[28]

On June 6 Robert Lovett held a press conference at which he said that it was "a very grave situation," that the strike was "just about as serious a blow as you could get," and he hoped something was done quickly to get production resumed. "A work stoppage in the steel industry," he said, "is important to the Defense Department, whether for one day or one week." Assuming that the arms program uses nine million tons of steel a month, he went on, with a strike of twenty days, "you lose six million tons."[29] Nevertheless, the strike proceeded and the steel mills shut down. On July 7 Robert Lovett was admitted to Walter Reed Army Hospital after a couple of days of lightheadedness, chills, and dark bloody stools. After consideration of his past medical history, the peptic ulcer, the November 1946 gallbladder surgery, and pancreatitis, it was determined that the cause of his problems was in fact a duodenal ulcer. After ten days, three diagnostic operations and blood transfusions,

Lovett was discharged from Walter Reed for three or four days' rest at home, followed by part-time in the office for a week.[30]

Finally, on July 23 and back to work, Lovett held an hour-long press conference at which he said the steel strike was "a darn sight worse than any bombing raid anybody ever launched." He said the situation was so serious that the president had "authorized and directed me to give you an accurate picture of what is going on." "This is the 52nd day of the strike," he said, "and military production is beginning to grind to the halt you were apprehensive about all the way through. No enemy nation could have inflicted more damage. This is a calamity and let's make no mistake about it."[31] With these words suddenly placed before the public, President Truman summoned the union and industry leaders to Washington and demanded an immediate settlement of the strike. Twenty-four hours later Truman was able to make the dramatic announcement that the strike had been settled, with the steel companies granted a price increase of as much as $5.65 per ton. Six hundred thousand steel workers would return to their jobs, and the defense industry would resume its work.

Top government officials felt that the man who had forced the settlement of the steel strike was not Truman but Lovett, that his press-conference statements were "a bombshell that shook the White House to its political foundations," its effectiveness multiplied by the fact that the Democratic National Convention was in session in Chicago and that Truman was scheduled to appear before it (although he had disclaimed any interest in another nomination). Some of the White House advisers were furious over Lovett's statements and their timing but felt that Truman had been "smart enough to follow the only course that would not have been politically disastrous."[32]

In any event, the steel strike was over. Fortunately, events in Korea had slowed down to the point that American arms shortages were not devastating, but in March 1953 Van Fleet, commanding the U.S. troops, "complained that his troops had been short of certain types of ammunition in the summer and early fall of 1952."[33] In September Robert Lovett expressed grave concern at strikes in California in the Lockheed and Douglas aircraft plants. "These two plants are very important elements in our production complex," he said. "Any stoppage of work has a very bad effect on our general program. We are very much concerned. There has been a rash of strikes which have done us much harm."[34]

On April 18, 1952, Lovett spoke to the American Society of Newspaper Editors in Washington. The United States, Lovett said, was developing new weapons, "so destructive as to raise serious doubts as to what would remain of civilization as we know it." These "bold new developments," he said, should make it obvious that it would not be enough to win the next war: "We must, if at all possible, stop World War III before it starts."[35]

Two weeks later Bob Lovett was back before the Senate Appropriations subcommittee, after the House of Representatives had cut the military budget to $46,000,000,000, a cut he said would force the country "to demobilize a substantial part of our armed forces." He urged the Senate to rebuff the House ceiling because it would "raise a serious question as to our ability to maintain troops" in Europe and Korea, would strike a "critical blow to military preparedness efforts and the defense of our country," and would wipe out much defense production capacity and make it necessary to spend up to eighteen months to get production rolling again in case of war. The Senate eventually got the budget back up to where it had been set by the Defense Department.[36]

There were still memories of Bob Lovett's close friend Jim Forrestal. On May 4, 1951, Lovett had turned over to Princeton University president Harold Dodds a check for $28,296 for the establishment of a "living memorial" to Forrestal, the remainder of the Forrestal Memorial Fund raised by one-dollar contributions from Defense Department workers and servicemen. An earlier donation from the fund of $5,700 had been used for a bust of Forrestal, sculpted by Kalervo Kallio and placed on the steps of an entrance to the Pentagon.[37] This donation was followed up on May 17, 1952, by Lovett's address to 800 representatives of business, government, industry, science, and education at the Armed Forces Day dedication of the James Forrestal Research Center at Princeton. Jim Forrestal, Lovett said, more than any other man, struggled to make unification of the armed forces a reality. "Many of the advances being made today in the Department of Defense," he pointed out, "will be rightly recorded in history as monuments to the wisdom, ability and patriotism of our first Secretary of Defense." Lovett went on: "I talked with Forrestal countless times on how to stop the aggression of world Communism. One conclusion ran through each of our talks. That conclusion was that weakness would lead us nowhere. The only solution was in the restoration of adequate strength."[38]

A couple of days later, Lovett was called to the White House, along with Dean Acheson and General Bradley, to discuss Indochina with President Truman. As a result of this meeting, Acheson was given several points to discuss with Anthony Eden of England and Robert Schuman of France, including "further development of indigenous forces and our willingness to give additional help to the effort." Ho Chi Minh's revolutionary efforts had not yet reached the crisis stage, and there was still hope that France might keep a lid on things there.[39]

On June 1 Dwight Eisenhower arrived in Washington, and his old friend Bob Lovett arranged a press conference for him at the Pentagon. Because the newly announced presidential candidate was still in uniform and "speaking under military auspices" he told the reporters "that I could comment only on military subjects…. Of course the reporters there that day were far more interested in politics than in NATO; nevertheless they understood the limitations."[40]

June turned out to be a very busy month for Bob Lovett, as he was awarded four honorary degrees, from Amherst College and the Ivy League Big Three—Yale, Princeton, and Harvard. Yale's commencement was on June 9, and Lovett happily heard President A. Whitney Griswold proclaim, "Honoring you as one of the most useful and trusted citizens of our time, Yale confers upon you the degree of Doctor of Laws."[41] On June 17 Lovett returned to Princeton, where he was presented with the honorary degree of doctor of laws by Harold Dodds. Two days later President Conant of Harvard conferred the same degree upon him.[42]

Several months later Lovett responded to germ-warfare charges coming out of Korea. "It is simply another tiresome episode in the rather shoddy and sinister swindle the Communists are perpetrating on the rest of the world by giving currency to these complete lies," Lovett said. The germ-warfare charges, he explained, coincided with the "discovery" by the Soviet youth magazine *Smena* that "beizbol" was not American in origin but a distortion of the Russian village sport of "lapta," played well before America's settlement. "We can stand almost anything," he said, "but having our national pastime called lapta. They live in a ridiculous land of make-believe." Getting back to the germ-warfare charges and their possible intention to use it themselves, Lovett continued, "It is their habit to charge some one else with crimes they propose to commit."[43]

Along with Korea and Europe there were troubles aplenty in the Middle East. On May 1, 1951, Mohammed Mossadegh, the prime minister of Iran, had nationalized the Anglo-Iranian Oil Company, setting off conflict and confusion in the country. While pushing a wide range of social reforms, Mossadegh struck hard at the British-owned oil company, cancelling its oil concessions and expropriating its assets.[44] Over the next couple of years, the conflict between Great Britain and the Iranians involved the United States in numerous ways, as Truman, Acheson, Lovett, and other American leaders attempted to devise possible methods to relieve the British-Iranian troubles and, in particular, to prevent Mossadegh from moving his country (and its vast oil resources) toward the Russians. Lovett worked on these problems with Acheson, stressing the need to avoid military confrontations as the conflict stretched out over many months.

After the uproar in Iran in July 1952, Mossadegh resigning and being reappointed, Lovett, as he wrote in a letter on August 16 to Undersecretary of State David Bruce, was concerned that the political current "is running toward even more extreme and irresponsible anti–Westernism and dangers of a coup d'etat, whether by the communists alone or in combination with the National Front, are more serious than had been believed." He went on: "The risks of continuing our present policy [depending on the British to intervene if necessary], have become unacceptable, and ... it must be discarded in favor of a policy of action to prevent Iran from falling to communism."[45]

While Acheson continued to try for some sort of amicable arrangement with Mossadegh and the Iranians, the British continued to obstruct such moves. After the change of administrations in January 1953, the State Department and the CIA changed American policy, joining with British intelligence groups working within Iran toward an overthrow of Mossadegh. This they, along with the Shah of Iran, were able to achieve in August 1953. Unfortunately, ousting and imprisoning the popular Mossadegh contributed to growing anti-Western feeling in Iran, which has led to increasing problems with that country over the years since.

On September 23 Robert Lovett was back in his old home town of Huntsville, Texas, where he was honored by the Huntsville Walker County Chamber of Commerce and the Board of Regents Texas State Teachers Colleges, as Sam Houston State Teachers College presented him with an honorary doctor of laws degree. That evening the Houston Chamber of Commerce gave a dinner in Lovett's honor, as Governor Allan Shivers had proclaimed "Robert A. Lovett Day" in the state of Texas. Harmon Lowman, the college president, said Robert Lovett Day was "the biggest thing our campus has ever experienced." As Lovett, in his speech at the dinner, recalled his early childhood in Huntsville, two elderly ladies present remembered him as a baby, one recalling "holding him in my arms."[46]

In November 1952 the nation went to the polls and ended twenty years of Democratic occupancy of the White House, electing Dwight Eisenhower president over Governor Adlai E. Stevenson of Illinois. In September, Lovett had responded to newsmen who had asked him if he would stay in the Defense Department if an invitation to do so were tendered by the president-elect with a firm reply: "'No,' said Lovett, he would not; his tour of duty would be over." He had made this position crystal clear in August. Walter Millis, in the *Herald Tribune*, had pointed out that while Lovett, as a Republican who had served in Democratic administrations, might be eligible for reappointment no matter who won the election, "unfortunately, there is no secret—and no doubt—about his determination to resign."[47]

Learning of Lovett's decision to leave the Defense Department in January, Bunny Harriman wrote him: "I've just come out of a partners meeting [at Brown Brothers] at which all those present expressed delight over your public statement appearing in yesterday's paper which confirmed what you told me last week about your personal plans. They want me to tell you we are getting out the welcome mat & polishing up a plate with your name on it at your desk."[48]

With his tenure as Defense Secretary scheduled to end on January 20, 1953, Robert Lovett sat down on November 18 and wrote a long letter to Harry Truman, setting forth his recommendations for improving the operation and administration of the Defense Department. The basic purpose of Lovett's letter was for it to be given to President-elect Eisenhower, in private, so that if he chose not to adopt some of Lovett's suggestions he would be under no pressure. However, contrary to Lovett's intentions, his letter was released to the press on January 8, 1953, when he presented it to a closed-door session of the House Armed Service Committee.[49] In his letter Lovett stressed that the opinions expressed were his own, not the result of any coordinated staff study, and that they were set down to give "my successor a running start on certain problems." He began by stating that "the quality of our professional military officers and the permanent civilian staff is remarkably high.... I have great respect and affection for our professional military men and having had an opportunity of seeing them both at the council table and in the field, I know of no country more fortunately situated in this respect than ours."[50] Lovett strongly recommended (1) the establishment of universal military training, (2) the reorganization of the Joint Chiefs of Staff to remove some of their paperwork and to lessen their dual capacity of serving both as military planners and as the administrative chiefs of their respective services, (3) the secretary be permitted to create his own staff of military advisers, (4) the supply services of the army be trimmed to get rid of overlapping functions and a survey be made of the organization of all services to see if they could be streamlined, and (5) an effort be made to reduce the ever-growing number of military headquarters throughout the world. There were far too many levels of headquarters in the various services, "thus adding to the overhead and inevitably causing delay." Protecting official secrets, Lovett said, was important, and a great hazard to national security was "the apparent inadequacy of existing legislation to protect this country against traitors, spies and blabber-mouths."[51] Finally, Robert Lovett concluded that another person in the job with different work habits might disagree with all of what he had said. Regardless of that, he said, "I will do my utmost to see that my successor is fully briefed and I will gladly hold myself at his disposal for any assistance I can give in making his take-over of responsibilities smooth and effective."[52]

Two weeks after the election Eisenhower came to Washington for a get-together with Harry Truman. Eisenhower brought with him two aides, while Truman had with him Lovett, Acheson, Snyder, and Harriman. It was a rather chilly meeting, and after Acheson's presentation on foreign affairs, Eisenhower cut short the gathering because he was following it up with a meeting at the Pentagon with Lovett and the Joint Chiefs of Staff, a consultation that came off much better because of Eisenhower's and Lovett's long-time relationship.

Eisenhower had promised as a part of his presidential campaign a trip to Korea, to see what he could do to bring matters there to a close. Robert Lovett, as Defense Secretary, sent his old friend immediately after the election what Ike called a "kind and thoughtful letter" regarding arrangements. Eisenhower said Lovett's letter "creates a feeling of confidence that is not characteristic of some that I have been receiving." With all the security measures in hand, the journey came off well, although it changed little in Korea. After it was over, Lovett thanked the American media for help in protecting Eisenhower's security there: "Their self-restraint ... was a necessary part of the program for providing all possible protection during the President-designate's trip to the war zone in Korea."[53]

For his choice to head the Defense Department, Eisenhower felt that he needed a strong, head-cracking secretary. "We have tried two investment bankers [Forrestal and Lovett], a politician [Johnson] and a military man [Marshall]," he told his aide, Henry Cabot Lodge. "Maybe we should try an industrialist." They wound up with the head of General Motors, Charles E. Wilson, and after Wilson was designated, Bob Lovett did what he could to acquaint him with the workings of the department. Wilson, though, did not turn out to be one of the better defense secretaries.[54]

On January 8 Prime Minister Winston Churchill paid another visit to the United States. His principal purpose was to meet with Eisenhower prior to Eisenhower's swearing-in, to be followed by a vacation in Jamaica. However, he also paid a visit to Harry Truman, who was serving his last weeks in the White House. Also there at the time were Acheson, Snyder, and Lovett. That evening, Truman, George Marshall, Lovett, Harriman, Bradley, and some members of Churchill's staff dined with the prime minister at the British embassy. Acheson recounted it: "The Prime Minister got the dinner off to an unpromising start by asking the President whether he would have his answer ready when they both stood before St. Peter to account for their part in dropping the atomic bombs on Japan. Before the President could answer, Bob Lovett, with admirable presence of mind, provided a diversion from this lugubri- ous subject. Was the Prime Minister sure," Lovett asked, "that he and the President would undergo that interrogation in the same place?" Churchill insisted that God "would not con- demn him without a hearing." "True," said Lovett, "but not in the Supreme Court to begin with; and, possibly, in quite a different jurisdiction." "By this time," said Acheson, "everyone had relaxed and the Prime Minister, with the aid of his champagne, was enjoying the game. He admitted the possibility suggested, but insisted that wherever the hearing might take place it would be conducted in accordance with the principles of the English common law." Lovett and Acheson then began putting together a jury of Churchill's peers, including Alexan- der, Caesar, Socrates and Aristotle, though Churchill balked at Voltaire and Cromwell. Ulti- mately, President Truman intervened, but the evening had been saved by Bob Lovett's diversion, and everyone had a light-hearted time thereafter.[55]

As he was preparing to return to private life, Bob Lovett even found himself in the Supreme Court, the result of a rape and murder of a young lady employee of a government store on the island of Guam by three soldiers who tried to get the death sentences imposed by courts-martial on Guam overturned by the civil courts. The district court in Washington turned them down, as did the Court of Appeals for the D.C. Circuit. From this came an appeal to the Supreme Court, with a writ of certiorari granted on December 15, 1952. Although Lovett had not a thing to do with the case, which involved the courts discussing the merits of courts-martial and how they were to be treated in civilian courts, the case was entitled *Burns and Dennis vs. Robert A. Lovett, Secretary of Defense*, 344 U.S. 903. The case was argued in the high court on February 5, 1953, and an opinion was handed down by Chief Justice Vinson on June 15, 1953, affirming the circuit court's ruling. By this time, however, the case was entitled *Burns & Dennis vs. Wilson*, 346 U.S. 137, reflecting the change at the head of the Defense Department.[56]

In any event, Robert Lovett did a very competent job as head of the Defense Department. On January 29, nine days after leaving his job, Lovett wrote to George Marshall telling him he had been unable to get through the crowd surrounding Marshall at the Eisenhower inauguration ceremony on the 20th; "when I tried to find you, you had disappeared into thin air through some mysterious means of egress, and I found myself hemmed in in the row by a pushing and determined crowd." So Lovett's letter was to serve a dual purpose—"to greet you, and also to give you a one paragraph report on my stewardship in office," although it actually ran to two paragraphs:

> I believe most of the goals you set in October 1950 were in general attained. Our total military strength rose from 1,460,000 (7/1/50) to about 3,600,000, with twenty well-trained divisions, eighteen regimental combat teams and their full complement of supporting units; a Navy of 1,150 active vessels, including over 400 warships as compared with 238 two years ago. The Air Force of 98 wings, as compared with 48, is on the way to the goal of 143 wings. Our man-power policy has been superbly carried out by Anna [Rosenberg], and we will rotate out of the service this fiscal year about ⅓ of the total—that is, about 1,003,000. We actually in the last quarter of the calendar year let out 49,000 more people than we took in. On the production side, our aircraft has gone up to about one thousand planes a month. Our jet engine program is in good shape. We are producing more medium tanks in two months than we lost in the entire Korean War, and more light tanks in two weeks than we lost since the beginning of Korea. The industrial base has a firm foundation, and out of a total of 444 Government plants, 408 have been put back into operation. The 36 remaining are very likely TNT plants which are being maintained on a reserve status. We will actually begin to go on a sustaining rate of production in March on many of our major items of procurement, and the cutting back of our schedules will, I think, be one of the first things Mr. Wilson must face in a field in which he should be uniquely very competent.
>
> You may recall that we promised, in November 1950, to bring down the requests for appropriations as rapidly as possible after our initial investment and purchase of assets had been completed. Our F.Y. 1954 requisitions for appropriations total 41.2 billion dollars as compared with 60.8 billion dollars in F.Y. 1952. There is, therefore, a reduction of about 20 billion dollars in two years, much to the astonishment of Ike and the Congress.

Lovett said he wanted "to make this hasty report to you as my boss, and to say that to the best of our abilities, we have tried to see that the wise policies you laid down for the Department ... have been carried forward." He added, "I would not have missed the opportunity of serving you for worlds," noted that Adele was laid up with the flu, and that they would soon be headed to Hobe Sound the next week.[57]

George Marshall, in his response from his home in Pinehurst, North Carolina, said, "I doubt if any man commanded more devoted loyalty combined with remarkable efficiency than I did in you. We had a good many years close together burdened with crises of world wide proportions. Few men in the world have had such an experience, and its authentic history, so far as we were concerned, is a record of complete cooperation, mutual accord and delightful friendship that I cherish and find in it a source of satisfaction in living."[58]

As Robert Lovett saw his days in Washington coming to an end, he wrote to Hazel Pierson at Brown Brothers Harriman: "As soon as possible after this tour of duty ends at noon on January 20th, Adele and I will go back to Locust Valley and I will expect to come in town every day or so during the ten days or two weeks before we go down to Hobe Sound for a long rest. This will give me a chance to catch up on some personal affairs and also to make some of my business arrangements." He said he hoped "to re-enter the firm about the 1st of March on a formal basis and to come back to work sometime in April."[59]

25

Out of the Government,
Technically

As of January 20, 1953, Robert Lovett figured that he was done with service to the United States government. There had certainly been plenty of it—from flying for the navy in World War I, backing up Henry Stimson as assistant secretary for air in World War II, working on Greek-Turkish aid, the Marshall Plan, the Berlin Airlift, NATO, and intergovernmental affairs for the State Department, and getting the U.S. military in proper shape in the Defense Department. Asked by Doris Condit in a 1976 interview what he considered his greatest contribution to the government, Bob Lovett thought about it and answered at some length:

> I think that my contribution, if any, was a result of unique training. After all, there was nobody prior to that time who had been trained through college and a graduate school afterwards, two graduate schools, and then been thrown into international banking in this turbulent period where you went out to foreign countries and were compelled to know at least one other foreign language and knew people abroad. I lived and worked in London two years, Paris the same thing. With that as a background, it was very much easier to deal with international affairs. To give you an example, the firm from which we got the basic raw materials for the atomic bomb was the Union Miniere du Haut-Katanga, a Belgian concern operating in Africa, in Katanga. The head of that was a friend of mine, because we—Brown Brothers in those days—had an account from them, and I used to go over and visit with them twice a year. I spent two months a year abroad. Since there were only steamboats then, it took about three-and-a-half months out of your life for that service. I had served with the British in World War I under their command, so I knew the British air men and the Navy men because I was serving in a naval squadron which was on land. I trained in France, and I knew the French Command at that time, not the political, but the basic military man.... From that I stepped into the AF business, which I had been in since 1915.... I knew exactly, or thought I knew, what the British reaction would be if we did this, and what the French reaction would be if we did that. I knew whom we could talk to. When I moved into the War Department, I began to learn something about our own system, about which I must confess I was abysmally ignorant. I said somewhere ... that I thought it would take a fellow two years to learn his way around this absurd governmental machinery we have.... So, going back and trying to answer fully your question, it was an unusual series of coincidences in background and previous experience that brought me into this thing at just the right time to be useful.[1]

Now, it would be back to Brown Brothers Harriman (after resting up for a while at Hobe Sound), to go back into private banking and to live out the rest of his days in private life. Back on Wall Street, Lovett summed up his career as a partner at Brown Brothers from January 1, 1926, to December 31, 1940, from June 1, 1946, to May 15, 1947, from April 1, 1949, to October 3, 1950, and a resumption on March 1, 1953. He looked forward to many years ahead in private banking. Well, perhaps not quite. President Eisenhower knew enough about his friend Bob Lovett to make sure that he utilized him as much as he could. If Lovett had not made it quite publicly clear that he would not be anyone's secretary of defense after January 20, 1953, Eisenhower might very well have kept him on in that position. Without that option, Ike nevertheless took advantage of his friend's well-known willingness to serve the public by appointing him to several committees at the start of the new administration.

In February, March, and April 1953, Robert Lovett made four trips to Washington—two from Hobe Sound and back, two from New York—to attend meetings of the Committee on Organization of the Defense Department, the President's Committee on the National Security Council, and the Committee Investigating Ammunition Shortages in Korea. Certainly for each of these committees, with Lovett's work in the Defense Department and the numerous meetings of the National Security Council he had attended, he was a very valuable and helpful member. Later he served on the Board of Consultants on Foreign Intelligence Activities, which he described as "the so-called watchdog committee concerned with the activities of the entire intelligence community." And there would be more.[2]

In addition, after Eisenhower set up the President's Advisory Committee on Government Organization (called the Rockefeller Committee after its chairman, Nelson Rockefeller), Plan No. 6 drafted by the committee, covering the Defense Department, drew heavily on proposals left by Robert Lovett. The plan, which went into effect on June 30, 1953, abolished various boards, transferred their duties to the secretary, and authorized the secretary to name a general counsel and eight assistant secretaries to cover separate areas of the defense business.[3]

On March 1, 1953, Lovett returned from Washington and Hobe Sound, his health hopefully the better for the Florida stay, to take up again his duties as a partner at Brown Brothers Harriman & Co., with the Harriman brothers, Knight Woolley, Prescott Bush, and numerous others with whom he had worked so well before. Along with the banking business, investments, loans, and all that went with it, Robert Lovett soon had another major business interest thrust upon him. He had served off and on—depending on government employment—as a member of the executive committee of the Union Pacific Railroad. Since 1931, of course, when Lovett's father died while chairman of the Union Pacific board, the company had been run by the Harrimans, first Averell and then Roland. When Lovett left the Defense Department he let Roland "Bunny" Harriman know that he could return to the railroad. In four months Roland made him chairman of the executive committee, a position Lovett probably did not particularly want, but he was unable to turn down Roland Harriman's insistence that he take the job. He would hold the position for fourteen years, "investing it with grace and style as well as a genius for grasping the essentials of a problem," the railroad's historian declared. One director said that Lovett "was our patron saint. Roland maybe should have been, but the guy you went to in the final clutches was Lovett, and Lovett always communicated with Roland. So there was total communication between them."[4] Roland later wrote, "Happily Bob Lovett agreed to take on the chairmanship of the executive committee. From that moment until our joint retirement from our official posts ... we worked not as a team but as one man. We made decisions jointly if we were both available. If not, one of us would decide for both."[5]

The Union Pacific of course was well known as one of the country's premier rail lines. While its corporate headquarters were in New York City, its operating center was in Omaha, Nebraska, where its president and supporting staff were located and from which its rail lines spread out across the West. The unusual corporate setup meant that the decisions and schedules relating to actual trains running came out of Omaha, while overall corporate and financial policies were fixed in New York. This kind of operation was fine with Robert Lovett.

Lovett's health issues continued to cause him trouble. In June 1954, he wrote as follows:

> I went in for a hemorrhoidectomy, which, I was told, was a minor but painful operation. Out of abundant caution, I suggested that they do some exploratory work while I was under the anesthesia, and they removed a small growth which, fortunately, turned out to be benign, and they went on with the operation. Things went fine for seven days, and then all hell broke loose as the result of an infection which shot my fever up from nothing to 104 in two hours. Since I am allergic to penicillin, they were somewhat concerned but finally streptomycin brought this under control and a week later they sent me back to the operating room and did a job on the outside by removing what I gather was a cyst. They kept me in the Medical Center for an extra week, but I got out last week and I am in the office today, part time, sitting on a piece of sponge rubber that I carry with me and guard with my life. So much for my tale of woe.

He added that "the only permanent ill effects that I have is a sense of deep nausea as a result of the Army-McCarthy hearings which I watched continuously from May 13th until last week. A more shameful performance by the Army as well as McCarthy I have never seen."[6]

In the fall of 1955, Bob and Adele went on a six-week business trip for Brown Brothers to London, Paris, and western Germany, "to call on our business correspondents." It was Lovett's first trip abroad since leaving the government two-and-a-half years earlier.[7]

There were numerous problems afflicting the railroad industry in the years following World War II, and Bob Lovett was soon up to his ears in dealing with some of them. One was the law, going back to the Hepburn Act of 1906, that forbade railroads from engaging in any other business, such as selling their coal or oil or anything else. Lovett later described it: "Our problem was to get out of the iron maiden that we were in … the past construction of the law which prohibited a railroad from doing anything other than operating a railroad."[8] Part of this problem was the control of activities in Omaha, separate from the New York board; the railroad managers in Omaha had little interest and less skill in dealing with the nonrail assets. Lovett came up with a divisional plan, an organizational structure that routed nonrail business around Omaha. The new plan took effect on the first day of 1961. "There was a lot of yelling and screaming from Omaha," said Elbridge Gerry. "It didn't do them any good…. When they ceased to report to [Arthur E.] Stoddard [president in Omaha] and began to report to Lovett in New York, well that's when things began to move." The nonrail activities were now free to develop on their own, which they did, particularly after modifications of the divisions went into effect in January 1965, enabling them to function as independent units.[9] Robert Lovett's primary goal was "to protect existing company assets by putting them under managers that knew more about them. Under this arrangement the railroad always remained the primary business."[10]

One material Lovett got involved with was trona, a nonmarine evaporate mineral which is the primary source of sodium carbonate in the United States. Union Pacific operators had been digging up trona for decades, but development of the mining business aroused little enthusiasm in the company. Lovett took a different approach to trona, striking a deal with Stauffer Chemical to create a new subsidiary, of which Stauffer owned 51 percent and Union Pacific 49 percent, for mining and refining trona, an operation that soon blossomed. Lovett also encouraged expanded explorations of other minerals, and the natural resources division soon flourished.[11]

Union Pacific Railroad executives (left to right) Arthur E. Stoddard, E. Roland "Bunny" Harriman (Bob Lovett's close friend), and Lovett (Union Pacific Railroad).

Another traditional Union Pacific function Lovett assisted was in industrial development, purchasing land along its lines in an effort to fill such sites with businesses that would produce increased traffic for the railroad. In Lovett's first year, 1953, industrial development became a separate item in the company's annual report, and in the next dozen years a total of 2,527 industries were attracted to locations along the rail lines. In 1965 Union Pacific's land division began a new push for acquisitions, putting up $17 million for 3,270 acres of land in places ranging from Omaha to Muncie, Kansas, and Walnut, California.[12]

In October 1956 Lovett sent off a letter to his old boss, George Marshall, describing his activities: "I am Chairman of the Executive Committee of the Union Pacific, a post which delights me because my father held it for many years…. The Executive Committee is domiciled here in New York and is charged with general policy and, specifically, with all financial matters. The work is interesting, as a railroad is very much like a military establishment in its organization, as well as the manifold type of problems which arise as a result of operating through thirteen states and all kinds of terrain and weather conditions."[13]

Union Pacific's postwar life saw a notable decline in passenger business. With the increase in airline travel, long-distance railroad passenger service fell off substantially, with only postal and express business keeping it up. Lovett understood that the fight to save the passenger business was hopeless, and he did his best to move Union Pacific away from it. With the passenger business slipping away, there was less reason to preserve the company's resort and tour business—Averell Harriman's beloved Sun Valley, Idaho, and the Utah parks. As they declined, they attracted fewer and fewer customers, so in October 1964 Sun Valley was sold outright, and the Utah parks facilities were donated to the U.S. National Park Service in 1972.

A movement toward consolidation of railroad lines inevitably attracted the attention of the leaders of the Union Pacific, specifically Bob Lovett and the company's general counsel Frank Barnett. After much study it was determined that the company should reverse its historic outlook and go east of the Missouri River to Chicago and St. Louis. After much study and debate, they decided to merge with the Rock Island Line. The proposed merger required much negotiation, but it was finally approved. Consent of the Interstate Commerce Commission (ICC) was much more involved. The ICC hearings opened in May 1966, six years after the merger talks had begun. The first witness was Robert Lovett, who "handled it with his usual polish." His testimony consisted of 75 pages.[14] Lovett himself wrote, "I have been working on this merger for the past four years and have had to devote my time almost exclusively to it for the last nine months in preparation for the battle which has now been joined. My extra curricular activities have, therefore, been completely curtailed and I am afraid that I will not regain control of my time for many months."[15] The ICC hearings would continue until the final approval of the merger in 1974, at which point the Union Pacific would make a final inspection of the Rock Island, which had been deteriorating all through the ICC turmoil, and decide simply to walk away from the proposed merger.

Long before that, Robert Lovett stepped down. He announced to the board in October 1966 that he would retire as chairman of the Union Pacific executive committee on December 31, 1966, having reached the age of 71. Barnett succeeded him as chairman, and Reginald Sutton was named to a new office as vice president of finance, while continuing as controller. As Dean E. Courtney Brown of Columbia, head of the committee to nominate Lovett's successor, told the press, "We didn't precisely replace Bob Lovett. But we created two jobs where there was one before and used the two best-fitted executives we had to fill them."[16]

Lovett continued as a director and as a member of the executive committee, primarily as a favor to Roland Harriman. Despite his usual health problems, he stayed active for the Union Pacific. Late in his life, Roland "Bunny" Harriman published his memoirs, in the course of which he said that the Union Pacific "has been, I think, an outstandingly happy organization. We have worked together with little or no jealousies, all with the same goals in mind. I think this comes down from the atmosphere of professionalism that my father established, that Judge Lovett and Averell carried on, and that I and Bob Lovett do our best to maintain and extend."[17] Lovett stayed on the board until March 1978, resigning after Roland had died; he thought it "appropriate that our memberships on the Boards should both end in the same year."[18]

When asked later what his major accomplishments at the Union Pacific were, Lovett replied, "Reorganizing it so that now it became free from its bonds which kept it just as a railroad." He said, "I think the biggest thing there was we finally got out of the chains that were put around us and formed a corporation. We were given the right to go into business. We had oil. We had coal, minerals and a railroad, and land. And that was the best thing you could have."[19]

At the same time Bob Lovett was devoting many hours and many thoughts to the Union Pacific Railroad he continued to serve as a general partner of Brown Brothers Harriman & Co. on Wall Street. The Union Pacific, he said, took "at least a third of the time," but that still left many hours to carry on the private banking business, of which Brown Brothers was the nation's largest. Bob Lovett continued to specialize in international investment. One of the happenings that helped measurably to strengthen the firm was the entry in 1955 of Elbridge Gerry and his firm, Gerry Bros. & Co., which brought in more than $5 million in new capital.[20]

Lovett, long noted for being tall and slim, started having what he considered trouble with his weight, having developed a paunch in front. In May 1957 he wrote General Marshall about his efforts while he was down at Hobe Sound to fight it: "I undertook a personal battle of the bulge and tried to get my paunch down to a more convenient size by a combination of dieting and exercise. The dieting was easy for me but, being congenitally bone lazy, I had to rely on Adele as a taskmaster. She would march me up and down the beach for an average of about 3 miles almost every day and, to my amazement and delight, this treatment seemed to have some promise of success. The result was I returned from holiday not exactly sylphlike but able to tie my shoelaces without grunting and feeling in top form."[21]

In March 1958 Bob Lovett received a letter from William Lovett, a cousin living in Highlands, Texas, who told him for the first time of the Lovett cemetery in San Jacinto County, "on the home place of Grandfather William Lovett ... about five miles west of Shepherd, Texas." In a later letter William described the cemetery, two or three acres, with "125 feet square of this plot ... fenced in 1903, funds donated by your father and C.B. Udall, Sr." Robert Lovett had known nothing of this plot established by his grandfather, but he sent back $950 to help with cemetery expenses and upkeep, and he sent more in later years.[22]

And, of course, there were still many hours dedicated to the good of the government, as a consultant and advisor to Dwight Eisenhower. In 1956 Ike created the President's Board of Consultants on Foreign Intelligence Activities, composed of what he told Central Intelligence Agency (CIA) director Allen Dulles would be distinguished but discreet private citizens, to monitor intelligence operations at a time when there were increasing questions being raised about the activities around the world of the CIA.

With Robert Lovett as one of its principal members, the board held its first meeting, with the president, on January 24, 1956, under its chairman, President James Killian of the Massachusetts Institute of Technology. The board soon set to work with considerable diligence, digging into the many problems and activities of the CIA. Most of the board's activities were classified, but it met with Eisenhower five times. Killian selected two of the board's leading members, Lovett and David K.E. Bruce, to investigate the CIA's covert action programs against communism. Allen Dulles was not upset with this investigation, particularly since he regarded both Lovett and Bruce as friends. Bruce, a wealthy Virginia gentleman and a Princeton classmate of Allen's brother Foster, had a distinguished record in government service. He had headed the European branch of the Office of Strategic Services (OSS) during World War II, had been ambassador to France from 1949 to 1952, and undersecretary of state under Acheson (1952–53). In later years David Bruce would serve as ambassador to West Germany, the United Kingdom, and NATO, as well as emissary to China in 1973.

As soon as Lovett and Bruce got into matters they became concerned. "Bruce was very much disturbed," Lovett testified to the board of inquiry on the Bay of Pigs failure in 1961. "He approached it from the standpoint of 'what right have we to go barging around into other countries buying newspapers and handing money to opposition parties or supporting a candidate for this, that or the other office?' He felt this was an outrageous interference with friendly countries." Lovett went on: "He got me alarmed, so instead of completing the report in thirty days we took two months or more."[23] The Bruce-Lovett report, or as it was titled, "Covert Operations," condemned "the increased mingling in the internal affairs of other nations of bright, highly graded young men who must be doing something all the time to justify their reason for being.... Busy, moneyed and privileged, [the CIA] likes its 'King Making' responsibility (the intrigue is fascinating—considerable self-satisfaction, sometimes with applause, derives from 'successes'—no charge is made for 'failures'—and the whole business is very much simpler than collecting covert intelligence on the USSR through the usual CIA methods!)."[24]

There seemed to be no reliable system of control. "There are always, of course, on record the twin, well-born purposes of 'frustrating the Soviets' and keeping others 'prowestern' oriented," the report continued. "Under these almost any action can be and is being justified." It went on: "Once having been conceived, the final approval given to any project (at informal lunch meetings of the OCB [Operations Coordinating Board] inner group) can, at best, be described as pro forma." As a consequence, "no one, other than those in the CIA immediately concerned with their day to day operation, has any detailed knowledge of what is going on." With "a horde of CIA representatives" all over, CIA covert actions were exerting "significant, almost unilateral influences ... on the actual formulation of our foreign policies ... sometimes completely unknown" to the American ambassador to the country affected.[25]

The report brought up the unusual circumstance that the secretary of state and the head of the CIA were brothers: "At times, the Secretary of State/DCI brother relationship may arbitrarily set 'the US position' ... whether through personal arrangement between the Secretary of State and the DCI (deciding between them on any one occasion to use what they regard as the best 'assets' available) or undertaken at the personal discretion of the DCI." Further in this line, it said, "the State Department people feel that perhaps the greatest contribution this Board could make would be to bring to the attention of the President the significant, almost unilateral influences that CIA activities have on the actual formulation of our foreign policies." The report suggested moving Allen Dulles's office to the White House and appointing a deputy to administer the CIA's covert operations.[26] The report went on to an exasperated plea for correction: "Should not someone, somewhere in an authoritative position in our government, on a continuing basis, be ... calculating ... the long-range wisdom of activities which have entailed our virtual abandonment of the international 'golden rule,' and which, if successful to the degree claimed for them, are responsible in a great measure for stirring up the turmoil and raising the doubts about us that exist in many countries of the world today? ... Where will we be tomorrow?"[27] The Bruce-Lovett report was handed to Eisenhower by his board on December 20, 1956. The president apparently read it over, but he basically rejected its recommendations. Allen Dulles maintained his firm hold on the CIA and its operations, and the activities of the CIA were not materially changed.[28]

Soon 1956 faded into 1957, and the situation in the world began to look darker. The Russians, who had already developed their own atomic bomb, announced the successful testing of an intercontinental ballistic missile, the ICBM, and on October 4, 1957, the Soviets shocked the Western world with the lofting of Sputnik, the first man-made satellite to circle the earth. A month later, Sputnik II was launched, and in December the U.S. Vanguard rocket was an embarrassing failure. The vast physical distance between Russia and the United States no longer seemed as much of a protection as Americans had long assumed it to be. Racial problems and an economy sinking into recession spread disenchantment that, coupled with fears of the Soviet Union and its technological advances, cut into Dwight Eisenhower's hitherto unmatched popularity. The question of civil defense was one that greatly troubled the American populace, as well as the military leadership. There were questions raised about unforeseen attacks, radioactive fallout, creation of shelters and provisions for evacuation, and the stockpiling of emergency materials. The possibility of a nuclear exchange as well as the country's infrastructure and the government's ability to continue to function were all issues that were discussed.

In September 1952 Harry Truman's National Security Council had asked Secretary Acheson, Secretary Lovett, and Director of Mutual Security Averell Harriman to submit a report analyzing U.S. national security policies. The group presented its report, noted as NSC 141, to Truman in January 1953, recommending continuation of present policies and the funding of improvements in continental defenses. This was the starting point for several studies of the subject and led the NSC, on April 4, 1957, to order a series of studies on the balance between active and passive defense measures, which led to the setup of the Gaither Committee.

In May 1957 Eisenhower, with the assistance of the Science Advisory Committee of the Office of Defense Mobilization (ODM), went to work. He decided to establish a committee of experts to study American national security and defense programs and problems and to analyze possible dangers to the country, as set forth by the NSC. He asked James Killian of MIT, a member of the Science Advisory Committee, to select a project director, and Killian recommended the appointment of H. Rowan Gaither as the committee chair. Gaither, a native of Natchez, Mississippi, was a San Francisco lawyer, investment banker, trustee of the RAND Corporation, and administrator of the Ford Foundation. He had been, during World War II, assistant director of the Radiation Laboratory at MIT, where he and Killian became friends. He accepted the president's request to chair what was formally known as the Security Resources Panel but became generally known as the Gaither Committee.

After his appointment Gaither and the ODM started filling out the committee with well-regarded individual members, divided into two main groups, the steering committee and the advisory panel. Robert Sprague and William Foster (who had been Lovett's deputy in the Defense Department) led the steering committee, and the two of them directed the overall committee after Gaither was diagnosed with arterial thrombosis in August and stepped down as director. Robert Lovett was a member of the advisory panel, along with others like General Jimmy Doolittle, John McCloy, and Gaither after his departure as director. Another member was Mervin Kelly, who had been chosen in 1952 by Secretary Lovett to chair a panel studying American air defenses. As the historian of the Gaither Committee wrote, after listing the members and consultants to the committee and their accomplishments, "these men and the rest of the Gaither committee represented some of the best minds in the country."[29] Because of the secrecy associated with the committee as well as that imposed upon its members, there is little documentation of Robert Lovett's activities within the Gaither Committee. Nevertheless, it can be assumed, from his prior activities and his longtime interest in American defenses, that he was an active member of the advisory panel and a contributor to its investigations.

The Gaither Committee received briefings, studies, books and reports from many members of the military, the Defense Department, and the State Department, as well as civilian study groups committed to examination of national security measures. In addition, in looking into the possibility of a major program of shelter building, the committee heard from Treasury Department officials (who mainly opposed the construction of any such shelters because of its potential drain on federal revenues). Particular attention was paid to the situation of the Strategic Air Command (SAC), as the response of the SAC planes to a Soviet attack would be crucial to the nation's defense posture.

While the committee's final report was being prepared, the committee's advisory panel gave President Eisenhower a summary on November 4, 1957, of its conclusions and recommendations. Rowan Gaither himself spoke for the committee, setting forth six principal conclusions. He said the planned active defense system was not adequate, and the passive defenses set forth did not provide proper protection for the civilian populace. The Strategic Air Command, Gaither said, was vulnerable to a surprise attack by the Russians, and by 1959 our vulnerability would be much increased with the Soviet production of ICBMs. The risks to the nation would continue to grow without a workable arms control agreement. Gaither concluded, "The long-run peril to the U.S. civil population demands prompt and efficient measures for increasing our basic and inherent strengths and for melding the will and resources of the free world."[30]

With this background, the Gaither Committee presented its full report to the National Security Council several days later, on November 7, 1957. Recognizing the basic attitude that the Soviets sought world domination and that the current economic superiority of the United States was declining, the report emphasized that by the 1960s the Russians would surpass America in military spending. The active defense systems currently in place, the report said, offered little defense against a well-planned Soviet attack, and the passive defense measures provided for the civilian population offered little or no protection from a nuclear blast or radioactive fallout. And, with the Strategic Air Command as our primary defense, the vulnerability of SAC to a surprise attack was most worrisome.[31]

The report made several recommendations: a $25 billion program of fallout shelters and civil defense provisions; a reorganization of the Defense Department in order to incorporate effectively scientific and technological advances into its programs (surely Robert Lovett was behind this, as this recommendation mirrored departmental changes he had proposed late in his tenure in the department); the need for obtaining greater knowledge of Soviet intentions through hard intelligence; and that these changes should be combined with a foreign policy that would assure our allies that it was not a retreat to "Fortress America." These recommended changes, the committee estimated, including the radar and fallout shelters, would cost about $44 billion, spread over five years, an amount the U.S. could afford although it would require "an increase in taxes, a somewhat larger federal debt, substantial economies in other government expenditures, and curbs on inflation."[32]

The first three meetings of the National Security Council in 1958 dealt with the Gaither Committee, its report, and comments upon it by various government agencies. The NSC continued to examine issues raised by the committee for the next six months. President Eisenhower was not happy with the committee's report and findings, particularly as they would increase government spending, although he did implement some of the recommendations such as the dispersal of SAC airfields to reduce their vulnerability to attack. Defense secretary Neil McElroy agreed with several of the Gaither proposals, particularly those relating to SAC.

The White House on November 23 released a statement announcing that the Gaither Committee, whose members it named, had performed a secret study for the use of the Eisenhower administration and its defense components. The statement, though, did not set forth the actual activities of the committee or any of the contents of its final report. This statement naturally provoked widespread inquiries and digging to find out more about the Gaither Committee and its report. Finally, on December 20, a *Washington Post* article under the headline "Secret Report Sees U.S. in Grave Peril" disclosed the findings of the committee. The article, written by Chalmer Roberts, included the following: "The still top-secret Gaither Report portrays a United States in the gravest danger in its history. It pictures the nation moving in frightening course to the status of a second-hand power. It shows an America exposed to an almost immediate threat from the missile-bristling Soviet Union. It finds America's long-term prospect one of cataclysmic peril in the face of rocketing Soviet military might and of a powerful, growing Soviet economy and technology which will bring new political propaganda and psychological assaults on freedom all around the globe."[33] This article was naturally followed by increased pressure to make the Gaither report public. Ultimately, however, Eisenhower refused to release either the report itself or a sanitized version of it. Nevertheless, the findings and recommendations of the Gaither Committee did have considerable influence on varied defense policies and decisions in the times ahead.

One of the most dangerous features of the time was the availability of nuclear energy, now in the hands of both the United States and Soviet Russia. As 1957 faded into 1958 there were signs that Eisenhower was beginning to lean toward a nuclear test ban. Secretary of State Dulles decided to take a step of his own. On April 26, 1958, he invited a group of gentlemen to his home. His guests were Alfred Gruenther, Walter Bedell Smith, Jack McCloy, and Bob Lovett. Dulles had selected his guests with care; he knew that the president admired each member of the group and would be impressed with a policy recommendation from them. Dulles gave them a full briefing on the nuclear situation as it existed and as it looked for the time ahead, and then he got the assent of the four of them to urge Eisenhower to take the initiative in seeking a test-ban agreement.

With the four of them helping, Dulles put together a draft of a letter for Eisenhower to send to Nikita Khrushchev, repeating an earlier proposal for technical talks on an inspection system, and stating, "Studies of this kind are the necessary preliminaries to putting political decisions into effect." Thus, Dulles wanted to take a firm step in divorcing production of future weapons from a nuclear test ban, a fundamental change in the U.S. disarmament position. Eisenhower accepted the recommendation from Dulles (and his guests) and on April 28 sent the letter off to Khrushchev, who accepted Eisenhower's proposal for technical talks, which opened in early July in Geneva.[34]

As it developed, negotiation of a limited test-ban treaty took years to reach an agreement, with all sorts of problems—political, diplomatic, and scientific—blocking the way. Finally, with Averell Harriman as the principal U.S. negotiator, a treaty was agreed to and initialed on July 25, 1963. It was announced to the public the following day by President Kennedy. After considerable discussion, the Senate Foreign Relations Committee approved it on September 3, and the treaty headed to the Senate floor. On September 13, 1963, Senator Henry "Scoop" Jackson (D–Wash), in the course of a speech to the Senate in support of the treaty, quoted extensively from a letter written to Senator J. William Fulbright, chairman of the Foreign Relations Committee, by Bob Lovett, whom Jackson called "a great American ... eminently qualified to advise us and the country on the matter before us." Lovett's letter said "this administration has, first, the necessary will and determination to continue our research and developmental laboratories at the level of activity necessary to permit us to retain any nuclear superiority we may currently have and to improve, if possible, our relative position in this field ... and, secondly, that our policy, after signing the treaty, will be to continue actively those tests permitted under it and to maintain as insurance a program for atmospheric tests ... in the event of abrogation or other emergent events." Lovett then urged ratification of the treaty, which, on September 24, was given by the Senate by a vote of 80–14.[35]

September 1958 saw a major article in *Business Week* magazine about Brown Brothers Harriman, with a cover photo of Lovett, Bunny Harriman, and F.H. Kingsbury. Robert Lovett's comment on the picture on the cover was, "If the grim look of the partners on the cover doesn't drive away our customers, I will consider that we have been very lucky."[36] The article emphasized that Brown Brothers had been run as a private bank for 140 years, "mainly because it has been extremely profitable," and that its partners were determined "to keep it both profitable and private," which takes "a fine measure of experience, money, and nerve, for the partners are personally liable in case of failure." The article was a fine summing up of the firm's character, despite the "grim look" of the partners on the cover.[37]

Finally, late in the Eisenhower administration, defense secretary Neil McElroy put together a special advisory group on the Defense Department's implementation of the 1958 Reorganization Act. The original members of the panel were General Nathan F. Twining, chairman of the Joint Chiefs of Staff, General Alfred Gruenther, Admiral Arthur Radford, and General Omar Bradley. He added to the panel Nelson Rockefeller and Robert Lovett. It was one more opportunity for Lovett to push forward his ideas on developing a more streamlined and responsive military.[38]

In 1960 the years of Dwight Eisenhower as president were coming to an end. A very close election between his vice president, Richard M. Nixon, and Senator John F. Kennedy of Massachusetts resulted in a Democratic victory, and Washington prepared for another major governmental makeover. Bob Lovett had commented, "I can't recall having felt less enthusiasm for two Presidential candidates," but he eventually voted for Nixon, despite the fact that Senator Kennedy had even praised him for his distinguished service to President Truman in a press conference on August 29. Lovett did not realize it at the time, but this indicated that Kennedy might very well call upon him for additional service.[39]

26

Times with Kennedy
... and LBJ

As President-elect John F. Kennedy prepared to take office on January 20, 1961, he had a great many decisions to make regarding the composition of his cabinet. Despite Robert Lovett's Republican registration and leanings, he found himself right in the middle of it all. The three major positions, of course, were secretaries of state, defense, and treasury. Obviously, the Justice Department was also very important, but Senator Kennedy's father, the notorious Joseph P. Kennedy, was insisting that brother Robert should be named attorney general, although the president-elect was not necessarily listening to his father and would make up his own mind.

Bob Lovett had met Robert Kennedy some time earlier. As he told it, "the first time I met Robert Kennedy was during the McCarthy hearings," when young Kennedy was on McCarthy's committee staff. "He had accompanied his father to the airport, and he introduced us. I remember riding up to New York on the plane with Joe Kennedy, saying, 'That's pretty tough company he's traveling with,' having in mind particularly McCarthy, for whom I had absolutely no use at all, and young [Roy] Cohn, who seemed to be about as unpleasant a character as one could find in a day's march. Joe said, 'Well, put your mind at rest about that. Bobby is just as tough as a bootheel.'" Bobby, of course, did get away from McCarthy and Cohn quickly.[1]

Joseph Kennedy was also pushing another name for his son's consideration, and that was Robert Lovett. In 1956 Joe Kennedy had been named to serve on Eisenhower's Board of Consultants on Foreign Intelligence Activities (the future source of the Bruce-Lovett report). Although Kennedy served only briefly, he got to know fellow member Bob Lovett and was apparently quite impressed with him. (The feeling was not mutual, however; Lovett was later said to have "voted against Kennedy in 1960 because Joe Kennedy was his father.") So, after the 1960 election, Joe Kennedy urged the president-elect to give Lovett serious consideration for an important appointment.[2]

At one point late in November 1960 Senator Kennedy, in Palm Beach, was talking with Kenny O'Donnell and other close advisers, bemoaning the fact that they did not really know the right men for the jobs available. Kennedy went on to say that he wanted to become better acquainted with Robert Lovett. He admired Lovett for the work he had done during the war and after, and he thought of offering him any one of the top three cabinet posts. Kennedy was acutely conscious of his lack of personal contact with the leaders of the New York banking and legal establishment—men like Lovett and John McCloy—and he was willing to seek talent there. As O'Donnell argued with him, Kennedy said, "Henry Stimson was one of those New York Republicans, and Roosevelt was glad to get him. I'm going to talk with Lovett and see what he can do for me." "Anyway," he said, "we need a Secretary of the Treasury who can call a few of those people on Wall Street by their first names."[3]

Senator Kennedy talked with Dean Acheson about his cabinet issues and told Acheson that he was determined to get Bob Lovett for treasury. Acheson said later, "I told him, Bob won't take that job. He hates banking and figures." He suggested offering Lovett the Defense Department. "But Kennedy said no; he wanted him as Secretary of the Treasury."[4] The president-elect then called on Clark Clifford, asking him to go up to New York and talk with his old friend Bob Lovett about taking the treasury position. Clifford got together with Lovett on November 28. "At sixty-five," Clifford said of Lovett, "he was still the delightful, gracious, and charming man I remembered from the forties. As we talked over a leisurely lunch, I thought that no one would get along better with Kennedy than this wise and gentle man." Lovett told him, with a grin, that he could never keep up with "a bunch of forty-year-old touch-football players," reflecting what the media had been saying about the president-elect and his close followers. And he said his health problems would force him to turn down any cabinet appointment. Clifford urged him not to turn down Kennedy outright, even on health grounds, without seeing his doctors again. Clifford said, "You offer a unique package and your obligation to the government has not yet been fully discharged." With a laugh, Lovett agreed to consult his doctor once more.[5]

As soon as Clifford departed Lovett was off to Presbyterian Hospital to talk with his doctor, who, as expected, said he had serious reservations about Lovett's health holding up for full-time government service, "with a good possibility that correction would have to be made by major surgery." The next morning Lovett called Clifford to turn down the cabinet offer. Clifford then suggested Lovett should come to Washington for a personal meeting with Senator Kennedy. This was then set up for December 1 by a phone call from Kennedy himself.[6]

Robert Lovett caught a plane for Washington, took a taxi to Kennedy's house at 3307 N Street in Georgetown, and pushed his way through a crowd of reporters. When he got inside, he was greeted and bumped into by three-year-old Caroline Kennedy, carrying a football and wearing crimson overalls adorned with a large letter "H." Lovett turned to the senator and said, laughingly, "That's a hell of a way to treat a Yale man." That broke the ice, and the two men took to each other very well, despite their differences in age, background, and politics. Lovett soon saw that Kennedy thought much as he did, and the senator was turned on by Lovett's bluntness and wit, grinning broadly when Lovett quickly informed him that he had not voted for him.[7]

Jack Kennedy, during and after lunch, offered Lovett his choice of state, defense, or treasury, but Lovett quickly turned him down, saying, "No, sir, I can't. My bearings are burnt out." There was talk of Lovett taking the Defense Department for one year with Bobby Kennedy as his undersecretary so that Bobby could succeed him, but Lovett said he was unable to take a cabinet position for even one year. Lovett later said "that this show of trust and confidence was a very moving thing and I found it difficult to put into words the appreciation I felt for his attitude."[8]

Following "a quick discussion of the major problems in Defense, State and Treasury," the two men "spent quite a lot of time" on, first, "the type of attention which the departments needed, from my point of view, in order to be fully effective," and then on "samples of individuals who, in my opinion, could fulfill the requirements and turn in a good job in those positions." Kennedy, Lovett said, "was extremely interested in this portion of the conversation and we spent, I think, most of the time of the visit in conversation about the type of person he should try to get and the difference between intelligence or even brilliance on the one hand and the sine qua non of good judgment on the other.... I was delighted to see the President's obvious interest in exploring these elements in the process of selection of his Cabinet."[9]

When the senator then said that he just didn't know enough of the "right people," Lovett told him that he and his colleagues could introduce him to any number of the "right people." For example, he suggested several names for the treasury: Jack McCloy, his good friend Henry Alexander from Morgan Guaranty, Eugene Black from the World Bank, or Douglas Dillon, then serving as undersecretary of state. For the Defense Department, Lovett spoke of Robert McNamara, the newly appointed president of Ford Motors; Lovett had recruited McNamara into the War Department during the war and had been highly impressed with him.[10]

For secretary of state, Kennedy said, two other possible people were unable to serve and "as a consequence, he was coming around more to considering Dean Rusk, whom he had met but did not know at all well" and had been recommended by Acheson. He asked Lovett specifically "if Rusk's performance at the Rockefeller Foundation" (of which Rusk was president) "had been good. " Lovett, who was on the board of that foundation, said "that, in my opinion, it had been excellent; that he [Rusk] had handled himself with great tact in an atmosphere which had some of the aroma of a college faculty with all its peculiar cliques, and that ... he had a judicial mind and a deep conviction as to the position of the President in our governmental system evidenced, in part, by the series of lectures he had given on the office of the President, the Secretary of State, Foreign Policy, etc. I suggested that the President might learn a great deal about him through reading these." Kennedy laughed and said he had already done so.[11]

There was then a discussion of Dean Rusk's financial situation, because he was almost entirely dependent on his salary at the Rockefeller Foundation, which was considerably larger than what he would get as secretary of state. Lovett said that Rusk would be entitled to "some termination allowance ... in lieu of the funded pension to which he would be entitled within a year or so," and, in fact, Lovett and other members of the board did subsequently arrange for a substantial termination allowance in order that Rusk could take the State Department position.[12]

The discussion of the Department of State, in which Lovett spoke highly of the good service Rusk had performed there, terminated "the detailed portion of the visit." Here, Senator Kennedy "said that he wanted me to help—with whatever formal title I felt appropriate—as an adviser to him and that he would count on me heavily in trying to find the right man for the jobs we had been discussing. I, of course, agreed to do my best and to hold myself at his disposal." Kennedy was amused at Lovett's reluctance to serve on any committees. "When he suggested that I might serve as a consultant," Lovett said, "I readily agreed to do so, provided I was not on a Committee of Consultants or Advisers." The Senator said "that was the last thing he wanted and that he was, in fact, getting rid of a committee."[13]

As Lovett was preparing to leave, Kennedy warned him about the crowd of newsmen outside and said, "I had better come out with you then because they will have microphones shoved into your face the moment you step outdoors." Sure enough, when he opened the door to the icy cold outdoors, three microphones quickly blocked the way. Kennedy "stepped out, walked up to the microphones and told the press that he had invited me down for lunch, that he had hoped to get me to accept a post in the Cabinet and that, to his regret, it was not possible for me to do so for reasons of health." When asked what cabinet post had been offered, Kennedy "said that he would have been delighted to have me in any one of three—State, Defense, or Treasury—and repeated again that it had been necessary for me to withdraw from public service which he regretted but that he had assurances that I would serve as a personal advisor from time to time." Kennedy then steered Lovett away from a CBS fellow trying to get an interview, introduced him to a Secret Service man in a car across the street, walked Lovett to the car, and told the driver to take him to the airport. Robert Lovett summed up his visit: "In the conversation during the day the President [-elect] had shown flashes of a kind of telegraphic wit, a very keen insight into a number of problems and an aptitude for quick comprehension which was very impressive. His final courtesy at the front door was an act of graciousness I will never forget."[14]

Senator Kennedy had told Lovett during their meeting that Sargent Shriver, his brother-in-law, would visit him in New York to discuss possible cabinet appointments. Shriver in fact visited the Lovetts at their Locust Valley home and went over the lists of names. For defense, Lovett said, "I thought McNamara was outstanding among the group and said so, and was questioned closely by Shriver as to my recollections of him." He suggested calling Eugene Zuckert, then serving as an aide to Thomas Finletter in the air force, or C.B. "Tex" Thornton from the wartime air force for background on McNamara and his accomplishments. He went on to say "that his eagerness for facts could be turned to great advantage in the Department and that he was well equipped to do the analytical work which would necessarily follow this."[15]

Not long after the discussion with Shriver, McNamara himself, who had by this time been spoken to by Kennedy and accepted the appointment, called Bob Lovett and asked to get together with him "to talk things over." Lovett gladly agreed and soon met with McNamara, who "asked a number of searching questions, with a notebook on his knee into which he put down whatever bits of information seemed to him worth recording." The discussion that followed included various issues that would be involved in running the Defense Department.[16]

As to Robert Lovett's position as an adviser or consultant to President Kennedy, that was formalized by a statement issued by the president on February 10, 1961: "I am pleased to announce the names of four men who have agreed to serve as consultants on major issues affecting the structure and operations of government." The statement went on to name first Lovett, then Richard E. Neustadt of Columbia University, Don K. Price of Harvard, and Sidney Stein, Jr., an investment counselor from Chicago. "They will be consulted," the statement continued, "in matters where the disinterested advice of highly qualified and experienced men in private life may help us find effective solutions to problems of government organization and operation." While they would not act as a committee or hold meetings, the statement stressed that "they will be asked for advice as individuals, under flexible and informal arrangements suited to the needs of the problem at hand."[17] It should be noted, nevertheless, that Robert Lovett did serve on some committees for Kennedy—the Advisory Committee to the Arms Control and Disarmament Agency, the Randall Committee on Military Pay, and the Clay Committee on Foreign Assistance Programs, created to help push the Foreign Aid bill of 1963 through Congress.

After John Kennedy had been sworn in as president, one of the first major occurrences of his administration was the attack on Cuba at the Bay of Pigs. Bob Lovett had been consulted during the last months of the Eisenhower administration concerning the wisdom of trying to force Fidel Castro from power in Cuba; Lovett had quietly denounced the proposition. Nevertheless, Eisenhower had funded the operation and preparations for an attack went on under the supervision of the CIA. On April 13, 1961, the 1,400 paramilitaries set out from Guatemala by boat for Cuba, arriving at the Playa Giron beach in the Bay of Pigs the night of April 16. Fighting began on the 17th, and by April 20 the invaders were completely overwhelmed. Two days later, on April 22, President Kennedy created the Cuba Study Group, headed by General Maxwell Taylor, with Attorney General Kennedy, Admiral Arleigh Burke, and CIA director Allen Dulles, to investigate what had gone wrong. Robert Lovett did appear before this commission to testify at some length. He related that "a good bit of my testimony … was directed to the CIA aspects of the affair since the investigation dealt not only with the CIA planning but also with the CIA operation itself."[18]

The principal line of questioning to Lovett dealt with the Bruce-Lovett report from 1956 and in particular with an incident described therein (somewhat similar to the Cuban foray) that had taken place in Indonesia and had counted upon a local rising that had not taken place, the lack of which had caused the proceeding to fail. "As a consequence," Lovett said, "the questioning dealt with this report and with the extraordinary identification which takes place in the minds of many of our foreign station heads with the native political ambitions, the political figures and their problems. This," he went on, "obviously introduces an element of substantial distortion and, in my opinion, a review of the CIA papers must always bear in mind the possibility that enthusiasm and emotionalism may distort the judgment of the reporting officer and thereby make it possible for planners to become seriously misled as to the consequences of this or that course of action."[19]

A second subject the board of inquiry dealt with at some length with Lovett was whether or not it was reasonable to expect the CIA to undertake such an operation. "I felt very strongly," he answered, "that it should not embark on a venture of this size since it called for military skills which, obviously, these young men did not have." Lovett pointed out that many had never served in the military and "most of them were from academic backgrounds or otherwise insulated from the ugly problems of putting a group of men into jeopardy for a cause no matter how worthy." The CIA's programs, he told the board, were not always "worth the risk or the great expenditure of manpower, money, and other resources involved."[20] These were the main points of Lovett's testimony before Maxwell Taylor and his board, also "the basis for a number of later conversations with the President on details of the CIA operations in the light of the five years which I had spent observing them from the President's Board of Consultants" under Eisenhower.[21]

Taylor's board filed its report on June 13, while President Kennedy dealt with the public and international repercussions from the Bay of Pigs fiasco. The president called in Robert Lovett to talk about the Bay of Pigs and the CIA's part in it. Lovett told him the CIA was badly organized, dangerously amateurish, and excessively costly, and it ought to be run in a hard-boiled fashion. This, he said, had not been possible with Allen Dulles running it for Eisenhower.[22]

On December 7, 1961, and January 6, 1962, Senator John Stennis (D–Miss), chairman of a subcommittee of the Senate Committee on Armed Services, wrote to Bob Lovett asking for his views on the proper relationship between military and civilian authorities. On January 16 Lovett submitted to Stennis a lengthy and well-reasoned memorandum, which was lauded in a *Baltimore Sun* editorial and placed in the Congressional Record on January 25 as a "splendid statement," by Senator Mike Mansfield (D–Mont). Lovett, with his experience in the Defense Department, stated the many reasons for the civilian leaders of the department to abstain from strictly military decisions and why military officers should absolutely divorce themselves from political issues: "The great tradition of the proper role of the career officer is exemplified in the conduct and record of Pershing, Marshall, Eisenhower, Bradley, and, indeed, most of the great leaders of World War I and II, who took the view that the military should speak publicly only on military matters and that they should leave the public statement of foreign policy and national policy to the elected head of the state. Any other course, they believed, brought divided counsels and weakened the authority both of the Chief Executive and the military commanders."[23] Well after the Bay of Pigs disaster, Cuba remained a thorn in the side of the Kennedy administration, a thorn whose effects became ever more pronounced a year-and-a-half later with the discovery of Soviet-supplied ballistic missiles there.

On September 4, 1962, Russian ambassador Anatoly Dobrynin told Robert Kennedy that the Soviets had no intention of placing ground-to-ground or offensive missiles in Cuba. But on October 14 there was presented to President Kennedy aerial photographic proof that such missiles had been presented to and installed in Cuba. Kennedy over the next several days met with what his aide Kenny O'Donnell called "a carefully limited number of officials and advisers, the only people in the government, outside of a few military commanders and intelligence experts, who shared the secret of the discovery of the missiles in Cuba until the President delivered his public ultimatum to Khrushchev a week later."[24]

This group was later called the "Ex Comm," meaning the Executive Committee of the National Security Council. It included, of course, the president and Vice President Johnson, as well as Dean Rusk and four other State Department aides, Robert McNamara, Roswell Gilpatric, Paul Nitze, and General Maxwell Taylor from Defense, Robert Kennedy, treasury secretary Dillon, John McCone, and Marshall Carter from the CIA, as well as McGeorge Bundy, Ted Sorenson, and O'Donnell from the White House Staff. The president also invited Acheson, Adlai Stevenson, and Robert Lovett for some of the later meetings.

Lovett received a phone call from the president on October 17 telling him that Kennedy might want him to come down to Washington to discuss a very serious matter. "He would communicate with me later on," Lovett recalled. The next morning Lovett, at a meeting of the Carnegie Institution in New York, was called to the phone and told by Kennedy that he wanted him to come to Washington at once, emphasizing "at once." Lovett left immediately for the airport, took the shuttle to Washington, arriving shortly after lunch, and went directly to McGeorge Bundy's office as the president had instructed him to do. Bundy and a CIA representative showed Lovett the photographic evidence on hand of the missiles in Cuba; this was followed by a briefing by men from the Department of Defense, again as directed by President Kennedy. Lovett "tried to lay out a series of courses of action for discussion with the President scheduled for later that afternoon and early evening following the briefings." Lovett felt "the response to this startling new threat quite obviously would fall into three stages."[25]

The first stage, he felt, would be a tight blockade (or, "a better word," quarantine) "to exclude from Cuba not only all offensive weapons but also ... energy fuels, machinery, spare parts, etc., but not interfering with food stuffs or medicines." Second, "if this were not effective, we could step up one degree higher and take out the identified missiles by a series of air attacks, using conventional demolition and incendiary bombs." "The third and final step," he decided, "was obviously the landing of troops and invasion from a beachhead and the direct seizure of any such weapons and the defeat of Castro and his troops." This last "would be a bloody and lengthy business," requiring "something over 150,000 troops" and risking major escalation.[26] Lovett then noticed on Bundy's desk a photo of Henry Stimson, who had been Bundy's boss as well as Lovett's. Lovett said, "Mac, I think the best service we can do to President Kennedy is to try to approach this as Colonel Stimson would."[27]

Even while this was going on, the president was meeting with Dean Rusk and Llewellyn Thompson, until recently the ambassador to Russia and well acquainted with Nikita Khrushchev, as they discussed how to get the U.S. message to the Soviet boss. Rusk pointed out that Adlai Stevenson had suggested a special emissary, and Kennedy responded: "Let's say we ask Mr. Robert Lovett to go over there. [Long pause] You'd have to put him on a plane; you'd have to send him off there; you'd have to make an appointment with Khrushchev; all that would take…." The idea of Lovett as an emissary quietly disappeared.[28]

In the midst of his briefing, Bob Lovett was given a message that the president would like to see him after Soviet foreign minister Andrei Gromyko ended his visit. It was in the Gromyko meeting that the Russian stoutly denied that armaments furnished to Cuba were in any way offensive. Kennedy barely restrained himself from pulling out of his desk the photographs of the offensive missiles. As Gromyko left, the president whispered to Dean Rusk: "That lying bastard."[29]

With Gromyko gone, the president asked to have Robert Lovett brought into the Oval Office. Lovett entered with Bundy, finding there with the president, Rusk, and Llewellyn Thompson. The president asked Lovett if he had received the full briefing, and Lovett said he had. President Kennedy then said, "I ought to finish the story by telling you about Gromyko who, in this very room not over ten minutes ago, told more bare-faced lies than I have ever heard in so short a time."[30] The discussion then zeroed in on the Cuban situation. "I urged the quarantine route as the first step…," Lovett said, "and the matter was discussed in some detail with Rusk and Thompson joining in." (A "quarantine" was considered a less-aggressive form of action than a "blockade.")[31] Then the attorney general came in from the Rose Garden and joined the talk. "The President asked me to repeat what I had previously said," Lovett said, "and I did so." "Robert Kennedy asked two or three very searching questions about the application of any blockade," Lovett recalled, "and indicated that he felt as I did about the necessity for taking a less violent step at the outset because, as he said, we could always blow the place up if necessary but that might be unnecessary and we would then be in the position of having used too much force." Robert Kennedy also described other sources advocating a full-stage invasion or an air strike. With such an action doubtlessly resulting in a Russian seizure of Berlin, Lovett suggested that our NATO allies would blame the United States for losing Berlin "with *inadequate* provocation, they having lived with these intermediate-range ballistic missiles for years." Lovett added "that the President would undoubtedly receive two or three more opinions." Should an attack on Cuba resulted in a Soviet seizure of Berlin in retaliation, Lovett said, the president's options would be limited, other than the inception of nuclear war. After considerable further discussion, Lovett and the attorney general were asked to stay and join President Kennedy for dinner.[32] Robert Lovett, it might be noted, was not the first consultant to advise a blockade, but his recommendation was apparently one of the strongest and soundest.

Lovett took a late plane and arrived back at LaGuardia after midnight. But, as he recalled, "I commuted almost daily to Washington during the remainder of that week and the first half of the following week." One meeting that stood out in his recollection took place on Sunday, October 21, technically a meeting of the National Security Council. President Kennedy had phoned and asked Lovett to be in Washington for a meeting at the White House in his upstairs sitting room at two o'clock. He suggested that Lovett come down a bit early, that Robert Kennedy wanted to have lunch with him, and that he would be met at the airport. As Lovett remembered, "He neglected to say that the welcoming committee would consist of Ethel Kennedy [Robert's wife] and a small daughter." Mrs. Kennedy, standing at the doorway of the Eastern Airlines shuttle, "said that she was the representative of her husband and would I accept her escort in lieu of the Attorney General's. I told her this was not a hardship but a boon," and he was promptly driven out to their house in McLean, Virginia, to be joined by the attorney general and the rest of the family. From Robert Kennedy Lovett learned that the main subject for discussion at the meeting with the president was "the language and method of the Presidential announcement of the quarantine," the preference of the military men (and Dean Acheson) to bomb Cuba off the map having been rebuffed. "This statement," Lovett learned, "was scheduled for Monday, October 22nd, and the purpose of the meeting was to go over it and polish it."[33]

About halfway through that meeting of the 21st, President Kennedy motioned to Lovett to leave the room with him and go out on the porch. It had become clear through an exchange of messages with Khrushchev that some negotiating would soon be taking place. The president asked Lovett whether he thought it could be handled by the United States delegation at the UN. Lovett said that he did not think so, that the U.S. United Nations ambassador, Adlai Stevenson, was not strong enough to hold up under the pressures that would be brought against him. Lovett had been present at the meeting on the 20th at which Stevenson had discussed offering to withdraw missiles currently based in Italy and Turkey and to evacuate the Guantanamo naval base in Cuba, at which point Lovett and others had upbraided Stevenson. Lovett suggested to the president that John McCloy, then in Frankfurt, Germany, be brought back to America to work with Stevenson in the negotiations and, in effect, give him backbone. The president then asked Dean Rusk, McGeorge Bundy, and Robert Kwennedy their thoughts on this, and they agreed with Lovett to introduce McCloy to the negotiations. This was shortly carried out, with Lovett working out the details of McCloy's flight home from Europe.[34]

Lovett recalled another long meeting on October 24, two days after President Kennedy's public speech on the Cuban missiles, "by which time it became clear that the Russians were going to back down in a big way." Kennedy had received a letter from Khrushchev "indicating an almost hysterical wish to get out of the mess he had got himself into." At the 24th meeting, "all aspects of the problem and the basic requirements in the negotiation were gone over at some length and ... the end of the major crisis seemed to be in sight," although there were still some reservations. Lovett emphasized the advantage of the quarantine, that it gave Khrushchev and the Soviets "a couple of days while they make up their *own* minds what their intentions are." He joined with the president in warning once again against an air strike: "There's no such thing as a *small* military action, I don't think. Now the moment we start *anything* in this field, we have to be prepared to do *everything*." The Cuban Missile Crisis was just about over, though much work on its resolution remained to be carried out. The successful resolution was brought about primarily by the United States' decision to impose a quarantine on Russian shipping to Cuba, a decision for which one of the earliest and most forceful advocates was Robert A. Lovett.[35]

Over the course of the Kennedy administration, even after the Cuban Missile Crisis, Bob Lovett had numerous get-togethers with Jack Kennedy: "President Kennedy was certainly one of the most remarkable men I have ever been associated with, not only because of his enormous personal charm, a debonair quality and his wry humor but also because he possessed an extremely intelligent mind whose quickness seemed to be sharpened by an intuitive quality. He had a real thirst for knowledge which was wide ranging and engaging in its keenness. These qualities, coupled with the courage to look facts in the face, made him one of the most delightful men I have ever met and infused the office of President with a brightness and energetic atmosphere which was magnetic." "Our relationship," Lovett continued, "was, from my point-of-view, an unusually pleasant one and it was touched with a special Kennedy form of teasing humor which I loved." He recalled an early conversation in which Kennedy said "that he would want me to come down rather frequently on a wide variety of subjects, none of which he identified." When Lovett asked him what sort of things he had in mind, Kennedy "grinned and said ... that the government had spent an awful lot of money in training me in both the military departments and in the Department of State and that, as Chief Executive, he thought it must be obvious that one of his duties was to try to get his money's worth." As their meetings increased, Lovett "found that the natural respect which I had acquired for him grew into a real admiration for his qualities and his attitude toward the future and a strong affection for him as a person." Lovett said, "The overriding impressions which I have [of John F. Kennedy] are related to two rare qualities; his true and natural love of excellence and, secondly, a real generosity of spirit. He was considerate in every action I saw him take and he did not fall victim to the pervading virus of vanity which so frequently seems to attack the holders of great positions of power in any government."[36]

On April 23, 1963, Robert Lovett sent a letter to McGeorge Bundy asking to be excused from the three committees on which he was serving for reasons, once again, of health. Several days later he received a "Dear Bob" letter from the president, accepting his stepping down. "I do want you to know, however, that this relief from formal service is in no sense a full discharge from this Administration," Kennedy wrote. "I would like to feel free to call on you personally whenever there is a problem like the one on which I talked with you when you were last here.... In particular, when we get to the really tight moments on the Foreign Aid program, I think we will need your personal help with selected leaders on the Hill, and I hope you will be willing to let us call on you then.... I do think we will need your persuasive voice with a number of important individuals." Finishing up, President

Kennedy wrote, "Since I refuse to regard your resignation from these committees as anything but a change in the form of our relationship, I will not take time in this letter to tell you what I am sure you already know—that your counsel and your support are of the highest value to me, and that I am deeply grateful."[37]

Bob Lovett performed one last duty for Jack Kennedy in the summer of 1963. He reported to the president on some other matter, and the two of them got to talking about the hostile attitude President Charles de Gaulle of France was taking at the time toward both the United States and Britain. Since Lovett was planning his annual business trip to Europe on behalf of Brown Brothers Harriman, he decided to make up a list of French industrialists and bankers he knew he could trust and to "stop by and see them to learn what their views were on de Gaulle. I mentioned this to the President and he was so intrigued with it that he asked me if I would do a little research in depth for him as a corollary to the vacation which I had planned. I, of course, agreed to do so and to report to him on my return." Lovett in fact spoke with twelve of his French business friends—who "were inclined to speak with perfect frankness to me as just another businessman"—and he returned to Washington on a bright, sunny afternoon in late September "and read the President excerpts from the verbatim notes which I took."

This was Lovett's last meeting with John F. Kennedy. "Within a few weeks I ended up in the hospital in New York for serious major surgery, from which I returned to our apartment for convalescence only a few days before the President's assassination." His ulcer problem put him into Harkness Pavilion on October 4, his surgery was on October 17, and he did not leave the hospital until November 7. He related that "the doctors finally decided … to go in and do a major job on my stomach, thereby reducing the prospect of further hemorrhaging which has plagued me over the years."[38]

Obviously Robert Lovett was in no condition to take any part in the ceremonies following the president's death. He did write a letter of condolence to the president's brother Robert. Shortly thereafter, he received an undated letter from Robert Kennedy, telling him that "your letter meant so much to me. There were few people the President admired as much as you, and so for you to write such a kind and thoughtful letter is really greatly appreciated."[39] In June 1964 Robert Lovett donated $10,000 to the proposed John F. Kennedy Presidential Library and Museum, for which he received a lovely letter of thanks from Jacqueline Kennedy as well as another from Robert Kennedy. Subsequently, Lovett became a director of the library. It was a fitting conclusion to what had been a warm and productive relationship between Bob Lovett and the president.[40]

Lovett's relationship with Jack Kennedy's successor was much cooler and more formal. One of the first meetings of Robert Lovett with the newly inaugurated president, Lyndon B. Johnson, came about when Johnson carried out a function of John Kennedy's, the award to Lovett of the Presidential Medal of Freedom. Kennedy had named Lovett as a recipient of this award, "with distinction," but he was assassinated before the ceremony bestowing the award was held. President Kennedy named twenty-two recipients of the Medal of Freedom, only three of them "with distinction," one of whom was Robert Lovett.

Shortly after the assassination Lovett wrote the following to a business associate in London: "We have every reason to believe that President Johnson will continue the major Kennedy policies and the country has closed ranks behind him with full awareness of our good fortune in having a man of President Johnson's long political experience as an immediate successor." Johnson indeed was able to have several of Kennedy's domestic policies enacted into law; his problems would lie overseas.[41]

In Washington Johnson was forced to throw together his presidency in the wake of John Kennedy's murder, and not very long thereafter he had to prepare for the presidential election campaign of 1964. One of the measures taken was the creation of a panel of consultants on international affairs, a field in which Johnson had not distinguished himself. The group, known as "the Wise Men," was lined up by Johnson's adviser James H. Rowe for the campaign and included men like Eugene Black, John McCloy, Arthur Dean, Paul Hoffman, Roswell Gilpatric, James J. Wadsworth, and Robert Lovett.[42]

In view of the sorry Barry Goldwater campaign, it does not appear that the "Wise Men" were called upon to do very much for Johnson's effort, which of course won in an overwhelming electoral triumph. President Johnson did call the panel together for a meeting and lunch on September 23 "to offer his personal greetings to its members in an informal way." Lovett called McGeorge Bundy, who had sent out the invitation, and regretted that he would not be able to attend.[43] Over the next several years there were occasional gatherings of the group to discuss Vietnam, but Lovett usually declined to attend. At one get-together that included Lovett, he said that it was "not useful to talk about 'victory,' that what was really involved was preventing the expansion of Communism by force; in a sense avoiding defeat." Basically, Bob Lovett was unhappy that the U.S. had gotten involved in Vietnam, but the main task since it had was to protect our fighting men there.[44]

Lovett's relations with President Johnson were rather distant, although on September 14, 1965, Johnson sent him a telegram providing "warmest good wishes on your 70th birthday." He continued: "I think I am the fifth president who has been helped by your wisdom and cheered by your wit. You belong in the small group of major statesmen who have made the last 25 years a time of extraordinary American achievement in the world's affairs. Don't think for a moment that you will be allowed to quit now."[45]

In a letter to a friend in August 1967 about Vietnam, Lovett talked of the "feeling of frustration and exasperation at the situation that we have let ourselves be trapped into in that remote and difficult country." He noted that he had been out of touch with the Vietnam situation "for over two and a half years," but "I am pretty thoroughly disgusted with the whole affair and yet I can see no way out.... [A]ll I can see for us to do at the moment is play for time, refrain from pushing the offensive too hard, cultivate patience and wait for the break which may, sooner or later, turn up as a result of everybody's wish to get us out." When we get out, of course, he said, "the Communists or Nationalists—or whatever they are—will certainly take over." But, he added, "as long as our troops are in the field, I can't see that we can do anything other than give them maximum protection."[46]

While the Johnson administration was taking shape, Robert Lovett was receiving a signal honor. On March 21, 1964, the *New York Times* announced that the Association of Graduates of the United States Military Academy had selected Lovett as the recipient of the 1964 Sylvanus Thayer Award, named for the "father of the military academy," to be presented "to an outstanding citizen of the U.S. whose services and accomplishments in the national interest exemplify personal devotion to the ideals expressed in the West Point motto, 'Duty, Honor, Country.'" The award would be presented at a ceremony at West Point on May 2.[47] Among the many letters of congratulations Lovett received was one from Harry Truman, who wrote that "they could not have picked a better man for the Thayer Award."

Lovett responded, "I am aware that my good fortune stems from the period during which I had the great honor—and, I must confess, fun—of serving under your leadership."[48]

Lovett's old friend Ira Eaker wrote him on April 22: "I met Tooey [Spaatz] at the Army Navy Club yesterday afternoon after talking to you. He is making an effort to get Gene Zuckert, the Air Secretary, to send a plane up for all the old timers from this area, many of whom have expressed an urgent desire to be present, the last being Omar Bradley. I think you will find you will have quite a cheering section from these parts." Lovett got a letter from General Jacob L. Devers, one of the top army generals in Europe in World War II, telling him, "I have admired you greatly, particularly during the War, when your sound advice and your knack for getting the impossible done helped win that war."[49]

At the ceremony at West Point, General Leslie R. Groves read the citation for the Thayer Award, which began as follows: "As naval officer, cabinet officer, statesman, international banker, and business executive, Robert A. Lovett by his distinguished leadership has advanced his country's welfare in peace and in war for more than forty-seven years." It went on to recite Lovett's numerous accomplishments and to conclude that "this distinguished citizen has long served his country and the world outstandingly in the highest positions of responsibility."[50] Lovett's speech in response, to the audience of several thousand cadets and West Point graduates, "advised the military establishment ... to avoid becoming isolated within the American society." With the growth of the armed power of the country over the years, this growth "has made it all the more important for the military to see the issues of the cold war in a broad perspective rather than from the viewpoint of narrow professionalism."[51]

Ira Eaker, in writing up the story of the Thayer award, recalled Lovett's vision during World War II, when "under his inspired leadership, in little more than a year," after his visit in late 1942, "the Eighth Air Force had 1,000 bombers and 2,000 fighters and, as he had predicted, the West Wall came down, the Luftwaffe was driven from the skies."[52] Back home, Bob Lovett wrote a friend that "the whole affair ... was one of the most colorful and moving ceremonies I have ever seen, and I was surprised and touched by the fact that, unknown to me, the military had arranged to fly up from Washington a group of my World War II colleagues, so that it turned out to be 'old home week,' Tooey Spaatz, Ira Eaker, Pete Quesada, Larry Kuter, Orvil Cook, Rosy O'Donnell, etc., etc., and some of the Korean War vintage, including Bradley, Fechteler, Max Taylor, Lew Douglas, Jack McCloy, and so on.... The whole affair was beautifully handled. Adele commented that there was no group anywhere that understood pageantry and could handle such affairs as well as the military, and I am sure she is right."[53]

Some years later, asked to help on a study, Lovett responded, "Secondly, as to the question requesting my views on the comparison of President Truman and President Lyndon Johnson, I feel that the differences in these two men are far greater than their points of similarity. Regarding what I consider wide differences in temperament and character, I would prefer not to attempt to compare them." He then went on to point out that he "did work very closely with President Truman for a number of years, and I have the highest possible regard for him," stating that he was "simple, direct, courageous and had a deep abiding faith in the democratic process as it appears in this country." As he went on with his laudatory views of Truman, of course, Lovett tacitly emphasized what he felt were the differences between Truman and Johnson.[54]

27

The Later Years

Once he was out of the government Robert Lovett felt that he could make contributions to political campaigns when he favored a candidate. Though he was a Republican by registration, that party affiliation did not dictate the direction of his largesse. His first contribution was to his good buddy Averell Harriman, $500 to Averell's 1954 Democratic campaign for New York governor (despite the Brown Brothers' position that year that they would "take no part whatever in current political activities"). Over the years he contributed to Republicans like William Scranton, Kenneth Keating, John Lindsay, and John Sherman Cooper (a fellow Bonesman), running for the Senate in Kentucky, and he made several contributions to his friend Pres Bush's son, George. On the other side, though, he gave to the Johnson campaign in 1964, to Hubert Humphrey's presidential campaign in 1968, and several contributions to Henry "Scoop" Jackson, the Democratic senator from Washington with whom Bob Lovett had a good relationship.[1]

Over the years, Lovett also made numerous substantial contributions for educational purposes to institutions like the Columbia University College of Physicians and Surgeons (with a note thanking them for what they did for his innards), The Hill School, the Felix Frankfurter Fellowship at Balliol College, Williams College, Tufts University for a professorship honoring Vannevar Bush, the Margaret Mead Fund for the Advancement of Anthropology, Princeton for endowing a chair in honor of David K.E. Bruce; and the Harry S Truman Library.[2]

The Lovetts were greatly saddened in May of 1967 when their daughter, Evelyn Springer Lovett Brown, a Vassar College alumna, passed away at the age of forty-seven, leaving behind her husband, David S. Brown, a professor at George Washington University, three sons (David, Jr., born in 1944, Christopher, born in 1948, and Robert, born in 1951) and a daughter, Adele, born at the end of 1953. Early in 1966 it had been discovered that Evelyn had very serious and widespread cancer, a disease that took her life a year later.

The Lovetts' other child, their son, Robin, had attended St. Paul's School and Yale, where he graduated in 1949 summa cum laude with a degree in electrical engineering. He went on to get a master's degree in science from MIT in 1950 before going to work for the DuPont Company in Wilmington, Delaware. Robin married Dorothy deHaven, known as "Didi," on February 27, 1965, and they had three children— Evelyn, born in 1966, Virginia, born in 1968, and Robert Abercrombie Lovett II, born in 1979. Robin and his family lived in Greenville, Delaware, but they made frequent visits to Locust Valley to see Bob and Adele, whom they loved.

At a dinner at Harvard University in early June 1967, Bob Lovett was astonished to learn of the establishment of the Lovett-Learned Professorship of Business Administration at the

Harvard Business School, in honor of himself and Harvard professor Edmund P. Learned. Adele had known this was coming, but she managed to keep the secret from her husband until the dinner. The funding for the chair was raised by Charles "Tex" Thornton, Lovett's statistical aide during the war, and Thornton's partner in Litton Industries, Roy L. Ash.

With his service to the government terminated and his leadership role at Union Pacific toned down considerably, Robert Lovett was glad to be working at 59 Wall Street, where he continued as an active partner in Brown Brothers Harriman. He still had close friends in the partnership, men like Elbridge Gerry, Knight Woolley, Prescott Bush, Bunny Harriman, and others, and he still found private banking to be stimulating and profitable. He drove in to the city from Locust Valley four days a week. In addition, he was often requested to send out copies of his article, "Gilt-Edged Insecurity," which had appeared in the *Saturday Evening Post* back in 1937.

In 1968 Brown Brothers, getting a bit crowded on the business floor, moved its four oldest partners, Lovett, Woolley, Bush, and Bunny Harriman, "upstairs," literally having their desks moved up to the next floor. They were still general partners, involved in the firm's business but were now physically out of the way of the ever-growing younger element of the firm.

In addition, of course, Lovett had numerous connections with other companies and other institutions, both business and nonprofit, and these consumed a good bit of his time. Along with his long service with the Union Pacific Railroad and its affiliates, he served on the board of the Columbia Broadcasting System for many years, contributing his time and efforts to CBS's finance committee. He put in lengthy time on the boards of the Royal-Globe Insurance Companies, the New York Life Insurance Company, the North American Rockwell Corporation, and the Freeport Minerals Company. On November 21, 1966, Lovett testified at length to the Federal Communications Commission on behalf of the American Telephone and Telegraph Company, testimony that took up eight printed pages.

Lovett was affiliated as well with a number of nonprofit and charitable organizations such as the George C. Marshall Research Foundation (of which he was board chairman), the German Marshall Fund of the United States, the corporation of the Massachusetts Institute of Technology (MIT), eventually becoming a life member emeritus, the Carnegie Foundation for the Advancement of Teaching, the Rockefeller Foundation, for which he was a trustee from 1949 to 1961, the Presbyterian Hospital in New York, the Metropolitan Museum of Art, the John F. Kennedy Library, of which he was a director, the John Fitzgerald Kennedy School of Government, for which he served on the Advisory Committee, and the Committee for Economic Development. Bob Lovett did not spend much time looking for things to keep him busy.

Besides all these connections, he continued his membership in several private clubs, the Century Association and The Links in New York, the Creek Club in Locust Valley, the 1925 F Street Club, the Metropolitan Club in Washington, and the Yale Club of New York City. The Century Association, located in a Stanford White-designed clubhouse at 7 West 43rd Street in Manhattan, was regarded as a center of the city's intellectual and literary life, "the very embodiment of the East Coast old boys' network," as one historian designated it.[3]

One of the personal characteristics Robert Lovett frequently alluded to was what he considered his very homely appearance. Sending off a requested photo, he wrote, "In sending it, I want to urge you to take a good, hard look at it and remember that my sole claim to remembrance in Washington is that of being the most non-photogenic man in Government," a claim he often repeated. His appearance was not improved by a dive onto his nose early in 1963, which landed him back in the hospital "with a rebuilt nose which appears to satisfy Adele."[4]

Bob and Adele Lovett were happy to spend their remaining years in Locust Valley, particularly in the abundantly flowered Pleasance. They made friends among their neighbors. Lovett wrote in 1968, "Adele and I are members of the local church in Locust Valley—St. John's of Lattingtown—and we are reasonably active in the community." In addition, they lived out a happy wedded life.[5]

While Bob Lovett continued his work with Brown Brothers Harriman, he noted that "Adele spends a good solid six or seven hours in the garden daily at hard manual labor, which is probably why she looks spry and as colorful as a young girl."[6]

On April 19, 1969, the Lovetts celebrated their 50th wedding anniversary. They decided to mark the occasion "by getting some of our friends together who either attended our wedding or who had been childhood friends and neighbors for fifty years." Much to their "astonishment and delight" sixty-six celebrants turned up. With such a gathering, they were happy to move it from their house to the nearby Creek Club. "Certainly," he added, "after all my trips to the hospital, I never expected to see a fiftieth wedding anniversary—so the occasion was one of both thanksgiving and gaiety. We engaged the Meyer Davis orchestra, now run by the son of the man who played at our wedding reception, got a list of all the old tunes and had the time of our lives! I was utterly amazed to see about three-quarters of my ancient friends skipping about like teenagers."[7]

Several years later, Lovett wrote to a Yale classmate in response to a request to attend a class reunion. "After three tours of duty in Washington, after each of which I had some of my insides removed, my extra-curricular activities have been restricted by my doctors and, in observing the rules, I have not been able to attend class reunions." But he pointed out that Brown Brothers Harriman "is absolutely crawling with Yale graduates over a variety of years, but the three senior partners include Roland Harriman and Knight Woolley, Class of 1917, and myself."[8] Another Yale connection came to Lovett's mind when Goddard Lieberson, the president of Columbia Records, sent him a copy of the long-playing record "Cole," a collection of Cole Porter recordings. In thanking Lieberson, Lovett said, "I am delighted to have it as Cole was an old friend of mine." Porter, of course, was a Yale man of the Class of 1913 who had passed away in 1964.[9]

One lasting connection of Bob Lovett to his alma mater in New Haven was the 1985 creation in Yale's Department of History of the Robert Lovett Chair in Military and Naval History. In late 1985 Lovett was advised that $950,000 had been raised for the chair, including $50,000 from North American Rockwell, the same from the Harriman foundations and from the partners at Brown Brothers Harriman, individually, just short of $100,000. The Lovett Chair is an eminent function of the History Department to this day.[10]

Bob Lovett wrote to a friend in September 1974, a couple of days after his seventy-ninth birthday, telling him, "Now that I am approaching middle age, I am delighted to say that I don't feel a day over ninety." Not long after that, in February 1975, he had a pacemaker installed in his heart, which he called "a surprisingly easy operation." Several months later, unfortunately, Lovett came down with pneumonia, to add to his growing list of health woes.[11]

In fact, Robert Lovett continued working as a partner with Brown Brothers Harriman for another ten years. He was very saddened on February 16, 1978, when his closest friend of many years, Roland "Bunny" Harriman, passed away, but he carried on, although late in 1980 he wrote to Hanson Baldwin, the *Times* writer, that "some rather hard-boiled doctors have taken command of my activities and I have the feeling when they let me come to the office to catch up with things, they are really only letting me out on parole."[12]

Finally, on December 1, 1983, at the age of eighty-eight, Bob Lovett, with several other of his aged compatriots, was transferred to the status of a limited partner in the firm. He still kept his desk upstairs, and he still came into the office from time to time, fifty-seven years after being designated a general partner. For the firm, William Ray wrote to Lovett approaching this change: "As you undertake this metamorphosis from general to limited partnership and as you approach your 60th anniversary with the firm on January 15, I want you to be aware that every one of your partners—and the staff—is proud of what you have done to create and guide our firm. You are indeed the Best and the Brightest and you have added luster and bright renown to the sacred house."[13]

Prior to the change at the firm, Bob Lovett in the summer of 1983 broke a hip. Some time after that he wrote a friend that "the restrictions of loss of sight plus a broken hip and a cancer operation limit my physical activities but so far have not invaded my head so that Adele and I live a restricted life but a happy one." He was so accustomed to health problems, whether severe or less so, by then that he was able to live with them.[14]

In January 1979 Marx Leva, who had been an assistant secretary of defense through 1951, spoke to a gathering at the Defense Department, recalling that "Secretary Lovett had one favorite expression, whenever we had managed to get ourselves into deep trouble. It was: 'To hell with the cheese; let's get out of the trap!'" Leva also remembered General Marshall's favorite expression, which was "Clear it with Lovett." A bit later Lovett wrote to Leva that he "vividly recall[ed] the saying you correctly attribute to me which I meant from the bottom of my soul. Now that I am out of the trap, I find I miss it."[15]

On February 16, 1980, Archibald MacLeish wrote to the chairman of the Wallace Awards of the American-Scottish Foundation: "I hereby nominate, for the Wallace Award, Mr. Robert Abercrombie Lovett ... an American citizen of Scottish descent on both sides, whose record of public service is well known." He then set forth that record. The Wallace Award, established in 1970, was for citizens of Scottish descent with major contributions to the welfare of this country. On March 7, President Natalie Douglas-Hamilton of the foundation wrote to Lovett, advising him that he had been elected the recipient of the award. A partner at Brown Brothers accepted the award for him.[16]

As the years passed, with time spent in Locust Valley as well as on Wall Street, Robert Lovett enjoyed looking back on his life. In 1984 he wrote to Pat Carter (George Marshall's closest aide): "I have the happiest recollection of certain periods in history, particularly those which I spent in Washington working with great people in a great cause. In fact, my three tours of duty in Washington were among the happiest of our lives and Adele and I look back on them with grateful pleasure. A very large part of this feeling arises from the fact that in a period of grimness, I was working with you and was able to find work turning into fun. For this and a sense of pride in working with you for GCM and Colonel Stimson, I send you my lasting thanks and some chuckles worth sharing."[17]

On May 5, 1983, Evan Thomas and Walter Isaacson, coauthors working on a book about Lovett and his confreres, stopped by for a visit with Lovett in Locust Valley. Later Thomas wrote him, in September 1985: "Over the last three years Walter Isaacson and I have come out to Long Island several times to see you about the book we are writing...." From these visits—and numerous others to the other men—came the book *The Wise Men*, the story of Lovett, Acheson, McCloy, Kennan, Bohlen, and Averell Harriman and their overwhelming influence on America's postwar policies. The book came out in 1986, but Lovett, with an advance copy to read, wrote to the two authors: "As it turns out it is the best single account I have so far read of the years it covers which had incredible complexities and side issues."[18]

The years were taking their toll on Lovett's compatriots. In September 1983 "Scoop" Jackson passed away. Bob Lovett wrote that Jackson "was one of the finest men I have ever known and I greatly admired him not only as a leading Senator but especially as a man of enormous courage, integrity and energy."[19] In the meantime, however, the Lovetts were hit with another dreadful personal development. On June 15, 1984, their son, Robin, died at the Wilmington Medical Center at the age of fifty-seven after a long battle with cancer. Services were held at a church in Greenville, Delaware, as Adele and Robert Lovett mourned the loss of their only surviving child. Jack McCloy sent his warmest regrets, and the Lovetts responded with thanks for his "dear words of sympathy."[20]

On September 14, 1985, Robert Abercrombie Lovett observed his ninetieth birthday— quite a feat for a man plagued by serious health problems for some seventy years. He received many messages of congratulations from persons as diverse as Tooey Spaatz's widow, Lady Bird Johnson, George P. Shultz, Frank Pace, George H.W. Bush (Pres Bush's son, at the time vice president), Margaret Truman Daniel, and President Ronald Reagan. Ira Eaker sent congratulations "to our very favorite distinguished statesman," and Dean Rusk called Lovett "a shining example of a man of the highest honor who has lived for many years with complete integrity, a fine sense of humor, and a compassionate interest in one's fellow human beings." General James Van Fleet expressed his "admiration and appreciation for the great things you have done for our country throughout your illustrious career," and General Maxwell Taylor recalled "when you were an Assistant Secretary of War along with Jack McCloy under Mr. Stimson and I was an insignificant major down the hall in the office of General Marshall. Over the years I have often reflected on the good fortune of the nation in having this foursome to direct the Army in World War II." And there were more—from the board of the Union Pacific, from the Marshall Foundation, and from the current secretary of the air force.

Frank Hoch, from Brown Brothers, remembered "your return to 'prosperous anonymity' in 1953 after those strenuous 12 years or so in Washington. Your health was a bit frail, and we all worried about you. Having put another 32 years behind you, you have embodied the triumph of mind over matter. Surely your never failing humor did it, and we miss it. We just don't laugh as much as when you were around." As Didi Lovett remembered, "his extraordinary mind and humor continued to the end." And one last one, from Lovett's old secretary Hazel Pierson: "A great age for a great man, for whom I have had the privilege to work for more than fifty years. I often think of you and Mrs. Lovett and your many kindnesses to me."[21]

Three-and-a-half months after that birthday, Robert Lovett had another occasion of great sadness, when, on January 4, 1986, eight days shy of her 87th birthday, Adele passed away. As he sat sadly in her funeral service at the church of St. John's of Lattingtown, Robert reviewed in his mind so many moments of joy and of sorrow he and Adele had shared over the sixty-six years of what had been a very fine marriage.[22]

Robert Lovett was not to be made to spend much time as a widower. On May 7, 1986, still in his ninetieth year, his body, wracked with pain and troubles for so many years, finally yielded to mortality, to his cancer and kidney ailments, and he died in his home in Locust Valley. The funeral, held at the same church that had celebrated Adele's life, took place on May 10, with ten partners from Brown Brothers Harriman in attendance. Trubee Davison's son Daniel presented a eulogy dealing with Robert Lovett's public life and his great contributions to the nation, and David Brown, the eldest grandchild who had flown in from his home in Seattle, spoke of his grandfather's family life. It was a beautiful day and a well-attended service. Robert's body was interred in the Locust Valley Cemetery, as Adele's had been.

Didi Lovett, Robin's widow, called Brown Brothers on the following Monday to thank the partners for their attendance. "She said words to the effect that none of us would ever realize how much it meant to her and to all of the grandchildren to have so many BBH & Co partners/friends show up."[23]

So ended a life of service—service to the navy in World War I, flying in combat planes and handling assignments for others, service to the army in World War II, creating the mighty air force that helped so much in winning the war, service to the nation and to the European world in the foundation of the policies that guided the United States and Europe in the long confrontation with communism, service to the economy in his many years of excellence in the worlds of banking and railroading, and service to needy people in his many contributions to the works of charity and education that moved the world forward. Asked about the motivating causes for his service in government, Lovett referred to his alerting the government to the desperate need to prepare aviation for the oncoming war. He concluded: "My experience in government service was a rewarding one; I enjoyed it; I was stimulated by it, and I felt it a privilege to be asked to serve as a non-political executive in three different tours of duty."[24]

We finish up with the words of Admiral William M. Fechteler, former navy chief of staff: "Oh, I think Bob Lovett is an outstanding man in every respect. He has intelligence, is forthright, sincere, and a great patriot."[25]

Robert Lovett in his later years (Robert Abercrombie Lovett Papers [MS1617]. Manuscripts and Archives, Yale University Library).

Chapter Notes

Introduction

1. Isaacson, Walter, and Evan Thomas, *The Wise Men: Six Friends and the World They Made* (New York: Simon & Schuster, 1986, paperback 2013).
2. Parton, James, ed., *Impact: The Army Air Forces' Confidential Picture History of World War II* (Harrisburg, PA, National Historical Society, 1989), iv.
3. Olson, Lynne, *Those Angry Days: Roosevelt, Lindbergh and America's Fight Over World War II, 1939–1941* (New York: Random House, 2013), 141.
4. Parton, James, *"Air Force Spoken Here": General Ira Eaker and the Command of the Air* (Bethesda, MD: Adler & Adler, 1986), 269; Krock, Arthur, *Memoirs: Sixty Years on the Firing Line* (New York: Funk & Wagnalls, 1968), 240.
5. James Parton to Robert A. Lovett, Aug. 15, 1978, Robert A. Lovett Papers, Yale University Library (hereinafter referred to simply as Lovett Papers).
6. Lovett to Thomas S. Lamont, July 27, 1965, Lovett Papers.

Chapter 1

1. Baruch, Bernard M., *Baruch: The Public Years* (New York: Holt, Rinehart & Winston, 1960), 66.
2. Robert A. Lovett to Mary Bean; Robert A. Lovett to Ferdinand Lathrop Meyer, June 19, 1957, Lovett Papers.
3. Lovett, Robert A., *Forty Years After: An Appreciation of the Genius of Edward Henry Harriman, 1848–1909* (New York: Newcomen Society, 1949), 6–7.
4. Cutts, Norma E., and Nicholas Moseley, "Notes on Photographic Memory," *Journal of Psychology*, 1969, p. 9.
5. Lovett to Nicholas Mosely, July 6, 1966, Lovett Papers.
6. Lovett to Beatrice B. Schalit of CARE, Lovett Papers. After World War II, when Lovett learned that Mlle. Gay was in somewhat dire straits in postwar France he arranged to have $60 worth of food sent to her by CARE every three months, plus other items and amounts he shipped to her from time to time. After CARE stopped the arrangement in 1955 he sent Mlle. Gay regular checks. In 1967 she died at the age of 91, though before that she wrote Lovett many letters of thanks.
7. Abramson, Rudy, *Spanning the Century: The Life of W. Averell Harriman, 1891–1986* (New York: William Morrow, 1992), 107; Lovett interview by Jessica Holland for Brown Brothers Harriman, June, 1981, Lovett Papers,

1. This interview, which was conducted on June 8, 15, and 22, 1981, covers well over 120 pages.
8. *The Hill School News*, June 10, 1913.
9. Ibid., October 8, 1913.
10. *The Dial; 1914* (The Hill School yearbook), 43.
11. Margaret Case Harriman and John Bainbridge, "The Thirteenth Labor of Hercules," *New Yorker*, November 6, 1943. This was a two-part article, the second part of which appeared on November 13, 1943.
12. Lovett interview, Brown Brothers Harriman, 7–8.
13. Harriman, E.Roland, *I Reminisce* (Garden City, NY: Doubleday, 1975), 45.
14. Wortman, Marc, *The Millionaires' Unit: The Aristocratic Flyboys Who Fought the Great War and Invented American Airpower* (New York: Public Affairs, 2006), 30; Lovett to Isaac Thomas, The Hill School, October 19, 1928, Lovett Papers. The Phi Beta Kappa chapter at Yale took in all men who maintained a stand of 330 on a scale of 400 for any two consecutive years; *The Hill School News*, April 20, 1914.
15. Harriman and Bainbridge, *New Yorker*, November 13, 1943, loc. cit., 29.
16. Wortman, op. cit, 7.
17. Ibid., 73–77, for a vivid description of Yale's Junior Promenade.
18. In the presidential election of 2004, curiously, each party nominated a Bonesman, George W. Bush for the Republicans and John Kerry for the Democrats.
19. Robbins, Alexandra, *Secrets of the Tomb: Skull and Bones, the Ivy League, and the Hidden Paths of Power* (Boston and New York, Little, Brown, 2002), 84–85. Reading through Robert Lovett's letters in his papers at Yale, this researcher notes numerous letters to and from him with the "322" attached along with a signature.

Chapter 2

1. Paine, Ralph D., *The First Yale Unit: A Story of Naval Aviation, 1916–1919* (Cambridge, MA, Riverside Press, 1925), i, 10.
2. Wortman, op. cit., 41; Groom, Winston, *The Aviators: Eddie Rickenbacker, Jimmy Doolittle, Charles Lindbergh, and the Epic Age of Flight* (Washington, D.C., National Geographic, 2013), 38.
3. Wortman, op. cit., 4
4. *New York Times*, August 24, 1916.
5. Ibid.
6. *Yale Daily News*, November 14, 1916.

7. The journey south can be followed in Wortman, op. cit., 85–87.

8. F. Trubee Davison Papers, Yale University Library (hereinafter Davison Papers).

9. Ibid., 113.

10. Robbins, op. cit., 108–109.

11. *Saturday Evening Post*, September 1, 1917; *Washington Post*, October 21, 1917.

12. Rossano, Geoffrey L., ed., *Hero of the Angry Sky: The World War I Diary and Letters of David S. Ingalls, America's First Naval Ace* (Athens: Ohio University Press, 2013), 29.

13. Trubee Davison, using crutches to overcome his physical handicap, went to law school at Columbia, was admitted to the bar and elected to the New York legislature and in 1928 became assistant secretary of war for aviation. He even took up flying again (*New York Herald Tribune*, April 22, 1928).

14. Paine, op. cit., i, 190–191. On August 7, 1917, Mc-Donnell, by letter to the supervisor, Naval Reserve Flying Corps, had recommended that Lovett and Gates, "leaders in every way … of this detachment," be advanced immediately to the rank of lieutenant junior grade; Davison Papers.

Chapter 3

1. Lovett to F. Trubee Davison, August 23, 1917, Davison Papers.

2. Lovett to F. Trubee Davison, September 8, 1917, Lovett to Mrs. Kate Davison (Trubee's mother), September 16, 1917, Davison Papers.

3. Lovett to F. Trubee Davison, September 24, 1917, Davison Papers.

4. Dichman report, November 15, 1917, and letter, Lovett to F. Trubee Davison, September 24, 1917, Davison Papers.

5. Lovett to Mrs. Kate Davison, November 29, 1917, Davison Papers.

6. Lovett to F. Trubee Davison, February 4, 1918, Davison Papers; Ingalls diary, December 24, 1917, Rossano, *Hero of the Angry Sky*, 95.

7. Lovett to Adele Brown, March 7, 1918, and Gates to Davison, April 15, 1918, both in Wortman, op. cit.,182.

8. Davison Papers.

9. Rossano, Geoffrey L., ed., *The Price of Honor: The World War One Letters of Naval Aviator Kenneth MacLeish* (Annapolis, Naval Institue Press, 1991), 103.

10. Larrabee. Eric, *Commander in Chief: Franklin Delano Roosevelt, His Lieutenants, and Their War* (New York: Harper & Row, 1987), 32.

11. *Waterville (SD) Public Opinion*, November 11, 1964.

12. Lovett to F. Trubee Davison, February 4, 1918, Davison Papers.

13. Wortman, op. cit., 176.

14. Letter to Adele Brown, March 26, 1918, 201.

15. Letter to Adele Brown, March 19, 1918, 205; Rossano, Geoffrey, *Stalking the U-Boat: U.S. Naval Aviation in Europe in World War I* (Gainesville: University Press of Florida, 2010), 69.

16. Paine, op. cit., ii, 179.

17. MacLeish to Priscilla Murdoch, April 18, 1918, Rossano, *The Price of Honor*, 144.

18. Letter to Adele Brown, April 14, 1918, Wortman, op. cit., 207.

19. Paine, op. cit., ii, 186.

20. Lovett to F. Trubee Davison, June 28, 1918, Davison Papers.

21. Rossano, *The Price of Honor*, 216.

22. Wortman, op. cit., 214.

23. Letter to Mrs. Kate Davison, March 10, 1918, 214.

24. Lovett to F. Trubee Davison, May 17, 1918, Davison Papers.

25. Lovett to Adele Brown, October 14, 1918, Wortman, op. cit., 257.

26. November 19, 1918, D.C. Hanrahan, Davison Papers.

Chapter 4

1. Lovett wrote a lengthy reply on June 2, 1964, to the Rev. Wayne N. Metz, in Stillwater, Oklahoma, who was writing a thesis on the religious affiliations of cabinet members, describing his religious connections over the years but calling himself "unable to identify a specific church in the sense that I understand your inquiry" (Lovett Papers).

2. The wedding is described at some length in the *New York Times*, April 20, 1919, albeit with a few errors, like Lovett's graduation from Yale in 1916 and his having been at Harvard Law School when he went into the naval service.

3. Harvard Law School Questionnaire, Lovett Papers; Brown Brothers Harriman interview, June 8, 1981, p. 11. Lovett did contribute several $1,000 gifts to the law school over the years.

4. Cutts & Moseley, loc. cit., 10. The authors of this article interviewed Lovett personally.

5. David Mays to Lovett, November 17, 1970, Lovett Papers.

6. *New York Herald Tribune*, Jan. 1, 1951.

7. Lovett interview, Brown Brothers Harriman, June 1981, p. 13.

8. Ibid., 13–14.

9. Handwritten letter, Lovett to "Charlie," an unnamed partner and close friend at Brown Brothers, probably Charlie Dickey, October 20, 1925, Lovett Papers. Lovett's father-in-law James Brown died on June 9, 1935.

10. Lovett interview, Brown Brothers Harriman, June 1981, pp. 15, 16, 18.

11. Ibid., 19–20.

12. Harriman and Bainbridge, November 13, 1943, loc. cit., 32; Lovett interview, Brown Brothers Harriman, June 1981, p. 81.

13. *New York Herald Tribune*, Jan. 3, 1951.

14. Fromkin, David, *In the Time of the Americans: FDR, Truman, Eisenhower, Marshall, MacArthur; The Generation That Changed America's Role in the World* (New York: Alfred A. Knopf, 1995), 287.

15. Hoopes, Townsend, and Douglas Brinkley, *Driven Patriot: The Life and Times of James Forrestal* (New York: Alfred A. Knopf, 1992), 48.

16. Undated draft of letter, Lovett to Charles Murphy, sent to Edythe D. Holbrook, December 16, 1983, Lovett Papers; May 11, 1982, interview with Lovett in Hoopes & Brinkley, op. cit., 40.

17. Hoopes & Brinkley, op. cit., 77
18. Lovett to Major David MacIsaac, July 27, 1970, Lovett Papers.
19. Lovett to Natl. Aeronautic Association of U.S.A., Mar. 26, 1928; Lovett to C.F. Schory, Secretary, Natl. Aeronautic Assn. of USA, April 16, 1928; Schory to Lovett, Apr. 18, 1928; Lovett to Schory, Apr. 20, 1928; Schory to Lovett, Apr. 30, 1928; undated "Immediate Release" from Natl. Aeronautic Assn., all in Lovett Papers. In August 1928 Lovett applied for his own membership in the National Aeronautic Association of USA, sending along a $5 check for his dues; he remained a member for many years (Lovett to C.F. Schory, Aug. 13, 1928, Lovett Papers).
20. Lovett, *Forty Years After*, op. cit., 14.
21. Lovett to Henry A. Finch, September 19, 1932, Lovett Papers. Lovett's mother had died five years earlier.
22. E.H. Harriman had left his estate, which obviously included a huge amount of Union Pacific stock, to his wife, Mary, and upon her death in 1932 that stock passed to her children including Averell and Roland.
23. Olson, Lynne, *Citizens of London: The Americans Who Stood with Britain in Its Darkest, Finest Hour* (New York: Random House, 2010), 57.
24. Lovett to C.F. Schory, Aug. 13, 1928, Lovett Papers; Harriman and Bainbridge, loc. cit., November 13, 1943, 29; Klein, Maury, *Union Pacific: The Rebirth, 1894–1969* (New York: Doubleday, 1989), 325–326.
25. E.R. Harriman, op. cit., 74.
26. Lovett interview, Brown Brothers Harriman, June 1981, p. 36.
27. Ibid., 121–122.
28. Harriman and Bainbridge, loc. cit., November 13, 1943, 32.
29. Lovett to Peter C. Bryce, Esq., April 30, 1934, Lovett Papers.
30. Lovett to John Vorys, June 12, 1940, Lovett Papers.
31. Lovett to W.A. Harriman, Apr. 25, 1934, Abramson, op. cit., 252.
32. Lovett, Robert A., "Gilt-Edged Insecurity," *Saturday Evening Post*, Apr. 3, 1937, 20. Sixteen years later, Lovett said he saw no reasons "to alter the conclusions reached" in his article; Lovett to Joseph H. Meyers, July 6, 1953, Lovett Papers.
33. Harriman, E.R., op. cit., 92.
34. Harriman and Bainbridge, November 6, 1943, loc. cit., 38; Meade, Marion, *Dorothy Parker: What Fresh Hell Is This?* (New York: Villard Books,1988), 186–187; Gaines, James R., *Wit's End: Days and Nights of the Algonquin Round Table* (New York: Harcourt Brace Jovanovich, 1977), 235; *New York Times Book Review*, December 8, 2013. Parker dedicated *Laments for the Living* to Adele Lovett.
35. Lovett to Noel Polk, April 25, June 26, 1973, Lovett Papers.
36. Joseph Blotner to Lovett, Aug. 16, 1965, Lovett Papers.
37. Faulkner, William, "Turn About," *Saturday Evening Post*, March 5, 1932; Blotner, Joseph, *Faulkner: A Biography* (New York: Random House, 1984), 290–291.
38. Harriman and Bainbridge, loc. cit., 37.
39. Lovett to Isaac Thomas, The Hill School, October19, 1928, Lovett Papers; Harriman and Bainbridge, November 13, 1943, loc. cit., 33.

40. Ibid., 29; Lovett to Devon Francis, July 31, 1969, Lovett Papers.
41. "European Outlook—If Any," by Lovett, June 16, 1939, Lovett Papers. On December 16, 1938, Lovett's secretary Hazel Pierson sent a $30 check to Sam Harwill, Carnegie Hall Studios, for six piano lessons given Lovett through December 15 (Lovett Papers).

Chapter 5

1. Lovett interview by Donald Shaughnessy, Columbia University Library, January 15, p. 2; Lovett interview, Brown Brothers Harriman, June 1981, p. 106; Groom, op. cit. 182–185. At the close of the war, Milch was tried and convicted on two counts of war crimes and sentenced to life imprisonment, although he was released in 1954. Udet, a well-known womanizer and hard drinker, had a relationship with Martha Dodd, daughter of the U.S. ambassador to Germany. After Hermann Goering and Milch told Hitler that Udet was responsible for losing the Battle of Britain, Udet committed suicide by gunshot on November 17, 1941.
2. Shaughnessy interview, 3.
3. Borklund, Carl W., *Men of the Pentagon, from Forrestal to McNamara* (New York: Frederick A. Praeger, 1966), 14.
4. Lovett to Robert P. Patterson, November 22, 1940, Lovett Papers.
5. Patterson to Lovett, November 25, 1940; Lovett to Patterson, November 26, 1940, Lovett Papers.
6. Henry Lewis Stimson Diary, Library of Congress (hereinafter "Stimson Diary"), November 28, 1940.
7. Stimson Diary, December 18, 19, 1940.
8. Lovett to F.W. Charske, December 19, 1940, Lovett Papers.
9. The United States supplied Great Britain with about 1,500 military planes during the year 1940 and 500 more went to Canada, with half of those going to Britain as well (*Washington Times-Herald*, December 26, 1940).
10. Stimson Diary, December 20, 1940.
11. Patterson to Lovett, December 11, 1945, Lovett Papers.
12. *New York Times*, December 20, 1940.
13. Lovett to Archibald MacLeish, September 17, 1940, Lovett Papers.
14. *Congressional Record—Senate*, December 23, 1940, #21656. Holt, elected to the Senate in 1934 at the age of 29, the youngest man ever elected to the Senate, was a staunch isolationist who had opposed any increase in military spending, opposed the Selective Service Act of 1940, and had already been defeated for renomination earlier in 1940, making him a "lame duck" when he attacked Lovett. His son, Rush Holt, Jr., was a liberal congressman from New Jersey from 1999 to 2015. Lovett to Honorable Morris Sheppard (D-Tex), December 28, 1940, Lovett Papers.
15. Lovett interview by Shaughnessy, Jan. 15, 1959, p. 6; Kai Bird, *The Chairman: John J. McCloy, the Making of the American Establishment* (New York: Simon & Schuster, 1992), 121.
16. Alsop and Kintner column, *Philadelpha Evening Bulletin*, February 24, 1941.

17. Morison, Elting E., *Turmoil and Tradition: A Study of the Life and Times of Henry L. Stimson* (Boston: Houghton Mifflin, 1960), 493.

18. Ibid., 495; Snow, Richard, *A Measureless Peril: America in the Fight for the Atlantic, the Longest Battle of World War II* (New York, Scribner, 2010), 107.

Chapter 6

1. Harriman & Bainbridge, November 6, 1943, loc. cit., 30.

2. Stimson Diary, December 23 and 30, 1940.

3. Lovett to Stimson, December 30, 1940, Lovett Papers (National Archives).

4. Harriman & Bainbridge, November 6, 1943, loc. cit., 30.

5. McNamara, Robert S., with Brian VanDeMark, *In Retrospect: The Tragedy and Lessons of Vietnam* (New York: Times Books, 1995), 8.

6. Ibid., 9.

7. Ibid. McNamara, of course, became secretary of defense in 1961.

8. Stimson Diary, December 31, 1940.

9. *Washington Times-Herald*, Jan. 8, 1941; Cray, Ed, *General of the Army: George C. Marshall, Soldier and Statesman* (New York: Touchstone, 1990), 162.

10. Watson, Mark S., "Plane Engine Lag Is Grave, Watson Says," *Baltimore Sun*, Jan. 4, 1941; *Washington Post*, February 7, 1941.

11. *Philadelphia Evening Bulletin*, Apr. 10, 1941.

12. *New Orleans Times-Picayune*, Apr. 27, 1941.

13. *Washington Post*, Apr. 21, 1941; *Wall Street Journal*, Apr. 25, 1941; *New York Times*, Apr. 20, 1941; *New York Herald-Tribune*, Apr. 20, 1941; *Newark Sunday Call*, Apr. 20, 1941; *Baltimore Sun*, Apr. 20, 1941.

14. Stimson Diary, April 22, 1941.

15. Harriman & Bainbridge, November 13, 1943, loc. cit., 31.

16. *Chicago Tribune*, September 4, 1941.

17. *New York Herald Tribune*, September 20, 1941; Mosley, Leonard, *Marshall: Hero for Our Times* (New York: Hearst Books, 1982), 149. The Lovett-McCloy memorandum now sits in the Marshall Foundation.

18. Lovett interview with Shaughnessy, Jan. 15, 1959, 6.

19. Ibid., 7. Credit for such an organization must, of course, go primarily to Stimson.

20. Lovett to Henry Morgenthau, Jr., September 8, 1941, Lovett Papers; Eiler, Keith E., *Mobilizing America: Robert P. Patterson and the War Effort, 1940–1945* (Ithaca, NY: Cornell University Press, 1997), 103–104.

21. Lovett interview with Shaughnessy, Jan. 15, 1959, p. 5. The words appeared as "right field" in Shaughnessy's transcript, but undoubtedly Lovett was referring to the Ohio air base, nothing in baseball.

22. F.D. Roosevelt to Stimson, May 4, 1941, Lovett Papers (NA); Harriman & Bainbridge, November 6, 1943, loc. cit., 33.

23. Dr. Nathaniel F. Silsbee, *Aviation Angler*, May 15, 1941.

24. Lovett to Arnold, May 7, 1941, Lovett Papers (NA).

25. Lovett to Patterson, June 12, 1941, Lovett Papers (NA).

26. Lovett to Stimson, July 2, 1941, Lovett Papers (NA).

Towers was the same navy officer, much higher now in rank, who had given a big assist to the Yale Unit many years earlier.

27. Lovett to Patterson, Aug. 16, 1941, Lovett Papers (NA).

28. Lovett to Stimson, Aug. 12, 1941, Lovett Papers (NA).

29. Stimson Diary, February 10, 1941.

30. Lovett, interview with Shaughnessy, Jan. 15, 1959, p. 8.

31. Lovett interview with Shaughnessy, Jan. 15, 1959, p. 9; Harriman & Bainbridge, November 6, 1943, loc. cit., 31.

32. Lovett interview with Shaughnessy, Jan. 15, 1959, p. 10; Mets, David R., *Master of Airpower: General Carl A. Spaatz* (Novato, CA: Presidio Press, 1988).

33. *Washington Post*, Apr. 29, 1941.

34. *Salt Lake Tribune*, May 24, 1941.

35. *Time*, February 9, 1942.

36. Lovett interview with Shaughnessy, February 13, 1959, p. 25.

37. *Flying and Popular Aviation*, September 1941.

38. Stimson Diary, June 12, 1941.

39. *Washington Times-Herald*, July 3, 1941.

40. Stimson Diary, 13; Arnold, H.H., *Global Mission* (New York: Harper & Brothers, 1949), 195.

41. Ibid., 195–196; Daso, Dik Alan, *Hap Arnold and the Evolution of American Airpower* (Washington and London: Smithsonian Institution Press, 2000), 163.

42. Arnold, op. cit., 539; Harriman & Bainbridge, November 6, 1943, loc. cit., 31.

43. Emmet O'Donnell to Lovett, July 26, 1963, Lovett Papers.

44. Lovett interview with Shaughnessy, Jan. 15, 1959, p. 12.

Chapter 7

1. Craven & Cate, op. cit., vi, vii.

2. Reuther, Walter, "A Program for the Utilization of the Auto Industry for Mass Production of Defense Plants," submitted to the president by CIO head Philip Murray, December 20, 1940; Davis, Kenneth S., *FDR: The War President, 1940–1943* (New York: Random House, 2000), 436–438.

3. Lovett to Patterson, June 12, 1941, Lovett Papers (NA).

4. Harriman & Bainbridge, November 6, 1943, loc. cit., 31.

5. Lovett to Maj. Gen. Oliver P. Echols, July 18, 1941, Lovett Papers (NA).

6. Arnold, op. cit., 266.

7. Lovett Papers.

8. Lovett to Clayton Burt, October 15, 1941, Lovett Papers (NA).

9. Stimson Diary, September 11, 1941; *New York Sun*, September 12, 1941.

10. *Philadelphia Evening Bulletin*, September 18, 1941; Stimson Diary, September 23, 1941.

11. Lovett interview with Shaughnessy, February 13, 1959, 36–37; Davis, Richard G., *Carl A. Spaatz and the Air War in Europe* (Washington & London: Smithsonian Institute Press, 1992), 68.

12. Overy, Richard, *The Bombers and the Bombed: Al-*

lied War Over Europe, 1940–1945 (New York: Viking, 2013), 83.

13. Baime, A.J., The Arsenal of Democracy: FDR, Detroit, and an Epic Quest to Arm an America At War (Boston & New York, Houghton Mifflin, 2014), 130.

14. Stimson Diary, Jan. 1, 1942.

15. New York Times, Jan. 7, 1942; Brigante, John E., The Feasibility Dispute: Determination of War Production Objectives for 1942 and 1943 (Washington, Committee on Public Administration Cases, 1950).

16. Stimson Diary, Jan. 12, 1942.

17. Lovett to Harry Hopkins, March 25, 1943, Lovett Papers (NA).

18. Lovett to Patterson, Jan. 9, 1942, Lovett Papers (NA).

19. Harriman, W. Averell, and Elie Abel, Special Envoy to Churchill and Stalin, 1941–1946 (New York: Random House, 1975), 8–9.

20. Lovett to A.H. Bunker, February 5, 1942, Lovett Papers (NA).

21. Lovett to Harry Hopkins, March 18, 1942, Craven & Cate, op. cit., vi, 343.

22. Stimson Diary, Jan. 12, 1942; Berg, A. Scott, Lindbergh (New York: G.P. Putnam's Sons, 1998), 436; Stimson Diary, Jan. 13, 1942.

23. Berg, op. cit., 439. Lindbergh performed useful work for the air force in the Pacific, though without an official connection. In 1954 Dwight Eisenhower restored him to the air corps, with a commission as a brigadier general. Between 1958 and 1967 Lindbergh secretly fathered seven children with three mistresses in Europe.

24. Caroli, Betty Boyd, Lady Bird and Lyndon: The Hidden Story of a Marriage That Made a President (New York: Simon & Schuster, 2015), 132. On March 3, 1943, the base was renamed Bergstrom Army Air Field, in honor of Capt. John Bergstrom, the first Austinite killed in World War II, at Clark Field in the Philippines on December 8, 1941. The base, later called Bergstrom Air Force Base, was officially closed on September 30, 1993.

25. Transcript, telephone conversation with Wm. L. Batt, December 12, 1941, Lovett Papers (NA).

26. Lovett to Vincent Bendix, July 15, 1941, Lovett Papers (NA).

27. Transcript, telephone conversation with Sen. Harley Kilgore, Aug. 12, 1943, Lovett Papers (NA).

28. Robert Gross to Lovett, June 24, 1941, Lovett Papers (NA).

29. Time, February 9, 1942, 14.

Chapter 8

1. Lovett to Robert Patterson, Jan. 21, 1941, Lovett Papers (NA).

2. Lovett to George Brett, February 14, 1941, Lovett Papers (NA).

3. Julius A. "Jay" Stratton (1901–1994) was a professor in physics at MIT who was a specialist in electrical engineering and radar, organized technical advisory committees for the Air Force, was given the Medal of Merit by the air force in 1946 for his great help with radar, and went on to become MIT president from 1959 to 1966.

4. Lovett to Arnold, Aug. 25, 1941, Lovett Papers (NA).

5. Lovett to Arnold, November 17, 1941, Lovett Papers (NA).

6. Craven and Cate, vi, 490–91.

7. Wm. H. Hastie to Lovett, November 26, 1942; Lovett to Hastie, December 17, 1942, Lee, Ulysses, The Employment of Negro Troops (Washington, D.C.: Center of Military History, 1963, republished 1994), 170.

8. Hastie to Henry L. Stimson, Jan. 5, 1943; Lee, op. cit., 171.

9. Lovett and Artemus Gates to Robert Hinckley, in the Commerce Department, April 18, 1942, Lovett Papers (NA).

10. Lovett to Arnold, Aug. 28, 1942, Lovett Papers (NA).

11. Chicago Sun, October 7, 1943.

12. Lovett to Donald Douglas, Jan. 2, 1942, Lovett Papers (NA).

13. Lovett to Franklin K. Lane, October 31, 1942, Lovett Papers (NA).

14. Lovett to Edsel Ford, November 20, 1942, Lovett Papers (NA).

15. Lovett to Robert Patterson, July 31, 1943, Lovett Papers (NA).

16. Aircraft War Production Council to Paul V. McNutt and James F. Byrnes, September 1, 1943, Lovett Papers (NA).

17. Frank F. Russell to Lovett, November 23, 1943, Lovett Papers (NA).

Chapter 9

1. Toledo Times, Aug.12, 1943.

2. A.T. Harris to Lovett, December 2, 1941: Lovett to Harris, December 3, 1941, Lovett Papers.

3. deSeversky, Alexander P., Victory Through Air Power (New York: Simon and Schuster, 1942), 203–204.

4. Washington Post, April 25, 1942.

5. Michie, Allan A., The Air Offensive Against Germany (New York: Henry Holt, 1943).

6. Stimson Diary, September 11, 1942.

7. New York Daily Mirror, Jan. 17, 1942.

8. Time, February 9, 1942, p. 15.

9. Los Angeles Times, Apr. 17, 1942; New York Daily News, Apr. 18, 1942; Pittsburgh Sun-Telegraph; New York Times, Apr. 19, 1942; Washington Times-Herald, Apr. 20, 1942.

10. Current Biography, 1942, p. 532.

11. New York Herald Tribune, June 10, 1942.

12. George Harrison, born in 1887 in San Francisco and a 1909 graduate of Yale (and a Bonesman), had served for thirteen years as president of the Federal Reserve Bank of New York before becoming, in 1941, president of the New York Life Insurance Company. After Stimson recruited him, he used Harrison in various matters, the most important one as his special assistant on the atomic bomb developments.

13. Stimson Diary, December 24, 1942.

14. Stimson Diary, September 18, 1942.

15. Stimson Diary, October 20, 1942; Stimson, Henry L., and McGeorge Bundy, On Active Service in Peace and War (New York: Harper & Brothers, 1948), 426–427.

16. New York Times, November 11, 1942; Buffalo Courier Express, November 16, 1942; Rochester Democrat and Chronicle, November 16, 1942; Lewiston (ID) Tribune,

November 23, 1942; Lovett, Robert A., "The War Department Weighs Air Cargo," *Air Transportation*, December 1942, pp. 16–17; Lewis, Thos. E., "Cargo Plane Valuable But Not a Cure-all," *Philadelphia Evening Bulletin*, December 7, 1942.

17. *New York Herald Tribune*, Jan. 29, 1943; *Washington Post*, Jan. 29, 1943; *Jersey City Journal*, Jan. 30, 1943.

18. Lovett interview with Shaughnessy, Jan. 21, 1960, 42.

19. Ibid.

20. Stimson and Bundy, op. cit., 510.

21. Stimson Diary, July 7, 1942.

22. Stimson Diary, July 15, 1942.

23. Stimson Diary, Jan. 28, March 26, 1943.

24. Lovett to Carl Spaatz, June 18, 1943, Lovett Papers (NA).

25. Stimson Diary, June 14, 15, 1943; Morison, op. cit., 576–577.

26. Lovett War Department Memorandum, July 27, 1943, Stimson Diary.

Chapter 10

1. Lovett Scrapbooks, Truman Library; *Philadelphia Public Ledger*, Jan. 2, 1942.

2. Yenne, Bill, *Hap Arnold: The General Who Invented the U.S. Air Force* (Washington, D.C.: Regnery History, 2013), 64.

3. Levine, Alan J., *The Strategic Bombing of Germany, 1940–1945* (Westport, CT: Praeger, 1992), 36.

4. Perrett, Geoffrey, *Winged Victory: The Army Air Forces in World War II* (New York: Random House, 1993), 98; *London Times*, Aug. 16, 1942; Parton, James, "*Air Force Spoken Here*": *General Ira Eaker and the Command of the Air* (Bethesda, MD: Adler & Adler, 1986), 175. There had earlier been a raid by a small force on July 4 to conform to a pledge foolishly given to the British by Arnold, against Luftwaffe fields in the Netherlands, with little damage done and seven crewmen dying.

5. Hansell, Haywood S., Jr., *The Air Plan That Defeated Hitler* (Atlanta, GA: 1972), 23.

6. Craven & Cate, eds. i, 148.

7. Hansell, op. cit., 93, 94. The entire development of AWPD-1 is covered in the book by Hansell (one of the four members of George's team), pp. 67–97, as well as in Clodfelter, Mark, *Beneficial Bombing: The Progressive Foundations of American Air Power, 1917–1945* (Lincoln: Nebraska University Press, 2010), 89–98.

8. Lovett memorandum, March 9, 1942, Lovett Papers (NA).

9. Spaatz to Arnold, Aug. 27, 1944, Spaatz Papers.

10. Lovett to James Parton, October 5, 1983, Lovett Papers. On Jan. 9, 1978, Ira Eaker wrote to Lovett that "the nostalgic memories of our long friendship and association are among my most prized recollections" (Lovett Papers).

11. Lovett interview with Parton, December 14, 1983 (Parton, op. cit., 114).

12. Ibid., 270.

13. Stimson Diary, Aug. 18, 1942.

14. Stimson Diary, Aug. 13, 14, 1942.

15. Stimson Diary, September 2, 1942.

16. Parton, op. cit., 154.

Chapter 11

1. *New York Times*, January 3, 1943.

2. Drew Pearson, *Washington Post*, April 23, 1943.

3. *Summary Report: The United States Strategic Bombing Survey* (Washington, D.C.: United States Government Printing Office), 5.

4. *Washington Post*, April 18, 1943.

5. *Washington Times-Herald*, March 6, 1943; *New York Times*, March 6, 1943; Stimson Diary, March 5, 1943.

6. Walter Lippmann to Lovett, March 25, 1943, Lovett Papers (NA).

7. Lovett to Eaker, October 3, 1943, Eaker Papers.

8. Stimson Diary, February 26, 1943.

9. Stimson Diary, February 27, 1943.

10. *Miami Beach Daily Tropics*, March 14, 1943.

11. Lt. Col. Laigh C. Parker to Col. G.A. Brownell, May 7, 1943, Eaker Papers.

12. J.W. Sessums, Jr., to Lovett, July 25, 1977, Lovett Papers.

13. *New York Herald Tribune*, Jan. 3, 1951.

14. The descriptions of the trip as well as several quotes are from the longhand diary kept from the beginning to the end of the journey by Col. John W. Sessums, Jr., which he typed up and sent on to Lovett with his letter of July 25, 1977, Lovett Papers.

15. Eaker to Lovett, June 17, 1943, Eaker Papers.

16. Lovett to Eaker, June 18, 1943, Eaker Papers; Perret, op. cit., 261.

17. Lovett memorandum to Arnold, June 18, 19, 1943, Eaker Papers.

18. Olson, op. cit. 261–262.

19. Biddle, Tami Davis, *Rhetoric and Reality in Air Warfare: The Evolution of British and American Ideas About Strategic Bombing, 1914–1945* (Princeton: Princeton University Press, 2002), 227.

20. Coffey, Thomas M., *Hap: The Story of the U.S. Air Force and the Man Who Built It, General Henry H. "Hap" Arnold* (New York: Viking Press, 1982), 321

21. Parton interview with Lovett, December 14, 1983, Parton, op. cit., 279.

22. Lovett memorandum to Arnold, June 19, 1943, Eaker Papers.

23. Eaker to Lovett, July 6, 1943, Eaker Papers.

24. *Philadelphia Evening Bulletin*, December 8, 1943.

25. Olson, op. cit., 269.

26. Stimson Diary, July 6, 7, 1943.

27. Harriman & Bainbridge, November 6, 1943, loc. cit., 36.

28. Miller, Donald L., *Masters of the Air: America's Bomber Boys Who Fought the Air War Against Nazi Germany* (New York: Simon & Schuster, 2006), 204.

29. Stimson Diary, April 11, 1944. A government functionary named Stanton Griffis was assigned the duty of collecting information regarding Sweden's shipments of iron ore, ball bearings, and steel to Germany. He soon learned that "Sweden was pouring vast quantities of its industrial output directly into Germany." In the spring of 1944, Griffis flew to Sweden as the special representative of the Foreign Economic Administration to England and Sweden, negotiated with Swedish industrialists, and in the second week of June had the Swedes agree "to ship less than 10 per cent of its former

quotas to Germany and to send only types that our experts knew were of little value to the Nazi war machine." Griffis, Stanton, *Lying in State* (Garden City, NY: Doubleday, 1952), 104, 118. A later editorial comment said that what Griffis "did constituted one of the great economic coups of the war, depriving Germany of at least 51 percent of highgrade Swedish bearings—an indispensable, super-critical item in any military machine" (*Washington Star*, December 16, 1944).

30. Speer interview, May 5, 1975, quoted in Coffey, Thomas M., *Decision Over Schweinfurt: The U.S. 8th Air Force Battle for Daylight Bombing* (New York: David McKay, 1977), 329.

31. *Washington Post*, October 15, 1943.

32. *Washington Post*, October 16, 1943.

33. Stimson Diary, October 21, 1943.

34. Eaker to Lovett, July 15, 1977, Lovett Papers.

35. "Lovett Joins Cupid's Forces," *Washington Star*, Aug. 23, 1943.

36. *Chicago Daily Tribune*, October 7, 1943.

37. Lovett speech, "The Growth of the U.S. Army Air Forces During the Last Two Years," December 9, 1943, Eaker Papers.

38. Eaker to Lovett, December 15, 1943, Eaker Papers.

39. Stimson Diary, December 15, 1943.

Chapter 12

1. Earl O. Ewan, of Federal Shipbuilding & Drydock Co., to Lovett, November 20, 1945, Lovett Papers.

2. *Summary Report, United States Strategic Bombing Survey*, 7.

3. Baime, op. cit., 269.

4. Stimson Diary, March 10, 1944.

5. Ibid., 270. Among those on these bombing missions were movie stars Jimmy Stewart and Clark Gable, journalists Walter Cronkite and Andy Rooney, and future senator George McGovern.

6. Goddard, George W., with DeWitt S. Copp, *Overview: A Life-Long Adventure in Aerial Photography* (Garden City, NY: Doubleday, 1969), 319–320. Goddard, born in England, came to the U.S. in 1904 at the age of 15; he was naturalized in 1918, in order to be commissioned in the U.S. Army. He remained in the army long after World War II, was inducted into the National Aviation Hall of Fame in 1976, died in 1987 at the age of 98, and was buried at Arlington National Cemetery.

7. Ibid., 321, 331–332.

8. Goddard to Lovett, March 31, 1964, and Lovett to Goddard, April 7, 1964, both in Lovett Papers.

9. Memo, David Griggs to Lovett, March 7, 1944, Lovett Papers (NA).

10. Stimson Diary, April 10, 1944.

11. Craven & Cate, op. cit., vi, 209–210.

12. Stimson Diary, May 2, 1944.

13. Stimson Diary, June 1, 1944.

14. *Philadelphia Evening Bulletin*, March 20, 1944. The army had started building an airstrip in northeast Philadelphia but gave up on the idea and turned the project over to the city. The city was able to find some funding for it and opened a fairly primitive northeast Philadelphia airport in June of 1945.

15. Lovett to Carl Spaatz, February 12, 1944, Spaatz Papers, Library of Congress.

16. Draft Letter, Stimson to Knox, February 24, 1944, Lovett Papers (NA).

17. Testimony of Lovett, April 26, 1944, "Hearings on Proposal to Establish a Single Department of Armed Forces," 78th Congress, 2d Session, 1944, pp. 59–62.

18. Lovett to Eaker, May 22, 1944, Eaker Papers.

19. Lovett to L. Welch Pogue, Jan. 26, 1943, Lovett Papers (NA).

20. Leffler, Melvin P., *A Preponderance of Power: National Security, the Truman Administration, and the Cold War* (Stanford: Stanford University Press, 1992), 58.

21. Lovett to Harold George, Jan. 8, 1943, Lovett Papers (NA).

22. Lovett to Committee on International Civil Administration, March 11, 1943, Lovett Papers (NA).

23. Berle's minutes of meeting, November 11, 1943, Lovett Papers (NA); also Berle, ed., op. cit., 483–484.

24. Lovett to Harry Hopkins, June 15, 1943, Lovett Papers (NA). It is interesting to note, in view of the problems between Lovett and Juan Trippe, that Trippe was a graduate of The Hill School, that he had entered Yale in 1917 but left it in 1918 to become a naval aviator, returned to Yale to graduate in 1921, and was a member of Skull and Bones. He was also married to the sister of Undersecretary of State Edward Stettinius.

25. Lovett to Bernard Baruch, September 30, 1944, Lovett Papers (NA).

26. Lovett to Gates, October 23, 1944, Lovett Papers (NA).

Chapter 13

1. Lovett to W.L. Welsh, June 30, 1943, Lovett Papers (NA).

2. Bradley, Omar N., *A Soldier's Story* (New York: Henry Holt, 1951), 307–308.

3. Lovett to Doolittle, July 11, 1944, Lovett Papers (NA).

4. Lovett to Doolittle, July 13, 1944; Doolittle to Lovett, July 19, 1944, Lovett Papers (NA).

5. *Stars and Stripes*, and *Philadelphia Evening Bulletin*, both July 19, 1944.

6. Lovett to Spaatz, July 25, 1944, quoted in letter, Carlo W. D'Este to Lovett, September 17, 1980, Lovett Papers.

7. Stimson Diary, September 18, 1944. The technical name for the Morgenthau Plan was "Suggested Post-Surrender Program for Germany."

8. Arnold, op. cit., 490.

9. Lovett to Donald K. David, September 5, 1944, Lovett Papers (NA).

10. Lovett to Spaatz, Apr. 22, 1945, Spaatz Papers.

11. D'Olier, an 1898 graduate of Princeton, turned out to be the great-grandfather of *Superman* actor Christopher Reeve.

12. Lovett to Maj. David MacIsaac, July 27, 1970, Lovett Papers.

13. *Summary Report: The United States Strategic Bombing Survey*, September 30, 1945, ii.

14. Eaker to Spaatz, Jan. 1, 1945, Spaatz Papers.

15. Lovett to Arnold, Jan. 9, 1945, Spaatz Papers; Perret, op. cit., 370.

16. Stimson Diary, December 28, 1944.

Chapter 14

1. Perrett, op. cit., 374.

2. Lovett to Eaker, Jan. 28, 1945, Eaker Papers.

3. Grandison Gardner to Lovett, March 14, 1985, Lovett Papers (NA).

4. Lovett to Gardner, March 19, 1945; memo from Col. Leslie O. Peterson, April 11, 1945; Memo, Oliver Echols to Lovett, April 18, 1945; memo, Col. John G. Moore to Lovett, Aug. 20, 1945; all in Lovett Papers (NA).

5. Lovett to H.H. Arnold, Jan. 9, 1945, Lovett Papers (NA).

6. Lovett to Spaatz, Jan. 7, 1945, Spaatz Papers.

7. Spaatz to Lovett, February 21, 1945, Spaatz Papers.

8. Stimson Diary, March 13, 1944.

9. Lovett to Spaatz, May 6, 1945, in Parton, op. cit., 439–440.

10. Beschloss, Michael, *The Conquerors: Roosevelt, Truman and the Destruction of Hitler's Germany* (New York: Simon & Schuster, 2002), 230.

11. Spector, Ronald H., *Advice and Support: The Early Years of the U.S. Army in Vietnam, 1941–1960* (New York: Free Press, 1985), 44.

12. Lovett to Norstad, April 27, 1945, Lovett Papers (NA).

13. Stimson Diary, Aug. 11, 1945.

14. Lovett to Spaatz, August 19, 1945, Spaatz Papers.

15. Stimson Diary, September 21, 1945 (dictated December 11, 1945).

16. Stimson Diary, September 7, 13, 1945.

17. Stimson Diary, September 18, 1945.

18. *Survey Report, United States Strategic Bombing Survey*, 15–16.

19. FRUS 1945–1950, Retrospective Volume, Emergence of the Intelligence Establishment, Document 32.

20. Memorandum from the Lovett Committee to Secretary of War Patterson, November 3, 1945, FRUS 1945–1950, Retrospective Volume, cited above, Document 42.

21. Minutes of Meeting, November 14, 1945, FRUS 1945–1950, Retrospective Volume, cited above, Document 45.

22. Rear Admiral Roscoe H. Hillenkoetter was the first director of the Central Intelligence Agency, serving from May 1, 1947, to October 7, 1950, to be followed by General Walter Bedell Smith, from October 7, 1950, to February 9, 1953, when he was succeeded by Dulles.

23. Memorandum, George A. Brownell to Members of Lovett Committee, December 17, 1945, FRUS 1945–1950, Retrospective Volume, cited above, Document 58.

24. Lovett to Devereux C. Josephs, November 28, 1945, Lovett Papers.

25. Lovett to Francis Drake, November 28, 1945, Lovett Papers.

26. Stuart Symington to Lovett, E. Roland Harriman to Lovett, Donald W. Douglas to Lovett, all November 30, 1945, Lovett Papers.

27. Robert P. Patterson to Lovett, December 11, 1945, Lovett Papers.

28. Brownell speech, Lovett Papers. George Brownell, a former New York lawyer, was named in 1946 as Harry Truman's personal representative to India and the Middle East, and he remained a State Department consultant until 1957.

29. Lovett to Haywood S. Hansell, July 14, 1980, Lovett Papers

Chapter 15

1. Clinical Record, Doctor's Progress Notes, August 17, 1951 Lovett Papers.

2. Lovett Papers.

3. Acheson, Dean, *Present at the Creation: My Years in the State Department* (New York: W.W. Norton, 1969). 236.

4. George C. Marshall to Lovett, February 6, 1947, Lovett Papers.

5. Lovett to Marshall, February 11, 1947, Lovett Papers.

6. Marshall to Lovett, February 18, 1947, Lovett Papers.

7. Lovett to Dean Acheson, March 1, 1947, Dean Acheson Papers, Yale University Library.

8. Robert S. Lovett II to Robert A. Lovett, May 14, 1947, Lovett Papers.

9. *Philadelphia Evening Bulletin*, May 12, 1947.

10. Leffler, op. cit. 174–175.

11. Beisner, Robert L., *Dean Acheson: A Life in the Cold War* (New York: Oxford University Press, 2006), 79.

12. Leffler, op. cit., 180–181.

13. Millis, Walter, ed., *The Forrestal Diaries* (New York: Viking Press, 1951), 279.

14. Griffis, op. cit., 150.

15. Neustadt, Richard E., *Presidential Power and the Modern Presidents: The Politics of Leadership from Roosevelt to Reagan* (New York: Free Press, 1990), 41–42.

16. Beisner, op. cit., 79. Lovett kept a diary "and daily log sheet" during his tenure at the State Department, now a part of the Brown Brothers Harriman Collection at the New-York Historical Society. Rather than footnote every item from the diary, it has been thought sufficient to advise the reader that most references to activities during this time come from the diary entry of that date.

17. Leffler, op. cit., 175; *Philadelphia Evening Bulletin*, July 1, 1947.

18. Clifford, Clark, with Richard Holbrooke, *Counsel to the President: A Memoir* (New York: Random House, 1991), 16.

19. Marshall to embassy in Paris, July 3, 1947, FRUS 1947, III, 308.

20. Heymann, C. David, *The Georgetown Ladies' Social Club: Power, Passion, and Politics in the Nation's Capital* (New York: Atria Books, 2003), 33–34.

21. Graham, Katherine, *Personal History* (New York: Alfred A. Knopf, 1997), 164.

22. This club, named obviously for its street address in Washington, was once known as the Alexander Ray House, as it was built in Greek Revival style for a naval captain of that name in 1849. Purchased in 1935 by the 1925 F Street Club, Inc., it became a private members' club and a popular meeting place for prominent Wash-

ington figures, including presidents. Operated like an English country manor, it had no menu; guests ate whatever was prepared for that day. The club was closed in 1999, and the building now serves as the home of the president of George Washington University.

23. Millis, ed., op. cit., 320–321.

24. Unger, Debi, and Irwin, *George Marshall: A Biography* (New York: Harper Collins, 2014), 389.

25. Hamby, Alonzo L., *Man of the People: A Life of Harry S. Truman* (New York: Oxford University Press, 1995), 389.

26. Vandenberg, Arthur H., Jr., ed., *The Private Papers of Senator Vandenberg* (Boston: Houghton Mifflin, 1952), 360–361.

27. Mee, Charles L., Jr., *The Marshall Plan: The Launching of the Pax Americana* (New York: Simon & Schuster, 1984), 268.

28. Millis, ed., 308–309.

29. Pogue, Forrest C., *George C. Marshall: Statesman* (New York: Viking, 1987), 213–214. It should be noted that this book, the fourth and final in Dr. Pogue's multivolume biography of Marshall, is dedicated to Robert A. Lovett, "whose sense of duty and service to his country in war and peace paralleled that of the subject of this biography with whom he labored."

30. Weintraub, Stanley, *15 Stars: Eisenhower, MacArthur, Marshall; Three Generals Who Saved the American Century* (New York: Free Press, 2007), 403.

31. Truman statement, FRUS 1947, III, 264–266; Miscamble, Wilson D., *George F. Kennan and the Making of American Foreign Policy, 1947–1950* (Princeton: Princeton University Press, 1992), 58–60.

32. Lovett to Thomas Lamont, July 31, 1947, Thomas Lamont Papers, Harvard University, cited in Yergin, Daniel, *Shattered Peace: The Origins of the Cold War and the National Security State* (Boston: Houghton Mifflin, 1977), 328.

Chapter 16

1. Millis, ed., op. cit., 282.

2. Lovett to Thomas Lamont, July 31, 1947, Thomas Lamont Papers, Harvard University, cited in Yergin, op. cit., 309.

3. Mee, op. cit., 156.

4. Lovett to Clayton, July 10, 1947, FRUS 1947, III, 324–326.

5. Miscamble, op. cit., 60.

6. *New York Herald Tribune*, Aug. 2, 1947.

7. Lovett to Marshall, Aug. 5, 1947, FRUS 1947, II, 1017–1020.

8. Memorandum of Conversation, August 5, 1947, FRUS 1947, II, 1021–1022.

9. Lovett to Caffery, Aug. 14, 1947, FRUS 1947, III, 356, 358–359.

10. Hogan, Michael J., *The Marshall Plan: America, Britain, and the Reconstruction of Western Europe, 1947–1952* (New York: Cambridge University Press, 1987), 72–73.

11. FRUS 1947, III, 357.

12. Lovett to Marshall, Aug. 24, 1947, FRUS 1947, III, 372–373.

13. FRUS 1947, III, 374–375.

14. Lovett to Clayton, Lovett to Caffery, Aug. 24, 1947, FRUS 1947, III, 376–379.

15. Lovett to Embassy in France, Aug. 26, 1947, FRUS 1947, III, 383.

16. Ibid., 384–389.

17. Lovett eyes only to Marshall, Aug. 31, 1947, FRUS 1947, III, 396–397.

18. Lovett to Embassy in France, September 3, 1947, FRUS 1947, III, 734.

19. *Philadelphia Evening Bulletin*, September 3, 1947.

20. Millis, ed., op. cit., 311–312.

21. Memorandum by the director of the Policy Planning Staff (Kennan), September 4, 1947, FRUS 1947, III, 397–398.

22. Ibid., 405.

23. Lovett to "Diplomatic Representatives Accredited to Countries Participating in CEEC," September 7, 1947, FRUS 1947, III, Document 236.

24. Mee, op. cit., 225–226.

25. Lovett to Clayton, Caffery, Douglas, September 22, 1947, FRUS 1947, III, Document 258.

26. *Philadelphia Evening Bulletin*, October 8, 1947.

27. "Memorandum, Acting Secretary of State to President Truman," October 13, 1947, FRUS 1947, III, 479.

28. Ibid., 478–81; Pogue, op. cit., 235.

29. Truman, Margaret, *Bess W. Truman* (New York: Macmillan, 1986), 311; Truman, Harry S., *Memoirs by Harry S Truman: Years of Trial and Hope* (Garden City, NY: Doubleday, 1956), 116–117.

30. Chairman of CEEC Washington Delegation to Lovett, FRUS 1947, III, 446–450.

31. CEEC Washington Delegation to Participating Governments Not Represented in Washington, October 31, 1947, FRUS 1947, III, 456, 459.

32. Lovett to Franks, November 3, 1947, FRUS 1947, III, 461–463.

33. Record of a Meeting Between Members of the Advisory Steering Committee and the CEEC Delegation, November 4, 1947, FRUS 1947, III, 463–468.

Chapter 17

1. Bland and Stoler, eds., op. cit., 257.

2. Oral Interview with Robert Lovett, "International Negotiations Project," Columbia University Interview, September 15, 1975, 7.

3. On December 11, Senator Connally (D-Tex) asked Lovett how the department felt about the China amendment to the Interim Aid bill. Lovett said China needed a different kind of aid that did not conform to the purposes of the bill and should be the subject of an amendment to the relief act passed the prior July, not part of interim aid.

4. Lovett to Marshall, December 4, 1947, FRUS 1947, III, 482.

5. Ibid., 483.

6. Ibid., 484.

7. Ferrell, Robert H., ed., *Truman in the White House: The Diary of Eben A. Ayres*, Columbia: University of Missouri Press, 1991), 212.

8. Pogue, op. cit., 236; Donovan, op. cit., 287. Interestingly, to the secretary of state it was the European Recovery Program, never the Marshall Plan.

9. Lovett Interview, July 7, 1971, Richard D. McKinzie & Theodore A.Wilson, Truman Library, 3.

10. Lovett to Prof. Quentin L. Quade, March 5, 1963, Lovett Papers.

11. Ibid.

12. *New York Times*, Jan. 9, 1948.

13. Hogan, op. cit., 104. Lincoln Gordon had been vice chairman of the War Production Board in World War II before going into the State Department. Subsequently he had controversial tours of duty as ambassador to Brazil (with involvement in the coup of 1964) and as president of Johns Hopkins University until ousted by its board of trustees.

14. Nitze, Paul H., with Ann M. Smith and Steven L. Rearden, *From Hiroshima to Glasnost: At the Center of Decision* (New York: Grove Weidenfeld, 1989), 63, 65–66.

15. Lovett Diary, March 30, 1948, for Hoover bit; Vandenberg to Marshall, March 24, 1948, Clark Clifford Papers, Truman Library. The senator concluded by saying that "this job as ERP Administrator stands out by itself … as requiring particularly persuasive economic credentials unrelated to diplomacy."

16. Abramson, op. cit. 424–425.

17. Lovett to Howard Smith, BBC Television, November 1, 1984, Lovett Papers.

Chapter 18

1. *Public Papers of the Presidents of the United States: Harry S. Truman, 1946,* 442–44.

2. Memorandum, John H. Hilldring to Secretary of State, October 9, 1947, FRUS 1947, V, 1177–78.

3. Memorandum, Henderson to Secretary of State, November 10, 1947, FRUS 1947, V, 1249.

4. Lovett to U.S. Representative at the United Nations, November 19, 1947, FRUS 1947 V, 1269–70. It might be noted that an alternate spelling of the name of the desert region is "Negeb," which was what Robert Lovett used.

5. Ibid., Memorandum for File by Robert M. McClintock, 1271.

6. Ibid., Memorandum of Telephone Conversation by Lovett, November 24, 1947, 1283–84.

7. Ibid.

8. Millis, ed., op. cit., 346; Lovett Oral History Interview, May 13, 1974, OSD Historical Office, the Pentagon; Hoopes, and Brinkley, op. cit. 436.

9. Millis, ed, op. cit., 360.

10. Roosevelt, Elliott, and James Brough, *Mother R.: Eleanor Roosevelt's Untold Story* (New York: G.P. Putnam's Sons, 1977), 119.

11. From Lovett Diary, February 16, 1948.

12. Clark Clifford Memoranda, March 6, March 8, 1948, FRUS 1948, V, pt. 2, 687–696.

13. Clifford Memo, May 4, 1948, Clark M. Clifford Papers, Harry S. Truman Library.

14. Truman, Margaret, *Harry S. Truman* (New York: William Morrow, 1973), 388.

15. Judis, John B., *Genesis: Truman, American Jews, and the Origins of the Arab/Israeli Conflict* (New York: Farrar, Straus and Giroux, 2014), 303.

16. Cohen, Michael J., *Truman and Israel* (Berkeley: University of California Press, 1990), 193. Of course, by the time he said this, Clifford knew of Marshall's long-standing contempt for him.

17. Rusk, Dean, as told to Richard Rusk, *As I Saw It* (New York: W.W. Norton, 1990), 147. Rusk, it may be noted, supported a reversal of the earlier partition vote.

18. Memorandum by Director of Executive Secretariat to Secretary of State, March 22, 1948, FRUS 1948, V, pt. 2, 749–750.

19. Ibid., 750, from a memorandum of March 22, 1948, Marshall to Charles Bohlen.

20. *Time*, March 29, 1948, 25.

21. Lovett Diary, April 28, 1948.

22. Top Secret Memorandum dictated over phone by Lovett, May 3, 1948, Clifford Papers, Harry S Truman Library.

23. FRUS 1948, V, pt. 2, 906.

24. Clifford, op. cit., 5–6.

25. Benson, Michael T., *Harry S Truman and the Founding of Israel* (Westport, CT: Praeger, 1997), 154.

26. Clifford, op. cit., 3.

27. Memorandum for the President, May 11, 1948, Department of State, Clifford Papers, Harry S Truman Library.

28. These quotes, and others to come, are from Memorandum of Conversation, by Secretary of State, May 12, 1948, FRUS 1948, V, pt. 2, 973. The Memorandum, which runs from 972 to 976, was drafted by McClintock, presumably from notes he took while listening to the conversation.

29. Clifford, op. cit., 11.

30. Ibid., 974–975.

31. Clifford, op. cit., 12.

32. Ibid.

33. FRUS 1948, V, pt. 2, 975, for Marshall's statement. Also, Cray, Ed, *General of the Army: George C. Marshall Soldier and Statesman* (New York: Cooper Square Press, 2000), 659.

34. Clifford, op. cit., 13–14. Clifford later said that Marshall never spoke to him again, and Marshall's principal biographer noted that Marshall never even mentioned Clifford's name; Pogue, op. cit., 377.

35. Clifford, op. cit., 15–16.

36. Ibid., 17.

37. Ibid., 18.

38. Clifford address to American Historical Association, December 28, 1976, quoted in letter, Alfred M. Lilienthal to Lovett, September 29, 1977; Lovett to Lilienthal, October 3, 1977, Lovett Papers.

39. Memorandum of Conversation by Under Secretary of State, May 17, 1948, FRUS 1948, V, pt. 2, 1005–1006.

40. Clifford, op. cit., 19.

41. Ibid., 20.

42. Dean Rusk to Wm. M. Franklin, June 13, 1974, FRUS 1948, V, pt. 2, 993.

43. Ibid., 1007.

44. Secretary of State to Eliahu Epstein, May 14, 1948, FRUS 1948, V, pt. 2, 992.

45. Clifford, op. cit., 23.

46. Millis, op. cit., 440.

47. Hamby, op. cit., 409; Truman, Harry S, op. cit., 165.

48. Austin to Marshall, May 19, 1948, FRUS 1948, V, pt. 2, 1013–15.

49. Rusk to Franklin, cited in Note 40.

Chapter 19

1. Memorandum of Conversation, Lovett with Bonnet, May 21, 1948, FRUS 1948, II, 270–272.

2. Simpson, Christopher, *Blowback: America's Recruitment of Nazis and Its Effect on the Cold War* (New York: Collier Books, 1989), 100–104.

3. Culver, John C., and John Hyde, *American Dreamer: The Life and Times of Henry A. Wallace* (New York and London: W.W. Norton, 2000), 475–476.

4. Bland and Stoler, ed., vol. 6, op. cit., 459

5. Lovett Diary, June 2, 1948.

6. Adele Lovett attended Vandenberg's presentation on June 9 and told her husband that "she was not only terribly moved but that it was brilliantly handled."

7. Memorandum, Lovett to President, June 15, 1948, FRUS 1948, V, 1060n; Lovett Diary, June 22, 1948.

8. Lovett Diary, June 24–25, 1948.

9. Bradley, Omar N, and Clay Blair, *A General's Life* (New York: Simon & Schuster, 1983), 478; Millis, op. cit., 408.

10. *Philadelphia Evening Bulletin*, Jan. 14, 1948.

11. Cowley, Robert, ed., *The Cold War: A Military History* (New York: Random House, 2006), 25; Shlaim, Avi, *The United States and the Berlin Blockade, 1948–1949* (Berkeley: University of California Press, 1983), 182.

12. Two letters, August 4, 1971, Philip C. Jessup to Lovett, including four pages of Jessup's proposed book, annotated by Lovett, and Lovett to Jessup, August 5, 1971, Lovett Papers

13. Lovett Interview, May 4, 1971, Columbia University Oral History Research Office, 1, 4.

14. Ibid., 13.

15. Bradley and Blair, op. cit., 479–480; Millis, ed., op. cit., 452–454.

16. Millis, ed., op. cit., 454; Reeves, Richard, *Daring Young Men: The Heroism and Triumph of the Berlin Airlift, June 1948-May 1949* (New York: Simon & Schuster, 2010), 30.

17. McCullough, David, *Truman* (New York: Simon & Schuster, 1992), 630.

18. Feis, Herbert, *From Trust to Terror: The Onset of the Cold War, 1945–1950* (New York: W.W. Morrow, 1970), 342.

19. Jessup-Lovett correspondence cited earlier, August 4–5, 1971.

20. The Secretary of State to the Soviet Ambassador, July 6, 1948, FRUS 1948, II, 951–954; Vandenberg, op. cit., 453.

21. Bohlen, Charles E., *Witness to History 1929–1969* (New York: W.W. Norton, 1971), 277; Reeves, op. cit., 74–75.

22. Truman, Harry S, op. cit. 125. Lovett had lunch after the NSC meeting with Marshall and Clay.

23. Bohlen, op. cit., 280.

24. Divine, Robert A., *Foreign Policy and U.S. Presidential Elections, 1940–1948* (New York: New Viewpoints, 1974), 224.

25. Washington Embassy to British Foreign Office, July 21, 1948, FO 371/70503, Public Record Office, London, cited in Shlaim, op. cit., 305; Memorandum of Conversation by Under Secretary of State, July 14, 1948, and Message from British Secretary of State for Foreign Affairs,

as Transmitted by the British Ambassador, July 14, 1948, FRUS 1948, II, 965–966.

26. Dewey statement, *New York Times*, July 25, 1948.

27. Millis, ed., op. cit., 481–483

28. Truman, H.S., op. cit., 128.

29. Lovett Diary, September 15, 1948.

30. Tusa, Ann, and John Tusa, *The Berlin Airlift* (New York: Atheneum, 1988), 171.

31. Shlaim, op. cit., 362–363.

32. Memorandum for Executive Secretary, National Security Council, from Harry S Truman, October 22, 1948, Presidential Secretaries File, Harry S Truman Library.

Chapter 20

1. Pietrusza, David, *1948: Harry Truman's Improbable Victory and the Year That Transformed America's Role in the World* (New York: Union Square Press, 2011), 383.

2. Lovett to Graham, December 31, 1947, FRUS 1947, VI, 1099–1100.

3. Memorandum of Conversation, by Secretary of State, September 17, 1948, FRUS 1948, VI, 343, 345.

4. Pogue, op. cit., 150; Lovett Interview, June 7, 1976, by Doris E. Condit, 11. In the same interview, in answer to another question, Lovett said that Marshall never called Eisenhower anything but "Eisenhower."

5. Lovett Diary, July 12, 13, 14. In his call with Clifford on the 12th, Lovett said the language of the plank on Poland was "unfortunate" but assumed it had something to do with the Polish vote.

6. Lovett interview, May 13, 1974, with Goldberg and Yoshpe, 24–25.

7. The story was written up at great length by Carl W. McCardle of the Philadelphia *Evening Bulletin*, August 15, 1948. Twenty-five years later, Lovett wrote a letter to Chip Bohlen recalling the incident and his encounter with the Russian ambassador; Lovett to Bohlen, December 6, 1973, Lovett Papers.

8. Acting Secretary of State to Certain Diplomatic and Consular Offices, September 21, 1948, FRUS 1948, V, 1415–1416.

9. Diary entry of Edward Jacobson, September 28,1945, Papers of Edward Jacobson, Truman Library.

10. Memorandum of Telephone Conversation by Acting Secretary of State, September 29, 1948, FRUS 1948, V, 1430–31.

11. Donovan, op. cit., 429; Truman, Harry S, op. cit., 168; Abels, Jules, *Out of the Jaws of Victory* (New York: Henry Holt, 1959), 246. The Negev went to Israel and has ever since been a part of Israel.

12. Pogue, op. cit., 376–377.

13. *Philadelphia Evening Bulletin*, October 20, 1948.

14. Pogue, op. cit., 407–408.

15. Divine, op. cit., 257.

16. Lovett to Marshall at the Marshall Foundation, quoted in Mosley, op. cit., 432.

Chapter 21

1. Memorandum of Conversation by Lovett, Jan. 27, 1948, FRUS 1948, III, 13–14.

2. Lovett to Inverchapel, February 2, 1948, FRUS 1948, III, 18–19; Inverchapel to Lovett, February 6, 1948, FRUS 1948, III, 19–20.

3. Memorandum of Conversation, February 7, 1948, FRUS 1948, III, 22–24.

4. Phillips, Cabell, *The Truman Presidency: The History of a Triumphant Succession* (New York: Macmillan, 1966), 264

5. Memorandum of Conversation, April 5, 1948, FRUS 1948, III, 77–79.

6. Kennan, George F., *Memoirs 1925–1950* (Boston and Toronto: Little, Brown, 1967), 404–405. The discussions between Lovett and Vandenberg on that day are contained in Memorandum of Conversation, by the Acting Secretary of State, Apr. 11, 1948, FRUS 1948, III, 83–85.

7. Lovett to Forrest C. Pogue, August 17, 1981, Lovett Papers. Kennan, it should be noted, was opposed to the whole idea of a North Atlantic treaty.

8. Truman, M., *Harry Truman*, op. cit., 405.

9. Haas, Lawrence J., *Harry and Arthur: Truman, Vandenberg and the Partnership That Created the Free World* (Lincoln, NE: Potomac Books, 2016), 234.

10. Memorandum of Conversation, by the Acting Secretary of State, Apr. 18, 1948, FRUS 1948, III, 93–97.

11. Lovett Interview, September 15, 1975, Columbia University Oral History Research Office, 25–26.

12. Truman, H., op. cit., 244.

13. Ibid.

14. U.S. Senate Resolution 239, 80th Congress, 2nd Session, June 11, 1948. It might be noted that Chip Bohlen called it the Vandenberg-Lovett Resolution.

15. Truman, H., op. cit., 245.

16. It was understood at the time that the House, led by Foreign Relations chairman Eaton, was also in favor of the resolution but had been unable to act on it before adjourning.

17. Lovett to Daryl Hudson, May 10, 1976, Lovett Papers. Harry Truman said he never doubted that Vandenberg's "judgment and his discretion warranted discussion with him of the most sensitive diplomatic problems" (Truman, Harry, op. cit., 431).

18. *New York Times*, June 27, 1948.

19. One member of the British group was Donald MacLean, later to be revealed to be a Soviet spy—so much for security.

20. Minutes of the First Meeting of the Washington Exploratory Talks on Security, July 6, 1948, FRUS 1948, III, 149–152.

21. Minutes of the Second Meeting of the Washington Exploratory Talks on Security, July 6, 1948, 4:00 P.M., FRUS 1948, III, 154.

22. Minutes of the Fourth Meeting of the Washington Exploratory Talks on Security, July 8, 1948, 10:00 A.M., 168–169.

23. Minutes of the Fifth Meeting of the Washington Exploratory Talks on Security, July 9, 1948, 10:00 A.M., FRUS 1948, III, 182–183.

24. Memorandum of Conversation by the Under Secretary, July 26, 1948, FRUS 1948, III, 201–202.

25. Memorandum of Conversation by the Under Secretary, Aug. 20, 1948, FRUS 1948, III, 215–222.

26. Truman, H., op. cit., 249.

27. Minutes of the Seventh Meeting of the Washington Exploratory Talks on Security, September 10, 1948, FRUS 1948, III, 250–251.

28. Memorandum by Kennan, enclosing PPS/43, "Considerations Affecting the Conclusion of a North Atlantic Security Pact," November 24, 1948, FRUS 1948, III, 283–289; Acting Secretary of State to U.S. Special Representative in Europe (Harriman), December 3, 1948, FRUS 1948, III, 303.

29. Minutes of the Eighth Meeting of the Washington Exploratory Talks on Security, December 10, 1948, FRUS 1948, III, 310–315.

30. Minutes of the Ninth Meeting of the Washington Exploratory Talks on Security, December 13, 1948, FRUS 1948, III, 317.

31. Report of the International Working Group to the Ambassadors' Committee, December 24, 1948, FRUS 1948, III, 333–343.

32. Minutes of the Eleventh Meeting of the Washington Exploratory Talks on Security, Jan. 14, 1949, FRUS 1949, IV, 27, 35.

33. Bland & Stoler, ed., op. cit., 682; Haas, op.cit., 271.

34. Acheson, op. cit., 266.

35. Baron Silvercruys to Lovett, April 17, 1950, Lovett Papers.

36. Lukacs, John, *George Kennan: A Study of Character* (New Haven, CT: Yale University Press, 2007), 102.

37. Clifford, op. cit., 16.

Chapter 22

1. Lovett Diary, November 16, 17, 18, 1948.

2. Lovett Interview, June 7, 1976, with Doris E. Condit, 11.

3. Lovett to Embassy in France, Jan. 17, 1949, FRUS 1949, VII, 4–6.

4. Ibid.

5. Ibid., 250.

6. Nitze, op. cit., 68.

7. Ibid., 51.

8. Vandenberg, op. cit., 405.

9. Millis, ed., op. cit., 543.

10. Clifford, op. cit., 173.

11. Rogow, Arnold A., *James Forrestal: A Study of Personality, Politics and Policy* (New York: Macmillan, 1963), 4–5.

12. Lovett Oral History Interview, May 13, 1974, quoted in Hoopes & Brinkley, op. cit., 450–451; Cherny, op. cit., 518.

13. Lovett to Herbert, "Personal and Confidential," June 16, 1954, Lovett Papers.

14. Lovett to Marshall S. "Pat" Carter, April 27, 1949, Lovett Papers.

15. *New York Times*, May 11, 1949.

16. "Pleasance," by Adele Lovett, May 1975, Lovett Papers.

17. Gay Wagner, Building Structure Inventory Form, Division for Historic Preservation, New York State Parks and Recreation, July 20, 1978, Lovett Papers.

18. Adele Lovett, "Pleasance," op. cit.

19. Ibid.

20. *Philadelphia Inquirer*, May 3, 1949.

21. Lovett to Gen. Marshall S. "Pat" Carter, December 21, 1949, Lovett Papers.

22. Lovett's speech, together with a three-page intro-

duction by Bunny Harriman and a statement from General Marshall, describing Lovett's "integrity of the highest order, complete loyalty, and great wisdom, along with a selfless dedication of all his efforts to represent the Government and those serving me," was printed up in a cardboard-covered publication given the same title as Lovett's speech.

23. Lovett Papers.

24. Chace, op. cit., 228.

25. Lovett to Eisenhower, April 12, 1950, Lovett Papers.

26. James P. Baxter to Lovett, October 9, 1950; Lovett to Baxter, October 26, 1950, Lovett Papers.

27. Acheson, Dean, *Sketches from Life of Men I Have Known* (New York: Harper & Bros., 1960), 162.

28. Ferrell, op. cit. 369.

29. The tale of the phone call comes from an Oral History Interview Lovett gave to Richard D. McKinzie and Theodore A. Wilson, on July 7, 1971, now in the Truman Library in Independence, pp. 4–5, and from a Lovett interview by Alfred Goldberg and Harry B. Yoshpe, May 13, 1974, Department of Defense Historical Office, p. 7. In the interviews, Lovett recalled this as referring to his State Department appointment, but an assumption has been made here that his memory may have mixed the two appointments up, since the circumstances of the two appointments seem more clearly to attribute the phone call from the president to the Defense appointment. In the latter interview, he quickly alludes to coming to Defense; "But I didn't have any choice. The President said General Marshall would be Secretary of Defense if I would be his Deputy. There isn't that much of a choice when the Old Man says, 'Come on down,'" 8.

30. *New York Times*, September 29, 1950.

31. Lovett Interview, by Goldberg and Yoshpe, May 13, 1974, p. 8.

Chapter 23

1. These messages, and many others congratulating Lovett, are contained in a bound volume in the Lovett Papers in the Yale University Library.

2. Lovett Interview, June 7, 1976, by Doris E. Condit, 3, 5.

3. Lovett Interview, May 13, 1974, by Goldberg and Yoshpe, 19; Lovett Interview, July 7, 1971, by Richard D. McKinzie & Theodore A. Wilson, Truman Library, 30–31.

4. Lovett Remarks, Anna Rosenberg Hoffman Dinner, April 16, 1964, Lovett Papers.

5. "Memorandum of Conversations Between Mr. Acheson and Mr. Lovett, November 6, 1950, 10:20 A.M.," Acheson Papers, Truman Library.

6. Cray, op. cit., 701; Isaacson and Thomas, op. cit., 542.

7. Memorandum of Conversation, by the Ambassador at Large (Jessup), December 1, 1950, FRUS 1950, VII, 1280.

8. Truman, Harry, op. cit., 441.

9. Herman, Arthur, *Douglas MacArthur: American Warrior* (New York: Random House, 2016), 804.

10. Acheson, *Present*, op. cit., 519.

11. Truman, Harry., op. cit., 442, 443.

12. Ibid., 442.

13. Ibid., 445–446.

14. Childs, Marquis, "The Pentagon's Big Headache," *Philadelphia Evening Bulletin*, August 17, 1951.

15. Acheson, *Sketches*, op. cit., 165.

16. *Philadelphia Evening Bulletin*, September 12, 1951.

17. Pogue, op. cit., 490.

18. Lovett interview, June 7, 1976, Condit, 17.

19. *Time*, September 24, 1951. The article went on to say, "A man with a long history of stomach trouble [and] a deft sense of humor ... he likes movies, painting and jive, detests physical exercise, and reads everything from Thomas Mann to whodunits."

20. *Business Week*, September 22, 1951.

21. Ibid.

22. *Life*, September 1951.

23. Unidentified newspaper clipping, September 30, 1951.

Chapter 24

1. Lockett, Edward B., "There Is No Other Way but Strength," *New York Times Magazine*, September 23, 1951, 12; *New York Herald Tribune*, September 13, 1951.

2. Ibid.

3. Ibid.

4. Baldwin, Hanson W., "Lovett an Ideal Choice," *New York Times*, September 13, 1951.

5. Lovett interview, June 7, 1976, Condit, 13.

6. Ibid., 15.

7. *Philadelphia Evening Bulletin*, September 25, 26, 1951. It should be noted that almost all quotes from this paper are from Associated Press dispatches.

8. *Philadelphia Evening Bulletin*, October 15, 1951.

9. Lovett memo to Hazel Pierson, November 3, 1951, Lovett Papers.

10. *Stars and Stripes*, November 20, 21, 1951, *Stuttgarter Zeitung*, November 22, 1951; *Sentinel*, November 23, 1951.

11. "Draft Memorandum by the Secretary of State and the Secretary of Defense for the President," February 4, 1952, FRUS 1952–1954, XV, pt. 1, 36–37.

12. "Memorandum by the Secretary of State to the President," February 8, 1952, FRUS 1952–1954, XV, pt. 1, pp. 45–46.

13. "Memorandum of Conversation with President Truman and Secretary Lovett," February 8, 1952, FRUS 1952–1954, XV, pt. 1, pp. 44–45.

14. Sen. Francis Case to Pres. Truman, October 1, 1952, Official File, Truman Papers, Truman Library.

15. Lovett to Sen. Francis Case, October 30, 1952, Official File, Truman Papers, Truman Library.

16. *Philadelphia Evening Bulletin*, February 4, 1952.

17. Acheson, *Sketches*, op. cit., 119.

18. *Philadelphia Evening Bulletin*, February 29, 1952.

19. *Philadelphia Evening Bulletin*, March 16, 1952.

20. Borklund, op. cit., 120, 130.

21. Truman, Harry, op. cit., 466–467. Truman had created the Economic Stabilization Agency as provided in the Defense Production Act of 1950, and the Administrator of that agency, Alan Valentine, had established the Wage Stabilization Board (WSB), with the function of settling labor disputes affecting the national defense.

22. McConnell, Grant, "The Steel Seizure of 1952," *The Inter-University Case Program*, 12.

23. Truman, Harry, op. cit., 469.

24. Hamby, op. cit., 595; McCullough, op. cit., 898.

25. McConnell, loc. cit., 38.

26. Statement of Hon. Robert A. Lovett, April 24, 1952, U.S. Senate, Committee on Labor and Public Welfare, 505–506.

27. Ibid., 40.

28. The Supreme Court decision was officially *Youngstown Sheet and Tube Co. v. Sawyer*, 343 U.S. 579 (1952).

29. *Philadelphia Evening Bulletin*, June 6, 1952.

30. In July 1952 a treating physician wrote up a lengthy history of Robert Lovett's health problems, from his duodenal ulcer in 1932 through the gallbladder full of stones in the '40s, pancreatitis, pneumonia and bronchitis in 1949 and 1952, and the treatments for the various problems as well as Lovett's actions in response to his ailments, such as very limited smoking and drinking (Clinical Record and Diagnostic Summary, Dr. James A. Weir, July 18, 1952, Lovett Papers).

31. *Philadelphia Evening Bulletin*, July 23, 1952.

32. *New York Herald Tribune*, July 31, 1952.

33. Truman, Harry, op. cit., 477.

34. *New York Herald Tribune*, September 17, 1952.

35. *Philadelphia Inquirer*, Apr. 19, 1952.

36. *Philadelphia Evening Bulletin*, April 30, 1952.

37. *New York Times*, May 5, 1951.

38. *Philadelphia Evening Bulletin*, May 18, 1952.

39. Acheson, *Present*, op. cit., 675.

40. Eisenhower, Dwight D., *The White House Years: Mandate for Change, 1953–1956* (Garden City, NY: Doubleday, 1963), 31–32.

41. Lovett Papers.

42. It is interesting to note that Lovett declined honorary degrees offered by Union College, Dartmouth, Bowdoin, Lehigh, Pennsylvania Military College, University of Pittsburgh, New York University, Hamilton, Middlebury, and Washington University, mainly because their ceremonies conflicted with the others in which he was involved. In the future he would receive additional honorary degrees from Sam Houston State Teachers College, in his birth-town of Huntsville, Texas, and from Long Island University to go with the earlier degrees he had gotten from Columbia, Brown, and Williams (Lovett Papers).

43. *New York Herald Tribune*, September 17, 1952.

44. *Time* magazine had named Mossadegh its Man of the Year for 1951.

45. Lovett to David Bruce, Aug. 16, 1952, Leffler, op. cit., 482–483.

46. The *Houstonian*, Sept 20, September 24, 1952; *Fort-Worth Star-Telegram* (editorial), September 21, 1952; also the *Huntsville Item* and the Lovett Papers.

47. *Philadelphia Evening Bulletin*, September 11, 1952; *New York Herald Tribune*, Aug. 20, 1952.

48. E. Roland Harriman to Lovett, Aug. 25, 1952, Lovett Papers.

49. *Philadelphia Evening Bulletin*, Jan. 8, 1953.

50. Borklund, op. cit., 133–134.

51. Ibid., 136.

52. Ibid., 137.

53. Ambrose, Stephen E., *Eisenhower the President* (New York: Simon and Schuster, 1984), 14–15; *Philadelphia Evening Bulletin*, December 5, 1952.

54. Perret, Geoffrey, *Eisenhower* (New York: Random House, 1999), 423. As Carl Borklund wrote in his history of the Pentagon, "Wilson ignored a lot of Lovett's guidelines, made some of the same mistakes Forrestal had made about what he could expect of Defense people, and lost control of the organization" (Borklund, op. cit., 6).

55. Acheson, *Present*, op. cit., 715–716.

56. The parties to the litigation against Lovett were Robert W. Burns and Herman P. Dennis, Jr., and the young lady who was killed on December 11, 1948, was Ruth Farnsworth.

57. Lovett to Marshall, Jan. 29, 1953, Lovett Papers.

58. Marshall to Lovett, February 8, 1953, Lovett Papers.

59. Lovett to Hazel B. Pierson, Jan. 2, 1953, Lovett Papers.

Chapter 25

1. Lovett interview, June 7, 1976, Condit, 19–21.

2. Lovett to Gerald F. Beal, May 10, 1957, Lovett Papers.

3. Borklund, op. cit., 153.

4. Klein, Maury, *Union Pacific: The Rebirth*, op. cit. 474.

5. Harriman, op. cit., 132.

6. Lovett to William C. Foster, June 14, 1954, Lovett Papers.

7. Lovett to George C. Marshall, July 18, 1955, Lovett Papers.

8. Lovett telephone interview, June 13, 1982, Klein, op. cit., 475.

9. Ibid., 478.

10. Klein, Maury, *Union Pacific: The Reconfiguration: America's Greatest Railroad from 1969 to the Present* (New York: Oxford University Press, 2011), 201–202.

11. Klein, *Rebirth*, op. cit., 482–484.

12. Ibid., 484.

13. Lovett to G.C. Marshall, October 22, 1956, Lovett Papers.

14. Klein, *Rebirth*, op. cit., 530; Lovett Papers.

15. Lovett to Judith H. Higgins, May 31, 1966, Lovett Papers.

16. *New York Times*, December 4, 1966.

17. Harriman, op. cit., 146.

18. Klein, *Rebirth*, op. cit., 545; John S. Reed to Lovett, Apr. 11, 1978, Lovett Papers.

19. Lovett interview by Jessica Holland, 6/8/81, 6/15/81, 6/22/81, p. 119.

20. Holland interview, p. 118; "Hardy Survivor of a Dying Breed," *Business Week*, September 13, 1958, p. 60. Gerry was descended from James Madison's vice president, Elbridge T. Gerry, who became famous as Massachusetts governor for legislative redistricting that became known as "gerrymandering," and Gerry's mother, it may be noted, was a Harriman.

21. Lovett to George C. Marshall, May 14, 1957, Lovett Papers.

22. William Lovett to Robert Lovett, March 5, 1958, and May 10, 1958, Lovett Papers. William Lovett died July 4, 1959.

23. Lovett to Maxwell Taylor Board of Inquiry, May 11, 1961, Grose, Peter, *Gentleman Spy: The Life of Allen*

Dulles (Boston and New York: Houghton Mifflin, 1994), 446; Schlesinger, Arthur M., Jr., *Robert Kennedy and His Times*, vol. 1 (Boston: Houghton Mifflin, 1978), 474–475.

24. Ibid., 475.

25. Ibid.

26. DCI referred to the Director of Central Intelligence.

27. Ibid.

28. The ultimate whereabouts of the Bruce-Lovett report have remained a long-standing mystery. The CIA files have no copy of it nor does the Eisenhower Library, the National Archives, Bob Lovett's papers at Yale, or the Virginia Historical Society, the custodian of Bruce's papers. The text which is available comes from notes made by Arthur M. Schlesinger, Jr., for his biography of Robert Kennedy. Schlesinger said he had seen the Bruce-Lovett report in Robert Kennedy's papers before they were deposited at the John F. Kennedy Presidential Library. How did Robert Kennedy wind up with the report? He served on Maxwell Taylor's board of inquiry into the Bay of Pigs in 1961, and when Lovett testified before that board Kennedy may very well have asked him for a copy of the report and had it handed to him. Nevertheless, the Kennedy Presidential Library has searched the RFK papers for it without success. Interestingly, *The Last American Aristocrat: The Biography of Ambassador David K.E. Bruce, 1898–1977*, by Nelson D. Lankford (Little, Brown, 1996), deals with Bruce's appointment to Eisenhower's Board of Consultants and what it did, in one ten-line paragraph, on page 275. It does not refer to the Bruce-Lovett report but mentions "one bluntly worded report."

29. Snead, David L., *The Gaither Committee, Eisenhower, and the Cold War* (Columbus: Ohio State University Press, 1999), 48.

30. Snead, op. cit., 120.

31. Ibid., 121–122.

32. Ibid., 123–125.

33. *Washington Post*, December 20, 1957.

34. Ambrose, op. cit. 453.

35. Speech in Senate, September 13, 1963, by Sen. Henry Jackson, Fosdick, Dorothy, ed., *Henry M. Jackson and World Affairs: Selected Speeches, 1953–1983* (Seattle: University of Washington Press, 1990), 126.

36. "Hardy Survivor of a Dying Breed," *Business Week*, September 13, 1958; Lovett to W. Dale Clark, September 22, 1958, Lovett Papers.

37. "Hardy Survivor," loc. cit., 57–58.

38. Frisbee, John L., ed., *Makers of the United States Air Force* (McLean, VA: Pergamon-Brassey, 1989), 274.

39. Lovett to Dean Courtney C. Brown of Columbia, November 3, 1960, Lovett Papers.

Chapter 26

1. Stein, Jean, and George Plimpton, ed., *American Journey: The Times of Robert Kennedy* (New York: Harcourt Brace Jovanovich, 1970), 50. Robert Kennedy had gotten his position on the Senate committee staff through his father. Robert Kennedy even asked Senator McCarthy to be the godfather of his daughter Kathleen (Thomas, Evan, *Robert Kennedy: His Life* [New York: Simon & Schuster, 2000]), 68.

2. Hersh, Seymour M., *The Dark Side of Camelot* (Boston: Little, Brown, 1997). 150; May, Ernest R., and

Philip Zelikow, *The Kennedy Tapes: Inside the White House During the Cuban Missile Crisis* (Cambridge, MA: Belknap Press, 1997), 2.

3. Ibid., 235.

4. Lilienthal, David E., *The Journals of David E. Lilienthal: The Harvest Years. 1959–1963* (New York: Evanston & London, Harper and Row, 1971), 215.

5. Clifford, op. cit., 337–338; Lovett interview, July 20, 1964, p. 2, by Dorothy Fosdick, Kennedy Library.

6. Ibid.

7. Bird, op. cit. 496.

8. Lovett interview, July 20, 1964, by Fosdick, 5; O'Donnell and Powers, op. cit., 240.

9. Lovett interview, July 20, 1964, by Fosdick, 6.

10. Bird, op. cit., 496–497; Lovett interview, July 20, 1964, by Fosdick, 7; Lovett interview, Aug. 17, 1964, 14, by Fosdick.

11. Ibid., 17–18.

12. Ibid., 18–19.

13. Lovett interview, July 20, 1964, by Fosdick, 12; Lovett interview, Aug. 17, 1964, by Fosdick, 20.

14. Lovett interview, July 20, 1964, by Fosdick, 12–13.

15. Lovett interview, Aug. 17, 1964, by Fosdick, 14–15. McNamara subsequently recommended that Kennedy appoint Zuckert as secretary of the air force, and Kennedy did so.

16. Ibid., 16.

17. "Statement by the President upon Announcing the Appointment of Consultants on Government Organization and Operations," February 10, 1961, in Lovett interview, Aug. 17, 1964, by Fosdick, 21; *New York Times*, February 11, 1961.

18. Lovett interview, September 14, 1964, by Fosdick, 40.

19. Ibid., 41.

20. Ibid.; Bird, op. cit., 504.

21. Lovett interview, September 14, 1964, by Fosdick, 41–42.

22. Schlesinger, op. cit., v. 1, 477–478.

23. Mansfield motion, *Congressional Record—Senate*, January 25, 1962, pp. 743–746. At no point in his memorandum, obviously, did Lovett mention Douglas MacArthur.

24. O'Donnell and Powers, op. cit., 311.

25. Lovett interview, November 19, 1964, by Fosdick, 45.

26. Ibid., 45–46.

27. Ibid., 47.

28. May and Zelikow, op. cit., 154–155.

29. Brugioni, Dino A., *Eyeball to Eyeball: The Inside Story of the Cuban Missile Crisis* (New York: Random House, 1991), 286–287.

30. Lovett interview, November 19, 1964, by Fosdick, 50–51.

31. Leonard C. Meeker, deputy legal adviser to the State Department's United Nations Affairs office, presented on October 19 his legal analysis that a "blockade" would be perceived as an act of war, while a "quarantine" would not. From that point on, the proposed action was generally called a quarantine (*Ocracoke Observer*, December 4, 2014).

32. Fosdick interview, 51–52; Stern, Sheldon M., *The Week the World Stood Still: Inside the Secret Cuban Missile Crisis* (Stanford: Stanford University Press, 2005), 65.

33. Lovett interview, November 19, 1964, by Fosdick, 52–53. In his interview Lovett digressed to say of Robert Kennedy's family "that I never saw a finer-looking group of children in my life than the platoon of young Kennedys which surrounded the porch on which we gathered" (Ibid).

34. O'Brien, Michael, *John F. Kennedy: A Biography* (New York: St Martin's Press, 2005), 675; Bird, op. cit., 527.

35. Lovett interview, November 19, 1964, by Fosdick, 54; Stern, op. cit., 117–118, 230; May & Zelikow, op. cit., 380.

36. Lovett interview, November 19, 1964, by Fosdick, 56–57.

37. John F. Kennedy to Lovett, April 29, 1963, Lovett Papers.

38. Lovett interview, November 19, 1964, by Fosdick, 57–59; Lovett to Cecil B. Lyon, October 25, 1963, Lovett Papers.

39. Robert F. Kennedy to Lovett, undated, Lovett Papers.

40. Jacqueline Kennedy to Lovett, June 22, 1964; Robert F. Kennedy to Lovett, July 6, 1964, Lovett Papers.

41. Lovett to Ion H.T. Garrett-Orme at Brown Shipley & Co., December 2, 1963, Lovett Papers.

42. Arthur Krock, in the *New York Times*, September 11, 1964, listed the panel members.

43. McGeorge Bundy to Lovett, September 15, 1964, penciled "regrets," September 17, 1964, Lovett Papers.

44. Bird, op. cit., 578.

45. Telegram, Lyndon B. Johnson to Lovett, September 14, 1965, Lovett Papers.

46. Lovett to Louis Curtis, August 28, 1967, Lovett Papers.

47. New York Times, March 21, 1964; Eaker, Ira C., "West Pointers Honor Lovett," *San Antonio Express*, May 6, 1964.

48. Harry S Truman to Lovett, March 31, 1964, and Lovett to Truman, April 2, 1964, Lovett Papers.

49. Ira C. Eaker to Lovett, Apr. 22, 1964, and Jacob L. Devers to Lovett, Apr. 18, 1964, Lovett Papers.

50. "1964 Sylvanus Thayer Award Citation," Lovett Papers.

51. *New York Times*, May 3, 1964; *Congressional Record (Senate)*, May 6, 1964, pp. 9864–9866, where it was placed by Sen. Henry "Scoop" Jackson, who added that "no American is more worthy of this award, which comes from the officers with whom Mr. Lovett worked for so many years."

52. Eaker, loc. cit.

53. Lovett to Maj. Genl. Carey A. Randall, May 6, 1964, Lovett Papers.

54. Lovett to J.L. Pruett, July 21, 1975, Lovett Papers.

Chapter 27

1. Lovett to Roger Kent, October 13, 1954, on the firm's position re contributions, Lovett Papers. The author was unhappy to find that Lovett gave $100 to the (successful) reelection campaign in 1970 of Pennsylvania senator Hugh Scott, who ran against the author's good friend William Sesler.

2. These contributions are all recorded in the Lovett Papers, usually with letters or messages accompanying them.

3. Olson, Lynne, *Those Angry Days: Roosevelt, Lindbergh, and America's Fight Over World War II, 1939–1941* (New York: Random House, 2013), 139.

4. Lovett to Everett H. Bellows, July 3, 1968; Lovett to Ernest T. Hoch, Jan. 25, 1963, Lovett Papers.

5. Lovett to Helen Warner, April 1, 1968, Lovett Papers.

6. Lovett to Eelco N. van Kleffens, May 19, 1969, Lovett Papers.

7. Ibid.

8. Lovett to William W. Crapo, June 26, 1973, Lovett Papers.

9. Lovett to Goddard Lieberson, March 12, 1973, Lovett Papers.

10. Michael Kraynak, Jr., to Lovett, September 12, 1985; Arthur Hadley to Lovett, December 5, 1985, Lovett Papers. The current occupant of the chair is John Lewis Gaddis.

11. Lovett to W. Dale Clark, September 16, 1974; Lovett to Goddard Lieberson, March 5, 1975, Lovett Papers. He had a pacemaker installed later, in 1977, and wrote that he was "now running along on my improved second model" (Lovett to J.W. Sessums, Jr., Aug. 1, 1977, Lovett Papers).

12. Lovett to Hanson W. Baldwin, November 19, 1980, Lovett Papers.

13. William F. Ray to Lovett, December 30, 1982, Lovett Papers.

14. Lovett to James H. Douglas, October 17, 1983, Lovett Papers. Lovett had undergone eye surgery in November 1977, and in mid-1979 he was writing of "my serious loss of vision which requires me to read for only short periods and then through a large magnifying glass" (Lovett to Thomas D. Cabot, July 11, 1979, Lovett Papers).

15. Lovett to Marx Leva, March 19, 1979, Lovett Papers.

16. Archibald MacLeish to Thomas H. Stewart II, February 16, 1980; Natalie Douglas-Hamilton to Lovett, March 7, 1980, Lovett Papers.

17. Lovett to Mr. and Mrs. Marshall Carter, May 17, 1984, Lovett Papers.

18. Evan Thomas to Lovett, September 24, 1985; Lovett to Evan Thomas and Walter Isaacson, December 1, 1985, Lovett Papers.

19. Lovett to Dorothy Fosdick, September 6, 1983, Lovett Papers.

20. Notice of death, George C. Marshall Research Foundation, June 19, 1984; John J. McCloy to Mr. and Mrs. Robert Lovett, June 25, 1984,; Lovetts to McCloy, undated, John J. McCloy Papers, Amherst College Library.

21. All of these 90th birthday messages, and more, are in the Lovett Papers.

22. On February 3 Lovett sent off a check for $5,098 to pay for Adele's funeral.

23. Memorandum, R.L. Ireland III, Brown Brothers Harriman & Co., May 12, 1986, Lovett Papers.

24. Lovett to Sen. Thomas C. Desmond, February 23, 1961, Lovett Papers.

25. Paolo E. Coletta (on the faculty of the United States Naval Academy) to Lovett, July 16, 1977, quoting from transcript of interview with Fechteler, Lovett Papers.

Bibliography

Books

Abels, Jules. *Out of the Jaws of Victory*. New York: Henry Holt, 1959.

Abramson, Rudy. *Spanning the Century: The Life of W. Averell Harriman, 1891–1986*. New York: William Morrow, 1992.

Acacia, John. *Clark Clifford: The Wise Man of Washington*. Lexington: University Press of Kentucky, 2009.

Acheson, Dean. *Present At the Creation: My Years in the State Department*. New York: W.W. Norton, 1969.

_____. *Sketches from Life of Men I Have Known*. New York: Harper & Brothers, 1960.

Affection and Trust: The Personal Correspondence of Harry S. Truman and Dean Acheson, 1953–1971. New York: Alfred A. Knopf, 2010.

Allison, Graham, and Philip Zelikow. *Essence of Decision: Explaining the Cuban Missile Crisis*. 2nd ed. New York: Longman, 1999.

Alsop, Stewart. *The Center: People and Power in Political Washington*. New York: Harper & Row, 1968.

Ambrose, Stephen E. *Eisenhower: Soldier and President*. New York: Simon & Schuster, 1990.

_____. *Eisenhower: Soldier General of the Army President-Elect, 1890–1952*. New York: Simon & Schuster, 1983.

_____. *Eisenhower the President*. New York: Simon & Schuster, 1984.

Andrew, Christopher. *For the President's Eyes Only: Secret Intelligence and the American Presidency from Washington to Bush*. New York: HarperCollins, 2005.

Arkes, Hadley. *Bureaucracy, the Marshall Plan, and the National Interest*. Princeton: Princeton University Press, 1972.

Arnold, Henry H. *Global Mission*. New York: Harper & Brothers, 1949.

Atkinson, Rick. *The Guns at Last Light: The War in Western Europe, 1944–1945*. New York: Henry Holt, 2013.

Baime, A.J. *The Arsenal of Democracy: FDR, Detroit, and an Epic Quest to Arm an America at War*. Boston and New York: Houghton Mifflin, 2014.

Baldwin, Hanson W. *Battles Lost and Won: Great Campaigns of World War II*. New York: Konecky & Konecky, 1966.

Ball, George W. *The Past Has Another Pattern: Memoirs*. New York: W.W. Norton, 1982.

Bamford, James. *The Puzzle Palace: A Report on America's Most Secret Agency*. Boston: Houghton Mifflin, 1982.

Baruch, Bernard M. *Baruch: The Public Years*. New York: Holt, Rinehart & Winston, 1960.

Beisner, Robert L. *Dean Acheson: A Life in the Cold War*. New York: Oxford University Press, 2006.

Benson, Michael T. *Harry S Truman and the Founding of Israel*. Westport, CT: Praeger, 1997.

Berg, A. Scott. *Lindbergh*. New York: G.P. Putnam's Sons, 1998.

Berger, Carl. *B29: The Superfortress*. New York: Ballantine Books, 1970.

Berle, Beatrice Bishop, and Travis Beal Jacobs, eds. *Navigating the Rapids, 1918–1971: From the Papers of Adolf A. Berle*. New York: Harcourt Brace Jovanovich, 1973.

Bernstein, Barton J., and Allen J. Matusow, eds. *The Truman Administration: A Documentary History*. New York and London; Harper & Row, 1966.

Beschloss, Michael. *The Conquerors: Roosevelt, Truman and the Destruction of Hitler's Germany*. New York: Simon & Schuster, 2002.

_____. *The Crisis Years: Kennedy and Khrushchev, 1960–1963*. New York: Edward Burlingame Books, 1991.

Best, Richard A., Jr. *"Co-Operation With Like-Minded Peoples": British Influences on American Security Policy, 1945–1949*. Westport, CT: Greenwood Press, 1986.

Biddle, Tami Davis. *Rhetoric and Reality in Air Warfare: The Evolution of British and American Ideas About Strategic Bombing, 1914–1945*. Princeton, NJ: Princeton University Press, 2002.

Bird, Kai. *The Chairman: John J. McCloy: The Making of the American Establishment*. New York: Simon & Schuster, 1992.

_____, and Martin J. Sherwin. *American Prometheus: The Triumph and Tragedy of J. Robert Oppenheimer*. New York: Alfred A. Knopf, 2006.

Bland, Larry I., ed. *The Papers of George Catlett Marshall*. Vol. 4. Baltimore: Johns Hopkins Press, 1996.

_____, and Mark A. Stoler, eds. *The Papers of George Catlett Marshall*. Vol. 6. Baltimore: Johns Hopkins Press, 2013.

Blotner, Joseph. *Faulkner: A Biography*. New York: Random House, 1984.

Blum, John Morton. *V Was For Victory: Politics and American Culture During World War II*. New York and London: Harcourt Brace Jovanovich, 1976.

Blumenson, Martin. *Mark Clark*. New York: Congdon & Weed, 1984.

Bohlen, Charles E. *Witness to History, 1929–1969*. New York: W.W. Norton, 1971.

Borklund, Carl W. *The Department of Defense*. New York: Frederick A. Praeger, 1968.

_____. *Men of the Pentagon: From Forrestal to McNamara.* New York: Frederick A. Praeger, 1966.

Bradley, Omar N. *A Soldier's Story.* New York: Henry Holt, 1951.

_____, and Clay Blair. *A General's Life.* New York: Simon & Schuster, 1983.

Brands, H.W. *The General vs. the President: MacArthur and Truman at the Brink of Nuclear War.* New York: Doubleday, 2016.

Brigante, John E. *The Feasibility Dispute: Determination of War Production Objectives for 1942 and 1943.* Washington, Committee on Public Administration Cases, 1950.

Brinkley, Alan. *The Publisher: Henry Luce and His American Century.* New York: Alfred A. Knopf, 2010.

Brinkley, Douglas. *Dean Acheson: The Cold War Years, 1953–71.* New Haven, CT: Yale University Press, 1992.

Brown, Seyom. *The Faces of Power: Constancy and Change in United States Foreign Policy from Truman to Johnson.* Columbia University Press. New York: 1968.

Brownell, Herbert, with John P. Burke. *Advising Ike: The Memoirs of Attorney General Herbert Brownell.* Lawrence: University Press of Kansas, 1991.

Brugioni, Dino A. *Eyeball to Eyeball: The Inside Story of the Cuban Missile Crisis.* New York: Random House, 1991.

Budiansky, Stephen. *Air Power: The Men, Machines and Ideas That Revolutionized War, from Kitty Hawk to Gulf War II.* New York: Viking, 2004.

Caraley, Demetrios. *The Politics of Military Unification: A Study of Conflict and the Policy Process.* New York & London: Columbia University Press, 1966.

Caroli, Betty Boyd. *Lady Bird and Lyndon: The Hidden Story of a Marriage That Made a President.* New York: Simon & Schuster, 2015.

Chace, James. *Acheson: The Secretary of State Who Created the American World.* Cambridge: Harvard University Press, 1998.

Cherny, Andrei. *The Candy Bombers: The Untold Story of the Berlin Airlift and America's Finest Hour.* New York: G.P. Putnam's Sons, 2008.

Clay, Lucius D. *Decision in Germany.* Garden City, NY: Doubleday, 1950.

Clifford, Clark, with Richard Holbrooke. *Counsel to the President: A Memoir.* New York: Random House, 1991.

_____, Eugene V. Rostow and Barbara W. Tuchman. *The Palestine Question in American History.* New York: Arno Press, 1978.

Clodfelter, Mark. *Beneficial Bombing: The Progressive Foundations of American Air Power, 1917–1945.* Lincoln: University of Nebraska Press, 2010.

Cochran, Bert. *Harry Truman and the Crisis Presidency.* New York: Funk & Wagnalls, 1973.

Coffey, Thomas M. *Decision Over Schweinfurt: The U.S. 8th Air Force Battle for Daylight Bombing.* New York: David McKay, 1977.

_____. *Hap: The Story of the U.S. Air Force and the Man Who Built It, General Henry H. "Hap" Arnold.* New York: Viking Press, 1982.

Cohen, Michael J. *Truman and Israel.* Berkeley: University of California Press, 1990.

Coleman, David G. *The Fourteenth Day: JFK and the Aftermath of the Cuban Missile Crisis.* New York: W.W. Norton, 2012.

Collier, Peter, and David Horowitz. *The Kennedys: An American Drama.* New York: Summit Books, 1984.

Collier, Richard. *Bridge Across the Sky: The Berlin Blockade and Airlift, 1948–1949.* New York: McGraw-Hill, 1978.

Craven, Wesley Frank, and James Lea Cate, eds. *The Army Air Forces in World War II: Men and Planes.* Chicago: University of Chicago Press, 1955.

_____. *The Army Air Forces in World War II: Plans and Early Operations, January 1939 to August 1942.* Chicago: University of Chicago Press, 1948.

Cray, Ed. *General of the Army: George C. Marshall Soldier and Statesman.* New York: Touchstone, 1990.

Dallek, Robert. *Camelot's Court: Inside the Kennedy White House.* New York: Harper, 2013.

_____. *Harry S. Truman.* New York: Henry Holt, 2008.

_____. *The Lost Peace: Leadership in a Time of Horror and Hope, 1945–1953.* New York: HarperCollins, 2010.

_____. *An Unfinished Life: John F. Kennedy, 1917–1963.* Boston: Little, Brown, 2003.

Daniels, Jonathan. *The Man of Independence.* Philadelphia: J.B. Lippincott, 1950.

Daso, Dik Alan. *Hap Arnold and the Evolution of American Airpower.* Washington and London: Smithsonian Institution Press, 2000.

Davis, Kenneth S. *FDR: The War President 1940–1943.* New York: Random House, 2000.

Davis, Richard G. *Carl A. Spaatz and the Air War in Europe.* Washington and London: Smithsonian Institute Press, 1992.

de Seversky, Alexander P. *Victory Through Air Power.* New York: Simon & Schuster, 1942.

Divine, Robert A. *Foreign Policy and U.S. Presidential Elections, 1940 1948.* New York: New Viewpoints, 1974.

Domhoff, G. William. *Who Rules America?* Englewood Cliffs, NJ: Prentice-Hall, 1967.

Donovan, John C. *The Cold Warriors: A Policy-Making Elite.* Lexington, MA: D.C. Heath, 1974.

Donovan, Robert J. *Conflict and Crisis: The Presidency of Harry S Truman, 1945–1948.* New York: W.W. Norton, 1977.

_____. *Tumultuous Years: The Presidency of Harry S Truman, 1949–1953.* New York: W.W. Norton, 1982.

Druks, Herbert. *Harry S. Truman and the Russians, 1945–1953.* New York: Robert Speller & Sons, 1966.

_____. *The Uncertain Friendship: The U.S. and Israel from Roosevelt to Kennedy.* Westport, CT: Greenwood Press, 2001.

_____. *The U.S. and Israel, 1945–1973: A Diplomatic History.* New York: Robert Speller & Sons, 1979.

Eiler, Keith E. *Mobilizing America: Robert P. Patterson and the War Effort, 1940–1945.* Ithaca, NY: Cornell University Press, 1997.

Eisenhower, Dwight D. *The White House Years: Mandate for Change, 1953–1956.* Garden City, NY: Doubleday, 1963.

Elsey, George McKee. *An Unplanned Life.* Columbia: University of Missouri Press, 2005.

Ewald, William Bragg, Jr. *Eisenhower the President: Crucial Days, 1951–1960.* Englewood Cliffs, NJ: Prentice-Hall, 1981.

Fanton, Jonathan Foster. "Robert A. Lovett: The War Years." PhD diss., Yale University, 1978.

Feis, Herbert. *From Trust to Terror: The Onset of the Cold War, 1945–1950.* New York: W.W. Morrow, 1970.

Ferrell, Robert H., ed. *The Eisenhower Diaries.* New York: W.W. Norton, 1981.

_____. ed. *Truman in the White House: The Diary of Eben A. Ayers.* Columbia: University of Missouri Press, 1991.

Fleming, Thomas. *The New Dealers' War: Franklin D. Roosevelt and the War Within World War II.* New York: Basic Books, 2001.

Fosdick, Dorothy, ed. *Henry M. Jackson and World Affairs: Selected Speeches, 1953–1983.* Seattle: University of Washington Press, 1990.

Frank, Richard B. *Downfall: The End of the Imperial Japanese Empire.* New York: Random House, 1999.

Frankland, Noble. *Bomber Offensive: The Devastation of Europe.* New York: Ballantine, 1970.

_____. *The Bombing Offensive Against Germany.* London: Faber & Faber, 1965.

Frantz, Douglas, and David McKean. *Friends in High Places: The Rise and Fall of Clark Clifford.* Boston: Little, Brown, 1995.

Freedman, Lawrence. *Kennedy's Wars: Berlin, Cuba, Laos, and Vietnam.* New York & Oxford: Oxford University Press, 2000.

Freeman, Joshua B. *American Empire: The Rise of a Global Power; The Democratic Revolution at Home, 1945–2000.* New York: Viking, 2012.

Freeman, Roger A. *The Mighty Eighth: A History of the Units, Men and Machines of the US 8th Air Force.* New York: Orion Books, 1970.

Friedrich, Jorg. *The Fire: The Bombing of Germany, 1940–1945.* New York: Columbia University Press, 2006.

Frisbee, John L., ed. *Makers of the United States Air Force.* McLean, VA: Pergamon-Brassey, 1989.

Fromkin, David. *In the Time of the Americans: FDR, Truman, Eisenhower, Marshall, MacArthur; The Generation That Changed America's Role in the World.* New York: Alfred A. Knopf, 1995.

Gaddis, John Lewis. *George F. Kennan: An American Life.* New York: Penguin, 2011.

_____. *The United States and the Origins of the Cold War, 1941–1947.* New York and London: Columbia University Press, 1972.

Gimbel, John. *The Origins of the Marshall Plan.* Stanford: Stanford University Press, 1976.

Goddard, George W., with DeWitt S. Kopp. *Overview: A Life-Long Adventure in Aerial Photography.* Garden City, NY: Doubleday, 1969.

Goldman, Eric F. *The Crucial Decade: America, 1945–1955.* New York: Alfred A. Knopf, 1956.

Goulden, Joseph C. *Korea: The Untold Story of the War.* New York: Times Books, 1982.

Graham, Katharine. *Personal History.* New York: Alfred A. Knopf, 1997.

Grant, William Newby. *P-51 Mustang.* Troy, MI: Bison Books, 1980.

Griffis, Stanton. *Lying in State.* Garden City, NY: Doubleday, 1952.

Groom, Winston. *The Aviators: Eddie Rickenbacker, Jimmy Doolittle, Charles Lindbergh, and the Epic Age of Flight.* Washington, D.C.: National Geographic, 2013.

Grose, Peter. *Gentleman Spy: The Life of Allen Dulles.* Boston and New York: Houghton Mifflin, 1994.

Grosscup, Beau. *Strategic Terror: The Politics and Ethics of Aerial Bombardment.* Kuala Lumpur, London and New York: Sird and Zed Books, 2006.

Guthman, Edwin O., and Jeffrey Shulman, ed. *Robert Kennedy in His Own Words: The Unpublished Recollections of the Kennedy Years.* Toronto. New York: Bantam, 1988.

Haas, Lawrence J. *Harry and Arthur: Truman, Vandenberg, and the Partnership That Created the Free World.* Lincoln, NE: Potomac Books, 2016.

Halberstam, David. *The Best and the Brightest.* New York: Random House, 1972.

_____. *The Fifties.* New York: Villard Books, 1993.

Hamby, Alonzo L. *Man of the People: A Life of Harry S. Truman.* New York: Oxford University Press, 1995.

Hamilton, Nigel. *The Mantle of Command: FDR at War, 1941–1942.* Boston and New York: Houghton Mifflin, 2014.

Hammond, Paul Y. *Organizing for Defense: The American Military Establishment in the Twentieth Century.* Princeton, NJ: Princeton University Press, 1961.

Hansell, Haywood S., Jr. *The Air Plan That Defeated Hitler.* Atlanta, 1972.

_____. *The Strategic Air War Against Germany and Japan.* Washington, D.C.: Office of Air Force History, 1986.

Hansen, Randall. *Fire and Fury: The Allied Bombing of Germany, 1942–1945.* New York: NAL Caliber, 2008.

Harriman, E. Roland, *I Reminisce.* Garden City, NY: Doubleday, 1975.

Harriman, W. Averell. *America and Russia in a Changing World: A Half Century of Personal Observation.* Garden City, NY: Doubleday, 1971.

_____, and Elie Abel. *Special Envoy to Churchill and Stalin, 1941–1946.* New York: Random House, 1975.

Hastings, Max. *The Korean War.* New York: Simon & Schuster, 1987.

Hechler, Ken. *Working with Truman: A Personal Memoir of the White House Years.* New York: G.P. Putnam's Sons, 1982.

Heller, Francis H. *The Truman White House: The Administration of the Presidency, 1945–1953.* Lawrence: Regents Press of Kansas, 1980.

Henderson, Sir Nicholas. *The Birth of NATO.* Boulder: Westview Press, 1983.

Herken, Gregg. *The Georgetown Set: Friends and Rivals in Cold War Washington.* New York: Alfred A. Knopf, 2014.

_____. *The Winning Weapon: The Atomic Bomb in the Cold War, 1945–1950.* New York: Alfred A. Knopf, 1980.

Herman, Arthur. *Douglas MacArthur: American Warrior.* New York: Random House, 2016.

_____. *Joseph McCarthy: Reexamining the Life and Legacy of America's Most Hated Senator.* New York: Free Press, 1999.

Hersh, Seymour M. *The Dark Side of Camelot.* Boston: Little, Brown, 1997.

Heymann, C. David. *The Georgetown Ladies' Social Club: Power, Passion, and Politics in the Nation's Capital.* New York: Atria Books, 2003.

Hodgson, Godfrey. *The Colonel: The Life and Wars of Henry Stimson, 1867–1950.* Boston: Northeastern University Press, 1992.

Hogan, Michael J. *The Marshall Plan: America, Britain*

and the Reconstruction of Western Europe, 1947–1952. New York: Cambridge University Press, 1987.

Hoopes, Townsend. *The Devil and John Foster Dulles.* Boston: Little, Brown, 1973.

_____, and Douglas Brinkley. *Driven Patriot: The Life and Times of James Forrestal.* New York: Alfred A. Knopf, 1992.

Hughes, Thomas Alexander. *Over Lord: General Pete Quesada and the Triumph of Tactical Air Power in World War II.* New York: Free Press, 1995.

Hynes, Samuel. *The Unsubstantial Air: American Fliers in the First World War.* New York: Farrar, Straus and Giroux, 2014.

Isaacson, Walter, and Evan Thomas. *The Wise Men: Six Friends and the World They Made.* New York: Simon & Schuster, 2013.

Jenkins, Roy. *Truman.* New York: Harper & Row, 1986.

Jordan, Robert S. *Norstad: Cold War NATO Supreme Commander, Airman, Strategist, Diplomat.* New York: St. Martin's, 2000.

Judis, John B. *Genesis: Truman, American Jews, and the Origins of the Arab/Israeli Conflict.* New York: Farrar, Straus and Giroux, 2014.

Kaplan, Lawrence S. *NATO and the United States: The Enduring Alliance.* Boston: Twayne, 1988.

Kaufman, Burton I. *The Korean War: Challenges in Crisis, Credibility, and Command.* Philadelphia: Temple University Press, 1986.

Keegan, John. *The Second World War.* New York: Viking, 1989.

Kennan, George F. *Memoirs, 1925–1950.* Boston and Toronto: Little, Brown, 1967.

_____. *The Kennan Diaries.* Edited by Frank Costigliola. New York and London: W.W. Norton, 2014.

Kennedy, Paul. *Engineers of Victory: The Problem Solvers Who Turned the Tide in the Second World War.* New York: Random House, 2013.

Kennedy, Robert F. *Thirteen Days: A Memoir of the Cuban Missile Crisis.* New York: W.W. Norton, 1969

Kennett, Lee. *The First Air War, 1914–1918.* New York: Free Press, 1991.

Ketchum, Richard M. *The Borrowed Years, 1938–1941: America on the Way to War.* New York: Random House, 1989.

Kinnard, Douglas. *The Secretary of Defense.* Lexington: University Press of Kentucky, 1980.

Kinzer, Stephen. *The Brothers: John Foster Dulles, Allen Dulles, and Their Secret World War.* New York: Henry Holt, 2013.

Klein, Maury. *A Call to Arms: Mobilizing America for World War II.* New York: Bloomsbury, 2013.

_____. *Union Pacific: The Rebirth, 1894–1969.* New York: Doubleday, 1989.

_____. *Union Pacific: The Reconfiguration; America's Greatest Railroad from 1969 to the Present.* New York: Oxford University Press, 2011.

Kouwenhoven, John A. *Partners in Banking: An Historical Portrait of a Great Private Bank, Brown Brothers Harriman,1818–1968.* Garden City, NY: Doubleday, 1968.

Kozak, Warren. *LeMay: The Life and Wars of General Curtis LeMay.* Washington, D.C.: Regnery, 2009.

Krock, Arthur. *Memoirs: Sixty Years on the Firing Line.* New York: Funk & Wagnalls, 1968.

Lamont, Thomas W. *Henry P. Davison: The Record of a Useful Life.* New York and London: Harper and Bros., 1933.

Lankford, Nelson D. *The Last American Aristocrat: The Biography of Ambassador David K.E. Bruce, 1898–1977.* Boston and New York: Little, Brown, 1996.

Larrabee, Eric. *Commander in Chief: Franklin Delano Roosevelt, His Lieutenants, and Their War.* New York: Harper & Row, 1987.

Lash, Joseph P. *Eleanor: The Years Alone.* New York: W.W. Norton, 1972.

_____. *A World of Love: Eleanor Roosevelt and Her Friends.* Garden City, NY: Doubleday, 1984.

Leamer, Laurence. *The Kennedy Men, 1901–1963: The Laws of the Father.* New York: William Morrow, 2001.

Lee, Ulysses. *The Employment of Negro Troops.* Washington, D.C.: Center of Military History, 1963, reprt. 1994.

Leebaert, Derek. *The Fifty-Year Wound: The True Price of America's Cold War Victory.* Boston: Little, Brown, 2003.

Leffler, Melvyn P. *A Preponderance of Power: National Security, the Truman Administration, and the Cold War.* Stanford: Stanford University Press, 1992.

Leuchtenburg, William E. *In the Shadow of FDR: From Harry Truman to Ronald Reagan.* Ithaca, NY: Cornell University Press, 1983.

Levine, Alan J. *The Strategic Bombing of Germany, 1940–1945.* Westport, CT: Praeger, 1992.

Lilienthal, David E. *The Journals of David E. Lilienthal: The Atomic Energy Years, 1945–1950.* New York, Evanston, and London: Harper and Row, 1964.

_____. *The Journals of David E. Lilienthal: The Harvest Years, 1959–1963.* New York, Evanston, and London: Harper and Row, 1971.

Lindbergh, Charles A. *The Wartime Journals of Charles A. Lindbergh.* New York: Harcourt Brace Jovanovich, 1970.

Loftus, John, and Mark Aarons. *The Secret War Against the Jews: How Western Espionage Betrayed the Jewish People.* New York: St. Martin's, 1994.

Lovett, Robert A. *Forty Years After: An Appreciation of the Genius of Edward Henry Harriman (1848–1909).* New York: Newcomen Society, 1949.

Lukacs, John. *George Kennan: A Study of Character.* New Haven, CT: Yale University Press, 2007.

Manchester, William. *American Caesar.* New York: Dell, 1979.

Marcus, Maeva. *Truman and the Steel Seizure Case: The Limits of Presidential Power.* New York: Columbia University Press, 1977.

Marshall, Katherine Tupper. *Together: Annals of an Army Wife.* New York and Atlanta: Tupper and Love, 1946.

May, Ernest R., and Philip D. Zelikow. *The Kennedy Tapes: Inside the White House During the Cuban Missile Crisis.* Cambridge, MA: Belknap Press, 1997.

Mayne, Richard. *The Recovery of Europe: From Devastation to Unity.* New York: Harper & Row, 1970.

McCloy, John J. *The Atlantic Alliance: Its Origin and Its Future.* New York: Columbia University Press, 1968.

McConnell, Grant. *The Steel Seizure of 1952.* Indianapolis: Bobbs-Merrill, 1960.

McCoy, Donald R. *The Presidency of Harry S. Truman.* Lawrence: University Press of Kansas, 1984.

McCullough, David. *Truman.* New York: Simon & Schuster, 1992.

McFarland, Keith D., and David L. Roll. *Louis Johnson and the Arming of America: The Roosevelt and Truman Years*. Bloomington: Indiana University Press, 2005.

McLellan, David S. *Dean Acheson: The State Department Years*. New York: Dodd, Mead, 1976

McNamara, Robert S., with Brian VanDeMark. *In Retrospect: The Tragedy and Lessons of Vietnam*. New York: Times Books, 1995.

Meade, Marion. *Dorothy Parker: What Fresh Hell Is This?* New York: Villard Books, 1988.

Mee, Charles L., Jr. *The Marshall Plan: The Launching of the Pax Americana*. New York: Simon & Schuster, 1984.

Merry, Robert W. *Taking On the World: Joseph and Stewart Alsop, Guardians of the American Century*. New York: Viking, 1996.

Mets, David R. *Master of Airpower: General Carl A. Spaatz*. Novato, CA: Presidio Press, 1988.

Michie, Allan A. *The Air Offensive Against Germany*. New York: Henry Holt, 1943.

Miller, Donald L. *Masters of the Air: America's Bomber Boys Who Fought the Air War Against Nazi Germany*. New York: Simon & Schuster, 2006.

Miller, Nathan. *FDR: An Intimate History*. Garden City, NY: Doubleday, 1983.

Millis, Walter, ed. *The Forrestal Diaries*. New York: Viking Press, 1951.

Miscamble, Wilson D. *George F. Kennan and the Making of American Foreign Policy, 1947–1950*. Princeton, NJ: Princeton University Press, 1992.

Monk, Ray. *Robert Oppenheimer: A Life Inside the Center*. New York: Doubleday, 2012.

Morison, Elting E. *Turmoil and Tradition: A Study of the Life and Times of Henry L. Stimson*. Boston: Houghton Mifflin, 1960.

Morris, Roger. *Richard Milhous Nixon: The Rise of an American Politician*. New York: Henry Holt, 1990.

Mosley, Leonard. *Marshall: Hero for Our Times*. New York: Hearst, 1982.

Moss, Norman. *Picking Up the Reins*. New York: Overlook, 2008.

Mrazek, Robert J. *To Kingdom Come: An Epic Saga of Survival in the Air War Over Germany*. New York: New American History, 2011.

Murphy, Robert. *Diplomat Among Warriors*. Garden City, NY: Doubleday, 1964.

Neal, Steve. *Harry and Ike: The Partnership That Remade the Postwar World*. New York and London: Scribner's, 2001.

Nelson, Donald M. *Arsenal of Democracy: The Story of American War Production*. New York: Harcourt, Brace, 1946.

Neustadt, Richard E. *Presidential Power and the Modern Presidents: Leadership from Roosevelt to Reagan*. New York: Free Press, 1990.

Newton, Jim. *Eisenhower: The White House Years*. New York: Doubleday, 2011.

Nichols, Lee. *Breakthrough on the Color Front*. Colorado Springs: Three Continents, 1993.

Nitze, Paul H. *From Hiroshima to Glasnost: At the Center of Decision*. New York: Grove Weidenfeld, 1989.

O'Brien, Michael. *John F. Kennedy: A Biography*. New York: St. Martin's, 2005.

_____. *Rethinking Kennedy: An Interpretive Biography*. Chicago: Ivan R. Dee, 2009.

O'Donnell, Helen, with Kenneth O'Donnell, Sr. *The Irish Brotherhood: John F. Kennedy, His Inner Circle, and the Improbable Rise to the Presidency*. Berkeley: Counterpoint, 2015.

O'Donnell, Kenneth P., and David F. Powers, with Joe McCarthy. *"Johnny, We Hardly Knew Ye": Memories of John Fitzgerald Kennedy*. Boston: Little, Brown, 1970.

Offner, Arnold A. *Another Such Victory: President Truman and the Cold War, 1945–1953*. Stanford: Stanford University Press, 2002.

Olson, Lynne. *Citizens of London: The Americans Who Stood with Britain in Its Darkest, Finest Hour*. New York: Random House, 2010.

_____. *Those Angry Days: Roosevelt, Lindbergh, and America's Fight Over World II, 1939–1941*. New York: Random House, 2013.

Oren, Michael B. *Power, Faith, and Fantasy: America in the Middle East, 1776 to the Present*. New York: W.W. Norton, 2007.

Overy, Richard. *The Air War, 1939–1945*. New York: Stein and Day, 1980.

_____. *The Bombers and the Bombed: Allied Air War Over Europe, 1940–1945*. New York: Viking, 2013.

Paine, Ralph D. *The First Yale Unit: A Story of Naval Aviation, 1916–1919*. Cambridge, MA: Riverside Press, 1925.

Paper, Lewis J. *John F. Kennedy: The Promise and the Performance*. New York: DaCapo, 1979.

Parmet, Herbert S. *JFK: The Presidency of John F. Kennedy*. New York: Dial Press, 1983.

Parrish, Thomas. *Roosevelt and Marshall: Partners in Politics and War*. New York: William Morrow, 1989.

Parton, James. *"Air Force Spoken Here": General Ira Eaker and the Command of the Air*. Bethesda, MD: Adler & Adler, 1986.

_____. consulting ed. *Impact: Bombing Fortress Europe*. Harrisburg, PA: National Historical Society, 1989

Patterson, James T. *Grand Expectations: The United States, 1945–1974*. New York and Oxford: Oxford University Press, 1996.

Pearlman, Michael D. *Truman and MacArthur: Policy, Politics, and the Hunger for Honor and Renown*. Bloomington: Indiana University Press, 2008.

Pelling, Henry. *Britain and the Marshall Plan*. New York: St. Martin's, 1988.

Perret, Geoffrey. *Eisenhower*. New York: Random House, 1999.

_____. *There's a War to Be Won: The United States Army in World War II*. New York: Random House, 1991.

_____. *Winged Victory: The Army Air Forces in World War II*. New York: Random House, 1993.

Phillips, Cabell. *The Truman Presidency: The History of a Triumphant Succession*. New York: Macmillan, 1966.

Pierpaoli, Paul G., Jr. *Truman and Korea: The Political Culture of the Early Cold War*. Columbia: University of Missouri Press, 1999.

Pietrusza, David. *1948: Harry Truman's Improbable Victory and the Year That Transfomed America's Role in the World*. New York: Union Square Press, 2011.

Pogue, Forrest C. *George C. Marshall: Ordeal and Hope, 1939–1942*. New York: Viking Press, 1966.

_____. *George C. Marshall: Organizer of Victory, 1943–1945*. New York: Viking Press, 1973.

_____. *George C. Marshall: Statesman, 1945–1959*. New York: Viking, 1987.

Reeves, Richard. *Daring Young Men: The Heroism and Triumph of the Berlin Airlift, June 1948–May 1949*. New York: Simon & Schuster, 2010.

Reeves, Thomas C. *A Question of Character: A Life of John F. Kennedy*. New York: Free Press, 1991.

Riddle, Donald H. *The Truman Committee*. New Brunswick, NJ: Rutgers University Press, 1964.

Rigole, Julius A. "The Strategic Bombing Campaign Against Germany During World War II." Master's thesis, Louisiana State University, 2002.

Robbins, Alexandra. *Secrets of the Tomb: Skull and Bones, the Ivy League, and the Hidden Paths of Power*. Boston and New York: Little, Brown, 2002.

Rogow, Arnold A. *James Forrestal: A Study of Personality, Politics and Policy*. New York: Macmillan, 1963.

Roosevelt, Elliott, and James Brough. *Mother R.: Eleanor Roosevelt's Untold Story*. New York: G.P. Putnam's Sons, 1977.

Rose, Lisle A. *The Cold War Comes to Main Street: America in 1950*. Lawrence: University Press of Kansas, 1999.

Rossano, Geoffrey L., ed. *Hero of the Angry Sky: The World War I Diary and Letters of David S. Ingalls, America's First Naval Ace*. Athens: Ohio University Press, 2013.

_____. *The Price of Honor: The World War One Letters of Naval Aviator Kenneth MacLeish*. Annapolis: Naval Institute Press, 1991.

Rusk, Dean. *As I Saw It*. As told to Richard Rusk. New York: W.W. Norton, 1990.

Schaffer, Ronald. *Wings of Judgment: American Bombing in World War II*. New York and Oxford, Oxford University Press, 1985.

Schaller, Michael. *Douglas MacArthur: The Far Eastern General*. New York and Oxford: Oxford University Press, 1989.

Schlesinger, Andrew, and Stephen Schlesinger, eds. *The Letters of Arthur Schlesinger, Jr*. New York: Random House, 2013.

Schlesinger, Arthur M., Jr. *Robert Kennedy and His Times*. 2 vols. Boston: Houghton Mifflin, 1978.

_____. *A Thousand Days: John F. Kennedy in the White House*. Boston: Houghton Mifflin, 1965.

Schweizer, Peter, and Rochelle Schweizer. *The Bushes: Portrait of a Dynasty*. New York: Doubleday, 2004.

Sebestyen, Victor. *1946: The Making of the Modern World*. New York: Pantheon Books, 2014.

Sestanovich, Stephen. *Maximalist: America in the World from Truman to Obama*. New York: Alfred A. Knopf, 2014.

Sheely, Lawrence D., ed. *Sailor of the Air: The 1917–1919 Letters and Diary of USN CMM/A Irving Edward Sheely*. Tuscaloosa: University of Alabama Press, 1993.

Sherwood, Robert E. *Roosevelt and Hopkins; An Intimate History*. 2 vols. New York: Bantam, 1950.

Shlaim, Avi. *The United States and the Berlin Blockade, 1948–1949*. Berkeley: University of California Press, 1983.

Silk, Leonard, and Mark Silk. *The American Establishment*. New York: Basic Books, 1980.

Simpson, Christopher. *Blowback: America's Recruitment of Nazis and Its Effect on the Cold War*. New York: Collier Books, 1989.

Smith, Jean Edward. *FDR*. New York: Random House, 2007.

Smith, Richard Norton. *On His Own Terms: A Life of Nelson Rockefeller*. New York: Random House, 2014.

Snead, David L. *The Gaither Committee, Eisenhower, and the Cold War*. Columbus: Ohio State University Press, 1999.

Snetsinger, John. *Truman, the Jewish Vote, and the Creation of Israel*. Stanford: Hoover Institution Press, 1974.

Snow, Richard. *A Measureless Peril: America in the Fight for the Atlantic, the Longest Battle of World War II*. New York: Scribner's, 2010.

Sorensen, Theodore C. *Kennedy*. New York: Harper & Row, 1965.

Spanier, John W. *The Truman-MacArthur Controversy and the Korean War*. Cambridge: Belknap Press of Harvard University Press, 1959.

Spector, Ronald H. *Advice and Support: The Early Years of the United States Army in Vietnam*. New York: Free Press, 1985.

Stein, Jean, and George Plimpton, ed. *American Journey: The Times of Robert Kennedy*. New York: Harcourt Brace Jovanovich, 1970.

Stern, Sheldon M. *Averting 'The Final Failure': John F. Kennedy and the Secret Cuban Missile Crisis Meetings*. Stanford: Stanford University Press, 2003.

_____. *The Week the World Stood Still: Inside the Secret Cuban Missile Crisis*. Stanford: Stanford University Press, 2005.

Stimson, Henry L., and McGeorge Bundy. *On Active Service in Peace and War*. New York: Harper & Brothers, 1948.

Talbot, David. *The Devil's Chessboard: Allen Dulles, the CIA, and the Rise of America's Secret Government*. New York: HarperCollins, 2015.

Thomas, Evan. *Ike's Bluff: President Eisenhower's Secret Battle to Save the World*. New York: Little, Brown, 2012.

_____. *Robert Kennedy: His Life*. New York: Simon & Schuster, 2000.

Thompson, Nicholas. *The Hawk and the Dove: Paul Nitze, George Kennan, and the History of the Cold War*. New York: Henry Holt, 2009.

Thompson, Robert Smith. *The Missiles of October: The Declassified Story of John F. Kennedy and the Cuban Missile Crisis*. New York: Simon & Schuster, 1992.

Toland, John. *In Mortal Combat: Korea, 1950–1953*. New York: William Morrow, 1991.

Truman, Harry S. *Memoirs by Harry S. Truman: Years of Trial and Hope*. Garden City, NY: Doubleday, 1956.

Truman, Margaret. *Bess W. Truman*. New York: Macmillan, 1986.

_____. *Harry S. Truman*. New York: William Morrow, 1973.

Tusa, Ann, and John Tusa. *The Berlin Airlift*. New York: Atheneum, 1988.

Uebelhor, Tracy S. *Presidential Profiles: The Truman Years*. New York: Facts on File, 2006.

Unger, Debi, and Irwin Unger. *George Marshall: A Biography*. New York: HarperCollins, 2014.

_____. *LBJ: A Life*. New York: John Wiley, 1999.

Vandenberg, Arthur H., Jr., ed. *The Private Papers of Senator Vandenberg*. Boston: Houghton Mifflin, 1952.

Vogel, Steve. *The Pentagon: A History*. New York: Random House, 2007.

Weiner, Tim. *Legacy of Ashes: The History of the CIA*. New York: Doubleday, 2007.

Weintraub, Stanley. *15 Stars: Eisenhower, MacArthur, Marshall, Three Generals Who Saved the American Century*. New York: Free Press, 2007.

Whitney, Courtney. *MacArthur: His Rendezvous with History*. New York: Alfred A. Knopf, 1956.

Widmer, Ted (selected and introduced by). *Listening In: The Secret White House Recordings of John F. Kennedy*. New York: Hyperion, 2012.

Wittner, Lawrence S. *Cold War America: From Hiroshima to Watergate*. New York: Praeger, 1974.

Wortman, Marc. *The Millionaires' Unit: The Aristocratic Flyboys Who Fought the Great War and Invented American Airpower*. New York: Public Affairs, 2006.

Yenne, Bill. *Big Week: Six Days that Changed the Course of World War II*. New York: Berkley Caliber, 2012.

_____. *Hap Arnold: The General Who Invented the U.S. Air Force*. Washington, D.C.: Regnery, 2013.

Yergin, Daniel. *The Prize: The Epic Quest for Oil, Money and Power*. New York: Touchstone, 1991.

_____. *Shattered Peace: The Origins of the Cold War and the National Security State*. Boston: Houghton Mifflin, 1977.

Articles

Allert, Johannes R. "Northwest Airlines' Modification Center in World War II." *Minnesota History* (Winter 2013–14).

Alsop, Joseph, and Stewart Alsop. "The Lesson of Korea." *Saturday Evening Post*, September 2, 1950.

Baldwin, Hanson W. "Lovett an Ideal Choice," *New York Times*, September 13, 1951.

Blumenschine, Leonard. "F. Trubee Davison and the Yale Units." *Foundation* (Fall 1982).

Browne, O'Brien. "Ernst Udet: The Rise and Fall of a German World War I Ace." *Aviation History* (November 1999).

Curtiss, Richard H. "Truman Adviser Recalls May 14, 1948 US Decision to Recognize Israel." *Washington Report on Middle East Affairs* (May/June 1991).

Cutts, Norma E., and Nicholas Moseley. "Notes on Photographic Memory." *Journal of Psychology* (1969).

Evans, Medford. "Coup d'Etat, November 22, 1963." *American Opinion* (September 1967).

Franklin, Jay. "Harry Truman's Foreign Policy," *Life*, January 10, 1949.

"Hardy Survivor of a Dying Breed. " *Business Week*, September 13, 1958.

Harriman, Margaret Case, and John Bainbridge. "The Thirteenth Labor of Hercules." *New Yorker*, November 6, 13, 1943.

Jessup, Philip C. "The Berlin Blockade and the Use of the United Nations." *Foreign Affairs* (October 1971).

Krebs, Albin. "R.A. Lovett, Ex-Chief of Defense Who Pressed Buildup In 50's, Dies," *New York Times*, May 8, 1986.

Lewis, Thomas E. "Cargo Plane Valuable but Not a Cure-all," *(Philadelphia) Evening Bulletin*, December 7, 1942.

Lockett, Edward B. "There Is No Other Way But Strength," *New York Times Magazine*, September 23, 1951.

Lovett, Robert A. "The War Department Weighs Air Cargo." *Air Transportation* (December 1942).

McConnell, Grant. "The Steel Seizure of 1952." *The Inter-University Case Program*.

McDonald, Amy Athey. "Defending Allied Skies: Yale's Pioneering Pilots Form First Naval Aviation Unit," *Yale News*, August 17, 2014.

"New Policy, New Broom," *Time*, March 29, 1948.

"Robert A. Lovett Now Secretary of Defense." *U.S. Air Services* (October 1951).

Schaffer, Ronald. "American Military Ethics in World War II: The Bombing of German Civilians." *Journal of American History* (September 1980).

"'Scrawny, Ill-Fed Eagle' Takes Over the Pentagon," *Business Week*, September 22, 1951.

West, F.J., Jr. "Secretaries of Defense: Why Most Have Failed." *Naval War College Review* (July 1981).

White, Theodore H. "A Voters' Choice of Millionaires," *Life*, September 22, 1958.

Wolff, Jerry. "The First Yale Unit: Aeroplanes Enter the Naval Reserve." *Naval Reservist* (Winter 1973–74).

Wortman, Marc. "Flight to Glory." *Yale Alumni Magazine* (September/October 2003).

Documents

Foreign Relations of the United States, 1945–1950.
Foreign Relations of the United States, 1947.
Foreign Relations of the United States, 1948.
The United States Strategic Bombing Survey, Washington, D.C. United States Government Printing Office.

Newspapers and Periodicals

Air Transportation
American Metal Market
Army and Navy Register
"Aviation Angles"
Baltimore Sun
Buffalo (NY) Courier Express
Business Week
Cascade (ID) News
Chicago Sun
Chicago Tribune
Christian Science Monitor
Cincinnati Enquirer
Cleveland Plain Dealer
Dallas Morning News
Detroit Free Press
Detroit News
Flying and Popular Aviation
Fort Worth Star-Telegram
Foundation
Houston Post
Houstonian
Huntsville (TX) Item
Idaho Daily Statesman
Jackson (MI) Citizen Patriot
Jackson (MS) Clarion-Ledger
Jersey City (NJ) Journal
Journal of American History
Journal of Commerce (New York)
Kansas City Star
Lewiston (Idaho) Tribune

Life
Los Angeles Times
Louisville Courier-Journal
Miami Beach Daily Tropics
Miami News
Minneapolis Tribune and Star Journal
Minnesota History
Nashville Tennessean
Neue Zeitung (Frankfurt Edition)
Newark (NJ) Sunday Call
New Haven (CT) Register
New Orleans Times-Picayune
Newsweek
New York Daily Mirror
New York Herald Tribune
New York Journal American
(New York) Journal of Commerce
New York Star
New York Sun
New York Times
New York World-Telegram
Omaha World-Herald
Ocracoke (FL) Observer
Pensacola (FL) News-Journal
Pensacola (FL) Times
(Philadelphia) Evening Bulletin
Philadelphia Inquirer
Philadelphia Public Ledger
Pittsburgh Press
Pittsburgh Sun-Telegraph
Port Arthur (TX) News
Providence (RI) Sunday Journal
Richmond (VA) News Leader
Roanoke (VA) Times
Rochester (NY) Democrat and Chronicle
St. Louis Post-Dispatch
Salt Lake Tribune
Seattle Journal of Commerce
Seattle Post-Intelligencer
Seattle Times
Sentinel
Shreveport (LA) Times
Sioux Falls (SD) Daily Argus Leader
Stars and Stripes
Stuttgarter Zeitung
Tacoma (WA) News Tribune
The Hill School News
Time
Toledo (OH) Times
U.S. Air Services
United States News

Wall Street Journal
Washington Daily News
Washington Post
Washington Star
Washington Times-Herald
Watertown (SD) Public Opinion
Wichita (KS) Eagle
Yale Daily News

Manuscript Collections

Dean G. Acheson Papers, Harry S. Truman Library
Dean G. Acheson Papers, Yale University Library
Philip Barry Papers, Beinecke Rare Book Library, Yale University
Brown Brothers Harriman Collection, New-York Historical Society
Clark M. Clifford Papers, Harry S. Truman Library
Matthew J. Connelly Papers, Harry S. Truman Library
F. Trubee Davison Papers, Yale University Library
Ira Clarence Eaker Papers, Library of Congress
Robert A. Lovett Papers, National Archives
Robert A. Lovett Papers, Harry S. Truman Library
Robert A. Lovett Papers, Yale University Library
John J. McCloy Papers, Amherst College Library
Presidential Secretaries' Files, Harry S Truman Library
Carl A. Spaatz Papers, Library of Congress
Henry Lewis Stimson Diary, Library of Congress
Henry Lewis Stimson Papers, Library of Congress
Harry S Truman Papers, Harry S Truman Library

Oral History Interviews

David K.E. Bruce, Harry S. Truman Library, March 1, 1972
Paul G. Hoffman, Harry S. Truman Library, October 25, 1964.
Robert A. Lovett, Brown Brothers Harriman, June 8, 15, 22, 1981.
Robert A. Lovett, Columbia University Oral History Research Office, Jan. 15, 1959, Feb. 13, 1959, Jan. 21, 1960, May 4, 1971. Sept. 15, 1975.
Robert A. Lovett, by Doris E. Condit, June 7, 1976.
Robert A. Lovett, by Alfred Goldberg and Harry B. Yoshpe, May 13, 1974.
Robert A. Lovett, John F. Kennedy Library, July 20, 1964; August 17, 1964; September 14, 1964; November 19, 1964.
Robert A. Lovett, Harry S. Truman Library, July 7, 1971.

Index